THE HISTORY
OF
LORD SEATON'S REGIMENT,
(THE 52ND LIGHT INFANTRY,)
AT
THE BATTLE OF WATERLOO;

TOGETHER WITH VARIOUS

Incidents connected with that Regiment,

NOT ONLY AT WATERLOO, BUT ALSO AT PARIS, IN THE NORTH OF FRANCE, AND
FOR SEVERAL YEARS AFTERWARDS:

TO WHICH ARE ADDED MANY OF

THE AUTHOR'S REMINISCENCES OF HIS MILITARY AND CLERICAL CAREERS,

DURING A PERIOD OF MORE THAN FIFTY YEARS.

BY THE

REV. WILLIAM LEEKE, M.A.,

(OF QUEEN'S COLLEGE, CAMBRIDGE,) INCUMBENT OF HOLBROOKE, DERBYSHIRE, AND RURAL DEAN,
WHO CARRIED THE 52ND REGIMENTAL COLOUR AT WATERLOO.

THE AUTHOR CLAIMS FOR LORD SEATON AND THE 52ND THE HONOUR OF HAVING
DEFEATED, SINGLE-HANDED, WITHOUT THE ASSISTANCE OF THE 1ST BRITISH
GUARDS OR ANY OTHER TROOPS, THAT PORTION OF THE IMPERIAL
GUARD OF FRANCE, ABOUT 10,000 IN NUMBER, WHICH ADVANCED
TO MAKE THE LAST ATTACK ON THE BRITISH POSITION;

THE 3RD BATTALION OF THE 1ST FOOT GUARDS, BY THE DUKE OF WELLINGTON'S ORDER, DROVE
THE SKIRMISHERS OF THE IMPERIAL GUARD OFF THE BRITISH POSITION,
THE OTHER BATTALION OF GENERAL MAITLAND'S BRIGADE OF GUARDS REMAINING STATIONARY.

IN TWO VOLUMES.—VOL. I.

WITH A PORTRAIT OF FIELD-MARSHAL LORD SEATON,
AND THREE PLANS OF WATERLOO, SHEWING THE POSITIONS AND
MOVEMENTS OF THE 52ND DURING THE ACTION.

LONDON:
HATCHARD AND CO., 187, PICCADILLY.
1866.

Publishing Statement:

This important reprint was made from an old and scarce book.

Therefore, it may have defects such as missing pages, erroneous pagination, blurred pages, missing text, poor pictures, markings, marginalia and other issues beyond our control.

Because this is such an important and rare work, we believe it is best to reproduce this book regardless of its original condition.

Thank you for your understanding and enjoy this unique book!

PREFACE.

It is beginning to be more and more widely understood that very great injustice has been done to Lord Seaton and the 52nd Light Infantry, which regiment he commanded at Waterloo, by those who have attempted, in subsequent years, to write the history of that great battle.

My only reason for thinking of writing these volumes was that I had always felt this injustice very strongly, and that with other officers of the regiment I thought, if it were possible, the truth, with regard to what we knew the 52nd had achieved at Waterloo, ought to see the light.

We knew that it had moved down 300 or 400 yards from the British position by itself, and had, single-handed, attacked and routed two heavy columns of the French Imperial Guard, consisting of about 10,000 men, and further we saw with our own eyes that this defeat was followed by the flight of the whole French army: why should this daring feat of their great commander not be made known to the British army and to the British nation?

The having a very vivid recollection of the scenes and events I witnessed at Waterloo, and the having the written recollections of several 52nd officers, and also other sources of information, led me to think I had a mass of materials for the work I was contemplating, which justified my proceeding with it; and I more particularly felt justified in doing so, when I considered, that amongst the few remaining officers of the regiment, who served at Waterloo, from various circumstances there was no one else who would feel at all disposed to encounter the labour, and difficulties, and perhaps annoyances, which such an undertaking would involve.

My first idea was only to write about the 52nd at Waterloo, and then I thought I would give some little account of the regiment during the time that it formed part of the army of occupation in the North of France. I found, as I proceeded, that my work took up more of my time than I felt justified in giving to it, unless I could hope in some way to make it not only interesting, but also calculated to be useful in a religious point of view, to those who might read it; and thus I was led on to adopt the plan set forth in the title page.

There have been three subjects, to which, in addition to my duties as a clergyman, I have given a great deal of time and earnest attention now for more than thirty years. The first, to which I have devoted more time than to anything else, and which I have always considered to be one of the most important objects which can engage the attention of a Christian community, has been the endeavouring to assist in promoting, amongst all classes of persons throughout the country, more correct views of the Divine Authority and of the perpetual and universal obligation of the Lord's Day, or the Christian Sabbath, and of the benefits, temporal, spiritual, and eternal, which result to nations and individuals from its due observance.

Another object of great solicitude with me has been the setting free the Protestant officers and men, of the British army, from their forced attendance on the idolatrous ceremonies of the Roman Catholic and Greek Churches.

The third object, which at one time engaged a great deal of my time and attention, was, what I considered to be a great blot on the escutcheon of our Established Church: I mean the plurality system, or the holding, by the same clergyman, of more livings than one, merely for his own personal advantage. This system, I am thankful to say, now appears to be in a fair way of gradual extinction.

It is natural, therefore, that, in such a work as this, I should have devoted some chapters to these subjects, which I trust will not be without interest and instruction to the reader.

I shall be grieved if anything I have written should occasion pain to any one. It is obvious that I could not ask the permission of individuals, with regard to the introducing particular names, or subjects, or letters, without running the risk of placing myself in a most difficult position.

There are two persons, to whom I, at one time, thought of applying as to the desirableness (of which I had no doubt myself) of stating certain details in these volumes; but I felt that such application would only embarrass them, as well as myself, whether they might or might not take the same view of the matter which I did.

I did not originally contemplate the introduction of the early and subsequent history of the 52nd into this work, but it has lately occurred to me that I should not be performing my duty to my countrymen, (only a very few of whom can have access to the 52nd "Record,") if I did not take advantage of my present opportunity to lay before them many most interesting particulars relating to the high character, military bearing and martial prowess of that old "Light Division Regiment," which General Sir William Napier, the celebrated historian of the Peninsular War, has described as, "A REGIMENT NEVER SURPASSED IN "ARMS, SINCE ARMS WERE FIRST BORNE BY MEN!"

It will not be necessary to apologize to the reader for writing in the first person singular, for it very soon became evident that the doing so was a necessity, but I should rather apologize to the printer, who has been so frequently forced, in his proofs, to find substitutes, in some of the chapters, for quite a company of capital fellows, whom I have no better way of designating than by calling them No. 9. This little double enigma the reader will not fully understand till he has read well on in the book.

And here I think I must plead guilty of having introduced into this work some few puerilities, some repetitions, and many defects, which I trust will be forgiven; and I must also claim indulgence for the style of writing: which I found could not very well be other than that of the common familiar letter-writing style, beyond which I have seldom attempted to soar.

In giving an account of the various incidents which came under my observation at Waterloo, I have been compelled to speak of myself and of my own feelings, and in detailing many of the reminiscences of both my military and my clerical careers, I must I think, as a matter of course, lay myself open to the charge of vanity; but it must be allowed, in extenuation of what may appear to be a palpable fault in that direction, that it is absolutely necessary that the author of a book of this description, containing as it does such a medley of subjects, and which is written chiefly for the purpose of proving a particular point with regard to Waterloo, but also with an earnest desire to make it religiously useful to those who may read it—it is absolutely necessary, that a person so circumstanced should have a fair character, in the eyes of those whom he desires to convince, and entertain, and benefit, for a certain amount of military intelligence, and also for uprightness of purpose: this must be my apology for letting many things appear in this work which bear favourably on my character both as an officer and as a clergyman.

I cannot quite agree with one of my old and valued brother-officers, that "he, who praises his "regiment praises himself," and that that would be a reason for not retaining in my book Napier's words about the 52nd, already mentioned; for a person may assuredly have a comparatively humble view of himself, who may at the same time think, that his regiment, or his ship, or his wife, cannot be surpassed by any other.

I cannot expect, indeed I know it must be otherwise, that any person can read this work without being annoyed at many things in it which he will consider to be in bad taste; such persons must, however, try and bear with, or pass over, what they dislike, and see if there is not much which they approve of, and which, by God's mercy, may be not without benefit to them.

I wish to call special attention to Chapter LV of this work, in which there is a strong recapitulation of much that I have said, in the early chapters, about the single-handed attack of the 52nd on the columns of the French Guard, without the assistance of the British Guards or any other troops. Some additional points of interest are also brought forward in it.

I think all my readers will be pleased with the fine portrait of Field Marshal Lord Seaton, which I am enabled to present to them through the kindness of Mr. Graves, the eminent engraver, of 6, Pall Mall. Photographers must not copy it without his permission, which I only have for its introduction into this work, and any further edition of it.

My military readers especially will admire the three plans of Waterloo, which very accurately represent the various movements and positions of the 52nd throughout the battle. They, the 52nd, must be looked for first of all at Merbe Braine, in the north-western corner of Plan I, and then in the same plan they may be traced, over the Allied position, to the slope in rear of Hougomont, where they were formed into two squares, and proceeded, with their gallant friends the 71st and 95th Rifles, to the north-east of Hougomont, where they remained for two hours and a half. In Plan II their place on the position, which they reached about seven o'clock, is marked by a dotted line from which their advance, about eight o'clock, may be traced to the flank of the French Imperial Guard. In Plan III they will been seen, at 8.30, close to the Charleroi road, in front of, and two hundred yards from, the Old French Guard; from that spot their track will be found to the left of the Charleroi road and La Belle Alliance as far as the farm of Rosomme where they halted for the night at 9.15.

WILLIAM LEEKE.

HOLBROOKE HALL, NEAR DERBY,
November 27, 1866.

CONTENTS OF VOL. I.

CHAPTER I.

1815.

52ND LIGHT INFANTRY AT WATERLOO.

Selection of a profession—Death of my eldest brother—Bonaparte's landing in the South of France—Joining 52nd Light Infantry in Flanders as a volunteer—Sir John Colborne (Lord Seaton)—June 16, March to Enghein—Cannonade at Quatre Bras—March to Waterloo—Bivouac on the night of the 17th—Position of troops before the battle—Ordered to carry the 52nd regimental colour 1

CHAPTER II.

1815.

52ND LIGHT INFANTRY AT WATERLOO.

Commencement of the battle at twelve o'clock—52nd in reserve—Chalmers's horse shot—Several casualties—First narrow escape—Attack on Hougomont—Attack on La Haye Sainte and Picton's division—Charge of the Union Brigade and of the Life Guards—Grand charge of 6000 French cavalry—British guns deserted—52nd form square, and advance over and down the British position—Brunswickers—French cavalry rally and are supported by 7000 fresh horsemen—Adam's brigade in squares to the left of Hougomont—52nd in two squares—Cannonade—French cuirassiers—Various incidents—La Haye Sainte taken by the French—The squares of the brigade ordered to retire up to the position 23

xiv   CONTENTS.

CHAPTER III.
1815.
DEFEAT OF THE IMPERIAL GUARD BY THE 52ND LIGHT INFANTRY.

PAGE

Form a four-deep line—Wounded men of the 52nd—Spent round-shot—
Duke of Wellington—French officer of cuirassiers—Advance of the
Imperial Guard—52nd advances singly to meet them—3rd battalion of
1st Guards drives a mass of skirmishers down the position—Defeat of
the whole of the Imperial Guard by the 52nd alone—No other English
troops within 300 yards of them—Flight of the French army—52nd
passes over the killed and the wounded of the French Guard—Various
incidents—Charge of cavalry—52nd suffer from grape—Prussian round
-shot—Serious thoughts   39

CHAPTER IV.
1815.
52ND ATTACK AND DEFEAT THE IMPERIAL GRENADIERS.

52nd attack and drive off Old Guard—Duke of Wellington arrives—Lord
Uxbridge wounded—The Duke and Napoleon in nearest proximity—
52nd pass La Belle Alliance—No other troops in sight—Pass 75 pieces
of deserted cannon—Encounter a French division and guns—Their
surrender—Fire on French staff-officers—Last infantry shots at Waterloo
—Bivouac at Rosomme—The Duke and Blucher—The 1st Guards
between La Belle Alliance and British position—Sir John Byng's speech
about 52nd—Wounded officers at the village of Waterloo—Sir Thomas
Reynell's letter—Wounded hussar and Imperial grenadier—Ammunition
waggon blown up—Various other incidents on the 19th   .   .   . 55

CHAPTER V.
1815.
DEFEAT OF THE FRENCH IMPERIAL GUARD BY THE 52ND ALONE.

Defeat of the Imperial Guard by the 52nd, and not by the 1st British Guards
—Lord Seaton and Sir John Byng—Steadiness of 52nd when wheeling
in line, &c.—The Duke's despatch written on the night of the 18th—
Duke of Richmond—Colonel Gawler—Siborne's mistakes—Sir W.
Napier's statement about treachery and secret politics in connexion with
Waterloo—Napier's letter about officers being drilled with men, and
Lord Seaton with 52nd at Waterloo—Colonel Bentham and Minie rifle—
Bentham and Waterloo—Lieutenant Sharpin of the Artillery contra-
dicts Siborne—Lord Seaton's letter to Bentham on defeat of French
Guard by 52nd—Mr. Yonge's conversation with Lord Seaton—Colonel
Brotherton   79

CHAPTER VI.

1815.

SIBORNE'S, ALISON'S, AND SHAW KENNEDY'S MISTAKES REFUTED.

The Duke's memorandum of 1836 about Waterloo—Much confusion in it—Confidence in the truth of history much shaken—Siborne, Alison, the Chaplain-General, Gleig, make great mistakes—Hooper's account more correct—Amount of the French Guard from 1804 to 1815—52nd, "a "bright beam of red light, &c."—Baron Muffling—Shaw Kennedy—What the 1st Guards did really do at the crisis of Waterloo—Killed and wounded of each battalion of the 1st Guards—How came Sir John Byng to allow the 52nd *to go on alone!*—Great injustice perpetrated against light infantry regiments—Letter to "The Times" in 1855—Brevet rank of the Guards injurious to the service 105

CHAPTER VII.

1815.

MARCH TO PARIS.

Nivelles—Letters to England—News of battle—Lists of killed and wounded—Mother ill—Alarm of sisters—March to Binche—Coal pit—Enter France—Le Cateau—Loss of baggage—Claim for remuneration—Other claims rejected—Fate of the baggage—Officers on baggage-guard—Marshal Monçey's Chateau—Distant view of Paris—Montmartre—52nd alone at Argenteuil—Pontoon bridge—Convention—Bridge and graveyard of Neuilly—Enter Paris—Encamp in the Champs Elysées . 138

CHAPTER VIII.

1815.

PARIS. THE 52ND ENCAMPED IN THE CHAMPS ELYSÉES.

Two companies a guard to the Duke's house—Colonel W. Rowan commandant—Bonaparte finds refuge on board the Bellerophon—Entry of Louis XVIII into Paris—The Imperial Guard—Position of 52nd in Paris—Cricket and drill—Dine with Sir John Colborne—Restoration of pictures, &c., taken by the French—Review of Russian Guards—Accident—Cossacks of the Don—Ecole de Natation—Practical jokes—Row in the Palais Royal—Row at St. Cloud—Gaming-houses—Observations on the evil of letting children play at games for money—Soldier condemned to be shot—Caricatures of English—"Les Anglaises pour rire"—Monsieur Calico"—Playhouses to be avoided. 154

CHAPTER IX.
1815, 1816.
THE 52ND QUARTERED AT VERSAILLES, ST. GERMAIN, AND CLERMONT.

Quarter at Versailles—Palace—St. Germain—Sir John Colborne goes on leave—His good advice—Clermont—Anniversary of the death of Louis XVI—A guard of honour in the church—Atchison and Dawson of the artillery 174

CHAPTER X.
1816.
CANTONMENTS IN THE NORTH OF FRANCE.

Villages around Thérouenne—Henry VIII—Siege of Thérouenne and Battle of Spurs three hundred years before—Honours gained by ancestors—Alarming occurrence—Periodical encampment and march to Valenciennes—Kind feeling between the villagers and our men—Meadow at Thérouenne—Bathing in the river Lys—Sir Denis Pack's inspection—Brigade orders—Curious occurrence—Remarkable case of one of the men becoming religious 180

CHAPTER XI.
1816.
AMUSEMENTS IN CANTONMENTS.

The regiment start a pack of fox-hounds—Anecdotes connected with our hunting—Accident—Go over to the cavalry quarters—Commandant of St. Omer and his staff—Lord Combermere joins the party—His regret at not having been at Waterloo—Dissertation on cruelty to the animals hunted—A singular argument on the subject—Extinction of poaching —A trumpeter-boy of the Life Guards 191

CHAPTER XII.
1816.
AMUSEMENTS AND INCIDENTS IN THE NORTH OF FRANCE.

Hunting at Callone—Captain English—Duke of Wellington's boar-hounds—Lord Hill and his brother—Gymnastic club near St. Pol—52nd play the rest of Colville's division at cricket—Fatal accident—Mess at Thérouenne in the summer—Accident to a friend in the 71st—Medals for Waterloo served out—Two of us wear them on going to Aire—Death of a poor woman in the Grande Place—Curious anecdote about the 18th of June, 1816, by a corporal of the 23rd Fusileers—Ball given by the English officers at St. Omer—My servant drowned—Remarkable dreams—Holman's servant shot—A corporal stabbed by a French officer —Capture of thieves—Winterbottom and his former comrade—Anecdote of the master tailor 204

CHAPTER XIII.
1816, 1817, 1818.
LEAVE TO ENGLAND AND PARIS. RETURN OF THE ARMY TO ENGLAND.

Cheltenham—Duke of Wellington—Paris in 1817—French family—Chef d'escadron—Labédoyère's tomb—Ball at the English Ambassador's—Denain—General Beckwith—Encampment again at St. Omer in 1818—Sir John Colborne joins—Purchases a horse from me—The horse's proceedings on parade—Last visit to Valenciennes—52nd occupy citadel—Review by the Emperor of Russia—52nd the last regiment in France—March to Calais—Embarkation—Arrival in England, November 29, 1818 221

CHAPTER XIV.
1818, 1819.
THE 52ND MARCH TO CHESTER AND ARE STATIONED THERE.

Dover—Deal—Ramsgate—Custom-house—Scene at Canterbury—Start for Sheerness—Short visit to friends—Sir John Moore's mother—Various incidents—Balls—Races—Hunting—The Bishop and Archdeacon—Special assize—Lord Lyndhurst commandant of the garrison—Fire, and amusing incident—52nd ball given to the town and county—Several incidents—Visit to Bold Hall—Obtain leave to go to Germany—Proceed to Plymouth—Ball at General Brown's—Sail in Myrmidon to Spithead—Bishop Crowther rescued from slavery by Myrmidon—Incidents connected with his deliverance 232

CHAPTER XV.
1819, 1820.
GERMANY, ENGLAND, PARIS, NICE.

Calais to Brussels—Murder of English gentlemen—How discovered—Tradition about the fight at Cheriton in the time of Charles I.—Visit the field of Waterloo—Corn rank where we defeated the Imperial Guard—The Rhine—Ehrenbreitstein, beautiful scenery—University of Gottingen—Curious funeral ceremonies—Hanover—The Jäger Guards—Colonel Reynett—Leave Hanover for Sottrum—Arrangements for learning German—Alarming illness—Religious feeling—Return to Hanover—Difficulty in speaking English properly—Advised to return to England—Paper written on my 22nd birthday—Ludicrous difficulty at Yarmouth—Thames frozen over—Anecdote connected with the loss of the Royal George—Unpleasant occurrence at races—Think of going on half-pay—Kind remonstrance from the regiment—Proceed to Nice—Bonaparte at Frejus in 1814—Religious friends, &c.—Adventure with a mosquito—The climate of the south of France and Italy . . 245

CHAPTER XVI.
1821.
ITALY.

Proceed by water to Genoa—From Genoa to Pisa—Cross a portion of the Apennines — Misunderstanding with a *vetturino* — Bridge over the Serchio carried away—The leaning tower at Pisa, etc.—The death of a student—The Carnival, etc.—Florence to Rome—Austrians bivouacked around Terni — St. Peter's at Rome—Curious scene—From Rome to Naples — Appii Forum — Cicero's villa and tomb— Naples — Portici, Pompeii—Go up Vesuvius—English squadron—Sir Graham Moore—Return by Rome, Florence, Milan, Turin, and Geneva to England—Dr. Malan at Geneva—Narrow escape at the mortar-practice there . 268

CHAPTER XVII.
1821.
AT HOME, AND THEN REJOIN THE 52ND AT DUBLIN.

Feelings of my relatives with regard to my religious views—Family prayers—Testimony of some now gone—Sir John Colborne—Coronation of George IV—Queen Caroline—Feelings of the people—Rejoin the 52nd at Dublin—My altered feelings with regard to religion—Found Gawler a religious man—Several incidents connected with his change—First intimation to the other officers of my altered views—Attendance at mess—The King's visit to Dublin—Incidents on his landing—Levee at the castle—A judge awkwardly circumstanced—43rd and 52nd reviewed by the King—In command of McNair's company that day—A ramrod accidentally discharged—Charge of cavalry, shewing that the horses would be willing to go on to the bayonets—The King's visit to St. Patrick's Cathedral—Mr. Guinness 292

CHAPTER XVIII.
1821.
DUELLING.

Major Oliver of the artillery—Is sent to "Coventry" by the artillery officers of the Dublin district—I become acquainted with him—Discussions on duelling, at the 52nd mess—Colonel Rowan's opinion—Remarkable instance of apology—Recent additions to the Articles of War—Roman Catholic officers of the Prussian Guards removed for declaring they would not fight a duel—Severe sentence on officers of the Russian Guards for fighting a duel—Belgian Minister of War sentenced to imprisonment for engaging in a duel 305

CHAPTER XIX.
1821, 1822.
THE 52ND AT DUBLIN.

Meeting of naval and military officers for reading the Scriptures—Lady Grey, Mr. Mathias, Mr. Nixon—Scripture argument against balls—Village dances—Refuse an invitation to a ball at Dublin—Difficulties and plan with regard to intercourse with the families of any neighbourhood . 314

CHAPTER XX.
1821, 1822.
THE 52ND AT DUBLIN.

The castle guard—The Montagus of the 71st and 52nd—Irritation of the King about a sentry—Amusing order handed down by the sentries on the bridge to the garden—Tracts and books for the men taken away by the captain of the guard—Some reason to hope they were made useful to him—Several anecdotes connected with that proceeding—Winterbottom and religious tracts at the bank guard; curious and important dialogue—Anecdote connected with Winterbottom's wound at Waterloo—Mention of his services in 52nd record—Peculiarities of religious people—Definition of a Methodist—A clergyman and his wife each considering the other to be free from sin—What a blessing that we have the first prayer of the liturgy—Expected Whiteboy attack on the barracks—On detachment at the Pigeon-house Fort—Boldness and discomfiture of rats—Detached to Wicklow—Rudiments of a savings' bank 318

CHAPTER XXI.
1821, 1822.
DUBLIN. PARTICULARS RELATING TO THREE 52ND SOLDIERS.

Pat Kelly's proceedings in Spain and France—Remarkable visitation—Becomes a religious man—One of the guard of honour to the King—Selected as a trustworthy man—His suspicious death at the Pigeon-house—Dogherty—Houghton's remarkable case—Benefit arising from the distribution of the Scriptures—My visits to him in the hospital—He leaves the army—His letter to me—Enters Trinity College, Dublin—Becomes a devoted minister of the Church of England—His death . 334

CHAPTER XXII.
1822.
THE 52ND IN THE SOUTH OF IRELAND.

March from Dublin—Fair at Ballynahill—The county of Tipperary under the Insurrection Act—Detached to New Birmingham—The Rev. John Galway—Set up a school for the men—Two drunken men shot by sentry near Carrick—Refuse invitation to dine out on Sunday—Extracts from journal—The priest prohibits my tracts—Tracts given to beggars to sell—Benefit arising from this—Interesting details—Introduced to a very clever nailer—Comes to compare Roman Catholic catechism with Bible—Praying to angels—Hopeful state of several persons—Joined at night by a stranger on the road—The priest burns the tracts—Give Bibles and Douay Testaments—Instance lately discovered of good done by the tracts given to the soldiers—Relieved by Gawler—Clonmel, Ballynamult—Escort prisoners to Fermoy—On duty to Dublin—Return to New Birmingham for a short time—Account in after years of one of the New Birmingham converts—Converts become protestant Scripture readers—Establishment of a regimental savings' bank—Compliment to my efficiency—First epistle of St. Peter—Lord Seaton . . . 344

CHAPTER XXIII.
1823.
SANDHURST.

Senior department at Sandhurst—Determined to work hard—Religious duties—Strict observance of the Lord's Day—Boerhave—Diggle's wound—Serjeant Housley met him wounded at Waterloo—Diggle's anecdote about a toast in Sicily—My order to join 52nd, and to embark for America—Sir George Murray, the governor, opposes it, but without success—Asks me to dine with him on Sunday—Correspondence with the Horse Guards—Proceed to Cork—Find 52nd embarking . . 363

CHAPTER XXIV.
1823.
THE 52ND GO TO NEWFOUNDLAND AND NEW BRUNSWICK.

Explanation with Sir John Tylden—Proceed with three companies to Newfoundland—Off Kinsale and Castle Townsend—Sea sickness—Calm—Visit timber vessel—Sudden squall—Shark—A bonnet overboard—Cards—Bible—Banks of Newfoundland—Fogs—Vessels—74th at St. John's—Found an order to proceed to New Brunswick—Naval officer—Rencontre—Frigate—Go on board—Leave Newfoundland—Bay of Fundy—St. John's—Annapolis—Proceed with one company to St. Andrew's—Barracks—Expel vermin—Level a road—Prayer for the people—Snow-shoes—Frost-bites—Kindness of the people—Many joined us in meeting to read the Scriptures—Party kept up for many years . 378

CHAPTER XXV.
1823, 1824.
ST. ANDREW'S, NEW BRUNSWICK.

Benefit of religious tracts—One lent in twenty-two houses—Man with cart—Tract given to one man, the means of the conversion of another—Sermons—Mr. Simeon—Description of a good minister—H.M.S. Sparrowhawk—Smuggled provisions—Smuggled fowl for dinner—Meat preserved by becoming frozen—Expedition into the uncleared woods—American General—Charlotte county militia—Voyage to St. John's—Find half the town on fire—Of some use in stopping the conflagration—Armine Mountain 397

LIST OF PLATES.

Portrait of Field-Marshal Lord Seaton, G.C.B. . . *Frontispiece.*
Plan of Waterloo, No. I 29
Plan of Waterloo, No. II 43
Plan of Waterloo, No. III 55

CHAPTER I.

1815.

52ND LIGHT INFANTRY AT WATERLOO.

Selection of a profession—Death of my eldest brother—Bonaparte's landing in the South of France—Joining 52nd Light Infantry in Flanders as a volunteer—Sir John Colborne (Lord Seaton)—June 16, March to Enghien—Cannonade at Quatre Bras—March to Waterloo—Bivouac on the night of the 17th—Position of troops before the battle—Ordered to carry the 52nd regimental colour.

It was intended that I should have been a sailor, in which profession my two elder brothers were, but my eldest brother having been killed in action in 1810,* my mother no longer thought of that career for me, and it was never mentioned to me; she then intended me for the church, but to this arrangement I had a great repugnance, as I considered myself altogether unfit to be a clergyman; then the law was very seriously thought of, and I turned my attention to it for some months after leaving school at the age of sixteen; but all intentions in that direction were completely upset by my meeting at a ball a young officer of the 51st Light Infantry, who had just returned from Spain, and to whose account of his adventures I listened with the greatest avidity for two or three hours, and then immediately determined that I would go into the army. Our friend and relative, Sir John Colborne, afterwards Lord Seaton, then in command of the 52nd, was written to; but before any course could be recommended, the Peninsular war came to an end. He, some time after, advised that I should go to a military

* See Appendix No. 1.

institution, at which Captain Malortie de Martemont received few young men who were preparing for the army. Captain Malortie was a French royalist, and professor of fortification at the Woolwich Academy. I was there for several months, and made some little progress in fortification and military plan drawing, &c.

In the early part of 1815, Sir Theophilus and Lady Pritzler and their family were staying with my mother, preparatory to their embarking for India; they were relatives of ours, and he commanded the 22nd Light Dragoons. On hearing of my plans, they proposed that I should purchase a vacant cornetcy in the 22nd, and follow them to India. Arrangements were made accordingly at the Horse Guards, and I was written to, and a little time was allowed for my decision. It had, however, been before arranged with Sir John Colborne that, if the American war continued, I should proceed with the 52nd to America.

Just at the time that the cornetcy in the 22nd Dragoons was mentioned to me, we were daily expecting to receive the account of the ratification of peace with America, so that, although I was much pleased with the arrangement about India, I felt that I had better not take the decided step about going there, until there was an end of all hope of seeing active service on the other side of the Atlantic. In a short time, the news of the ratification of peace with America appeared in a second edition of the papers; and, in the very same papers, was a third edition, announcing the landing of Bonaparte in the south of France from Elba, on the 1st of March. If the intelligence of Bonaparte's return to France had reached me four-and-twenty hours later, all my steps for getting my cornetcy and for proceeding to India would have been taken, and probably mine would have been an Indian life for many years. As it was, I determined on doing nothing until I saw what success Bonaparte's enterprise met with. I knew that, if it succeeded, the 1st battalion of the 52nd, already embarked at Cork, would most probably be ordered with other troops to reinforce the 10,000 men we already had in Flanders under the Prince of Orange.

When we heard of Bonaparte's arrival at Paris on the 20th of March, I immediately wrote to Sir John Colborne, who was military secretary to the Prince of Orange, to beg of him to let me know what I had better do under the circumstances. Several weeks passed away, and I received no reply to my letter, and I hardly knew what to think of Sir John Colborne's silence, when, towards the end of April, a letter arrived from him, but it was directed to my mother, who opened it with considerable anxiety, and then produced the one which had been sent in answer to my first letter some weeks before. My poor mother had felt justified, considering my youth, (I was rather more than seventeen,) in opening and keeping back from me my own letter, until she should again communicate with Sir John Colborne on the subject. His reply was, that he could not give any other advice than that which he had already given in his letter to me. The advice he had given, which so alarmed my mother, and which he still gave, was that I should at once lodge my money for an ensigncy in the 52nd, and come out immediately and join the 1st battalion as a volunteer.

The day after the arrival of Sir John Colborne's letter, on Friday, the 28th of April, I left home for London. I am writing this more than fifty years after that first step in my military career, and so rapidly has the time passed away, that it seems to be only a few years since my dear mother, when the carriage was at the door, to convey me to the place where I should meet the coach for London, pressed me to her, and begged me with many tears not to go, saying, it was not necessary that I should run into such danger, or that I should go into any profession whatever. I felt this parting very much, but of course it was impossible for me to yield to her wish, dearly as I loved her. The kind relatives, at whose house I was during the few days that I remained in London, had secured for me the assistance of a colonel in the Guards, who kindly devoted to me many hours on the day after my arrival, and went with me to the several tradesmen to order my outfit. During my short stay in town I saw Mrs. and Miss Moore, the mother and sister of General Sir John Moore, who fell at Corunna, and who had been so much respected and beloved by the 52nd. At the house of my aunt, I met with the widow of my cousin, Captain Bogue, who had fallen at the battle of Leipsic about eighteen months before, in command of the British Rocket Brigade.* I recollect she regarded me and my enthusiasm about the 52nd, and my commencing career, with much kind and melancholy interest.

On Tuesday, May 2nd, I left London for Dover by the evening coach, with all my outfit, as a 52nd officer, complete. I was to embark for Ostend on the evening of the 3rd, and did not know very well what to do with myself during the day. The 2nd battalion of the 52nd was stationed at Dover, and, under my circumstances, I was not anxious to fall in with any of the officers, having some undefinable fear that something might turn up to prevent my getting out at once to the 1st battalion. However, I only came across one solitary bugler of the regiment the whole day. I was in a military great coat, with 52nd cap and sword. After seeing what there was to be seen, I strolled into a billiard room, where I found several officers of the old 95th, (now the Rifle Brigade); they were very civil and kind, and I played with them for some hours. I was rather a good player at billiards, and consequently won almost every game we played; and, although we played for small sums, I was ashamed to find, when it was nearly time for me to embark, that I was a winner of between four and five pounds. I had hardly time for another game, but still I arranged to play one, and contrived, by offering odds, to have quite as much at stake as I had won altogether, with the full intention of losing the game. When I had got about half way through it, and was rather behind-hand in my score, I told them I feared I should be too late for the packet, and that, as I was sure to lose the game, I would pay my losses and not play it out. My 95th friends, however, I think rather suspecting what I was aiming at, begged me to finish it, which I did to save appearances, and to prevent them from refusing to take the money I had won from them. I soon managed, by making two or three bad hits, to lose the game, and, putting down my money, I hastened off, and was just in time not to lose my passage. I must not conclude this without referring my readers to the Appendix,† for my opinions on the subject of the immense evils which arise from young persons being allowed to learn and play at games of chance.

* See Appendix No. 2. † See Appendix No. 3.

I left Dover for Ostend on the evening of the 3rd of May. I recollect little more of the voyage than that I was dreadfully sea-sick—so much so, that it was a great trouble to me to think that I could not reach England again without passing through the same fearful ordeal. We had rather a head wind and a short chopping sea; and the first time we tacked and were in stays, when I was half asleep in my berth in the middle of the night, I, who had never been at sea before, fancied, for a few seconds, that the ship had met with some disaster and was settling down and sinking. I well remember that the first thought was, Oh, then, I shall get rid of this horrid sea-sickness!

I arrived at Ostend in the forenoon of Thursday, the 4th of May, which, as I afterwards found, was the date of my commission as ensign in the 52nd. As I landed on the quay, they were unloading cannon-balls from an arsenal transport, pitching them up as bricklayers do bricks; I thought it looked very warlike. At Ostend I found Lieutenant Cottingham, and four men just come out of hospital, who were going up in four days from that, to join the regiment at Lessines; I arranged to wait and go with them. The only thing I recollect doing at Ostend was the buying a baggage-horse; I took a fancy to him from his very superior powers in leaping over the very broad gutters across the street, which were filled with water by the pouring rain.

I went part of the way to Ghent in the canal-boat; my only fellow-passenger was Major-General Sir James Kempt, who was going up to the army to take the command of a brigade in Picton's division. He was very kind to me: when, after some hours' abstinence, we began to feel hungry I volunteered to go and see what was the state of the larder, and came back with the report that there was literally nothing to eat on board, the general produced two gingerbread nuts from a paper, and gave me one of them. Even little kindnesses of that sort are often remembered for years afterwards.

The having fallen in with Cottingham made my march up from Ghent very agreeable, and also took off from the awkwardness attending my first introduction to the officers of the regiment. We reached Lessines on the 11th of May, exactly five weeks and three days before the Battle of Waterloo. When we arrived the regiment had marched out some miles, and we only found a serjeant's guard at the entrance of the town. Soon, however, we heard the martial notes of the bugles, and I had the great delight of seeing a regiment of upwards of 1000 men, whom I looked upon as the finest soldiers in the world, come winding down the road amongst the corn, marching to the sound of one of those stirring tunes, which one always connected with feats of arms and deeds of daring.

When the regiment was dismissed, many of the officers gathered round Cottingham and me, and he talked away with them for three or four minutes, quite forgetting that he was leaving me in a somewhat awkward position, as I was unknown to any of them, till at last one of them said, "Cottingham, will you not introduce your friend to us?" when, they of course, received me very kindly. That afternoon I was put in orders, as Volunteer Leeke, and attached to Captain McNair's company.

During the Peninsular war, and how long before I know not, it was very occasionally permitted to young men, who had difficulty in getting a commission, with the consent of the commanding officer, to join some regiment on service before the enemy. In action the volunteer acted as a private soldier, carrying his musket and wearing his cross belts like any other man. After a campaign or two, or after having distinguished himself at the storming of some fort or fortress, he would probably obtain a commission. He messed with the officers of the company to which he was attached. His dress was the same as that of an officer, except that, instead of wings or epaulettes, he wore shoulder straps of silver or gold, to confine the cross belts.

My case was somewhat different; my money was lodged for the purchase of my commission, and it was known that only a short time would elapse before I was gazetted, and that I had come out as a volunteer to avoid being sent to the 2nd battalion in England, with which I should have had to remain for at least six months. In fact, the notification of my having been gazetted as an ensign in the regiment appeared in orders about ten days after I joined. Under the circumstances Colonel Charles Rowan desired me not to have the wings removed from my jacket. I was an anomalous sort of personage; and I recollect at first some of the men saluted me, and others did not, when they passed me in the streets.

Two or three days after I arrived, Sir John Colborne joined from Brussels, and took the command of the regiment. I had only seen him once before, and stood in considerable awe of him, though I was thoroughly convinced that he had the kindest feeling towards me. He was a sort of nephew of my mother's, her brother having married his mother. He told me, I remember, that he thought, from Sir James Kempt's description of the person he had met in the canal-boat, that I had arrived out. He recommended me to purchase a riding-horse in addition to the one I had for my baggage; I told him I had been intending to try and do without a horse, until after the first action, in which, no doubt, many officers would be killed, and then a horse would be purchased at a cheap rate; he smiled, I suppose at my war-like and sanguinary ideas, and merely said, "You had better get "a horse at once." This I did, and purchased a black horse with a long tail, very much like those used by the Life Guards and Blues; he was consequently called in the regiment "the Life "Guardsman."

Sir John Colborne always strongly advocated the importance of infantry officers, when on active service, having riding-horses, and used to say, that if, from insufficiency of income, they found it difficult to manage this, still they should stint themselves in wine, and in every thing else, in order to keep a horse if possible. As mounted officers they were more useful, under very many circumstances; they were less tired at the end of a day's march, and more ready for any duty which might be required of them; they could be more effective in bringing up stragglers on a long and weary march; some of them might be usefully employed when extra staff officers were required. I think, on the long march of upwards of fifty miles, which we had from Quevres-au-camps to Waterloo, all but two of the officers of the 52nd were mounted.

During the five weeks between my joining at Lessines and our start for Waterloo, I went through some portion of my drill, which, soon after our arrival at Paris, was completed in the Champs Elysées.

At Lessines, on one occasion when the regiment was at ball-practice not far from the bank of the Dender, and were firing volleys by companies at targets set close to a very thick wood, we were all astonished and horrified, and our firing put a stop to, by the appearance, round the side of the wood, of a man and woman with uplifted arms and horror-stricken countenances. No one had the least idea that there was any habitation in the wood; but it turned out that these poor people occupied a cottage somewhere within it. No wonder that they were alarmed, for, before they could get round the skirts of the wood, several volleys had been fired into it by the ten companies, each consisting of about one hundred men.

There were fully sixty officers with the regiment at that time. We messed at the same hotel, in two separate rooms; after mess, each day, between thirty and forty horses were usually paraded, and we used to have some excellent steeple-chasing or rather brook-leaping in the meadows adjoining the town. I recollect particularly Whichcote, now General Whichcote, as the most determined rider on those occasions; it was really a very pleasant and happy time.

About 150 of the 52nd had volunteered from the South Hants Militia, and I selected a servant from amongst them, that I might have one who came from the same part of the country that I did. I recollect well the being laughed at by my brother officers, when first I joined, for talking of the right or left "side" of the company instead of the "flank," and of being "behind" instead of being "in the rear" of it. In our company's mess, they voted me a very good messmate, for not liking eggs, or strong tea, or brandy. When furnishing a canteen which I purchased in London, I was wise enough, although I was going to the continent, to desire the two large bottles, containing about three pints each, to be filled with the best brandy which the canteen maker could procure. Before I lost my canteen, which I did with the rest of my baggage at Waterloo, I found that, although I did not drink brandy myself, some of my friends had no objection to it, for without being particularly invited to do so, they had emptied my bottles of brandy in no very long space of time. One of their jokes with me was that, if I was a lucky fellow, I should get made "a field officer" before Lille, by which they meant that I should perhaps be killed and buried under the sod before Lille.

Whilst we were at Lessines there was a grand review of the greater portion of the splendid cavalry and horse-artillery of Great Britain and of the King's German Legion. This took place near Grammont, about eight or nine miles from Lessines. There were about 7000 men present. There were no particular incidents; but we were exposed to a most drenching rain for some time. The Prince of Orange and his brother, who were on a break with some young Englishmen, were placed by them, well wrapped up in great coats and tolerably well exposed to the storm, on the box of the break, the seat of honour, whilst their young friends got a much better berth themselves under the body of the vehicle.

When I had been four weeks at Lessines, I one day asked Sir John Colborne if he had any objection to my going for a day to Brussels, which was about twenty miles off, as possibly I might not again have so good an opportunity of seeing it. He told me he thought I had better be getting on with my drill; he however kindly added, "but you can go if you like." As I saw he had some reason for thinking I had better not go there at that time, I gave it up; and it was well that I was not there on the 16th of June, for two of the 52nd captains, who were at Brussels on leave at that time, had the misfortune not to be able to find their regiment. They probably, misled by various reports, rode about in vain on the roads between Brussels, Lessines, Ath, Enghien, and Quatre Bras. One of them never reached the regiment at all, until after the action at Waterloo; the other only reached it in the evening, just at the moment it was advancing to charge the French Imperial Guard, and thereby, to the regret of his brother officers, lost his brevet-lieutenant-colonelcy, which fell to the lot of a junior brevet-major.

Towards the latter end of May, Sir Henry Clinton's division, of which Adam's light brigade, in which the 52nd was, formed a part, proceeded to occupy the country beyond Ath towards the French fortress of Condé, and they assembled for division drill in a large domain, surrounded by extensive plantations, in the neighbourhood of Quevres-au-camps. Here they practised the formation of an encampment by means of blanket tents, which appeared to be a most troublesome affair, and did not meet with much favour on the part of officers or men.

We remained there only a few days, and then returned to our former cantonments. About the 12th of June, the 52nd finally left Lessines, and the 2nd division of the British army made another demonstration towards Condé.

It was known that the Emperor Napoleon was likely soon to make his attack either on the Prussian or the English army, and great watchfulness was exercised along the front of both armies, which extended over a length of upwards of 100 miles. Regular information also reached the Duke of Wellington of the movements of various bodies of the French troops; but still all was uncertainty as to the point at which Bonaparte would strike his first blow.

Sir Henry Clinton's division had been some days near Quevres-au-camps, occupying the villages near that place in the direction of Ath, and were preparing for a division field day, on the morning of the 16th of June. The 52nd were at Elleguies St. Ann, and were assembling on the various company parades at ten o'clock. I was on the parade of No. 9, Captain McNair's company, with one man and one bugler only besides myself, when the general's aide-de-camp came cantering down the village, and delivered the following order to me, "Your company, Sir, is to "be a mile on the Ath road in twenty minutes from this time." He then rode forward, the bugler sounded the assembly, and the men who were close at hand, came pouring in immediately, and the company was at the rendezvous on the Ath road at the time appointed. Every one was on the qui vive, and various reports of the advance of the enemy were afloat. After halting a short time, that the baggage might come up, we were ordered to move on Ath and Enghien; we reached the latter place a little after two o'clock. There we halted for two or three hours, and the men cooked their ration beef. During this time we distinctly heard the cannonade of Quatre Bras, although it was twenty-two miles from us. Yet strange to say, two days afterwards, the troops at Hal, under Sir Charles Colville, though they were only eight miles distant, never heard the firing or anything about the action at Waterloo, till the morning of the 19th. When we first heard the cannonade at Quatre Bras, one of the old soldiers exclaimed, "there they go shaking their blankets again." The sound of a distant cannonade is not unlike that arising from the shaking of a carpet or a blanket.

From Enghien we marched a considerable distance on the Hal road, passing the road leading back towards Mons. After proceeding several miles towards Hal, we countermarched, and I think retraced our steps till, about two miles before reaching Enghien again, we struck into the above-mentioned road leading to Mons, and afterwards, leaving that road, we must have got, by some cross road to the left, to Braine-le-comte, without going through Soignies, which place I have no recollection of. I remember one good halt after leaving Enghien, which we made from about eight till half-past nine. There was also another halt on the 16th, which took place in a large open wood. As we moved off again, the band struck up a march, the horse in a sutler's light covered cart, frightened by the band, dashed off amongst the trees, and the last I saw of the occurrence was that the body of the cart separated from the wheels and axletree and shafts, with which the horse ran off, leaving the poor woman inside the body of the cart. I think she could not have been much hurt; but it would probably be some considerable time before she and her husband, if she had one, would be able to join the division again.

We reached Braine-le-comte at midnight, on the 16th, and remained there till a little after two on the morning of the 17th, in the midst of torrents of rain. It was with some difficulty that I got my horse under cover. I found there were some persons in a large barn, and, on making some attempt to open the large door, was told in a strong Scotch accent, "There's no room here, "we are all full here;" however by kicking up a great row and insisting on having the door opened, I at last succeeded, and found within only two men of the 71st Highlanders. The lower room of an adjacent auberge I found crowded with men of the brigade waiting for their turn to purchase something to eat; I was directed to a room upstairs, where I found some bread and cheese on the table, and two 71st officers lying their full length on two beds fast asleep. After eating some bread and cheese, I took the liberty of lying down by the side of one of them, although they were perfect strangers to me, judging that, according to the laws of war, the one half of the bed fairly belonged to me. I could not sleep, so, after lying there about an hour and getting a good rest, I left my friends of the 71st not at all aware of the honour I had conferred upon them.

We reached Nivelles about seven o'clock; the narrow streets were full of cavalry horses tied to the doors and windows of the houses. The morning had become fine, and the 52nd got into a large orchard. Here we got our breakfast, and here about thirty of the officers of the 52nd, I being amongst the number, saw their baggage for the last time. There was much confusion on the road between Waterloo and Brussels on the 18th, and thus the baggage of nearly half the officers of the army was plundered, either by foreign allies running away from the action or by the Belgian peasantry.

In the middle of the day on the 17th we moved off from Nivelles along the direct road from that place to Hougomont, Waterloo, and Brussels; this road joins the road from Charleroi, Quatre Bras, and Genappe, on which the French were advancing, near the farm of Mont St. Jean. Shortly after leaving Nivelles, we found ourselves marching in a parallel line with British artillery and cavalry, we being on the road and they moving for some distance along the fields on either side. At the same time a Dutch Belgian battalion was trying to cross our line of march in the direction of Genappe. We moved very slowly, the men being wearied with their long march, and by the heavy load which each had to carry; this consisted of the knapsack, containing the kit and blanket, (the great coats had been sent to England,) the musket, and bayonet, and 120 rounds of ball-cartridge, sixty rounds of the latter being in the knapsack; this was a wise precaution adopted by the commanding officer. Had the Germans, posted in the farm house of La Haye Sainte on the 18th, been thus provided with the reserve of ammunition in their knapsacks, it is very probable that the French would never have taken that important post; and had the brigade of the 1st British Guards been similarly provided, the 52nd would probably not have been left without support in their single-handed attack on the columns of the French Imperial Guard. Sir John Byng, who succeeded to the command of the two brigades of Guards when General Cooke was wounded, gave this to Sir John Colborne as his reason for not advancing Maitland's brigade to his support.

Colonel Hall tells me, "Near Nivelles we overtook Barlow, "captain in the 69th. He had been promoted from the 52nd "about a year before. Through the fault of the Prince of Orange, "the 69th, in the act of changing position, had been charged by "French dragoons. Barlow, and many others, lay down and "escaped hurt, except from the trampling of the horses. He "was limping along, very sore and lame, and feelingly declaimed "against the common notion, that a horse will not tread on a "man lying on the ground. His jacket was blackened with the "marks of horse shoes. I suppose in such a case the horse has "no choice and cannot pick its way."

About midway between Nivelles and Hougomont, the 52nd halted for rather more than two hours, 200 yards to the left of the road. I heard Sir John Colborne (for the future I think I shall call him Lord Seaton,) asking if any of the officers could lend him the cape of a boat-cloak, as he wished to lie down for a couple of hours, and try and get some sleep; I had a very large boat-cloak with a cape and hood to it, I unhooked the cape and hood and handed them to him. He wore them over his uniform during the whole of the Battle of Waterloo.

Whilst we were halted on this occasion, several waggons, with those wounded at Quatre Bras, passed along the main road towards Waterloo and Brussels.

After our halt we came on to the road again just ahead of a regiment of Dutch Belgians, and formed open column of companies from subdivisions as each company reached it, so that our allies had to halt till we were all on the road. Each side of the road was now *lined* with soldiers of different regiments, and with some women and drummer boys, who had fallen out from fatigue. From this time until some time after we had reached the entrance to Hougomont, no less than five mounted officers were sent, one after the other, to bring up stragglers belonging to the 52nd.

About a mile and a half before we reached Hougomont, we saw something of the French troops on our right, marching on the Charleroi road, towards Maison du Roi and Rosomme. This was the first we had seen of them. Shortly after this we halted, still in open column of companies, and loaded. Two French staff officers rode down to within 200 yards of us to reconnoitre, and one of them I saw writing down what he observed. On our arriving at the avenue leading to the Chateau of Hougomont, the head of the column turned to the right, and had advanced some distance down the avenue, when it was halted and countermarched, from which it was supposed that the original intention was that our brigade should occupy Hougomont for the night.

About this time, half-past seven, the British and French armies were taking up their positions on the Field of Waterloo. The French, at first, appeared not quite to understand that the English had arrived at their position, and had to be restrained by Picton, from behind La Haye Sainte, opening a cannonade from two brigades of artillery upon a mass of French infantry, which had advanced along the Charleroi road to some little distance in front of La Belle Alliance. In other parts of the field, between the two positions, there were some spirited little affairs of cavalry at intervals, in which our troops, forming part of the rear-guard under the Earl of Uxbridge, very much distinguished themselves. When we were on the slope, to the rear of Hougomont, looking towards La Belle Alliance, we had close to us a British light dragoon regiment with white facings, who appeared to have just come up the slope after one of these encounters. As they faced about and re-formed on our position there was some cheering amongst them. As we were marching at ease across the slope just about this time, and appeared to be not far from the French, I heard one of our men say we were likely to be engaged at once, when another replied, "There will be no battle to night, but "to morrow; all the Duke of Wellington's great battles have been "fought on a Sunday."

Whilst we were halted near Hougomont, a heavy clap of thunder from the direction of Mont Plaisir startled us all; my first idea was that the French artillery in that direction were opening upon us. Siborne speaks of there having been much thunder and lightning during the evening and night of the 17th of June, but that was the only clap of thunder I heard; there was much rain during the night. Just after this, when it was decided to what part of the ground we should move, Lord Seaton directed me to ride and see if the regiment could get through a hedge about two hundred yards off, in the direction of the village of Merbe Braine; it was a stiff hedge cut down to stakes nearly five feet high, with gaps here and there through which a single file might pass, and I was somewhat afraid if I reported that the regiment might pass through it, I might get into a scrape, if the column should be brought up by it. I reported it passable, and we marched through it without any great difficulty, and took up our position in a ploughed field, just in advance of Merbe Braine, looking towards Hougomont, and at about two miles to the eastward of the town of Braine-la-leud.

I was ordered with a fatigue party to go into the village to bring straw for the company. As we passed along the street we saw lying in the middle of the road, opposite to one of the cottages, the dead body of one of the 95th Rifles; I supposed he had been plundering and had been killed by one of the inhabitants. I proceeded with my fatigue party to the principal farm, where I found our general of brigade, Adam, who had taken up his quarters there. We could find no straw in the barn, and so, as "necessitas non habet leges," we took the straw from the roof of the barn itself, which had been recently thatched. A German soldier was walking off with a fine calf about a month old, when the mistress of the house appealed to us for assistance, and the general's aide-de-camp, Campbell, coming out at the moment, gave the fellow a good kicking, and took the calf from him.

On my return to the bivouac, our servants made a bed of straw on the wet ploughed field, and all four of us, McNair, Hall, Yonge, and I, lay down and, being covered with our boat cloaks, tried to go to sleep; it was very hot and there was heavy rain, and the straw conducted the rain into the inside of my stock, so that I was soon glad to get up. I think it was a little after ten o'clock when we were ordered to fall in again, as we were going to move, and each man was to take his straw with him. I don't know where the others were, but I found myself to be for a short time the only officer with the company. We moved in file, left in front, and I was very proud of my command, when Colonel Charles Rowan rode up to me, as No. 9 formed up into line on the left of No. 10, and said to me, "Leeke, dress your company in a line with that distant fire." Our line then faced the French position, and was about 400 yards in rear of the crest of the British position, and about 500 yards from Merbe Braine. Here, having formed open column of companies, we piled arms and remained for the night. My friend Yonge shared my boat-cloak and straw with me, and we consequently both of us got very wet. The horses were picketed near us, and very soon some half-dozen of them got loose and galloped away towards Hougomont and the French position, and then came back again at speed towards the horses they had left, nearly passing over us, and only being prevented from doing so by our jumping up; they galloped about in this way the whole night, and thus made this wretched night still more wretched. I fell asleep several times, then dreamt we were advancing and closing with the enemy, then started up again, then thought of home and all my beloved ones there; again I dozed off, then came our horses like a furious charge of cavalry, and we had to start up and scare them off; and this kind of thing went on till the night had passed, and the morning of the 18th broke upon us.

As the morning of this eventful day advanced, the heavy rain of the preceding night passed off and was succeeded by fine weather. The men of the regiment were soon to be seen in every direction in their shirt sleeves, drawing the charges from their muskets and cleaning and drying their arms, and thus preparing for the coming conflict. The French line of battle was about three-quarters of a mile from that of the English. The great road from Charleroi to Brussels ran through the centres of each line, dividing the right wing of each army from the left. On the right of the British army were the chateau and farm and grounds of Hougomont, the whole in a square each side of which was a quarter of a mile in length. The northern side of the inclosure towards Brussels was nearly a quarter of a mile from the British position; the southern side of the inclosure was about the same distance from the position occupied by General Foy's 9th division of the French army, and the western side was a quarter of a mile from Prince Jerome's division. In the centre of the British position, 300 yards down the slope and close to the right of the Charleroi road, was the farm house of La Haye Sainte; its yard and orchard extended nearly a quarter of a mile along the right of the road, and the inclosure, in its whole length, was about eighty yards in width; the left of the British position extended about a mile and a half from the centre above La Haye Sainte, and was composed of Picton's division (in which were Kempt's and Pack's British, and Von Vincke's Hanoverian brigades) containing upwards of 7000 men; and of Lambert's and Best's brigades of Cole's division, containing upwards of 5000 men, and, further to the left, of Vandeleur's and Vivian's brigades of light cavalry, containing 2500 men. Along the front of the left wing, and extending down to the farm of Papelotte and the village of Smohain, were Perponcher's Dutch Belgian division, in which were Bylandt's and Prince Bernhard of Saxe-Weimar's brigades, containing 7500 men; a quarter of a mile in rear of Kempt's infantry brigade was Sir William Ponsonby's Union Brigade, containing the Scots Greys, the Enniskillens, and 1st Royal Dragoons, about 1200 heavy cavalry; 300 yards to the rear of these, to the left of the farm of Mont St. Jean, were a reserve of upwards of 1000 Belgian horse under General Ghigny; so that from the left of La Haye Sainte and of the Charleroi road to the extreme left of the British position there were stationed about 24,000 men, who formed the left wing of the army.

The right wing of the army extended away, from the centre to the right, for about the same distance of a mile and a half. Colonel Von Ompteda's brigade of four battalions of the King's German Legion, had its left resting on the Charleroi road. To the right of Ompteda's brigade stood Count Kielmansegge's brigade of six battalions of Hanoverian landwehr or militia; and further to the right was Sir Colin Halkett's British brigade of four battalions. These three brigades formed Count Alten's division, and occupied about 800 yards of the British position, from the centre towards the right; they contained about 8000 men. In rear of Alten's division were General Von Kruse's Nassau contingent of 3000 infantry, Lord Edward Somerset's brigade of the Life Guards, Blues, and 1st Dragoon Guards, Trip's and Van Merlen's brigades of Dutch Belgian cavalry, and Arentschildt's light cavalry brigade. On the right of Alten's division were Cooke's 1st division of the British army, composed of Maitland's and Byng's brigades of Guards. Maitland's brigade consisted of the 2nd and 3rd battalions of the 1st regiment of Guards, and Byng's consisted of the 2nd battalion of the 2nd or Coldstream Guards, and of the 2nd battalion of the 3rd Guards. The division was nearly 4000 strong; Byng's brigade was posted on the higher ground above Hougomont; the light companies of all the four battalions of the division occupied the farm house and buildings, and the garden of Hougomont; there were also in the inclosure of Hougomont a battalion of the Nassau troops and two companies of Hanoverians. To the right of the Guards and to the rear and north-west of the grounds and inclosure of Hougomont, Mitchell's brigade, of Sir Charles Colville's division was posted; it consisted of the 51st Light Infantry, and of a battalion of the 14th regiment and another of the 23rd Fusileers, and was about 1800 strong.

Between these last mentioned troops and the village of Merbe Braine, on the reverse slope of the British position, there was a most imposing force, which formed a very strong reserve; and which, if the French had attempted to advance upon Brussels to their left of Hougomont and by Hal, as the Duke of Wellington expected, would most completely have intercepted them and defeated their intention. These troops were composed of the three brigades of Sir Henry Clinton's division, namely, General Adam's brigade, consisting of the 52nd Light Infantry, the 71st Highland Light Infantry, six companies of the 2nd battalion of the old 95th Rifles (now the Rifle Brigade), and of two companies of the 3rd battalion of the 95th Rifles; these fine regiments contained 2600 men. The other two brigades of Clinton's division, amounting together to 4000 men, were Colonel Du Plat's 1st brigade of the King's German Legion, and Colonel Halket's Hanoverian brigade. To the left of Merbe Braine and between it and the road from Nivelles to Brussels, were the

Brunswickers, infantry, cavalry, and artillery, making up 6000 or 7000 men; in rear of the guard, also, were Grant's, and Dornberg's, and other brigades of cavalry. The British and Allied artillery, amounting to 196 guns and upwards of 8000 men, were attached to their several divisions or brigades.

The above is a rough but tolerably accurate account of the positions occupied by the British and Allied troops on the morning of the 18th of June; but whilst some of the troops occupied the same ground the whole day, others, and more especially our own brigade, passed over a large portion both of the British and French positions.

Here I beg leave to state, that I do not profess to give any detailed account of any other regiment than my own. I may have occasion to mention some of those other glorious regiments, but I have scarcely any details which I could give, if I wished to do so, excepting such as relate to the 52nd; and those statements which I may make respecting the 52nd at the battle of Waterloo will be almost all such as I witnessed myself.

Early on the 18th, Captain Diggle's company, No. 1 of the 52nd, was sent with two or three companies of the 95th into the inclosures of the village of Merbe Braine, facing Braine-la-leud; they were withdrawn sometime before the action commenced. Some little time after we were all stirring, I wandered off a short distance to a fire belonging to the 71st, at which one or two officers were standing; I was very glad to get the opportunity of warming and drying myself. I found a plank, of about my own length, near the fire; where it came from I have no idea, but I took the liberty, as no one was using it, of laying myself at full length on it before the fire; I very soon fell asleep and must have slept three hours, which much refreshed me, when my servant came to tell me some breakfast was going on amongst the officers of Captain Mc Nair's company, the company to which I belonged. Our breakfast consisted of a biscuit each and some soup, which was in one of the servants' mess tins; I was, unintentionally on his part, done out of my drink of broth by one of the officers exclaiming, just as I put my lips to the tin, " Come, " Master Leeke, I think you have had your share of that." This half-mouthful of broth and a biscuit were all I tasted that day until after nine o'clock, when I got a lump of bread about as big as my fist from a French loaf. About ten o'clock, Lord Hill, with his staff, came galloping along, about fifty yards in the rear of the 52nd, through the high corn; he was riding towards the extreme right of our position; as he passed me, I recollect he gave me one of his pleasant smiles. Shortly after this we got under arms, and Nettles and I were warned by Winterbottom, the adjutant, that we were to carry the colours; on our taking them over from the serjeants, we both agreed that it was not our turn to carry the colours, and wondered why we had been told off to them. I recollect observing, that it would suit me very well, that I had not been long enough in the regiment (I had only joined five weeks before) to be of any other use, but that I *could* carry a colour. Major William Chalmers rode up to us and said, "The regiment is going to act in separate wings; I am going to "command the right wing, and one of you gentlemen will go to "my wing," and addressing me, he added, "You, sir, will go to the "right wing." Now I was anxious, as I did not know so much of the other officers as I did of those belonging to my own company, No. 9, to be in the left wing with them, which I knew was the proper wing for the regimental colour, carried by me as the junior ensign of the two. I therefore ventured to tell Major Chalmers that mine was the regimental colour which should be with the left wing, but he did not choose to rectify the immaterial mistake, which nobody else, probably, discovered at the time, for our colours, which had been with the regiment and the light division all through the Peninsular War, were little more than bare poles. Immediately afterwards, poor Nettles and I separated, not to meet again; he was killed by a cannon-shot, about seven o'clock in the evening. There were two brevet-majors by the name of William Chalmers in the 52nd; the one at Waterloo, being a dark man, was always called "Black Will," the other, "White "Will."

The following extracts, from a letter I have lately received from Captain the Hon. William Ogilvie, relates to circumstances which occurred before the action commenced, and should find insertion here, and will be read with interest:—"I was in Robert "Campbell's company, commanded by Captain Cross, afterwards

"Lieut.-Colonel of the 68th. I was the senior subaltern, poor
"Nettles also belonged to the company, I am not sure if we had
"any other officer at this time. I happen to have preserved the
"parade state of the company on the 16th of June, on which
"morning I dare say you will remember we turned out for one of
"Sir H. Clinton's field days. Cross, not being very well, did not
"come out, and, by the time I had inspected the company, a
"cavalry man was seen on a jaded horse coming up the road, and,
"it was soon known that he brought an order for the division to
"march on Enghien, &c. In the agreeable excitement at the news,
"Winterbottom did not collect the states. The state is interest-
"ing from shewing the splendid condition of the corps then. The
"company, 87 rank and file, under arms, five tailors left at Les-
"sines employed on the soldiers' clothing,* and only one man
"sick; officers' servants, bâtmen, band, &c. making a total of 104
"rank and file. I have no doubt the other companies were equally
"strong. What a noble battalion it was!

"One additional circumstance, which I have not seen anywhere
"mentioned, occurred shortly before the action. An order came
"for a working party from the brigade with intrenching tools; it
"was accordingly paraded; William Rowan, now General Sir
"William Rowan, commanded it, and it chanced to be my turn for
"that duty also. When ready, I heard the brigade-major direct
"Rowan to march on a single tree, far to our left, where he would
"receive further orders. The party, however, had proceeded but a
"very short way, when the French attack on Hougomont com-
"menced, and we were immediately recalled. I have since had
"very little doubt that the purpose was to have used the working
"party to strengthen the post of La Haye Sainte, had time allowed,
"and it was unfortunate it was not thought of a few hours
"sooner."

About eleven o'clock the 52nd moved from the ground on which it had bivouacked, about 300 yards more to the rear. The right wing of the regiment was in column of subdivisions, about twenty yards in front of the steep bank between it and Merbe

---

* The men at Lessines, amounting to between forty and fifty, probably joined us at Enghien or Nivelles. Siborne states, that the 52nd had 1038 men at Waterloo, which amount would agree with this company's parade state.

Braine; the left wing was in line to the left of the front subdivision of the right wing, with an interval of a few paces between the wings. Captain Siborne, in his first plan of the field of Waterloo, places the 52nd, when in reserve, 200 yards more in advance, and 100 yards more to the eastward than they were.

CHAPTER II.

1815.

52ND LIGHT INFANTRY AT WATERLOO.

Commencement of the battle at twelve o'clock—52nd in reserve—Chalmers's horse shot—Several casualties—First narrow escape—Attack on Hougomont—Attack on La Haye Sainte and Picton's division—Charge of the Union Brigade and of the Life Guards—Grand charge of 6000 French cavalry—British guns deserted—52nd form square, and advance over and down the British position—Brunswickers—French cavalry rally and are supported by 7000 fresh horsemen—Adam's brigade in squares to the left of Hougomont—52nd in two squares—Cannonade—French cuirassiers—Various incidents—La Haye Sainte taken by the French—The squares of the brigade ordered to retire up to the position.

EXACTLY at twelve o'clock, by Chalmers's watch, the battle was begun by a cannon shot fired from the French position at the Duke of Wellington, who, with a numerous assemblage of general and other staff officers, had taken post about a third of a mile in our front on the high ground in rear of the north-eastern corner of the enclosure of Hougomont, from whence he could see the greater part of the French position. Such an assemblage was sure to attract the attention of the enemy, and unnecessarily to bring on itself the opening cannonade. It was said the Duke told some of the generals they were "rather too thick upon "the ground."

Whilst we were in reserve above the village of Merbe Braine, the regiment suffered several casualties from the shot and shell which passed over the British position in our front. I think the first occurred to Major Chalmers. The regiment was lying down; I was forced to remain with the colour in rear of the centre subdivision of the right wing, but several of the officers were standing in a group round Chalmers's horse when a ricochet shot came lobbing in amongst them, but fortunately did no other injury than that of breaking the horse's leg; Chalmers drew a pistol from his holster and put the animal out of his misery.

Most of our casualties at this time were occasioned by shell bursting over us, but we saw many cannon-shot ploughing up the ground near us: I had been already regarding several of them with great respect, when my colour-serjeant, Rhodes, who took great care of me and shewed me much kindness all the day, said, pointing to a shot passing through the standing corn, on the right of the column, "There, Mr. Leeke, is a cannon-shot, if you "never saw one before, Sir!" Serjeant Houseley,* whilst standing in rear of the column, narrowly escaped having a round shot through him, by stooping just as he saw it in a line with him at some little distance; this was quite allowable when his comrades were lying down at their ease. One of my narrow escapes occurred whilst we were lying here in reserve; I had my head against my colour-serjeant's knapsack, and was trying, but in vain, to get some sleep, when all at once there was a great rattle against the mess-tins, which, fitting one within the other, were strapped to the back of every man's knapsack; a piece of shell about the size and about as thick as the half of the palm of one's hand, had struck, and lodged in the inner tin; we both sat up, and he extracted the inner tin and the piece of shell, saying, as he pitched them both away, "If that had hit either you or me "on the head, Sir, I think it would have settled our business for "us." On our leaving this ground I looked back and saw we had left two poor fellows in 52nd uniform lying dead under a tree, and could scarcely refrain from shedding tears at the melancholy sight; one of them was the assistant serjeant-major, a man greatly respected in the regiment. We lost, whilst in reserve, these two men killed, and I think about ten or twelve men wounded, who were taken to Merbe Braine.

Colonel Hall, speaking of the casualties which occurred at this time in the 52nd, says:—" A young lad, (Kearns) of our com-"pany was struck by a cannon-shot, and was borne off motionless "and white as a sheet. Those about me and myself concluded he "was dying. Two or three days afterwards I could scarcely be-

* See Appendix No. 4.

"lieve my eyes, when I saw him walk into the bivouac. The shot
" had carried away his pouch so cleanly, that he suffered no injury
" beyond the temporary shock and fright."

The 52nd remained about three hours in reserve just above Merbe Braine, and during that time three of the principal attacks of the French took place on our position. The first of these was made on the post of Hougomont, by large bodies of skirmishers and their supports detached from Prince Jerome Bonaparte's and General Foy's divisions. Hougomont was defended by the light companies of the two brigades of the British Guards, by the Hanoverian riflemen, and by the Nassau battalion. The French and English skirmishers advanced on and gave way before each other with alternate success. At one time the French, superior in numbers, had almost got into the farm yard of Hougomont, but were repulsed by the light company of the Coldstream Guards; the French did actually pass round to the northern side of the inclosures near to the British position. Some of the masses sent forward by Foy and Prince Jerome, were forced to retire by the fire opened on them from the British and German guns and howitzers. Some companies from the Coldstream and 3rd Guards, having reinforced the gallant defenders of Hougomont, the enemy were driven off from the chateau to the lower inclosures of the place.

The attack on Hougomont was preparatory to, and appears also to have been, in a great measure, a feint to draw off attention from, a grand attack which the Emperor caused to be made about half-past one or two on La Haye Sainte and the centre of the Allied position, by the whole of Count d'Erlon's corps, which formed the right wing of the French army, supported by a division of cavalry from the left wing and by the fire of no less than seventy-four pieces of cannon, intended, whilst the troops were forming for the attack in advance of La Belle Alliance, and whilst they crossed the lower ground and the first rise of the British position, to draw off the fire of the British artillery from them. In the latter part of the action, the most of these pieces and many others were abandoned by the French, in consequence of the rapid advance of the 52nd to the British left of La Belle Alliance between eight and nine o'clock in the evening, after they had defeated the columns of the French Imperial Guard.

This attack of the centre and left wing of the Allied position was made by about 17,500 infantry supported by cavalry. The left division of this force under General Donzelot tried in its advance to gain possession of the farm of La Haye Sainte, but were successfully resisted at that time by Major Baring and his Hanoverians. The French attack embraced the whole of the left wing, so that the Nassau troops under Prince Bernhard, of Saxe Weimar, were driven by the French skirmishers from the farm of Papelotte, which, however, they speadily retook.

The first and chief brunt of the attack appears to have fallen on Kempt's brigade of Picton's division, composed of the battalions of those fine regiments, the 28th, 32nd, 79th Highlanders, and (those old friends of the 52nd in the light division in Spain) the 95th Rifles. The French sent forward as usual a mass of skirmishers. Bylandt's Dutch Belgian brigade was in advance of the interval between Kempt's and Pack's brigades, and shamefully fled past the British brigades, notwithstanding the efforts of their officers to restrain them, directly they felt the fire of the advancing skirmishers; Picton ordered Kempt's brigade to advance on the enemy, which they did, and fired on them and charged them as they were reaching the crest of the position and completely routed them. In this *melée* the gallant Sir Thomas Picton was killed.* The 1st light battalion of the King's German Legion, belonging to Colonel Von Ompteda's brigade, crossed to their left of the Charleroi road, and joined Kempt's brigade in this charge. The French advancing in front of Pack's brigade were repulsed with equal gallantry by that brigade, consisting of the 1st Royals, the 42nd, and 92nd Highlanders, and the 44th regiment.

* After his death it was discovered that his hip had been very severely contused by a spent cannon shot at the action of Quatre Bras, two days before; this wound he had concealed, that he might not be absent from the grand battle, which was fought at Waterloo. In the United Service Museum, on the wall just above Captain Siborne's model of the battle of Waterloo, hangs the map of Belgium which poor Picton carried in the breast of his coat when he was killed. It is stained in several places with his blood.

Some of the French supporting cavalry advanced to their left of La Haye Sainte and inflicted severe loss on one of Kielmansegge's Hanoverian regiments, which had been sent by the Duke to reinforce the troops holding La Haye Sainte. Whilst this was taking place, and during the advance of Kempt's and Pack's brigades, Lord Uxbridge ordered forward the Household Brigade of cavalry under Lord Edward Somerset, consisting of the Life Guards, Blues, and the 1st Dragoon Guards; and also Sir William Ponsonby's brigade, consisting of the Enniskillen Dragoons, the Scots Greys, and 1st or Royal Dragoons. Ponsonby's brigade charged to the left of Kempt's brigade and was somewhat mixed up with Pack's. They took two eagles, and with Somerset's brigade, which advanced more to the right, greatly contributed to consummate the rout of this large French force, which Picton's division had initiated. The French fled in in all directions, leaving two eagles and 3000 prisoners in our hands, and having many pieces of cannon disabled.

The English had two generals, Sir Thomas Picton and Sir William Ponsonby, killed on this occasion. The Union Brigade, as Ponsonby's was called, from its consisting of an English, an Irish, and a Scotch regiment, and also a portion of the Household Brigade, after the rout of the French, did not know when to pull up, but followed them on to the French position, and thereby, after causing much confusion, suffered most severely, when attacked in their scattered state and cut off by the formed cavalry of the enemy. Sir Colin Campbell, who was on the Duke of Wellington's staff, told me that he saw what I have attempted briefly to state, respecting the attack and defeat of the French on this occasion, including the splendid charge of the two brigades of cavalry, and that he saw the white horses of the Scots Greys carrying confusion into the French ranks, as far as the eye could reach; he saw also the enemy detaching troops in various directions to cut them off in detail. The supporting regiment of the Union Brigade in charging got mixed up with those in advance, and Vandeleur consequently moved down two of the regiments of his brigade, the 12th and 16th Light Dragoons, in support, and by charging and routing the French lancers, secured the retreat of some of the scattered remnants of Ponsonby's brigade. In the charge of the 12th Light Dragoons, Colonel the Hon. Frederick Ponsonby was disabled in both arms, and his horse carried him on to the French position where he was struck to the ground by a sabre cut.*

About three o'clock, the Emperor ordered Marshal Ney to make a grand attack with 6000 cavalry on the right wing of the British; it extended from La Haye Sainte in the centre to Hougomont on the right of the position; as these troops advanced they could only see the British artillery standing to their guns on the crest of the position; the infantry was in battalion squares on the reverse incline of the position. The Duke had moved up the Brunswickers from their place in reserve, and also Colonel Du Plat's brigade of the King's German Legion. After firing round shot and grape into the advancing cavalry of the enemy till they could no longer stand to their guns, the British and German artillerymen took refuge in the squares nearest to them. The French, on reaching the summit of the position, found the whole line of guns deserted, and found themselves in presence of the British, German, and Brunswick squares, which they charged and which opened fire upon them. The French cavalry did not attempt to charge home on any one of the squares, but inclined to the right and left and rode between them, receiving the fire of the four faces of almost every square. They were thrown into much confusion, which the Allied cavalry taking advantage of, charged and drove them from the position. Directly this occurred, the artillerymen ran to their guns and opened a most destructive fire on the retiring squadrons. The French soon rallied, and supported by 7000 fresh cavalry, again attacked the guns and the squares with the same result, suffering very severe loss in killed and wounded and being thrown into very great and irretrievable confusion by the mixing up of various divisions, and various brigades, and regiments. On one of these occasions, Sir Colin Campbell told me, that he, having lost his horse, got under an ammunition waggon near the centre of the position, to avoid the charge of the French cavalry. Directly the French cavalry had fled, the French artillery again opened a tremendous fire on our position, under cover of which the

* See Appendix No. 5.

enemy sent forward a large force of infantry and cavalry, which maintained itself in the hollow to the Allied right of La Haye Sainte until nearly the close of the action.

During the occurrence of nearly all the stirring events briefly recorded in the foregoing portion of the chapter, the 52nd were lying down in reserve in front of Merbe Braine. About three o'clock or a little after, the whole regiment formed open column of companies to the left, and proceeded about a quarter of a mile along the right of the road from Braine-la-leud, in an eastern direction, nearly to the angle formed by the junction of that road with that running from Nivelles to Brussels, and formed square on No. 10 company. We there saw the grand charge of the French cavalry, before described, all along the British position, a quarter of a mile in our front, and numbers of our guns deserted. Colonel Charles Rowan addressed the regiment, and said, he did not think "those fellows would come near us, but "that if they did we would give them a warm reception." Sir John Colborne was somewhere away in front at that time. Almost immediately after the formation of the square, the 52nd advanced in square, up to, and over the British position. Some little time before it crossed the position, Cottingham, who was the first officer wounded, was struck by a spent cannon-ball on the right ankle. He had a trick of continually exclaiming "By "Jove!" and was often joked about it. I had a little joke against him on the subject, as on our march up from Ostend, in describing to me an attack by a German regiment of cavalry on a body of French, he concluded by saying, "By Jove, they cut them up "like sparrows." When he received this very severe contusion, he was immediately supported by one of the serjeants, and hopped about on his other foot, crying out "Oh, by Jove, by Jove!" One could hardly help smiling at the exclamation. This shot must have been fired from the extreme left of the French army, at the troops of Mitchell's or Du Plat's brigade, stationed on the higher ground in rear of Hougomont, and have first taken the ground near them. It passed over, or through the lengthened-out right face of the 52nd square, and spent its strength on poor Cottingham's ankle. I was marching about five or six feet behind him; and first of all thought it was a shell, but, on looking at it, I found it to be a round-shot, from one of the French twelve-pounder batteries.

On the position we passed over the spot on which one of the Brunswick squares had stood, and found lying there many of their killed and badly-wounded men. They had suffered most severely from round-shot and shells. It was one of the most shocking sights we saw even on that most blood-stained battle field. One poor fellow, whose thigh was completely taken off high up, by the explosion of a shell at the moment it struck him, and who was black in the face, raised himself and caught hold of the hand of one of our men, and then fell dead. Another, who had not long to live, shook the hand of another 52nd man, as we were passing to the front, and cried "Brave Anglais." Close to this was a Brunswick square, prepared to receive cavalry, with the front rank kneeling, as steady as a rock; but whether it was the square these wounded men belonged to, which had been removed out of its exposed position, or another square, I know not. We must have passed here near to the right square of Maitland's brigade of Guards, but we saw nothing of them. Our advance was just at the close of the first attack of the French cavalry on the Allied squares. I think, but am not sure, that we saw at this time, the 13th Light Dragoons, of Grant's brigade, ride down the slope on our left, to charge some French cavalry on their left front.

Immediately on descending the slope of the position towards the enemy, the regiment, almost concealed by the tall rye, which was then for the first time trampled down, formed two squares. I remember that when we formed these two squares, we were not far from the north-eastern point of the Hougomont inclosure, and on the narrow white road which, passing within 100 yards of that point, crosses the interval between the British and French positions in the direction of La Belle Alliance.

The squares of Adam's brigade advanced till the 71st were nearly half way down the inclosure of Hougomont, and about 300 yards from it; the right square of the 52nd was nearly 150 yards down the line of the inclosure and about 400 yards from it, the left square of the 52nd being on its left, and more up the British position, whilst the square of the 2nd battalion of the

95th Rifles, was the left square of the whole brigade, and was still further up the position.

When I was talking with Sir Colin Campbell on the subject of the battle of Waterloo, he said he never understood why Adam's brigade was placed in that advanced and exposed position, and inquired if I knew what the object of it was. I told him that we had supposed we were placed there as a support to the troops in Hougomont. It has, however, occurred to me whilst I have been writing this portion of my book, that this brigade posted in squares in the manner above described, if it could maintain its ground, in spite of the tremendous cannonade to which it must necessarily be exposed, would so break the force of any fresh cavalry attack on the English guns and squares on the crest of the position, as to render it abortive; and also, that its maintaining its ground so far in advance of the other troops, many of whom were young battalions who had never been in action before, would tend to inspire them with confidence. In the next chapter I shall bring before my readers many events of interest which occurred in connexion with the 52nd squares. Of the 71st and 95th squares I only know that they suffered very severely from the fire of the French artillery; and they appeared, as the French General Foy said of the squares of this brigade, to be rooted to the ground, so steady were they, under the tremendous fire to which they were exposed.

The old officers, who had served during the whole of the Peninsula war, stated that they were never exposed to such a cannonade as that which the 52nd squares had to undergo on this occasion for two hours and a half, from the French artillery planted about half a mile in their front. Our own artillery, on, or just under the crest of our position, were also firing over our heads the whole time, either at the enemy's troops or at their guns. Some shrapnel-shells burst short, and wounded some of the 52nd men; but the firing of these shells was discontinued, on our sending notice of what they were doing to the artillery above us. In the right square of the 52nd, and I suppose it was the same in all the squares of our brigade, there was one incessant roar of round-shot and shells passing over or close to us on either flank; occasionally they made gaps in the square. The only interval that occurred in the cannonade, was when we were charged by the French cavalry, for they, of course, could not fire on our squares for fear of injuring their own squadrons, so that the charges of cavalry were a great relief to us all I believe, at least, I know they were so to me.

The standing to be cannonaded, and having nothing else to do, is about the most unpleasant thing that can happen to soldiers in an engagement. I frequently tried to follow, with my eye, the course of the balls from our own guns, which were firing over us. It is much more easy to see a round-shot passing away from you over your head, than to catch sight of one coming through the air towards you, though this also occurs occasionally. I speak of shot fired from six, eight, nine, or twelve-pounder guns. Some of the artillery above us were firing at one time, over our square, at a body of cuirassiers drawn up to their right and rear of the lower inclosure of Hougomont; one of the round-shot, which I caught sight of, made a regular gap, and occasioned some confusion in their front squadron. After this, as the officer in command of the regiment was riding up and down about twenty yards in front of the leading squadron, I saw a round-shot which I thought would have struck his horse's head; it however appeared to pass about half a foot from his head, causing him to start back affrighted, and in a way calculated to have unseated his rider had he not been a superior horseman.

My position in the right square was in the rear of the centre of the front face. I have before stated that it is only very occasionally that a person can see a round-shot coming from a twelve-pounder gun, or from one of smaller calibre. After we had been stationed for more than an hour so far down in front of the British position, a gleam of sunshine, falling on them, particularly attracted my attention to some brass guns in our front which appeared to be placed lower down the French slope, and nearer to us, than the others; I distinctly saw the French artilleryman go through the whole process of spunging out one of the guns and reloading it; I could see that it was pointed at our square, and when it was discharged

I caught sight of the ball, which appeared to be in a direct line for me. I thought, Shall I move? No! I gathered myself up, and stood firm, with the colour in my right hand. I do not exactly know the rapidity with which cannon-balls fly, but I think that two seconds elapsed from the time that I saw this shot leave the gun until it struck the front face of the square. It did not strike the four men in rear of whom I was standing, but the four poor fellows on their right. It was fired at some elevation, and struck the front man about the knees, and coming to the ground under the feet of the rear man of the four, whom it most severely wounded, it rose and, passing within an inch or two of the colour pole, went over the rear face of the square without doing further injury. The two men in the first and second rank fell outward, I fear they did not survive long; the two others fell within the square. The rear man made a considerable outcry on being wounded, but on one of the officers saying kindly to him, "O man, don't "make a noise," he instantly recollected himself, and was quiet. This was the only noise, except the "By Jove!" mentioned before, which I heard from any wounded man during the battle, although I must have been within hearing distance of many hundreds of the wounded, particularly later in the day, when we passed over the killed and wounded of the French Imperial Guard. The story one used to hear in one's boyhood, of the bands of regiments playing during the raging of a battle to drown the cries of the wounded, is a myth. The men of the band and some of the buglers generally make themselves useful in action, in attending to the wounded. This cannon-shot coming through the centre of the front rank of our square without touching me was, I think, my narrowest escape up to that period of the action. I should not omit to mention that it was said, after the action, that a round-shot had expended its force in the solid square of the 71st Highland Light Infantry on our right front, and only stopped when it had killed or wounded seventeen men; I can easily suppose this to be possible from what I saw of the effects of the shot which passed so close to me.

We stood in the right square, not on rye, or wheat trampled

down, but, I think, on clover or seeds which had been recently mown. I furnished information to Captain Siborne with regard to this crop, and to that on which we afterwards stood on the British position, when he was forming his beautiful model of the Field of Waterloo, and was very anxious to procure accurate information on the subject. It was generally supposed that there would have been a much greater loss in killed and wounded at Waterloo, if the heavy rain on the nights of the 16th and 17th had not well saturated the ground. Many of the shells which fell near the troops went so far into the ground, perhaps a foot or more, that they exploded without doing any injury. This was the case in and near our squares. A company of the 95th Rifles were extended in front of the brigade at one time, that they might fire into the French cuirassiers, who were drawn up some three hundred yards from us. One of the files was about ten paces in front of our right square; they were both kneeling, and the front rank man was taking aim at the cuirassiers, when a shell pitched two or three feet before them; they hastily retired towards our square, when, from its not exploding, they supposed it was a round-shot, and returned to the spot and knelt down, and the front rank man was just raising his rifle again to take aim, when the shell exploded, covering them with dirt, and they retired, the front rank man having evidently been wounded.

It was said some little time after the action, but I did not observe it myself, that in one of the squares, probably the left, whilst Colonel Nicolay or some other officer who had come down from the position, was speaking to Colonel Charles Rowan, a shell fell in the midst of the square, when on Colonel Rowan saying, "Steady, men!" Colonel Nicolay observed, "I "never saw men steadier in my life." The shell burst, and seven poor fellows were struck by the fragments.

Speaking of the left square of the 52nd, Colonel Hall writes, " A French half battery (*i.e.* two guns) about 600 yards distant from " the farthest advance of this square, made it their especial object. " They hit us several times whilst we stood halted, yet the " casualties were not so numerous as might have been expected. " I should say the enemy fired well but not with rapidity. Did

"you notice any of the cannon-shot wounds? While the left
"wing square stood under the cannonade, one of Shedden's
"company (Woods I think) was struck down by a ball full on
"the knee. He was removed into the centre of the square. I
"observed the limb above the knee quickly swell till it became
"the size of his body. The poor fellow was left upon the ground,
"I suppose to die there." In addition to one or two advanced
batteries, the brigade, being almost the only British infantry in
sight, must have been cannonaded by a considerable portion of
the artillery of the left wing of the French army.

I have a very vivid recollection of the charge of the French
cavalry. Those who advanced on the right square of the 52nd
were cuirassiers, having not only a steel breastplate but the
same covering for the back. As I observed before, the pleasing
part of the charge was that, for several minutes, perhaps ten, we
were relieved from the cannonade which the French had kept up
upon us, except when their cavalry charged. They came on in
very gallant style and in very steady order, first of all at the
trot, then at a gallop, till they were within forty or fifty yards of
the front face of the square, when, one or two horses having
been brought down, in clearing the obstacle they got a somewhat
new direction, which carried them to either flank of the face of
the square, which direction they one and all preferred to the
charging home and riding on to our bayonets. Notwithstanding
their armour many of the men were laid low, many horses
also were brought down, and the men had a difficulty in disen-
tangling themselves from them. The cuirassiers passed the
square, receiving the fire of all the four faces, and proceeded up
to the crest of the British position. They then re-formed, and
came down the slope again upon us in the same way, and again
avoiding to charge home upon the rear face of the square, as
they could scarcely hope to penetrate the squares; possibly it
was a *reconnoisance* ordered to be made by the Emperor, who
had no other means of ascertaining what force the Duke of
Wellington had at that time on the reverse slope of the position.
From the French position scarcely any of the British troops
could at that time be seen, except our own and the other
regiments of General Adam's brigade.

An interesting anecdote was mentioned to me not long ago, by the late General Sir Frederick Love, who was a captain and brevet-major in the 52nd at Waterloo:—"Some years ago he and "his brother were returning through the South of France, from a "trip they had been taking to the Pyrenees, when they fell in "with a nice gentlemanly Frenchman in one of the public "conveyances, who, in the course of conversation, told them that "he also had served at Waterloo; and it turned out, on their com- "paring notes, that he had been an officer of some standing in the "very regiment of cuirassiers which had charged the right square "of the 52nd in that action. Amongst other things, the French "officer said that whilst the cuirassiers were re-forming, just under "the British position, preparatory to renewing their attack "upon us, he observed that the men had ordered their arms and "were standing at ease, and that he said to a young officer near "him, 'See how coolly those fellows take it; depend upon it that "'is one of the old Spanish regiments, and we shall make no "'impression on them.'"

This officer added, that on charging back again he rode close to the right face of our square, so close, that a young fellow sprang from the square and wounded him with his bayonet, on the left side of his neck, it was a slight wound, but he showed them the scar which it had left. My attention, when the cuirassiers charged back upon us, was chiefly directed to those who were brought down by our fire, about twenty yards from the angle formed by the front and right faces; but I have a recollection of something having occurred at that time, without knowing what it was, in the front ranks of the right face of the square, not far from its junction with the rear face.

When we were in squares of wings, to the left of Hougomont, the French had two divisions, consisting of 12,000 men and some cavalry, in the neighbourhood of La Haye Sainte, from which, about six o'clock, they, after a severe fight, succeeded in driving the Germans under Major Baring, who had expended all their ammunition. The left square of the 52nd was not much more than a quarter of a mile from La Haye Sainte, and in much closer proximity to General Donzelot's division, which was between La Haye Sainte and the square. At one time some skirmishers from Donzelot's division crept up through the high standing corn and fired into this left square. There being some difficulty about the 3rd battalion of the 95th Rifles sending out skirmishers to drive them in, Lord Seaton ordered the front rank of the left face of the 52nd square to do so, thus leaving that face of the square with only three ranks for a short time.

Captain Yorke of the 52nd, who served at Waterloo as extra aide-de-camp to General Adam commanding our brigade, had his horse killed by a cannon-shot or a shell, when riding near the 52nd squares.

The following circumstance mentioned to me by Lord Seaton, when I was dining with him in London some years ago, will help to shew that the cannonade our squares were exposed to at Waterloo was something out of the common way. His words were, "I recollect a friend of mine, Beckwith of the 95th, riding "down to the square in which I was, and when the men had "opened out and let him pass into the square, he threw his bridle "on his horse's neck, and said, 'I hope you *are* satisfied now, I "'hope you *are* satisfied.'" Major Beckwith was an assistant quartermaster-general, and, after leaving the square, lost his leg by the explosion of a shell. I recollect his dining with us, when we were encamped some miles from Valenciennes in the autumn of 1816, and keeping the whole mess in roars of laughter, with anecdotes relating to the light division in Spain. At one time Lord Seaton desired the right square to kneel, thinking, from the peculiar formation of the ground in front, that it would thereby be somewhat protected from the enemy's fire. We were told, when we arrived at Paris, that Napoleon had said of the British squares, that they stood like walls, and that the French cannon-balls seemed to make no impression on them.

About half-past six o'clock, the Duke of Wellington sent an order by his aide-de-camp, Colonel Hervey, to the commanding officer, that the 52nd should retire; but he replied that, if it was necessary, he could remain, for although the squares appeared very much exposed, the shot generally passed over them. Immediately afterwards, however, when the Nassau troops were driven back in the inclosures of Hougomont, the 52nd squares were ordered to retire up and over the position. Whilst this movement was taking place, the fire of the French artillery was more furious than ever, and several casualties occurred. In the left square Colonel William Rowan was wounded in the elbow by a shot which passed through his horse's neck and killed it, bringing its rider very heavily to the ground. Poor Nettles, who carried the king's colour, was killed just before reaching the summit of the position, by a cannon-shot through his body; and it was said that his colour-serjeant was killed at or about the same time; and, in some unaccountable way, the colour was left under the body of poor Nettles till the next morning, when it was discovered by a serjeant of Captain Mercer's troop of horse-artillery. The other two serjeants attached to that colour, I presume, were in front of it when retiring in square, and poor Nettles, if he kept his relative position, would be just in front of the rear rank of what had been the front face of the square before it faced about to retire. As we neared the summit of our position, it seemed as if the whole of the French artillery was firing round-shot at our devoted squares. Almost every shot which took effect, brought death or some dreadful wound to the person struck. It certainly was a pleasant relief from "one "of the most murderous cannonades ever recorded in the annals "of war," when, on passing the crest of the position, we found ourselves, at forty paces from it, out of fire on its reverse slope.

CHAPTER III.

DEFEAT OF THE IMPERIAL GUARD BY THE 52ND LIGHT INFANTRY.

Form a four-deep line—Wounded men of the 52nd—Spent round-shot—Duke of Wellington—French officer of cuirassiers—Advance of the Imperial Guard—52nd advances singly to meet them—3rd battalion of 1st Guards drives a mass of skirmishers down the position—Defeat of the whole of the Imperial Guard by the 52nd alone—No other English troops within 300 yards of them—Flight of the French army—52nd passes over the killed and the wounded of the French Guard—Various incidents—Charge of cavalry—52nd suffer from grape—Prussian round-shot—Serious thoughts.

It was now getting on for seven o'clock. The 52nd formed line four deep, the right wing being in the front line, and the left wing having closed up upon it. The regiment stood about forty paces below the crest of the position, so that it was nearly or quite out of fire. The roar of round-shot still continued, many only just clearing our heads—others striking the top of the position and bounding over us—others, again, almost spent and rolling down gently towards us. One of these, when we were standing in line, came rolling down like a cricket-ball, so slowly that I was putting out my foot to stop it, when my colour-serjeant quickly begged me not to do so, and told me it might have seriously injured my foot. Exactly in front of me, when standing in line, lay, at the distance of two yards, a dead tortoise-shell kitten. It had probably been frightened out of Hougomont, which was the nearest house to us, and about a quarter of a mile off. The circumstance led me to think of my friends at home.

For some little time there was a lull in the battle all along the British line, excepting that the French artillery kept up their fire on the British artillery, almost the only force which could then be seen by them. No shells were at that time directed against the troops posted just behind the summit of the British position. Here was a most interesting scene! Everything was wild and strange, yet everything was quiet and natural. This is rather a bold paradox! Bounding our view, about forty paces in our front, was a bank not quite three feet high; there was a stunted hedge on it away to the right of our centre, but not so to the left. Under this bank and hedge to the right lay some twenty of our badly and mortally wounded men, covered by their blankets, which some of the poor fellows had got out from their knapsacks. I particularly remember at that time two poor fellows passing through the line to the rear, who, I think, must have had their arms carried away by the same cannon-shot, for they were both struck exactly in the same place, about four inches below the shoulder, the wounded arm being attached to the upper part by a very small portion of skin and flesh, and being supported by the man taking hold of the hand of that arm with his other hand. About the same time, I made way also for one of the Rifles, who was seriously wounded in the head, to pass to the rear. Lieut.-Colonel George Hall, then a lieutenant in McNair's company, tells me that at that time most of the buglers had, with the permission of the officers, gone to the rear with wounded men; and that Captain Cross, at his request, allowed his last remaining bugler to take charge of and convey to the rear a severely wounded man of McNair's company.

In front of our left company were several killed and wounded horses; some of the latter were lying, some standing, but some of both were eating the trodden down wheat or rye, notwithstanding that their legs were shot off, or that they were otherwise badly wounded. I observed a brigade of artillery, coming from our left, pass over the bank into action in a very cool and gallant style. In doing this, some of the guns went over the legs of the wounded horses—the wounded *men* were out of their way. It often happens in action that, in charges of cavalry and in rapid advances of artillery, wounded men are ridden or run over. It is mentioned that at the battle of Ligny, two days before Waterloo, Blucher's horse fell, and that, before he could disentangle himself from it, the French and Prussian cavalry charged each other twice, passing over him and his horse without his being hurt. There was a peculiar smell at this time, arising from a mingling of the smell of the wheat trodden flat down with the smell of gunpowder.

Half an hour, or perhaps three-quarters of an hour, had elapsed after our return to the position, when a French cuirassier officer came galloping up the slope and down the bank in our front, near to Sir John Colborne, crying, "Vive le Roi!" He was a chef d'escadron, and took that opportunity of escaping from the French left wing, that he might shew his loyalty to Louis XVIII. He told Sir John Colborne that the French Imperial Guard were about to advance, and would be led by the Emperor. I think the officer of cuirassiers was sent, under the charge of a serjeant, to the Duke of Wellington.

Soon after this, when it was nearly eight o'clock, the Duke rode across our front from the left of the line quite alone, and spoke to Sir John Colborne, as they were both sitting on their horses observing the enemy. The Duke's dress consisted of a blue surtout coat, white kerseymere pantaloons, and Hessian boots. He wore a sword with a waist-belt, but no sash, and had a small extended telescope in his right hand. He rode a chestnut horse. He rode across our front within fifteen paces of our centre, so that I had a complete view of him. I remember him and his cool, quiet demeanour as well as if I had seen him only yesterday. This was the first time the 52nd had seen him on the 18th. He wore no cloak, but Sir John Colborne wore then and during the whole of the action, as a short cloak, the cape and hood of my blue camlet boat-cloak, which I had lent him on the afternoon of the 17th. After speaking for a short time to Sir John Colborne, the Duke rode quietly away again in the direction of the centre of the position, still unattended.

We heard what the officer of cuirassiers had said to Sir John Colborne about the attack of the Imperial Guard, and not long after we heard them advancing with continued shouts of "Vive "l'Empereur" away to our left front. The drummers were beating the "pas de charge," which sounded, as well as I recollect, very much like this, "the rum dum, the rum dum, the rumma- "dum dummadum, dum, dum," then "Vive l'Empereur." This was repeated again and again, till, in about a quarter of an hour or twenty minutes, we put an end to it in the manner mentioned a little further on.

The Imperial Guard advanced from the low ground in front of La Belle Alliance, and on the French left of the Charleroi road. At the same time a forward movement, in support of this attack, was made both by the right and left wings of the French army, whilst the troops forming the centre of their left wing under Foy, made a corresponding advance within the inclosures of Hougomont. The French had maintained themselves in force for several hours to the right and left of La Haye Sainte, about 300 yards under the crest of the British position, and had taken that post from the Germans about six o'clock. Thus, when the Imperial Guard were advancing from the low ground towards the right centre of the position, the Duke could not withdraw any of his brigades of infantry from any other part of the line. A mass of skirmishers was sent forward from the Imperial Guard, who were joined on their right by skirmishers from Donzelot's division; both sets of skirmishers getting, I believe, intermingled in some measure. Whether the Imperial Guard skirmishers fired into the right regiment of the 1st British Guards, that is, the 2nd battalion, and into the left of the 2nd battalion of the Rifles, I am uncertain, but the brunt of the attack from the French skirmishers fell upon the 3rd battalion of the 1st Guards.

Under these circumstances, when the leading battalion of the first column of the Imperial Guard was about 400 yards from that part of the British position occupied by Maitland's brigade of Guards, Sir John Colborne, who had been watching his opportunity, ordered No. 5 company of the 52nd, under Lieutenants Anderson, Campbell, and F. W. Love, to extend and move down and fire into the enemy's columns, looking to the regiment for support.*

---

* The left of the skirmishers of the 52nd and the left of those of the Imperial Guard could not have passed very far from each other, for only the four-deep line of the six companies of the 95th Rifles intervened, between the left of the 52nd and the right battalion of Maitland's brigade of Guards, yet the hostile skirmishers did not meet or even see each other; probably when the 52nd skirmishers advanced from the left of the regiment, which, owing to the formation of the ground, was more forward on the British position than the troops on its left, the French skirmishers were just surmounting the more retired crest of the position in front of the British Guards, and had commenced firing into them.

He then, without having received any orders from the Duke or any other superior officer, moved forward the 52nd, in quick time, directly to its front. As we passed over the low bank and the crest of our position, we plainly saw, about 300 or 400 yards from us, in the direction of La Belle Alliance, midway between the inclosures of Hougomont and La Haye Sainte, and about a quarter of a mile from each of those places, two long columns of the Imperial Guard of France, of about *equal* length, advancing at right angles with the position and in the direction of Maitland's brigade of Guards, stationed on our left. The whole number of these two columns of the French Guard appeared to us to amount to about 10,000 men. There was a small interval of apparently not more than twenty paces between the first and second column; from the left centre of our line we did not at any time see through this interval; I think they were all in close column.

As the 52nd moved down towards the enemy it answered the cries of "Vive l'Empereur," with three tremendous British cheers. When the left of the regiment was in a line with the leading company of the Imperial Guard, it began to mark time, and the men touched in to their left, every one seeing the necessity for such a movement, and that, if they proceeded, they would be outflanked by the French column, which was then not quite two hundred yards from us. In two or three seconds the word of command, "Right shoulders forward," came down the line from Sir John Colborne, repeated by the mounted officers, and the officers commanding the front companies; the movement was soon completed, and the 52nd four-deep line became parallel to the left flank of the leading column of the French Guard, there being a slight dip and rise again of the ground between us and the enemy. The 52nd was alone, the other regiments of Adam's brigade having been thrown out by the suddenness and peculiarity of the movement. In this dangerous and exposed advance Sir John Colborne was on the right of the regiment, anxiously watching a large mass of the enemy's cavalry, which was seen between us and the French position. From the left centre of the 52nd line we saw a numerous body of skirmishers of the Imperial Guard running towards, and then

forming about 100 yards in front of, their leading column.*
These appear not to have been seen by the 52nd officers on the
right; possibly the head of the French column intervened. I
recollect seeing a French officer strike, with the flat of his sword,
a skirmisher, who was running farther to the rear than the point
at which the others were forming; at that time I could see 300
yards up the slope of the British position to our left, and not a
British regiment or a British soldier was in sight. These
skirmishers no doubt were the troops driven in from the British
position, by the 3rd battalion of the 1st Guards, which was the
left battalion of Maitland's brigade; Lord Hill was on the right
of the 2nd battalion of the 1st Guards, which was the other and
right battalion of the brigade, and it was "stationary and not
"firing." The 3rd battalion of this brigade of Guards was lying
down in square, on the reverse incline of the position, to the
left of their 2nd battalion and at some distance from it, when
the Duke, coming back from the centre of the position, and
seeing how they were fired into by a large mass of skirmishers of
the Imperial Guard, desired the commanding officer "to form
"line on the front face of the square, and to drive those fellows
"in," (this was the origin of "Up Guards, and at them," words
which were never uttered.) The Duke's order was immediately
obeyed, and the 2nd battalion of the Guards drove them some
little distance down the slope, when there was a cry of "cavalry,"
and the Guards retired up and over the British position in some
disorder. This agrees with Colonel Gurwood's statement, that as
the 10th Hussars, in which he commanded a troop, were moving
from the left to the right centre of the position, they saw the
Guards retiring in some confusion. This, from all accounts, was
the only movement made against the enemy by Maitland's
brigade of Guards (and this was made by one battalion of
it only) during the action. They suffered severely from the
cannonade, and were charged, as all the troops were, by the
French cavalry, and suffered very much from the fire of these
skirmishers of the Imperial Guard, whom they drove in; but
this was the only forward movement they made against the

* This was erroneously spoken of after the battle, as "an attempt at
"deployment."

enemy. Gurwood must have seen them at some distance down the reverse slope of the British position, just about the time that the 52nd were completing their right-shoulder-forward movement, and that the skirmishers of the Imperial Guard were forming in front of their leading column. I must not now stop to prove that the story of Maitland's brigade of Guards having attacked and routed the leading column of the Imperial Guard is a mere myth, and that this has been all along well known to every officer of the 52nd who was present at Waterloo, from Lord Seaton down to myself, the youngest ensign, but will hereafter devote a chapter or two to the subject.

This advance of the 52nd line and its right-shoulder-forward movement was seen from the height above, and was spoken of by Lord Hill as one of the most beautiful advances he had ever seen. Sir John Byng, who had succeeded to the command of the whole division of the Guards when General Cooke was wounded, and was at the time near Maitland's brigade, said of it to one of the 52nd officers that night, "*We* saw the 52nd "advancing gloriously, as they always do." The Duke of Wellington also was much pleased with it, as I shall have to state more particularly in a subsequent chapter.

It is very difficult to calculate time during the progress of a battle; one officer told me that the whole action only appeared to him to last two hours, whereas it commenced exactly at twelve o'clock at noon, and lasted till a quarter after nine at night. It must have been nearly a quarter past eight when the 52nd stood parallel with the left flank of the Imperial Guard.

Our artillery on the British position, 300 yards above, had been playing upon the masses of the French Guard, but when we saw them there appeared to be no confusion amongst them; our advance put a stop to the fire of our artillery; it was not till the 52nd skirmishers fired into them that the Imperial Guard halted, then as many files as possible, on the left of each company of their leading column, faced outwards and returned the fire; as the 52nd approached, our skirmishers fell back to the regiment, two of the three officers being severely wounded, and many of the men being either killed or wounded. The regiment opened fire upon the enemy without halting; the men fired, then partly halted to load, whilst those in the rear slipped round them in a sort of skirmishing order, though they maintained a compact line, occupying, however, nearly double the extent of ground, from front to rear, which a four-deep line usually requires.

The French writer, Quinet, although his account of this action contains all kinds of mistakes, speaks of this attack of the 52nd on the flank of the Imperial Guard as follows: "Le 52e régiment Anglais en profite pour venir audacieusement "se déployer sur le flanc gauche. Quand le régiment Anglais "l'eut débordée tout entière, il ouvrit son feu à brûle-pourpoint "......qui l'écrasait."

Here was a most exciting as well as a most critical period in this famous battle. The far-famed Imperial Guard of France, led on by the gallant Marshal Ney, whom the French styled "Le plus brave des braves," came into contact with that British regiment, of which Sir William Napier, the historian of the Peninsular War, had written that it was "a regiment never sur-"passed in arms, since arms were first borne by men;" and this regiment was commanded by Colonel Sir John Colborne (afterwards Field-Marshal Lord Seaton) one of the most experienced, steady, cool, and at the same time, gallant and dashing officers of the British or any other army.

The mounted officers rode to the front of the line. There were Colonel Sir John Colborne, Lieut.-Colonel Charles Rowan, Major Wm. Chalmers, Adjutant Winterbottom, and Assistant-Adjutant Nixon, also our general of brigade, Adam, who had just come up, and some of his staff, Lieutenant Campbell, 7th Fusileers, and Major Hunter Blair, 91st regiment, brigade-major. Chalmers, in front of the right of No. 4 company, placed his cap on the point of his sword, and, standing up in his stirrups, cheered the regiment on. Here I saw Winterbottom badly wounded in the head, and brought by his horse through the line, without his cap, the blood streaming down him; the poor fellow managed to hold on by the pommel of his saddle. Captain Diggle, commanding No. 1 company, had been desperately wounded just before on the left temple. Lieutenant Dawson was shot through the lungs; Anderson lost a leg. Major Love was severely wounded in the head, and afterwards, as he lay on the ground, in the foot and in two other places. Lieutenant Campbell, who had been skirmishing, came through the line severely wounded in the groin; General Adam was severely wounded in the leg, but did not quit the field. Colonel Charles Rowan was also slightly wounded; Sir John Colborne had his horse killed under him, and was grazed in the hand and on the foot. Several of the other officers were very slightly hit, but were not returned as wounded; I consider that about 140 of our men were killed or wounded at this time, in the course of five or six minutes. I missed Sir John Colborne for two or three minutes, and felt very anxious about him, but presently he came quickly down the front on foot, giving directions, still wearing a portion of my cloak, and wiping his mouth with his white handkerchief.

As we closed towards the French Guard, they did not wait for our charge, but the leading column at first somewhat receded from us, and then broke and fled; a portion of the rear column also broke and ran; but three or four battalions of the Old Guard, forming part of this second column, retired hastily, in some degree of order, towards the rising ground in front of La Belle Alliance, with a few pieces of the artillery of the Guard, which must have been on their right flank when they advanced, as we did not see them, and those which were left by the gunners on the ground, until the French Guard had given way; indeed, had these guns been on the left flank of the columns of the Imperial Guard, when we were bringing our right shoulders forward, they might have plied our line with grape, and have caused us the most serious loss; or, possibly, had they been there, Sir John Colborne would not have ventured on the movement at all. With the exception of these battalions of the Old Guard, the whole French army, as far as the eye could reach, appeared to us to be in utter confusion.

The 52nd still advanced by itself, in the direction of the lower inclosure of La Haye Sainte, towards the Charleroi road, and nearly at right angles with that part of the British position behind which, on the reverse slope, stood Maitland's brigade of Guards, and Sir Colin Halkett's, Count Kielmansegge's, and Colonel Von Ompteda's brigades, at a distance from the 52nd varying, as the regiment continued to advance, from 350 to 700 yards.

Immediately after the defeat of the Imperial Guard, the 52nd passed over their killed and wounded, who, poor fellows, were lying very thick upon the ground, where I passed on a breadth of about fifty yards; in some places I had to spring over heaps of them lying over each other. One of the 52nd officers, who has now been dead for many years, told me, some time after the action, that an occurrence had taken place as we passed the killed and wounded of the French Guard, which had since given him at times some uneasiness. It was this:—As he was advancing in rear of the regiment, he saw a Belgian soldier, who was following us in pursuit of plunder, try to take money from a wounded Frenchman, who begged him to let him keep what little he had; on which the Belgian dealt him a heavy blow on the head with the butt end of his musket, which appeared to kill him, and that he was so indignant at this atrocity, that he immediately ran the Belgian through the body with his sword. He asked me what I should have done under the circumstances, and I replied, that I most likely should have done the same; but that I was not sure it was the right thing to do; yet, as the scoundrel had left his own corps in search of plunder, and had under those circumstances taken away life, his own life seemed to be fairly forfeited. I saw a man of the 40th regiment about the same time, who also was probably on the same sort of errand, and I only mention him, because I observe that in Colonel Ponsonby's account of what happened to him when he was lying wounded on the ground, he mentions amongst other things that a soldier of the 40th came across him late at night, and took care of him till the morning of the 19th. This was probably the same man we had seen earlier in the evening.*

The 52nd had only got a very short distance from the killed and wounded of the Imperial Guard, when suddenly, through the smoke, it saw a charge of cavalry coming upon its flanks and centre. They consisted of British and German light dragoons, mingled with French cuirassiers, before whom they were retiring at speed. We took them all for the enemy, and they were fired on and lost some men before it was discovered that many of them were English. Some went round the flanks, but many

* See Appendix No. 5, again.

rode at the centre of the regiment, and, when they were about twenty yards off, the line opened about six or eight feet in the centre to let them pass. I thought at the moment that the men were not right in making an opening for those whom we regarded as enemies, and should have received the charge on their bayonets; I, therefore, stood to the front, on the right of the formed line and to the left of the opening, and attempted to draw my sword from the scabbard that I might attack the leading horseman. It was hanging on my left side, hooked up to the waistbelt, as officers carrying the colours do not draw their swords in action, except in cases of emergency. To my great dismay, the looped sword-knot was entangled in the button of the scabbard, and I could not get my sword out, and therefore I instantly took the colour in both hands with the intention of using it as a lance against the foremost dragoon. The poor fellow was, however, shot dead by our men, and fell headlong from his horse on his back, with his head towards us, about six feet in front of the opening; I then saw by his three stripes that he was a serjeant. The horse passed through the centre of the interval, and, as he was at speed, the stirrups flew out at right angles from the saddle, and the right one nearly struck me in the face. There was then a cry, "They are English," and the firing ceased. Opposite to the centre of the 52nd, the cuirassiers were seen to draw off in admirable order. On the right, one gallant cuirassier penetrated the line and was cut down, just as he got through it, by the serjeant-major.

Just clear of the right of our line, an encounter was witnessed between a cuirassier officer and a cadet, (answering to a volunteer in our service,) attached to one of the German light dragoon regiments of Dornberg's brigade. The latter was retreating at speed before his antagonist, with his head down on his horse's neck and his sword over his own neck. The German cadet was watching his opportunity, and on finding himself near his friends, on the right of our line, suddenly pulled his horse up upon his haunches, and dealt the cuirassier a blow across his face; he wheeled round and engaged the cadet in single combat, who managed to strike him again on his face, so that he fell over on one side, and was pierced under the arm and killed.

Colonel Hall, writes as follows, on the subject of this passage of the light dragoons through our centre:—" The uniform of the "light dragoons had just been altered, and they were dressed as "the French chasseurs, so it was quite natural that they should "receive a volley. I remarked that but few fell in front of the "line, but a considerable number in the rear. The coolness of "our men in this unfortunate mistake was admirable; in the "smoke and noise and confusion, no one knew if his comrade was "cut down or not, but there was no thought of dispersing or of "lying down for safety; they just faced about and prepared to "fire on the supposed enemy in the rear. I believe some did do "so before the officers, who had discovered the error, could stop "them. Anderson told me that the dragoons who rode through "our line, re-formed close to where he was sitting wounded, and "that he heard the commanding officer exclaim, in a tone of "vexation, 'It's always the case, we always lose more men by "'our own people than we do by the enemy.'"

It was said that some of the 23rd Light Dragoons (and it seems there were German light dragoons with them) had attacked a body of French infantry, probably some of the defeated Imperial Guard, and that being consequently somewhat broken, they were charged by a formed body of cuirassiers, before whom they had to retire, in order that they might re-form. They did good service in engaging the enemy, but when they had to retire, they ought to have ridden round the flanks, and not through the line, of one of their own infantry regiments. I may remark that if all our soldiers, cavalry and infantry, wore the scarlet uniform, these unfortunate mistakes of taking friends for foes would be of less frequent occurrence.

Almost immediately after we had become disengaged from the above-mentioned cavalry, we suddenly found that some guns on our right, towards La Belle Alliance, were firing grape into the front of the regiment, and making some serious gaps in our line. One discharge came into the centre, and the rattle of the grape against arms, accoutrements, and men, was something very different from the roar of round-shot, the noise from the explosion of shells, and the whistling and humming of bullets, which we had hitherto been accustomed to. Sir John Colborne, who was not then mounted, anxiously exclaimed, as he went quickly towards the right of the line, " Where are these guns? "they are destroying the regiment." Lieutenant Gawler, who, after Captain Diggle was wounded, had taken command of the right company, told him they were not far away on the right, and asked if he should take the right section and drive them in; Sir John Colborne told him to do so, and he then wheeled the right section to the right, extended it, and advanced towards them. As soon as the French gunners saw the red coats through the smoke, they immediately limbered up and retired. Gawler found a considerable body of French infantry in front of him, at 200 or 300 yards distance, and collected his men and waited for the regiment, which in the meantime had brought its left shoulder rather more forward.

When the discharge of grape came into the centre, I saw a man spring behind to take the musket of one who was killed, as his own would not go off. Another man near me said, in an undertone to his comrade, " the top of ——'s skull was taken off," mentioning the poor fellow's name, which I do not now recollect. Shortly after, as we were advancing, (there was no halt,) I found about a foot-and-a-half of my colour-pole was very wet with blood, about the height of my shoulder, and that there was blood on the buff cuff of the left sleeve of my jacket. It was not my own blood. The next morning I found that the thumb of my left hand was black and sore. I think my left hand and the colour-pole must have been struck, without my perceiving it at the moment, by a part of the skull of the man mentioned above, for the contusion could not have been occasioned merely by blood. I believe it was at this time that Lieutenant Holman had three musket-balls through the blade of his sword, without being touched himself. I have often seen the sword, and the holes made by the balls are connected with each other, as if they had been made by canister-shot; the thick rim of the sword holding the two parts of the blade so strongly together, that Holman used the sword for several years afterwards whenever he was on duty. He was the brother of Mr. Holman the blind traveller, whom I afterwards met at Nice and Rome.

I have mentioned that Sir John Colborne was on foot when

the French fired grape into our line. Just before this, both he and the present Lieut.-General Sir William Rowan, G.C.B., now colonel of the 52nd, made an ineffectual attempt again to become mounted officers. I think I may venture to relate the circumstance in Sir William Rowan's own words:—" I was "mounted, and my horse shot under me by a grape shot,* which "first grazed my right arm and then passed through my horse's "head. The fall stunned me a good deal. Sir John Colborne's "horse was also (afterwards) shot, which led to a laughable scene. "On our coming up to an abandoned French gun, with the horses "still attached to it, Sir John and I mounted two of the horses, "calling to our men to cut the traces, which they were unable to "accomplish; and as the regiment was advancing rapidly, we had "to dismount and follow as fast as we could. Shortly after we "met plenty of horses with empty saddles."

It has been said that the guns which retired with the rear battalions of the second column, and which afterwards, as I have related, fired grape into us, were directed to open fire on the advancing 52nd line by the Emperor himself; but I think it more likely they were directed to take up their ground by General Drouot, who was with the Imperial Guard when they gave way. The Emperor was then on the height above, in front of La Belle Alliance. Drouot had commanded the artillery of the Guard in several of the former campaigns of the Emperor, and had accompanied him to Elba, and afterwards went with him to St. Helena. At Waterloo he was the " Général aide-de-camp " de l'Empereur."†

Directly after the guns were driven in on our right by Gawler, we distinctly saw on our left, 300 or 400 yards up the British

* I think it must have been a round-shot.

† It is recorded of Drouot that he always carried a small Bible with him to read, which constituted his chief delight; and he avowed it openly to the persons in the imperial suite, a peculiarity not a little remarkable on that staff, and the admission of which required no small degree of moral courage. Napoleon often placed him in the most exposed positions, so that his situation was full of peril. He was said to be somewhat superstitious, because in action he took care to wear his old uniform of general of artillery, as he had long worn it and had never been wounded. The probability is, that he considered it unwise to draw the fire of the enemy upon himself by wearing a splendid uniform. He also always dismounted when near the enemy.

position, and on the Hougomont side of La Haye Sainte, four battalions in column, apparently French, standing with ordered arms. According to all accounts they were too far down the British position to be Dutch Belgians; they certainly were not English. It was thought they were French, and part of Donzelot's division, who did not know how to get away, and therefore remained quietly where they were until the 52nd had passed. We were then about 200 yards from the Charleroi road, and I think a line in prolongation of our front would on the left have cut the farm house of La Haye Sainte, at 300 yards distance, and on our right the south-eastern point of the inclosures of Hougomont, at a distance of rather more than half a mile from us. The 52nd was then, as before, quite alone, and had these four battalions of Donzelot's division come down upon our left flank with a regular British charge, they would possibly have prevented the rout of the French army from becoming so complete as it was. The brigades of Alten's division could not at this time have made any forward movement down a portion of the British position, which they did afterwards, when the Duke ordered the whole line to advance, or we should have seen them. I think the 71st, the right regiment of our brigade, and the left regiment, the 2nd battalion of the Rifles, both of which had been thrown out by the sudden advance of the 52nd, and perhaps the Osnabruck landwehr battalion, under Colonel Halkett, were the only British troops which had left the crest of the British position at this time; and we saw nothing even of these till the next morning, though Captain Siborne and other historians of the battle place the 71st and Rifles in line with us in our attack on the battalion of the Old Guard, which will presently be described.

When we were about 200 yards from the Charleroi road, the Prussian round-shot, directed either at our line or at the French extreme right, began to strike near us, one about fifteen yards from the centre, but apparently none of them touched the regiment. The Prussians had come up on the right flank of the French from the direction of Wavre, and at that time were trying to drive them out of the village of Planchenoit; rather later they succeeded in doing so, at an immense loss to themselves.

The Prussian guns were more than a mile from us; they soon discovered that we were friends, and ceased to cannonade us.

I well remember thinking, when I saw some of these Prussian round-shot striking the ground not far from us, that it would be very unfortunate to be killed or wounded just at the close of the action, when the enemy were in full retreat. I think it must have been at a rather earlier period of our advance, that my first thought occurred, of what would become of my soul in case I should be killed; I recollect I quieted the thought at once, by thinking that those who believed in the Saviour, the Lord Jesus Christ, would be saved; and that, as I believed in Him, all would be right if I should be killed that day. Of course most of my readers will be aware that such a mere belief in the history given in the Bible of what our Saviour did and said and suffered is not that saving faith or trust in Him, spoken of in John i, 11, 12; in John iii, 14—16; in Romans viii, 1; in 2 Corinthians v, 17; and in many other passages of the word of God. My careless and sinful life for several years afterwards, evidently shewed that, though I believed the history of the Saviour's life and death, I had, at the time referred to, no saving knowledge of Him. As I write this, I desire and pray that those of my readers, who have not hitherto laid this matter to heart, will look out these passages and consider them and the whole subject, with humble prayer that their God will, by means of His word, guide them into the way of salvation, holiness, peace, and eternal life.

CHAPTER IV.

52ND ATTACK AND DEFEAT THE IMPERIAL GRENADIERS.

52nd attack and drive off Old Guard—Duke of Wellington arrives—Lord Uxbridge wounded—The Duke and Napoleon in nearest proximity—52nd pass La Belle Alliance—No other troops in sight—Pass 75 pieces of deserted cannon—Encounter a French division and guns—Their surrender—Fire on French staff-officers——Last infantry shots at Waterloo—Bivouac at Rosomme—The Duke and Blucher—The 1st Guards between La Belle Alliance and British position—Sir John Byng's speech about 52nd—Wounded officers at the village of Waterloo—Sir Thomas Reynell's letter—Wounded hussar and Imperial grenadier—Ammunition waggon blown up—Various other incidents on the 19th.

It was about twenty minutes after eight, when Sir John Colborne seeing a considerable body of troops in his front inclined to make a stand, halted the 52nd in the low ground close to the Charleroi road, for the purpose of dressing the line, which had then advanced more than half a mile without any halt from the time it had left the British position. The regimental colour and the covering-serjeants were ordered out, and Nixon, the acting adjutant, had just dressed them, when the Duke of Wellington, attended by Sir Colin Campbell, rode up to Sir John Colborne, who was in the rear of the centre of the 52nd, and I heard him say, as I looked back from my position in front of the centre, "Well done, Colborne! Well done! Go on, don't give them "time to rally."*

* The Duke, referring to this part of the action in a memorandum written in October, 1836, twenty-one years after the Battle of Waterloo, has shown perhaps a very pardonable forgetfulness of the exact circumstance here related. He writes, " The infantry was advanced in line. I halted them for a moment in " the bottom, that they might be in order to attack some battalions of the enemy

The French had then opened fire on our line at about 200 yards distance, and I well recollect that several bullets streaked the ground close to me, many others seemed to whiz very close to my ears, so that I suspected the French were directing more attention than was quite pleasant to me and my colour. It may however have been principally attracted by the Duke, and Sir Colin Campbell and Sir John Colborne, who were immediately in my rear and about ten paces from me. The colour and the covering serjeants were immediately called in, without the line being dressed, and the regiment advanced and drove off the enemy. It was here that the Marquis of Anglesea, then Lord Uxbridge, rode up to the Duke and said, " For God's sake, Duke, "don't expose yourself so, you know what a valuable life yours "is," and that the Duke replied, " I'll be satisfied, when I see "those fellows go." Lord Uxbridge was wounded by a grape or musket-shot in the knee. I did not see it, nor was it observed by Sir John Colborne or by any of the officers of the regiment, our attention being engaged by the enemy's troops in our front. Sir Colin Campbell told me, several years afterwards, that, on observing that Lord Uxbridge was wounded, he rode up to him and laid hold of him by his collar and held him on his horse till his aide-de-camp took charge of him.

These troops, who acted as a rear guard to the French army now retiring in the greatest confusion, were, it is said, three battalions of the Old Guard, a small body of cuirassiers of the Guard, and a few pieces of artillery, probably the same guns which had been driven off by the right section of the 52nd under Lieutenant Gawler. It has been stated and is supposed that the Emperor Napoleon was with these troops. If so, the Emperor and the Duke were at this time in closer proximity, than they ever were at any other time ; and I am not sure that

---

"still on the heights." This is altogether incorrect. The Duke found the 52nd already halted, and said "Go on, don't give them time to rally." I find that after the lapse of several years, almost all those who were present at Waterloo forget many circumstances, which one is perfectly astonished at, whilst they are very clear about other points even of very minor importance. The being always able to distinguish between what they themselves witnessed and what they have heard from others or read of, is a great difficulty with some of my friends, after the lapse of fifty years. I do not experience the same difficulty myself.

I have not a good claim to having been at this time, for a few seconds, for the second time the foremost man of the British army, and the one nearest to the French Emperor; excepting of course the three or four persons who had been taken prisoners during the action and had been brought before him to see what information he could draw from them.

Here again was a most interesting period of the Battle of Waterloo, a battle of which the Duke of Wellington wrote, that being "possibly the most important single military event in "modern times, it was attended by advantages sufficient for the "glory of many such armies, as the two great Allied armies en-"gaged." Here the 52nd, certainly a most distinguished regiment in the British army, and one of the regiments formerly composing the famous light division in Spain, were opposed to the Old Guard, which was recruited from the Young Guard and from the other French regiments, not a man being admitted into it, who had not seen twelve years' service and who was not distinguished for good and gallant conduct. No man was admitted into the Young Guard who had not been in the army for four years. These fine fellows had never met with any defeat before, unless such had happened to them in other corps of the French army. Twenty minutes before this they had witnessed the defeat by the 52nd of the first column of their Guard and of the leading portion of their own column, from which they had hastily retired to their present position, where they were making something of a stand against us.

As I have observed above, here were the choicest troops of France, opposed to one of England's choicest regiments. Many fine and gallant officers had fallen on both sides, but here were on one side the Duke of Wellington, the Earl of Uxbridge, Commander-in-Chief of the British cavalry, Lord Seaton (then Sir John Colborne), an officer of the very highest repute in the English army, and Sir Colin Campbell (not the one who was afterwards Lord Clyde), Chief of the Duke's staff. On the other side were the Emperor Napoleon, Marshal Ney, Prince of Moskowa, Bertrand, General Drouot, Count D'Erlon, and probably Soult. From my point of view, I saw in front of us two or three bodies of men on the rising ground before us, but I could not see clearly their formation, for they were either kneeling, or no more of their bodies could be seen than to about a foot below their shoulders, owing to the ruggedness of the ground; they are, however, described by others of the 52nd as having been three squares, with a body of cavalry on their right; they had three guns on their left, which fired a round or two of grape at us. The 52nd did not return the fire of these troops of the Old Guard. On our advancing, the French retired in good order. The cavalry on their right faced about to cover the retreat of their squares, but, on our pressing on in pursuit, they prudently refused the encounter with our compact four-deep line. Only one of their squares retreated by our left of La Belle Alliance and the Charleroi road; and this square the 52nd kept in view for nearly a mile further, until they lost sight of it about a quarter of a mile before it reached the farm house of Rosomme, where we brought up for the night.

Sir Colin Campbell told me that, when Lord Uxbridge was wounded, he himself again pressed the Duke not to expose, as he was doing, his valuable life, and that he received the same reply which the Duke had immediately before given to Lord Uxbridge, that "he would be satisfied when he saw those fellows "go." He told me several other things about the Duke, most of which I noted down the day after I had the conversation with him. He told me that, when the 52nd advanced, the Duke and he went off to our right, which would probably be towards the lower part of the inclosures of Hougomont, and that some little time afterwards they crossed over some rising ground to their left, where they witnessed the unsuccessful charge by Major Howard and a party of the 10th Hussars upon a body of French infantry, and that the Duke was very angry when he saw them make the attack without having any support. Before he had accompanied the Duke down to the rear of the 52nd and about twenty minutes after we had advanced from the British position, he had taken an order from the Duke of Wellington to Sir Hussey Vivian to bring forward his hussar brigade, consisting of the 10th, 18th, and 1st German Hussars. He met him coming down the slope of the position and Vivian told him his brigade was just behind him. It appears from Vivian's correspondence with Gawler of the 52nd in 1833, that he must have come down the British position, through the interval made by the sudden advance of the 52nd, and that he saw no British troops as he advanced at right angles with the position, either to his right or left, and that his brigade came upon and charged a large body of cavalry somewhere in front of the 2nd French corps. These cavalry were mixed; there were cuirassiers, lancers, and guns with their horses attached. Colonel Gurwood, who had been in the 52nd, but at Waterloo commanded a troop in the 10th Hussars and was wounded, told me that, as he lay on the ground, he saw poor Howard's charge; that Vivian, after the charge of the 10th, observing some formed infantry in front, desired Howard to collect as many men as he could of those who had got into confusion in their charge on the French cavalry and to attack this infantry. This was looked upon as a very desperate service, as cavalry have rarely been known to defeat regularly formed and steady infantry. Gurwood told me that a young officer said to Howard, "If I were you, Howard, I would'nt do "it," and that Howard replied, "You heard the General's order, "and you know my position in the regiment." The charge was made and repulsed, Howard being killed. The infantry they attacked appears to have been one of the squares of the Grenadiers of the Imperial Guard, which had retired just to the right of La Belle Alliance and Primotion, when the square, followed by the 52nd, retired to the left of those houses, and to the left of the Charleroi road. As far as I can make out, this square and another were under Cambronne, and were closely followed, when he came near them, by Colonel Hugh Halkett with the Osnabruck battalion, one of the regiments of his Hanoverian brigade. Halkett had seen the sudden movement of the 52nd, and having sent his brigade-major* to order the rest of the brigade to follow, he moved the Osnabruck battalion down the slope of our position from the right of the 71st, and came away to the right of the 52nd, when these squares of the Imperial Guard were attacked by us; Halkett with his Hanoverian battalion got so near to one of these, that he made a dash at General Cambronne, who was at some little distance from the square, and took him prisoner with his

* The brigade-major was killed before he could deliver his order.

own hands.* The other square, which Major Howard charged, was farther to the rear of the French position, and more to our right than the square which Halkett was so close to. Vivian, in his correspondence with Gawler, eighteen years after the action, mentions that he expected a regiment of Hanoverians, on his left and rear, to have advanced to attack the square that Howard charged, but that this regiment, instead of doing so, followed another square more to its left.

I must now return to the account of the advance of the 52nd in its pursuit of the square of the Old Guard to our left of the Charleroi road. It gradually brought its left shoulders more forward, till opposite to La Belle Alliance the line was exactly at right angles with this road, the British position being about a mile directly in our rear. We passed great numbers of guns and ammunition waggons, which had been deserted in consequence of our rapid advance. Lord Seaton stated that at this time we passed no less than "seventy-five pieces of French "artillery, and that very shortly after the French columns dis-"persed."

Leaving La Belle Alliance and, farther on, the farm of Primotion on its right, the 52nd advanced in pursuit to the left of the Charleroi road, and at no great distance from it. It had been

* French writers assert that General Cambronne never exclaimed, "La Garde "meurt et ne se rend pas" (The Guard dies and does not surrender), but that these memorable words were uttered by General Michel, "who was killed at Waterloo "at the head of the square of the grenadiers of the Old Guard." In 1845, the two sons of General Michel addressed a request to the French King that a royal ordinance which authorised the town of Nantes to erect a statue to the memory of General Cambronne might be modified, that is to say, that the commission, charged with the erection of this monument, should not be authorised to cause to be engraven on the base of this statue those admirable words, "La Garde meurt et ne se rend pas." In support of their request, the sons of General Michel brought forward many witnesses to prove that Cambronne himself had denied using these words, and others to prove that they heard General Michel use them. Amongst these last was Baron Martenot, who commanded the battalion in which the Emperor took refuge "for a moment at the "end of the battle." Bertrand presented to General Michel's widow a stone detached from the Emperor's tomb, at Sainte Helena, on which he had inscribed these words and signed them :—" A la Baronne Michel, veuve du Général Michel, "tué à Waterloo, où il répondit aux sommations de l'ennemi par ces paroles "sublimes—'La Garde meurt et ne se rend pas'!

"Pierre du tombeau de Sainte Hélène.   [Signé,] BERTRAND."

quite alone since it left the British position, and continued so till it halted for the night.

I think it was after passing the farm of Primotion that I remember seeing, on the other side of the Charleroi road about 300 yards to our right, a small body of cavalry riding to the charge, probably it was poor Howard's charge, before referred to. Sir Colin Campbell thought, on examining with me a plan of the Field of Waterloo, that this charge took place not far from Primotion; he remembered there were some trees there near to a house, and that it then wanted a quarter to nine by his watch.*

One hundred yards to the south of the inclosures of Primotion, we being about the same distance to the left of the Charleroi road, the 52nd found itself on the edge of a deep hollow road with steep banks, in which were a large body of French infantry retiring from their right. In the centre it appeared to be a mutual surprise; they threw down their arms in token of surrender, and we rapidly passed through them. In the centre not a shot was exchanged. Captain McNair, however, made the men break some of the French muskets by knocking them against the ground, thinking it unwise to leave so large an armed body of the enemy in our rear, but there was no time for much of this, and probably not more than a dozen muskets were smashed. What took place on the right of the 52nd was thus graphically described by Colonel Gawler, in his "Crisis of Waterloo," thirty years ago :—" A hundred yards to the Allied left of

---

* The following letter from the Duke of York to the Duke of Wellington is published in the tenth volume of the Duke's supplementary despatches :—

"HORSE GUARDS, *June 30th*, 1815.

"MY DEAR LORD DUKE,—The family of the late Major Howard, of the "10th Hussars, have urged so earnestly that every possible measure should "be adopted for finding the body of that officer, as to induce me to desire that the "officer commanding at Bruxelles should be written to on the subject. I under-"stood that two serjeants of his regiment were employed to bury him ; and if you "will give orders that one of them should be sent back to Bruxelles to give any "information on the subject, the family will feel that both your Grace and "myself have done all that is practicable to effect their wishes.

"I remain, my dear Lord Duke, yours sincerely,
"FREDERICK."

[" *Let inquiry be made on this subject at the regiment for the two serjeants* "*mentioned.* WELLINGTON."]

"La Belle Alliance, a hollow road runs, nearly at right angles
"towards the chaussée, up which a column of artillery and infan-
"try was hastily retreating. The square (of the Imperial Guard)
"crossed the head of this body, but the high bank concealed the
"approach of the 52nd, until the distance became too small to admit
"of any but a hand-to-hand contest. The column seemed not suffi-
"ciently aware of its desperate circumstances to surrender without
"hesitation, and for a moment the scene was singularly wild. The
"infantry, before they threw down their arms, made an effort
"either at defence or escape. The artillery dashed at the opposite
"bank, but some of the horses of each gun were in an instant brought
"down. A subaltern of the battery, threw his sword on the
"ground in token of surrender; but the commander, standing in
"the centre of his guns, waved *his* above his head in defiance. A
"soldier sprang from the British ranks, parried his thrust, closed
"with him, threw him on the ground, and keeping him down with
"his foot, reversed his musket in both hands to bayonet him;
"when that repugnance to shedding of blood, which so often rises
"in the hearts of British soldiers even under circumstances of
"personal danger and prudential necessity, burst forth in a groan
"of disgust from his surrounding comrades; it came, however, in
"this case too late, the fatal thrust was sped, and the legion of
"honour lost another member."

On the left flank of the 52nd line, at no very great distance from it, a French officer brought up and formed about a hundred men from the hollow road, apparently with the view of making some attack upon us, but, on this being observed, the left company of the 52nd brought up its right shoulders to drive them in, when they retired back into the hollow road much faster than they came out of it; there was no firing on either side.

I was the first up on the top of the opposite bank, and the regiment formed on the colour. It was then getting somewhat duskish, and must have been close upon nine o'clock. At a distance of about 200 yards we observed four French staff-officers. McNair who was on the right of No. 4, (his own company, No. 9, being in the rear) gave the word, "No. 4, make ready," when I, who was next to him on his right, begged him to "let those poor "fellows off." He replied, "I dare not, I know not who they "may be." He then completed the word of command, and No. 4 fired a volley; No. 3, on the right did the same. The "cease firing" sounded down the line from the right, and I believe these were the last infantry-shots fired at Waterloo. The horse of one of the French officers fell, and we soon lost sight of them. I have thought it was probably Marshal Ney, who thus had his horse shot under him. It tallies with his own account; he speaks of lingering on the field, and of all his horses being shot. When McNair said, "He did not know who they might be," he was thinking of Napoleon, and thought it was not right to let him get away, if he could prevent it. It is very possible that the Emperor did form one of this group, for in the note at page 60, he is spoken of as having *at the end of the battle* been, "for a moment," in one of the squares of the Old Guard. Now one of them was retiring before the 52nd, and the other two or three were in our immediate vicinity on the other side of the Charleroi road. He may have been in the square we pursued, and have left it when they halted for a moment to throw off their knapsacks. This they were seen to do I think before we reached the hollow road. Being thus lightened they gained on us and we no longer saw them when, from the top of the hollow road, the two centre companies, 3 and 4, fired on the four mounted French officers.

There was no pursuing-cavalry on our side of the main road. Vivian's brigade of cavalry came up into line with us, far away to the right, when we were somewhere abreast of Primotion. Vandeleur's brigade of cavalry, came up rather later in pursuit. Halkett, with the Osnabruck battalion, must have been not very far in our rear, on the other side of the chaussée; and I conjecture from Colonel Reynell's letter that when we were at Primotion, or at the hollow road beyond it, the 71st, one of the two other regiments of our brigade, must have been away on the other side of Vivian's brigade, in a line with us, but at a distance from us of nearly 700 yards. The 71st, [perhaps the 2nd and 3rd Rifles,] and Halkett's Osnabruck battalion, afforded a most important support to the 52nd in its single-handed attack on the French Imperial Guard, but none of them nor any other regiment of the British or Allied troops were at all engaged with them. As far as I have been able to make matters out, the above mentioned regiments were the only infantry which advanced that night beyond the low ground between the French and British positions. The rest of the infantry bivouacked on the lower part of the slope of our own position; the enemy having been fairly routed and dispersed, long before the rest of the British and Allied army passed over the crest of that position.

In the advance of the 52nd from the hollow road to the farm of Rosomme, where it halted for the night, it passed at one place within a quarter of a mile of the nearest houses of Planchenoit, but saw nothing of the French who nearly up to that time had been keeping the Prussians in check in that village, and had inflicted severe loss upon them. They had now made off, with the rest of the French army who could get away, in the direction of Genappe and somewhat to their right of it, between it and Maison du Roi. About a quarter of a mile before we reached Rosomme we came upon the knapsacks of the square of the Old Guard. My colour-serjeant took possession of a *havre-sac* and afterwards took from it a loaf, from which he cut a good slice of bread, and offering it to me said, "Won't you have a slice of bread, Mr. Leeke? I am sure you deserve it, sir!" I was very glad of the bread, for I had eaten nothing but one biscuit for more than twenty-four hours; and I was pleased also with the kind and approving words of the serjeant. Shortly after this we reached Rosomme, and forming column of companies on the northern side of the farm, we halted in the angle formed by the Charleroi road and the road leading into it from Planchenoit, and piling arms bivouacked there for the night. It was a quarter after nine o'clock.

The farm of Rosomme is three-quarters of a mile from La Belle Alliance, and exactly the same distance from the church of Planchenoit. On this ground we found the straw which the French Imperial Guard had collected for themselves, and slept on the night before. The Duke himself must have ordered Sir John Colborne to halt there, for General Adam had not been with us since the defeat of the 10,000 men of the Imperial Guard, but had, notwithstanding he was severely wounded, been away to look after the 71st, who had been so much separated from the 52nd. I did not see the Duke at that time, but I recollect hearing that when he came up to the regiment at Rosomme, he asked Sir John Colborne "if there was anything he could do for the "52nd," and that Colborne replied he should be very glad if the Duke could send them a barrel of biscuits; which he promised to do.

As there has been so much controversy as to whether or not the Duke of Wellington and Marshal Blucher met, after the battle, at La Belle Alliance, the Duke himself even having declared that they met first at Genappe, and his memory evidently having been confused about it, I will copy verbatim the note I made of the information I got from Sir Colin Campbell the very day after I had the conversation with him in 1833. It is as follows: —"The Duke, seeing where *we* (the 52nd) were to halt for the "night, returned to La Belle Alliance and arranged with Blucher "that the Prussians should undertake the pursuit."

Soon after we halted a large fire was lighted, round which the officers stood, and talked over the events of the battle. Whilst we were thus engaged, we heard some cheering away in our rear, near La Belle Alliance, and May, of the 52nd, coming up shortly afterwards, told us that it proceeded from those who were present when Wellington and Blucher met.*

One of the first duties attended to when the regiment had piled arms and were lying down in column, was the calling the roll by a serjeant of each company. I observed that in almost every case of absence, some of the men could say what had happened to the man, whether they knew him to be killed or only wounded. We had left, including officers, exactly 206 of our

* The following is from the "Edinburgh Review" for *April*, 1864:—"In a letter "to Mr. Mudford, dated June 8th, 1816, he (the Duke) wrote :—'A remarkable "instance of the falsehoods, circulated through the evidence of unofficial des- "'patches, is to be found in the report of a meeting between Marshal Blucher "'and me at La Belle Alliance, (and some have gone so far as to have seen the "'chair in which I sat down in the farm house.) It happens that the meeting "'took place after ten at night, at the village of Genappe, and anybody who "'attempts to describe with truth the operations of the different armies will see "'that it could not be otherwise.'

"Captain Gronow has gone so far as to say that he was present, with other "officers, at the meeting at La Belle Alliance. Confidently as the Duke writes, "there are strong reasons for suspecting that he was mistaken as to the precise "place. It is clear, from French official accounts, that the French did not "abandon Genappe till past eleven; from the Prussian, that Blucher and his "staff did not reach it till near midnight."

F

poor fellows on the Field of Waterloo. Many of the wounded, I believe, but not all, got into houses at Merbe Braine or at the village of Waterloo.

The following was the return of the casualties of the 52nd at Waterloo:—

GENERAL RETURN.	OFFICERS' NAMES.	
Killed.	*Killed.*	
1 Ensign	Ensign Nettles	
1 Serjeant	*Wounded.*	
36 Rank and File	Major and Bt.-Lieut.-Col. Charles Rowan	Slightly
	Capt. Charles Diggle	Severely
Wounded.	Capt. and Bt.-Major J. F. Love	Severely
1 Major	Lieut. and Adjt. John Winterbottom	Severely
2 Captains	Lieut. Charles Dawson	Severely
5 Lieutenants	Lieut. Matthew Anderson	Severely
10 Serjeants	Lieut. George Campbell	Severely
150 Rank and File	Lieut. Thomas Cottingham	Severely

Major Hunter Blair, our brigade-major, who was in much concern about General Adam, whom he had not been able to find, came up to me about half an hour after we had halted, when I was near the men, and inquired if anybody had seen General Adam, and stated that he would reward any man who would find the general. This I made known, neither the brigade-major nor I thinking at the moment that by so doing we were giving an opportunity to any bad fellows, who might be so disposed, an opportunity of quitting the column for the purpose of plundering the killed and wounded they might meet with; I am not aware that any did so; but within half a minute, a man came to me in front of the general, who rode into the bivouac from the direction of Genappe, and said, "Here is General "Adam, sir!" Neither Blair nor I thought him entitled to the promised reward, as the general had found the regiment and was within a few paces of it when the man saw him. Adam had conducted himself with great gallantry in front of the 52nd when they took the French Imperial Guard in flank, and evinced his pluck also in not leaving the field, when severely wounded in the leg. As he sat on his horse for some little time near our fire, I heard him say that " he should never forget the honour of hav-"ing commanded the 52nd on that eventful day."

The following is taken from the 52nd record:—

"On returning to England for the recovery of his wounds, the "following extract of a letter from Major General Sir Frederick "Adam was communicated to the 52nd regiment:—

"'I request you will express in my name to the officers, non-"'commissioned officers and men of the brigade, (52nd, 71st, and "'95th regiments,) how much I regret my separation from them. "'The expectation of being early enabled to rejoin, and the hope "'of doing so, (which till within these last few days I have "'continually entertained,) have alone prevented my sooner ex-"'pressing to the several corps of the brigade the admiration I "'shall ever entertain of their intrepid and noble conduct in "'the battle of the 18th of June. To have had the good "'fortune of being at their head on so glorious an occasion "'will be to me a subject of increasing satisfaction. In pro-"'portion as I have regretted being separated from the light "'brigade, I shall look forward with anxiety to resuming that "'which through life it will be my pride to have held.

"(Signed) 'FREDERICK ADAM,
"'*Major-General.*'"

After our arrival at Rosomme I lay down for a few minutes on the flank of No. 9 company, and on my saying "Can any one "give me a drink of water," I was gratified with the kindness of the men, for there was no getting a supply of water where we were, yet four or five of them, directly they heard me, readily began to pass their canteens (wallets) towards me. I have always retained a grateful recollection of this little kindness. It is a rule with soldiers to go into action, if they can, with their canteens full of water, for, when a man is severely wounded, the desire for water is sometimes almost intolerable. I shall have to relate an instance of this presently.

About three-quarters of an hour after we had halted at Rosomme, the first column of the Prussians, by whom the pursuit was to be taken up, arrived from Planchenoit. As they marched round the column of the 52nd from Planchenoit into the Charleroi road, they broke into slow time, and their bands played, "God save the King." A mounted officer, who rode up the bank, and passed along the flank of the column, which was lying down, pulled up and asked me in French "if that was an "English colour;" (I still kept it in my possession, to give some poor tired fellow a little rest before he was placed on sentry over it.) On my replying that it was, he let go his bridle, and taking hold of the colour with both hands, pressed it to his bosom, and patted me on the back, exclaiming, "Brave Anglais."

The 52nd record relates the above occurrence as follows:—

"The Prussian regiments, as they came up the road from "Planchenoit and wheeled round into the great chaussée by "Rosomme, moved in slow time, their bands playing our National "Anthem, in compliment to our success; and a mounted officer at "the head of them embraced the 52nd colour, (which had been "carried that day by Ensign William Leeke,) to serve as the "expression of his tribute of admiration for the British army."

In a note from my name is the following: "Now the Rev. "W. Leeke, of Holbrooke, near Derby. The king's colour was "singularly lost for a time, buried under the body of Ensign "Nettles, who was killed in retiring from the square near "Hougomont, about 7 p.m. It was recovered on picking up the "wounded."

Some few of the Prussian soldiers passed up the bank and along the flank of our column with strings of three or four horses each, which they had picked up between Planchenoit and Rosomme. They were apparently horses taken from the French guns and ammunition waggons. One man, to whom I spoke, I found very ready to part with a couple of horses for a few francs. Probably the thinking he would have considerable difficulty in conducting his prizes very far, in the confused state of the roads by which the Prussians were to advance, may have had something to do with his willingness to part with them at so small a price. I had no defined object in the purchase, except that I thought it unfair that the Prussians should walk off with all the horses they came across, whilst we got none of them for our portion of the spoil. I took one of the horses for myself, and the other as a mess horse for the officers of the company. It turned out to be a very useful purchase; for half the officers of the regiment lost the whole of their baggage and baggage-horses, in the confusion which prevailed during the whole of the 18th on the road between Waterloo and Brussels. The officers of McNair's company were amongst the unfortunate sufferers. In a pocket on one of the saddles I found a quart bottle of brandy, which I suppose the Prussian soldier had not discovered. I do not think I tasted any of it myself, but I have no doubt it was properly appreciated by some of the more experienced officers, in the absence of anything else to drink or to eat.

Major Chalmers had a small straw hut constructed for himself just large enough to cover the upper half of his body. I took the liberty of lying down at the back of it with my head near to his and my legs stretched out in a contrary direction. I slept soundly and sweetly that night from eleven till about half-past two. How many thousands, within the space of two miles from us, British, Hanoverian, Brunswick, Nassau, Dutch, Belgian, Prussian and French, who bid as fair for life as any of us on the morning of the 18th, were now sleeping the sleep of death or lying desperately wounded on the field of Waterloo amidst what Marshal Ney described, as "the most frightful carnage he had ever witnessed!" Including the battle of Ligny, between the French and Prussians, on the 16th, and that on the same day between the French and English, &c., at Quatre Bras, the English, Germans, and Prussians lost about 33,857 in killed and wounded, from the 16th to the 18th inclusive. The loss of the French must have been much greater. Probably the whole amount of the loss on both sides during those three days would be about 75,000 men. Almost all the 52nd wounded officers were very "severely wounded." The late Lieut.-General Sir James Frederick Love, then a brevet-major, was wounded in the head in our attack upon the columns of the Imperial Guard. On falling, he lay on the ground stunned, for some moments; and, on recovering, he put his finger into the wound, and, in his confusion, it appeared to him to go straight down into his head, and, feeling convinced that no man could recover with such a wound, and seeing the 52nd advancing, he ran after them, thinking that he would die with his regiment, instead of lying to die where he was. He, however, after making the trial, had to succumb. He remained on the ground and there received another severe wound in the foot, besides two other slight wounds. There was some serious intention at one time of taking off his leg, but Bell, the eminent surgeon who wrote one of the "Bridgewater Treatises," to whom he was known and who had received some attention from him in the Peninsula, hearing that he was lying badly wounded at the village of Waterloo, went to see him, and by his advice the operation was delayed and the limb was saved.

Sir J. F. Love had two brothers in the 52nd, and they, hearing that their brother was severely wounded, obtained leave from Sir John Colborne, after the action, to go back and look for him. As people are so apt to do in the night, they completely missed their direction, and after wandering about for a considerable time, till they were regularly knocked up, they determined to remain for the night at a farm house which they had come to. Here the people, who were very glad of their protection, were very kind to them; and after getting something to eat, they had just laid themselves down on some straw in the large kitchen, when there was a loud knocking at the great gates of the farm, and, on these being opened, in stalked three grenadiers of the Imperial Guard with their firelocks and with bayonets fixed. They would not have been pleasant opponents perhaps for two young officers, but on the elder Love saying to them "Vous êtes prisonniers?" they very gladly acquiesced in the proposal, and their firelocks having been placed against the corner of the room, after a little time the five wearied soldiers, who had so lately met in mortal strife, were lying side by side on the same straw, and there slept together till daylight. The French soldiers, no doubt, were most thankful for the protection thus secured to them; for soldiers of a defeated army can never feel quite sure that their lives will be spared by any of their enemies whom they may fall in with; and I suspect the French were that night especially, to make use of an elegant expression recently imported from Cambridge, "awfully afraid" of the Prussians.

I may here mention that General Gneisenau, who had the command of the Prussian advanced troops on the night of the 18th, gave the French no rest. When his infantry, who had been on the march or in action since daybreak, were unable to march any further, he mounted a drummer on one of the horses taken rom Napoleon's carriage at Genappe, and made him every now and then beat his drum, to make the French, who did not care so much for the cavalry, think that the infantry were close at their heels. It is stated that in this manner Gneisenau drove the French from seven bivouacs which they had taken up, that he passed through Quatre Bras, which had been abandoned on his approach, and advanced beyond Frasne, a distance of eight miles from Rosomme, before he halted. The French army, completely scattered and disheartened, fled beyond the Sambre without venturing to make the least stand against their pursuers.

Soon after the 52nd had halted at Rosomme, the present Sir William Rowan, then a brevet-major, received permission from Sir John Colborne to go and look after his brother, the late Sir Charles Rowan, K.C.B., who had been wounded. After passing beyond La Belle Alliance and the ground beyond it, he found Maitland's brigade of Guards between the British and French positions, with their arms piled, he thought. He fell in with an officer of the 1st regiment of Guards, whom he knew; whilst he was speaking to him Sir John Byng rode up and asked "Who is "that?" and on the officer replying, "It is Rowan of the 52nd, "Sir," Sir John said, "Ah, we saw the 52nd advancing gloriously, "as they always do." Sir John Byng, in the early part of the action, commanded the brigade of Guards, composed of a battalion of the Coldstream and one of the 3rd Guards, which was posted in and to the rear of Hougomont. When General Cooke was wounded, Byng succeeded to the command of the whole division of the Guards, and was with Maitland's brigade when the 52nd attacked the Imperial Guard and advanced in the manner described by him in such glowing terms. Now this conversation happened about a quarter past ten o'clock, two hours after the 52nd had crossed the whole front of the right wing of the British army, 300 yards and more below the crest of the position; and the fact that Maitland's brigade was still at that late hour below the French position, helps to confirm the idea I have before advanced that scarcely more than four infantry regiments and two brigades of cavalry, Vivian's and Vandeleur's, advanced over the low ground towards the French position on the evening or night of the 18th of June, notwithstanding all that has been said about the Duke's advancing his whole line in support of those troops. I suppose that the greater portion of the British and Allied troops left their stations on the reverse slope of our position, and sought out for themselves ground on which to bivouac, more free, than that on which they had been stationed, from the melancholy sight of the slain and from the groans of the wounded and dying. I fear it was an unavoidable necessity that many of the wounded should be left for the night on the field of battle. One of the 52nd officers who was ordered on duty to Brussels the next morning, on passing over the ground by which we had advanced, was called upon by name by some of the 52nd men, who had been lying wounded all night, to get something done for them. He was unable to assist them, but at a very early hour a strong fatigue-party was sent out from the regiment to place them under the care of the surgeons. Another fatigue-party was sent out to collect the arms belonging to the regiment. I think by far the greater number of the wounded on our side were removed into houses at Waterloo, Merbe Braine, and other villages, before it became dark on the evening of the 18th. Sir William Rowan proceeded to Waterloo and there found his brother and all the 52nd wounded officers, except Anderson, in the same house.

At daylight on the 19th all were stirring. It was some time before we left our bivouac at Rosomme, perhaps an hour or two. On the opposite side of the Charleroi road was a battalion of the 95th Rifles, whom we had not seen the night before; probably they were the 2nd battalion of the 95th, who belonged to our brigade, and had come up some time after we had halted for the night.

About a third of a mile from the 52nd bivouac, near the farm of Rosomme to the south-east, is the house in which Bonaparte is said to have slept on the night of the 17th. On the other side of the Charleroi road, we found at some little distance some dead bodies, and swords and cuirasses which had been thrown away. This would be the ground over which some portions of Vandeleur's and Vivian's cavalry brigades must have passed in pursuit the night before. In one place were a number of letters strewn about which appeared to have been taken from the dead body of a French officer; they were the letters of a young lady in Scotland, to her husband, a French officer, who had *recently* left her to join the French army. They were just the tender affectionate letters which a young loving wife would write to a husband under such circumstances. I well remember the following sentence in one of them, "How I pity the poor English." Portions of these letters were listened to with great interest by several officers who were present, and all felt distressed at the thought that such a bitter cup of sorrow awaited the poor young widow. It was observed that one of those present took a peculiar interest in the writer of these letters; he frequently spoke of them, and of her afterwards, and it turned out that he had taken down her name and address, and that on his going on leave to Scotland some time after, he determined to go to the place in which she lived and to make enquiries about her. The sequel of the story is, that he was somewhat disappointed to find, that she and her husband were living most happily together. The husband had only been severely wounded at Waterloo, and had lost his letters.

If the French officer and his wife should be still living, and this should be read by them, the account of a matter, with which they were so closely mixed up, will be interesting to them, and it is hoped its public narration will not occasion them any annoyance. The Scotch officer died many years ago.

On moving from Rosomme, we passed through the burning village of Maison du Roi, about a quarter of a mile off, and joined the 71st on the other side of it. The following soldier-like letter to "The United Service Journal" from Sir Thomas Reynell, who commanded the 71st at Waterloo, will shew the good service that regiment performed when the 52nd moved down alone upon the two columns of the Imperial Guard. It also helps to shew that these columns were "*at the bottom of the declivity*," that is, *three or four hundred* yards from the crest of the British position, so that the 2nd battalion of the 1st Guards could not have come in contact with them, but only with their skirmishers:—

Sir Thomas Reynell on the Movement of the 71st during the
"Crisis" at Waterloo.

"MR. EDITOR,—I am induced to address you in consequence of some observations on Sir Hussey Vivian's Reply to 'The Crisis of Waterloo,' that appeared in your last Journal, which leave in

"doubt whether the 71st regiment was not that 'regiment in red'
"represented to have halted and opened a fire more destructive
"to their friends than foes, instead of charging at a very critical
"moment, and thus 'contributing to prevent the complete success
"' of the attack.'

"Although Sir Hussey adds that the officer whom he sent to
"stop the fire of this battalion reported it to be a regiment of the
"Hanoverian Legion, and asserts, in another part of his reply,
"that the impression on his mind has always been that they were
"so, and not the 71st regiment, still something less questionable
"seems indispensable for the honour and character of the latter
"distinguished corps; and I trust that I shall be able, in a few
"words, to supply that something.

"From having commanded the 71st regiment from the com-
"mencement to the close of that eventful day of Waterloo, and not
"having for a moment quitted its ranks, it may be presumed that
"no other person can speak with so much correctness as I can as
"to the part it performed during the battle.

"After the deployment from square, the 71st regiment moved
"in line, the right wing to the front, the left wing to the rear,
"forming a third and fourth rank. We passed Hougomont ob-
"liquely, throwing the right shoulders a little forward, as stated
"by the author of 'The Crisis,' and experienced some loss in the
"companies nearest to the orchard hedge from the fire of the
"tirailleurs posted there. We had in view, *at the bottom of the de-
"clivity, two columns of the enemy's infantry;* and my object, and
"I believe the object of every officer and soldier in the corps, was
"to come in contact with those columns, but they did not wait
"our approach, or afford us an opportunity of attacking them.

"I can positively assert that from the time the 71st regiment
"commenced this forward movement it never halted, but main-
"tained a steady advance upon the only enemy in front, until it
"reached the village of Caillon, against the walls of which were
"deposited a considerable quantity of arms, as if abandoned by
"the soldiers composing the enemy's two columns. It was becom-
"ing dark at this period, and after scouring the village of Caillon,
"we retired to a field to the right of it, where we bivouacked for
"the night, near to our friends the 52nd.

"I do not recollect to have seen in our advance any body of
"men, cavalry or infantry, to our front, but the *two columns of the
"enemy;* nor do I know that there was any on our right flank so
"much advanced as we were. I can well imagine that the move-
"ment of the 71st, conducted, as I trust it was, in a steady and
"soldier-like manner, must have afforded a very decided and im-
"portant support to the troops acting to our left, who approxi-
"mated closer to the point of the enemy's final attack.

"I have no desire whatever to attract notice to the services of
"the 71st regiment in the battle of Waterloo, firmly believing that
"every battalion and corps of the British army engaged did the
"duty assigned to it fully as well; but I confess that I have every
"wish to remove the possibility of its being supposed that at any
"moment the regiment could have hesitated to attack an enemy
"opposed to it; and I only hope that this plain statement of facts
"will convince the readers of your valuable Journal that the
"'regiment in red,' alluded to in Sir Hussey Vivian's Reply, was
"not the 71st Light Infantry.

"I remain, Sir, your most obedient humble Servant,

"Thos. Reynell, Major-General.
"Devonshire Place, 18th July, 1833."

The 52nd remained for several hours on the morning of the 19th near Maison du Roi, before they marched to Nivelles. Meat was served out, and the men cooked. I recollect having there first eaten "beefsteaks fried at the end of a ramrod." My servant brought some water for us to drink from a pond in which he said there were the dead bodies of two French soldiers, and that he could not find any other water. Some of our men had some orders and other things, which they had picked up on the field of battle; probably the men had belonged to one of the fatigue-parties sent out to take up any of our wounded who had remained on the ground all night, and to collect arms belonging to the regiment. I bought a pair of brass-barrelled pistols from one of the men. In a field about two hundred yards off, to the left of the chaussée, I found a French ammunition-waggon, and supplied myself with some cartridges, which fitted my pistols, for the purpose of putting an unfortunate horse, that had had its leg shot off, out of its misery. I did not succeed very well, as the horse, whenever I pulled the trigger, so suddenly moved his head that my aim did not take effect. Two Prussians coming up from Planchenoit, one of them a serjeant, shot the horse for me. After this I rode forward to a hamlet nearly half a mile in advance. I took three or four canteens with me to see if I could not get some water fit to drink; but one of our men whom I desired to fill them for me, told me when I was leaving the place afterwards, that he had filled them with beer, which he thought better than water. I remained in a farm house at this place for some time, as there were several wounded men filling all the lower rooms, to whom I and some of our men tried to render some little services. One was a man of the 7th Hussars who had received seven wounds when that regiment charged the French lancers, just to the north of Genappe, on the afternoon of the 17th. He described to me the manner and order in which he had received his wounds, all of which I do not distinctly recollect; but several of them, though not all, were lance wounds, inflicted whilst he was lying on the ground. There appears to have been much of this unnecessarily cruel work of piercing those lying on the ground wounded, carried on by the French lancers at Waterloo. Some of our cavalry regiments have since that time been armed with lances; but it may be worthy of the consideration of our own military authorities and of those of other nations, whether the use of a weapon, which appears to be chiefly used for the unmanly and cruel purpose of putting the wounded to death, might not be altogether given up. This 7th Hussar man, who had not till then been discovered and visited by any surgeon, was, whilst I was at the place, taken away by his own regiment. How he had got so far away from the ground on which he was wounded I do not know; but I think the distance from Genappe must have been nearly two miles. I had some hope that the man would recover.

On the other side of the fireplace, on a bed or mattrass, lay a poor fellow belonging to the grenadiers of the French Guard. He had, I thought, a fatal wound from which the bowels protruded. When he saw one of our men washing the wounds of the hussar, he begged that he would bring the water to him also; and on this being done, he eagerly seized the basin, and quenched his burning thirst by drinking deeply of the bloody water which it contained.

On my return to the regiment, with my canteens hanging on each side of my saddle, and my pistols stuck through the straps which fastened on my boat cloak in front of me, I saw our general of division, Sir Henry Clinton, and some of his staff coming towards me. He looked all the more formidable from a fashion he had adopted of wearing his cocked hat, not in the usual way, "fore and aft," but with the small ends over either shoulder. I thought I must look so much like a marauder, that I was rather ashamed of being seen by him. I soon disposed of my pistols by pitching them over a hedge on my right, never to see them again, and thus freed from the chief appendage I was ashamed of, I passed the general without attracting his particular attention.

Whilst I was away, a French ammunition-waggon was blown up not far from the regiment, and two men of the brigade were killed. I think one belonged to the 71st and the other to the 95th Rifles. They were on the top of the waggon, hacking at it with a hatchet or bill-hook to get some wood for cooking. I am not sure that it was not the same ammunition-waggon from which I had been helping myself to cartridges some little time before.

When the regiment fell in for the march to Nivelles, an inspection of knapsacks took place and several things were thrown away with which some of the men had encumbered themselves. We formed square either before or after this inspection, and some men were paraded as prisoners, who had fallen out drunk at Braine-le-comte on the morning of the 17th, in consequence of getting access to some wine vaults in that town, and had thus missed being with their regiment at Waterloo. Sir John Colborne addressed them, and said he should forgive them, as he considered it was a sufficient punishment for them that they had been absent from their regiment "*when they had the honour of defeat-*"*ing the Imperial Guard of France, led on by the Emperor* "*Napoleon Bonaparte in person.*" We supposed then, from what the French chef d'escadron had reported, that the Emperor was with his guard when we attacked them; but it afterwards appeared from the French accounts that it was not so, and that after they had marched past him in the low ground between the two armies, he had gone back to the French position, from which he only retired with the squares of the Old Guard.

CHAPTER V.

1815.

DEFEAT OF THE FRENCH IMPERIAL GUARD BY THE 52ND ALONE.

Defeat of the Imperial Guard by the 52nd, and not by the 1st British Guards—Lord Seaton and Sir John Byng—Steadiness of 52nd when wheeling in line, &c.—The Duke's despatch written on the night of the 18th—Duke of Richmond—Colonel Gawler—Siborne's mistakes—Sir W. Napier's statement about treachery and secret politics in connexion with Waterloo—Napier's letter about officers being drilled with men, and Lord Seaton with 52nd at Waterloo—Colonel Bentham and Minie rifle—Bentham and Waterloo—Lieutenant Sharpin of the Artillery contradicts Siborne—Lord Seaton's letter to Bentham on defeat of French Guard by 52nd—Mr. Yonge's conversation with Lord Seaton—Colonel Brotherton.

I MUST now, before I proceed to give the account of our march from Waterloo to Paris, enter upon the consideration of the following questions :—

1. Did the 52nd, as I have asserted in my account of what that regiment achieved at Waterloo, move down at least 300 yards from its position in the right wing of the Allied army, and defeat, single-handed, by an attack on their left flank, the two heavy columns of the Imperial Guard, apparently consisting of about 10,000 men?

2. Did the 1st Guards on that occasion, or on any other on that day, do anything beyond receiving and defeating various charges made by the French cavalry, and driving off, by an advance of their left battalion in line, the mass of skirmishers of the French Guard, and perhaps of Donzelot's division, who were firing into them?

I must endeavour to bring forward the various proofs I have of the correctness of my assertion relative to the defeat of the Imperial Guard by the 52nd alone, in the best order I can.

Every officer of the regiment who served at Waterloo has never had the least doubt of the correctness of the statement that the 52nd, and the 52nd alone, moved down upon the left flank of the Imperial Guard and defeated it, and when the Duke of Wellington's despatch reached us on our march to Paris, all considered themselves as most unjustly treated because Colborne's daring feat was not even alluded to.

Shortly after the 52nd reached Paris and were encamped in the Champs Elysées, Sir John Colborne gave us the following account of what Sir John Byng had said, on meeting him a day or two before. He said, "How do your fellows like our getting "the credit of doing what you did at Waterloo? I could not "advance when you did, because all our ammunition was gone." Some little time afterwards, when Sir John Colborne met Byng, and tried to lead him to speak on the subject again, he found him quite disinclined to do so. Many years afterwards, I think it was in 1850, when I was dining with Lord Seaton in town, one of his sons requested me to try and draw his father out to talk about Waterloo, saying that he often told them about his other battles, but they could not get him to speak much about that. I took an opportunity of asking him if he recollected much about Waterloo, and I suppose I particularized the charge of the 52nd on the Imperial Guard, for I remember he said, "Did you ever "hear what Sir John Byng said to me at Paris?" I replied that I had a very distinct recollection of it; but that I should be very much obliged if he would repeat to me what Sir John Byng had said, in order that I might see, if my recollection of it exactly tallied with his. Lord Seaton then gave me the account of what passed on the two occasions of his meeting Byng, just as I have related it above, and exactly as I remembered to have heard it from him five and thirty years before in the camp at Paris.

An old officer of the 52nd, who has now been dead for many years, wrote as follows in 1853, in reference to the advance of the 52nd on the the French Guard and to the subsequent unjust treatment the regiment received, in that the credit of, and the reward for, their splendid charge was given to the 1st regiment of the British Guards, *who really had nothing at all to do with it:*—

"The wheeling of a battalion in line, though under such cir-
"cumstances the only practicable mode of changing front, was
"altogether unprecedented, just one of those promptings of inspi-

"ration that mark the mind of a great general. Executed amid
"a continued roar of artillery that rendered words of command
"inaudible, trusting chiefly to the further companies that they
"would be guided by the touch to their inward flank, it could
"hardly have been ventured at all, but for the previous precaution
"of the commanding officer, who, when the order was given by the
"Duke, that all the regiments in the centre should form four deep,
"rather than loosen his files by that formation, had prepared to
"double his line by placing one wing closed up in rear of the
"other; another instance, to show how the knowledge of details,
"and constant attention to them, are essential in order to enable
"an officer to apply his men to the best purpose.

"Owing to the skill with which the movement was made,
"the very *acmé* of time being seized, never perhaps was more
"signal service done by a body of troops so disproportionate in
'number to the force attacked; that force being composed of the
'*élite* of the enemy's army, the most veteran troops in Europe.
A line on the flank of a column exhibits in the highest degree
the triumphs of skill over number. The column has only the
alternative of flight or destruction.

" This adventurous movement was undertaken upon his sole
responsibility, by the commanding officer of a single battalion,
and, from the first onset of the 52nd, that regiment and the
71st proceeded to the close of the day without receiving orders
from any general officer, whether of brigade or division*

" The successful charge and immediate pursuit of the broken
columns carried Adam's brigade far ahead of the other troops,
constituting them, as it were, an advanced guard to the main
body of the British army.

"We must not omit the admirable steadiness and intelligence
'of the men, mostly veterans of the Peninsula, enabling the com-
'manding officer in the first place to rely on them for taking up,
'amid a deafening fire, such a movement as a wheel in line,
'which every military man knows would in general be an awk-
'ward business for the first time on a quiet parade-ground, and

---

* The movement of the 71st in support of the advance of the 52nd is
described in Sir Thomas Reynell's letter, which will be found towards the close
of the last chapter.

"next exhibited in the cool way in which they treated the irrup-
"tion of cavalry on them, causing the officers to remark, that
"with such self possession, they need never be under any appre-
"hension from a charge.

"The Duke in his account of the battle entered but little
"into particulars. Of the period here referred to he says, 'These
"'attacks were repeated till about seven in the evening, when the
"'enemy made a desperate charge with cavalry and infantry, sup-
"'ported by the fire of artillery, to force our left centre near the
"'farm of La Haye Sainte, which, after a severe contest, was
"'defeated.' It is to be recollected that the despatch was written
"during the night succeeding the day of the battle in the house
"in which some of his staff were lying wounded and dying, and
"that it comprised also the action of Quatre Bras.

"These circumstances may account for its being somewhat
"brief, but certainly when the Gazette came out, a good deal of
"disappointment was felt that more detail had not been given. It
"was not only those who were engaged in that particular part of
"the fight we have been describing who were impressed with the
"importance of the service rendered in that conjuncture, but, two
"days after the battle, it so happened that sufficient means were
"afforded of learning something of the general sense of the army
"on the subject. Two officers from every regiment of cavalry and
"infantry were ordered back to Brussels to look after any missing
"soldiers, and among these, on their meeting there in the public
"rooms, discussing the events so fresh in their minds, it was the
"common consent that the charge of the 52nd was not only the
"decisive action of the day, but that it was one of the most gallant
"feats ever performed. And it may be said that a feeling stronger
"than disappointment arose, when it appeared that the defeat of
"Napoleon's last great effort was attributed to the Guards. The
"error was thus occasioned:—The battle commenced by the attack
"on Hougomont, which was occupied by a detachment of Byng's
"brigade of Guards, who held it during the day, had a hard service,
"and performed it well. So the Duke in his despatch said, 'The
"'Guards set an example which was followed by all.'

"This therefore was true enough, but Lord Bathurst, at that
"time Secretary for War and the Colonies, having to make a

"speech on the occasion in the House of Lords, founded a romance
"upon it, and said that the British Guards had encountered the
"grenadiers of the Imperial Guard and overthrown them. Then
"too was invented the story of 'Up, Guards, and at them,' a
"myth of the same baseless character with the ' Meurt mais ne
"' se *rend pas*' of the French. It was a piece of gossip picked
"up in the camp by Sir Walter Scott on his visit to Paris, first
"appearing in his 'Paul's letters to his kinsfolk,' and from
"thence gravely adopted by Alison as an historical fact.*

"However, these fictions served as an excuse for making the
"1st Guards grenadiers, and giving the ensigns of all three regi-
"ments precedence over those of the Line by lieutenant's rank.
"And as most writers of narratives of battles think it is excu-
"sable to cover their ignorance of facts, by the use of inflated
"language and figurative descriptions of unrealities, so these
"inventions have become the staple of almost every subsequent
"account of Waterloo, and this trash has been handed on from
"one to the other till, by force of repetition, there is risk that at a
"future day, when none remain to contradict, it may be recog-
"nized as authentic; while the knowledge of such a piece of
"generalship as the charge of the 52nd, so full of interest and
"instruction to military men, is in danger of being altogether
"lost."

The writer of the above says, in a letter I received from him
in June, 1853. "The Duke of Richmond,† I mean the present
"one, was with the Duke very near the Guards, and he says that
"until the 52nd began their movement the Duke was very
"anxious; that his anxiety was to be seen in his countenance,

---

* An instance of the common proneness to fiction respecting the events of great battles is to be observed in the repeated French assertions, that the British at Waterloo fought behind entrenchments. It had been proposed to the Duke, when he looked over the ground a month before, to throw up some redoubts, but he refused, saying, "No, no, that would tell them where we mean to fight." The choice was decided rather by the junction of the great roads to Brussels, than by any great advantage of the ground: so that Picton, half an hour before the action began, said, "I have just ridden along the whole length of the line, and I never saw a worse position."

† The Duke of Richmond was a captain in the 52nd at that time, but served on the staff of the Prince of Orange at Waterloo. After the Prince was wounded he attached himself it appears to the Duke of Wellington.

"and that he never saw such evident relief of mind as when the "52nd appeared moving across the ground so strong and "steady."

I have mentioned before that all the officers of the 52nd who served at Waterloo were fully convinced that a very great injustice had been done to the regiment by the attempt to give to the British Guards the credit of having repulsed the attack of the French Imperial Guard, or, as Captain Siborne has ventured to state, of having repulsed *the leading column* of the Imperial Guard.

In 1833 my friend and relative Colonel Gawler, then a major in the 52nd, published his admirably written work, "The Crisis of "Waterloo," and the wonder is how, with the few materials he had at command for such a work, he described so accurately, as he did, the movements of the two brigades of cavalry, and of the three or four regiments of infantry who were engaged at the crisis. From being on the extreme right of the 52nd he was not aware of the great distance (300 yards) of the left of our line from the British position, when it became parallel with the leading column of the French Guard, nor did he see, as we on the left and left centre of the 52nd line saw, the skirmishers of the Imperial Guard forming about a hundred yards in front of the leading battalion, when they had been driven down from the British position—no doubt by the 3rd battalion of the 1st Guards; he therefore fell into the mistake, which has been adopted by subsequent writers, of thinking and stating "that "the headmost companies of the Imperial Guard [those that the "52nd attacked] crowned the very summit of the position—their "dead bodies, the next day, bore unanswerable evidence to the "fact." When he wrote "The Crisis" he was not aware, that the columns of the Imperial Guard had been preceded by a mass of skirmishers, and that the bodies he saw the next morning on the summit of the position, must have been the bodies of some of these skirmishers. But Colonel Gawler, although supposing that the head of the columns of the Imperial Guard had reached the summit of the British position, never for a moment had the idea that these columns were repulsed by the British Guards, but solely by the flank attack of the 52nd. His book was only written to refute the claim put forward on the part of the Guards, and he thus expresses himself on the subject :—

"All the accounts of the battle which have hitherto come
"before the public, including those by the standard writers of the
"day, (and general opinion even in the army has much followed
"the same current), assert more or less directly, that the attack
"of the Imperial Guard was repulsed and the French army thrown
"into irretrievable confusion—either by a charge of General Mait-
"land's brigade of Guards—or by an advance of the whole line.
"But, if the leading points in the preceding account be, as they
"are maintained to be, correct, it follows, that the attack of the
"Imperial Guard was repulsed, and the French army thrown into
"consequent irretrievable confusion by neither of these causes,
"but by a charge of the 52nd covered by the 71st regiment, with-
"out the direct co-operation of any other portion of the Allied
"army. For as the 52nd charged across the whole front of attack
"from right to left, a simultaneous successful attack from any other
"corps must have crossed the charge of the 52nd, and no such event
"took place. These points are not advanced in a spirit either of
"display or dispute, but simply for the purposes before described.
"If incorrect they are open to refutation; and no one will be more
"gratified than the writer to see correction or refutation ably and
"thoroughly, if candidly attempted by any, who, having been
"eye-witnesses of these events, may conceive they have sufficient
"grounds for establishing either. If injustice in any shape has
"been done to the corps, to whom the credit of deciding the crisis
"has been hitherto more or less imputed, it is altogether uninten-
"tional. These battalions very hardly earned the honours justly
"due to them, *not* at the crisis and close, but by a most successful
"defence of their place in the position, during the reiterated
"attacks of the ordinary progress of the battle: they earned them
"well, and may they long, very long, continue to wear them un-
"tarnished. General Adam's brigade, posted during the early
"part of the day in reserve on the extreme right of the line,*

* It will be perceived that Colonel Gawler has here omitted to mention the advance of Adam's brigade over the British position and a quarter of a mile down the slope towards the enemy, and our standing there for nearly three hours, exposed to a furious cannonade from the artillery of the centre and of a part of the left wing of the French army.

86   DEFEAT OF THE FRENCH IMPERIAL GUARD

"came up to the right centre at an advanced period of the action,
"principally to meet the fresh and desperate masses of the enemy
"which pressed on for the crisis; it was *then their* opportunity,
"and why should they not also wear the laurels they then as fairly
"gained? The battalions first referred to, possess too many indis-
"putably their own, gathered on this and other fields, to require
"for the completion of their reputation a leaf to which they have
"no just title, while that leaf, torn as it was from the bearskin
"caps of imperial grenadiers at the grand crisis of the fate of
"Waterloo, of Napoleon, and of Europe, should not for ever be
"silently relinquished of those, by whom it was really won.

"Eighteen years* have elapsed without an effort to correct the
"error or to establish the claim, and if the attempt had further
"been deferred to any much later period, the generation of those
"who fought at Waterloo might so far have passed away, as to
"have left the question, without sufficient supporting evidence
"on either side, a standing subject of doubtful dispute and of
"historical obscurity."

It will have been observed from what has been stated, that those on the left of the 52nd line, when it was nearly parallel with the flank of the columns of the Imperial Guard, could see up the British position 200 yards beyond the ground on which the French skirmishers formed, when repulsed by the 3rd battalion of the Guards. This ground was entirely clear of anything in the shape of a defeated *column* of the Imperial Guard. And we were not a little astonished when we found that Siborne had stated in his "History of Waterloo" that the Guards had defeated the *leading column* of the French Guard. He was fully aware, when compiling his history, of what the 52nd claimed to have done; but yet, on weighing all the intricate and contradictory accounts which he received from officers of different corps, with whom he corresponded, he sought to reconcile them all by adopting this myth about a leading column having been defeated by our Guards.

The history of a great battle, especially if the materials for it are collected by one who did not see the principal events which he attempts to describe, must necessarily abound in mistakes. Captain Siborne took immense pains in collecting information,

* Colonel Gawler published "The Crisis of Waterloo" in 1833.

both when he first determined to construct his beautiful model of the Field of Waterloo, and afterwards when he was about to write the history of the battle, nearly thirty years after it was fought. Of course after the lapse of so many years, the greater portion of those he consulted could not be expected to recollect much that they had witnessed with any great degree of accuracy, or to be able always to distinguish between what they themselves had witnessed and what they had heard from others or had read of in accounts of the action.

In the preface to his history, dated March, 1844, he says:—

"Anxious to ensure the rigorous accuracy of my work, (the "model,) I ventured to apply for information to nearly all the "surviving eye-witnesses of the incidents which my model was "intended to represent. In every quarter, and amongst officers of "all ranks, from the general to the subaltern, my applications "were responded to in a most generous and liberal spirit, and the "result did indeed surprise me, so greatly at variance was this "historical evidence with the general notions which had prevailed "on the subject. Thus was suggested the *present* work. I was "induced by the success of this experiment, to embrace a wider "field, and to extend my inquiries over the entire battle, and "ultimately throughout the campaign itself, from its commence-"ment to its close.

"Having become the depositary of such valuable materials, I "felt a duty to the honourable profession of which I am a "humble member, to submit to it and to the world a true and "faithful account of this memorable epoch in the history of "Britain's military greatness.

"Though not so presumptuous as to imagine that I have fully "supplied so absolute a desideratum, yet I consider myself fortu-"nate in being the instrument of withdrawing so far the veil from "truth. One of my Waterloo correspondents has humourously "remarked that 'if ever truth lies at the bottom of a well, she "does so immediately after a great battle, and it takes an "amazingly long time before she can be lugged out.' The time "for her emerging appears to have at length arrived, but, while "I feel that I have brought to light much that was involved in "obscurity, I cannot but be sensible that I may have fallen into

" errors. Should such be the case, I shall be most ready, here-
" after, to make any corrections that may appear requisite, on
" my being favoured, *by eye-witnesses,* with further well authenti-
" cated information."

I find the following note written by me some years ago on the pages of my copy of Captain Siborne's work which contain the preface from which the above is extracted:—"Captain " Siborne appears to have consulted more than one officer, and in " some cases, several officers of the same regiment. Their accounts " would of course vary as to the exact time and as to circumstances. " In the case of the 52nd, and I think in the case of the 3rd " battalion of the 1st Guards, he mentions things somewhat similar " to each other, as having taken place on separate occasions, when " in fact they only occurred once." It may be well to remark here that in nothing have I found so much difference as in the ideas which people have formed respecting *the time occupied* by the several events, which occurred in connexion with the proceedings of the 52nd at Waterloo. Even under the long and severe cannonade we experienced, time passed much more quickly than it appeared to do. One intelligent 52nd officer, who, some years ago, was arguing with me about the time occupied by a certain movement or event—I forget now what it was—very soon gave way, saying, "I must not argue with you about the time it occu- " pied, for I confess the whole of the Battle of Waterloo appeared " to me only to last two hours."

The following are instances in which Captain Siborne has been led, in the arrangement of the immense amount of conflicting information supplied to him, to mention *the same event as having happened at two or three different times.* At page 116 of the second volume of the second edition of his work, in speaking of events which took place some considerable time before the advance of the Imperial Guard, he gives the following description of an event which resembles in some of its principal features, what did afterwards really take place as regards the 3rd battalion of the Guards,[*] with the exception that the skirmishers are not represented as being Imperial Guardsmen, but as having come from the hollow near La Haye Sainte:—

[*] See my account at page 44.

"A mass of *tirailleurs* now ascended by their left, from the
"hollow westward of La Haye Sainte, and pushed forward with
"great boldness against the advanced square of Maitland's British
"brigade formed by the 3rd battalion of the 1st Foot Guards.
"Their fire, concentrated upon the square, and maintained with
"astonishing rapidity and vigour, was most galling to the British
"Guards. Also upon their left another portion of their numbers
"poured a destructive fire upon the left square of Adam's brigade,
"formed by the 2nd battalion of the 95th Rifles. The exposed
"situation of the 3rd battalion of Guards, the fire from which in
"square was necessarily so vastly disproportioned to that by which
"it was assailed, caught the eye of the Duke of Wellington, who
"immediately rode up to the battalion, and ordered it to form line
"and drive the skirmishers down the slope. Its commander,
"Lieut.-Colonel D'Oyley, wheeled up the right and left faces of the
"square—the right half of the rear face accompanying the former,
"and the other half the left face—into line with the front face,
"and charged the enemy down the hill. A body of French cavalry
"was now seen approaching, but the battalion re-formed square
"with great rapidity and regularity. The cavalry refused the
"square, but receiving its fire, and then dashing along the front
"of the 52nd regiment, it exposed itself to another vigorous
"fire by which it was nearly destroyed; whilst the 3rd bat-
"talion of the Guard retired, in perfect order, to its original
"position."

As regards the 52nd, all that is said in the above paragraph is mere moonshine; the 52nd never fired on the enemy's cavalry at the time referred to; indeed they never fired, *whilst in line*, on any cavalry excepting on a mixed body of English and French, immediately after passing the killed and wounded of the Imperial Guard, and both on that occasion and when in square they were charged by the French cuirassiers, they were some hundreds of yards from the 3rd battalion of the 1st Guards.

It must be remembered that the 2nd battalion of the 1st Guards, which was the right battalion of Maitland's brigade, was stationary and not firing at the time of the attack of the Imperial Guard. This was Lord Hill's statement, who was on the right of the brigade, and from the position saw the advance of the

Imperial Guard and also the right-shoulder-forward movement and charge of the 52nd. The 3rd battalion of the 1st Guards only claimed to have advanced against the enemy once, and that was against what they called a column of the Imperial Guard, and that advance took place as I have before described it. Not only the Imperial Guard skirmishers, whom we saw form in front of their leading column, were driven in by this advance, but also the skirmishers and their supports said to have been sent forward from Donzelot's division to attack the right of Alten's division; this might account for their being called a column, and some of the skirmishers being Imperial Guardsmen may have led to its being called the *leading column of the Imperial Guard;* but as I have stated, and as will be shewn still more clearly hereafter, no *column* of the French Guard preceded those with which we came in contact.

At pages 168—171 of the second volume of Siborne's history, we have his account of the attack of the French Imperial Guard on the British Guards, and it will be seen from the following extracts, how it coincides, in various particulars, (such as the Duke riding up, the square forming line on its front face, the driving the enemy down the slope, the alarm of cavalry, and the retiring to the position,) with the advance of the 3rd battalion of the 1st Guards related above as having taken place a considerable time before:—

"Pressing boldly forward, they had arrived within fifty paces "of the spot on which the British Guards were lying down, when "Wellington gave the talismanic call, 'Up, Guards, make ready!'* "and ordered Maitland to attack."

"The British Guards had continued their charge some dis-"tance down the slope of the hill, when Maitland perceived the "second attacking column of the Imperial Guard advancing on "his right, and exposing his *brigade*† to the imminent risk of being

---

* Neither this, nor the more current expression of "Up, Guards, and at "them!" was ever used by the Duke of Wellington. He merely told the commanding officer of the 2nd battalion of the Guards to "form in line on the "front face of the square and drive those fellows in."

† Who would gather from this description the fact, that the 2nd battalion of the 1st Guards never moved from their place on the position all this time, as there is abundant testimony to prove, besides that of Lord Hill and Sir John

"turned on that flank. He accordingly gave the order to face
"about and retire; but amidst their victorious shouts, and the
"noise of the firing of cannon and other arms, the command was
"imperfectly understood, and the first sense of danger led to a cry
"of 'Form square' being passed along the line, it being naturally
"assumed that the enemy's cavalry would take advantage of their
"isolated position; which, however, was not the case. The flanks
"of battalions gave way as if to form square. Saltoun conspicu-
"ously exerted himself in endeavouring to rectify the mistake,
"but in vain; and the whole went to the rear."

At page 100 of his second volume, Captain Siborne, in attempting a description of the advance of our brigade over the British position, four hours before the driving in of the skirmishers of the Imperial Guard by the 3rd battalion of the 1st Guards, makes statements and brings forward expressions, so similar, in some respects, to those used in relation to this latter event, that I cannot but look upon them as really belonging to that period. They certainly do not at all properly describe what happened to Adam's brigade on that occasion, for the Duke was not then near them, nor were any French skirmishers attacked by them, and therefore the Duke could not order them, as Siborne states in the following extract, to "drive those fellows away;" but all these things did occur to the 3rd battalion of the 1st Guards, and the very words just mentioned were uttered by the Duke to Colonel D'Oyley, four hours afterwards, when they attacked and drove off the Imperial Guard skirmishers. This I had several years ago from a very intelligent officer of the 3rd battalion of the Guards, who was present in the action.

The extracts referred to above are as follows:—

"Suddenly the summit in front of Adam's brigade was crowded
"with the French skirmishers, who were almost as quickly con-
"cealed by the smoke from the rattling fire which they opened
"upon the Allied artillery and the squares. The gunners, whose
"numbers were fearfully diminished, were speedily driven back
"from their crippled batteries upon the nearest infantry, upon
"which the concentration of this most galling fire threatened the

Byng1 There were only two battalions in Maitland's brigade of the 1st regiment of Guards—the 2nd and 3rd battalions.

"most serious consequences. But succour was at hand. Welling-
"ton, in the midst of a shower of bullets, had galloped to the front
"of Adam's brigade, ordered it to form line, four deep, and then,
"pointing to the daring skirmishers on the height, called out, with
"perfect coolness and unaffected assurance, 'Drive those fellows
"'away.' With loud cheers the brigade moved rapidly up the slope,
"eager to obey the Duke's commands.

"The French skirmishers began to give way as the firm and
"intrepid front of the brigade presented itself to their view. Adam
"continued his advance, driving the French infantry before him."

I have thus endeavoured to point out how Captain Siborne has mentioned things as having taken place on two or three separate occasions, when in fact they only occurred once. In the case of the 3rd battalion of Maitland's brigade of Guards, they themselves only claim to have advanced and driven the enemy down the slope on one occasion, and that this advance was not an advance of the whole brigade, but only of one battalion, whereas Siborne makes them to have done so twice. And he has also scattered some leaves of laurel on the 52nd which they are not entitled to, whilst at the same time he has treated them most unfairly by attempting to deprive them of that full share of honour and glory, and of that very large branch of the emblematic evergreen, which so justly is their due, for having so steadily and "gloriously," under their noble and gallant commander, moved down upon and defeated, without the direct help of any other regiment or portion of a regiment, ten thousand of the best and most veteran troops of Europe, led on by Marshal Ney, "the bravest of the brave," and others of the most experienced officers of the French army, and accompanied by their artillery, and having large bodies of cavalry not far from them. Perhaps this was one of the most dashing exploits ever performed by a single regiment;— and I trust the 52nd will no longer be deprived of the laurels they so nobly and fairly won on the blood-stained field of Waterloo. It must be remembered also that the defeat of the two columns of the Imperial Guard by the 52nd led immediately to the flight of the whole French army. *The Prussians till then had been completely held at bay by the French at Planchenoit.*

Some time after the completion of the model of Waterloo, and when it was about to be removed from London for exhibition in the large towns of England and Scotland, I went to see it for the first time, and met Captain Siborne there. I had given him information, in consequence of his having applied to me through Colonel Gawler, as to the crops growing where we stood in square to the left of Hougomont, and where we stood in line on the reverse slope of the British position just before we advanced to the attack of the Imperial Guard, and with regard to some other matters connected with that attack. I therefore introduced myself to him, and spoke in terms of admiration of his beautiful model; but I told him that we of the 52nd were dissatisfied with the forward position he had given to Maitland's brigade of Guards, and to his representing a first French column as having been routed by them, and as flying in disorder towards and near to the Charleroi road, as we *knew both these things to be incorrect*. He merely shrugged his shoulders as much to say he could not now help it, and that there was no use now in discussing the matter. There was a serjeant there who was helping to exhibit the model: he had been in the 1st Guards at Waterloo; on my asking how far they had gone down the slope, from the British position, in pursuit of the French, he said "a few yards only, and that then "they retired again."

It seems somewhat astonishing that when Captain Siborne must have known that only the 3rd battalion of the 1st Guards made the forward movement, and that the 2nd battalion of that regiment was stationary at the time, he should have ventured to place the latter on his model in a forward position, and on a line with the 3rd battalion within 100 yards of the French Guard, at the moment that he represents the 52nd as being at exactly the same distance from the flank of the same Imperial column. When the 52nd was within that distance of the column of the Imperial Guard, the French skirmishers had just been driven in, the 3rd battalion of the Guards, on the cry of "cavalry," had retired over the British position and some considerable distance down the reverse slope to the point at which Vivian's hussar brigade had arrived, for they were seen by that brigade retiring in some disorder. They would have arrived at a point at some distance below the British position on its reverse slope, at the very time that the French skirmishers were seen by the 52nd to run in and form 100 yards in front of the leading column of the Imperial Guard, and 200 yards from the British position; these 300 yards being seen by us to be clear of all troops excepting these two or three companies of the Imperial Guard, containing perhaps three hundred men who had been skirmishing and firing into the square of the 3rd battalion of the Guards, and had then been driven off by them.

If there had been a first *column* of the Imperial Guards defeated and driven down the slope, as Siborne represents the case, how is it that the skirmishers, we saw, ran down to the long columns the 52nd attacked, and formed up in such a soldier-like and steady way a little a-head of that mass of troops? besides which, we must have seen such a defeated column, if there had been one at the time and on the ground indicated by Siborne both on his model and in his history of Waterloo.

In the "Life" of the late Lieut.-General Sir William Napier, the historian of the peninsular war, the following paragraph appears in one of his letters:—

" Depend upon it, Waterloo has a long story of treachery and " secret politics attached to it, which will not be made known in " our days, if ever."

I have frequently wondered if Sir William Napier wrote this in connexion with the wrong, which he knew very well had been perpetrated on the 52nd, in what has somewhat the appearance of a systematic plan to deprive that regiment of the honour of having done, what the world never saw before, in having made single-handed the most glorious advance against, and the most successful defeat of, ten times their own number, of the best disciplined troops of any age or country, barring always our own gallant army.

I shall here introduce what I had intended to place in the appendix—a letter, taken from Sir William Napier's "Life," on the regimental training of our young officers, written some time in 1853, in which he speaks of the defeat of the French Imperial Guard by the 52nd, under Lord Seaton, in connexion with Sir John Moore's system of training:—

"*To the Editor of 'The Naval and Military Gazette.'*

"Sir,—Introducing the letter of 'Veritas,' you say, the late Duke
" of Wellington opposed, '*as contrary to our national feelings,*'
" the having officers taught practically the whole routine of regi-
" mental discipline, from the first position of the drill-squad to
" marching in the ranks and mounting guard with the privates,
" which you nevertheless think would be useful.

"Did the Duke really object? He must have known that
" at Shorncliffe Sir John Moore introduced, and rigidly enforced
" that very system, and thus formed the British regiments of the
" light division, who were perhaps, or rather certainly, the best
" instructed, the most efficient military body in the field that
" modern times has produced—not excepting Napoleon's Guard,
" as Lord Seaton well proved with the 52nd regiment at Water-
" loo. The officers of those regiments, the 43rd, 52nd, and 95th
" Rifles, were never averse to, or mortified at, being made to
" acquire, amidst the private soldiers, a complete knowledge of
" what as officers they were to exact from, and superintend with,
" those privates. Never did the system lead to disrespect or un-
" due familiarity on the part of the soldiers; on the contrary, it
" produced the natural effect of knowledge, combined with power,
" willing and entire obedience from the soldiers, while the officers
" were proud of their acquirements, knew their men, and were
" known to them; knew when to exact and when to relax, and
" were in every sense commanders. This knowledge carried
" them through many a hard struggle, when ignorance would
" have gone to the wall.

"Much, very much, now forgotten and unknown, did Sir
" John Moore do for the British army, and I may perhaps here-
" after recall some of it to public recollection. At present I halt
" at this point."

Whilst reading Sir William Napier's "Life," I made also the following extract, as it bears upon my present object :—

"What would become of mankind if the arena where must
" be fought out the great battle of right against wrong should be
" deserted by the champions of the good cause?"

In accordance with this sentiment I have felt it to be my

duty to endeavour to set forth in its right and true light the great event which took place at the crisis of the battle of Waterloo—the defeat of the French Imperial Guard. I believe there is no one now remaining of the 52nd officers, but myself, who has both the recollections and the materials necessary for bringing before the public the "wrong" which was perpetrated against that regiment immediately after Waterloo, and which has continued to be perpetrated, though not to the same extent, ever since.

I think I have observed before, that the officers of the 52nd always felt, with great indignation, the wrong which had been inflicted on the regiment.

Lord Seaton was very decided in his statements on the subject, though he always spoke about the charge of the 52nd with his usual modesty.

The late Lieut.-Colonel John Bentham, who served in the 52nd for many years, and afterwards did himself so much credit, and rendered good service to his country, when in command of the 3rd regiment of Lancashire militia, and also by his unwearied efforts to introduce the use of the Minie rifle into the British army, took a most enthusiastic interest in the 52nd, and especially in its glorious advance on the French Imperial Guard at Waterloo. In a letter on this subject, written to me in 1853, he shews his strong feeling about it, when he says, "I hope to live to see this matter "made transparent." He entered into correspondence with many of the old officers of the regiment, and especially with Lord Seaton and Mr. Yonge, the latter a very intelligent officer who served in the 52nd, in the Peninsula and at Waterloo, and who also exerted himself for the introduction of the Minie rifle. The following testimonial was sent to Mrs. Bentham, sometime after the death of Colonel Bentham, by Lord Seaton:—"At the "request of Mrs. Bentham I have great satisfaction in stating "that the late Colonel Bentham served under my command in "the 52nd regiment; that he was one of the most active and "efficient officers in that distinguished corps; and that by his "exertions and perseverance, for ten years, he accelerated the "adoption of the Enfield rifle—having visited Vincennes fre- "quently, and established by his inspections of the rifle-practice

" at that military station, the superiority and precision of the
" Minie Rifle.

" I am persuaded that the attention of the authorities at the
" Horse Guards was first attracted to this subject, in consequence
" of his strong representations, and of his having, in conjunction
" with the late Mr. Yonge, of the 52nd, published the report of
" Colonel Sir Frederic Smith of the trial of the old musket at
" Chatham, proving its defects.

"SEATON, Field-Marshal.

"London, May 16, 1860."

As some acknowledgment of the service thus rendered by Colonel Bentham to the army in the above matter, the Government have given his son an appointment in the War Office.

The following are extracts from a letter written to me by Bentham, in November, 1853:—

" I read with very great interest and satisfaction your remi-
" niscences of Waterloo, forwarded to me by Yonge, and consider-
" ing the intense excitement and bustle at the period chiefly
" dwelt on, it is marvellous how closely all the statements of
" 52nd men agree thereon."

" It can hardly be conceived that the Duke, who witnessed
" the glorious swoop, and would not give the men time to inflate
" their lungs, but urged ' Colborne to go on,' could not only com-
" pletely ignore this astounding flight, but allow others to have
" the credit of it, by strong marks of distinction."

" I can fully bear you out as to Gurwood's declaration about
" the Guards. He was always very strong on this point. I met
" Gurwood in London, about 1828; he was then staying at
" Apsley House, and I asked him why he never drew the Duke
" out about the catastrophe at Waterloo. He said that he had
" repeatedly made the attempt, but that it was a subject which
" always excited great impatience. On the last attempt the
" Duke said, ' Oh, I know nothing of the services of particular
" ' regiments; there was glory enough for us all.' But had he
" written his annals true, Baron Muffling would not, as he has
" done recently, have charged him with '*policy*' in advancing
" his weak battalions to prevent the Prussians coming in for the

"victory. Baron Muffling and the world would have known that
" the genius and daring of Colborne gave the panic and death-
" blow, before the French began to yield to the Prussians. Let
" us yet have the whole truth."

In a letter I received from Colonel Bentham, dated May 16, 1854, he gives the account of an interview he had with Lieut. Sharpin, of Captain Bolton's brigade of artillery, attached to our division; it was stationed just to the left of the 52nd, and not far from the right of the 2nd battalion of the 1st Guards. It must be borne in mind that Captain Siborne, in his history of the Battle of Waterloo, has stated, on what the 52nd knew to be incorrect information, that a *first column* of the Imperial Guard was repulsed by Maitland's brigade of Guards, and that I maintain no such *column*, (but only the *skirmishers* of the Imperial Guard) reached within three hundred yards of the British Guards, and that these skirmishers were driven off the British position, not by an advance of the whole of Maitland's brigade, but by the advance of the 3rd battalion of the 1st Guards, whilst the 2nd battalion remained stationary. Captain Siborne has ventured to dress up his account of the supposed *column* (" which, as far as I can gather," writes Colonel Bentham, " was a column in buck-
" ram,") with several details, which belong to the advance of the two long columns of about 10,000 men, which the 52nd encountered and defeated. It must be borne in mind also that these two columns of the Imperial Guard were apparently of equal length, and were so close to each other that, although we could, in the left centre of the 52nd, see that there was an interval between them, we could not see through it. I should say that the interval did not exceed twenty paces.

Before I give the account of Colonel Bentham's interview with Lieutenant Sharpin, I must give the following extract from Siborne's history, in that part in which he is giving his account of what he calls a *first column* of the Imperial Guard :—

" Wellington rode up to the British foot battery, posted on
" the immediate right of Maitland's brigade of Guards, with its
" own right thrown somewhat forward, and addressing himself to
" an artillery officer, (Lieutenant Sharpin) hastily asked who
" commanded it. The latter replied that, Captain Bolton having

"just been killed, it was now under the command of Captain
" Napier. The Duke then said, 'Tell him to keep a look out to
"'his left, for the French will soon be with him.' The message
" had scarcely been communicated, when the bear-skin caps of
" the leading divisions of the column of the Imperial Guard
" appeared just above the summit of the hill. The cannonade,
" hitherto directed upon this point from the distant French bat-
" teries, now ceased, but *a swarm of skirmishers* opened a sharp
" and teasing fire among the British gunners. In the next
" moment, however, they were scattered and driven back upon
" the main body by a sudden shower of canister, grape, and
" schrapnel shells, poured forth from Napier's guns, which now
" kept up a terrific fire upon the column, within a distance of
" forty or fifty yards. Nevertheless the French Guards continued
" to advance. They had now topped the summit. To the
" astonishment of the officers who were at their head, there ap-
" peared, in their immediate front, no direct impediment to their
" further advance. They could only distinguish dimly through
" the smoke extending from Napier's battery, the cocked hats of
" a few mounted officers, little imagining, probably, that the most
" prominent of these was the great Duke himself. Pressing
" boldly forward, they had arrived within fifty paces of the spot
" on which the British Guards were lying down, when Wellington
" gave the talismanic call, 'Up, Guards, make ready,' and ordered
" Maitland to attack, &c., &c."

In contradiction of the above statement of Captain Siborne's, relating that Napier's battery fired into a *column* of the Imperial Guard which the British Guards had defeated, Colonel Bentham says, in his above-mentioned letter to me :—

"Since I wrote to you I ferretted out a Lieutenant Sharpin,
" of the artillery, who was attached to the battery in the angle
" made by the Guards and 52nd. He tells me that, until he saw
" the statement in Siborne, he never saw or heard of two attempts
" on our centre by the Imperial Guard; and subsequently in a
" detailed description, he says that Siborne was wrong in making
" his battery fire on any column but the one taken in flank by
" the infantry on the right. He is an excellent witness on our
" side."

I now introduce in extenso a letter written by the late Field-Marshal Lord Seaton, (formerly Sir John Colborne) to the late Colonel Bentham, on the subject of the defeat of the Imperial Guard of France solely by the flank attack of the 52nd on their columns. I prefer giving it in full, although I think there are one or two slight mistakes in it, which I can rectify in a note. I copy from the letter in Lord Seaton's own hand-writing:—

Deer Park, Honiton, October 15, 1853.

"MY DEAR BENTHAM,

"I forwarded to Lord Hardinge your letter addressed to "him, and your suggestions relative to the extension of the system "of education at Sandhurst. I do not, however, think that the "authorities will encourage the establishment of an 'Ecole de Tir' "at that college on the scale proposed by you.

"With reference to your letter of the 7th, it may be more "satisfactory to you, instead of replying to your queries, to draw "your attention to the principal movements which accelerated "the termination of the battle of Waterloo, and to the facts which "would have been admitted as evidence in support of the claims "of the 52nd, to the merit of having first checked the advance of "the Imperial Guard at the crisis of the battle, and of having "completed their *déroute*, by marching directly on their dense "columns, and by a flank movement charging them so vigorously, "that the whole gave way and retired in confusion. The state-"ments of officers, engaged at Waterloo, I found were generally "so different and conflicting, that it was impossible to draw up "any correct account of them. Captain Siborne, I believe, con-"sulted every officer in command with whom he was acquainted, "or to whom he was introduced, and endeavoured to make *their* "versions correspond with the facts generally known relative to "the movements of regiments, brigades, and divisions. I have "never read his account. If you bring the 52nd into a contest "with the Guards by attempting to prove from rumours that the "latter were retiring at the time they are said to have charged "and defeated the French troops, you will raise up a host of op-"ponents to your account, which would rather injure the cause "of the 52nd. I suppose the Guards must have made some for-

"ward movement, and that many officers must have seen it, but
"I contend that the French column had been checked and
"thrown into disorder before the Guards moved. I saw the
"column of the Imperial Guard steadily advancing to a certain
"point, and I observed them halt, which was *precisely* as the
"skirmishers of the 52nd opened fire on their flank. My atten-
"tion was so completely drawn to our position and dangerous
"advance—a large mass of cavalry having been seen on our
"right, exposed as it was, that I could see no movement what-
"ever on the part of the Guards, and indeed, as we advanced, I
"believe, we were too much under the position to have been able
"to have them in sight. Sir John Byng's brigade * remained in
"line without firing or making any movement, while we passed
"along its front, our line forming a right angle with that brigade,
"and being about two hundred yards nearer to the French. Sir
"John Byng told me afterwards at Paris, that he had his whole
"attention drawn to our movement, and that his brigade had no
"ammunition left. He gave *us*, at that time, full credit for our
"advance. Till the Duke of Wellington's dispatch was made
"known at Paris, *we* had never heard of the charge of the
"Guards; and I am inclined to believe that the attack of the
"French had been checked by the advance of the 52nd, and the
"movements afterwards of the whole of Sir H. Clinton's division,†
"before any forward movement had been made by the brigade
"commanded by Sir P. Maitland. This account corresponds
"with that given to me by Lord Hill, who was close to the

* It was Sir Peregrine Maitland's brigade, composed of the 2nd and 3rd battalions of the 1st Guards. Sir John Byng commanded the other brigade of Guards composed of the 2nd battalion of the Coldstream, and of the 2nd battalion of the 3rd Guards. This brigade was principally engaged in the defence of Hougomont. Major-General Cooke commanded the whole division, and on his being wounded, Byng succeeded to his command, and thus was with Maitland's brigade towards the close of the action. The whole of this brigade was not in line (possibly the right battalion was) when it was attacked and fired into by the skirmishers of the Imperial Guard; the 3rd battalion was at first in square, and was ordered by the Duke to "form line on its front face, and drive those fellows "in," which it immediately did, and the 2nd battalion remained stationary.

† Besides Adam's brigade, the Osnabruck battalion, under Colonel Hugh Halkett, was the only infantry regiment which advanced at that period of the close of the action. Vivian's hussar brigade appears to have come up with them somewhere between La Belle Alliance and Hougomont.

"Guards and 'saw us moving across the plain.' When we "followed the French towards La Belle Alliance, no troops from "the part of the position occupied by the Guards were near us, "and we passed eighty guns and carriages, a short time after the "French had retired, which they had left on the road between "La Haye Sainte and La Belle Alliance.

"I have written this, as circumstances have occurred to me "to remind me of the part we performed, without method—but "with these remarks and the facts mentioned in the inclosure, "you may be able to judge correctly of the claims of the 52nd.
"Yours very faithfully,
"SEATON."

The following passages, bearing upon the defeat of the French Imperial Guard by the single-handed attack of the 52nd, are extracted from some remarks on Waterloo by Lord Seaton:—

"The crisis may be called the period when the French columns, "advancing with the intention of penetrating our centre, were "checked and compelled to halt by the flank movement and fire "of the 52nd. This was the very first appearance of a change in "our favour. The attackers were attacked and checked in their "assault, and driven from the ground they had gained before "they could deploy. . . . . The whole of the Imperial Guard "advanced at the same time, and their flank was first attacked "by the 52nd, before any forward movement was made to check "them in front. . . . . The Prussians could not have attracted "the attention of the French, so as to cause the throwing back of "their right wing, until after the Imperial Guard had commenced "their attack on our centre. . . . . No regiment except the 52nd "fired on the flank of the Imperial Guard."

The late Mr. Wm. Crawley Yonge, of the 52nd, in a letter to Colonel Bentham written in November, 1853, says:—"He (Lord "Seaton) was saying here last week that after his conversation with "the French cuirassier officer, he kept watching the heavy column "advancing, saw it directed against a very weak part of the line, "saw no attempt at preparation to meet it, and therefore, (making "'light of his own exercise of judgment and decision,) he said, "there was nothing else to do, having such a strong battalion in

"hand, but to endeavour to stop them by a flank attack, for it
"seemed quite evident that, if something of that sort was not
"done, our line would unquestionably be penetrated. With a
"man looking on in this intelligent way, and acting on what he
"saw, how is it possible that all this fanfaronade, of Guards
"charging the head of this column, can have the smallest found-
"ation in truth?"

The same officer writes :—"It is the dearest wish of my heart
"to see that affair put to rights in the eyes of the world. As to
"Lord Seaton, I think there never was a man so ill-used as he
"was—only fancy how many men were there at any time,
"who would have done what he did, being only the commanding
"officer of his own regiment, without orders or sanction from any
"superior officer, his own general of brigade yet on the field, to
"take upon himself such responsibility; first, in acting without
"orders, and secondly, daring to expose his flank to the enemy
"as he did? How few would have seen and caught the right
"moment; and was there another man in the army who would
"have ventured on it, if he had seen it? As for the regiment, if
"they had their rights, they ought to have more credit for their
"exemplary steadiness under heavy fire for a good while previous
"to the charge, than for the charge and pursuit itself. It was
"capitally done, and few regiments could have borne to be so
"handled without getting into confusion, but it was easy work
"compared with the other."

On another occasion he speaks of Lord Seaton's characteristic
humility and modesty in the following terms:—"Meeting him
"in London a little while ago at the house of a lady, a mutual
"friend, she, hearing us talk over some of the occurrences of the
"war, remarked, 'How proud you gentlemen may feel at the
"'recollection that you had a share in those great events;' on
"which he replied very gently, 'Proud! No, rather humbled, I
"'think.' How characteristic this is, is it not? It puts me in
"mind of two lines in 'The Christian Year' on St. Philip and St.
"James's day. The stanza ends—

      "'Thankful for all God takes away,
      "'Humbled by all He gives.'"

In "The United Service Journal" for 1833, Colonel Gawler

104   DEFEAT OF THE FRENCH IMPERIAL GUARD.

published a letter from Colonel Brotherton, from which the following is an extract:—

"Some years ago, not long after the Battle of Waterloo, in
"conversation with a French officer of the staff, who had accom-
"panied the column led by Marshal Ney at the close of the day,
"we were describing the relative merits of our different modes of
"attack. I observed to him that to us it seemed surprising and
"unaccountable that our gallant opponents should obstinately
"persist in a practice, which experience must have taught them
"to be so unavailing and destructive to themselves, viz., their
"constant attacks in column against our infantry in line. I
"cited as a last and conclusive instance, the failure of the attack
"at the close of the day at Waterloo, where a column composed
"of such distinguished veterans, and led by such a man as Ney,
"was repulsed and upset by some comparatively young soldiers
"of our Guards, (for of such I understood the brigade in ques-
"tion to be composed,) adverting also to the singular coincidence
"of the Imperial Guard encountering our British Guards at such
"a crisis. Upon which he observed, without seeming in the
"least to detract from the merit of the troops which the column
"had to encounter in its front, who, he said, showed 'très bonne
"'contenance,'* that I was wrong in adducing *this* instance in
"support of my argument, or in supposing the attack was solely
"repulsed by the troops opposed to it in front; 'for,' added he,
"'nous fumes principalement repoussés *par une attaque de flanc,*
"'*très vive,* QUI NOUS ECRASA.' †

"As far as I can recollect, these were his very words. I retain
"all the feelings of a Guardsman, in which corps I served several
"years, and should feel as jealous of its honours as if still in
"its ranks, &c.

"Cavalry Depot, August 2nd, 1833."

* This expression would fairly apply to the driving in of the skirmishers by the charge of the 3rd battalion of the 1st Guards.
† "*We were chiefly repulsed by a very sharp flank attack*, WHICH DESTROYED "US."

These last words are the same as those employed by Quinet in describing the result of the fire of the 52nd, on the same occasion.

CHAPTER VI.

1815.

SIBORNE'S, ALISON'S, AND SHAW KENNEDY'S MISTAKES REFUTED.

The Duke's memorandum of 1836 about Waterloo—Much confusion in it—Confidence in the truth of history much shaken—Siborne, Alison, the Chaplain-General, Gleig, make great mistakes—Hooper's account more correct—Amount of the French Guard from 1804 to 1815—52nd, "a bright beam of red light, "&c."—Baron Muffling—Shaw Kennedy—What the 1st Guards did really do at the crisis of Waterloo—Killed and wounded of each battalion of the 1st Guards—How came Sir John Byng to allow the 52nd *to go on alone?*—Great injustice perpetrated against light infantry regiments—Letter to "The "Times" in 1855—Brevet rank of the Guards injurious to the service.

In reading over the numerous accounts, both printed and in manuscript, both English and French, of the *Crisis* of Waterloo, that is, of the advance of the two long columns of 10,000 men of the French Imperial Guard, towards the British position, supported by a forward movement of a great portion of the remainder of the French army, and of the total defeat of these columns, followed by the flight of the whole of the French army, one has been almost struck down with a feeling of despondency and of utter despair of being able to unravel the confused and complicated mass of detail, into which the various writers on the subject have together managed to work the history of that event.

Many of these writers have followed in the wake of Captain Siborne, who, not having had the good fortune to be at Waterloo, and not having witnessed the attack, was sure, as I have before shewn, to fall into the most terrible mistakes with regard to persons and time, in working up all the conflicting information which he received, so many years after the battle, from great numbers of officers who were present at it.

The Duke of Wellington, whose own memory, with regard to many things which occurred at Waterloo, has been found to be exceedingly defective in after years, wrote as follows to a person whom he wished to deter from attempting to write a history of the Battle of Waterloo:—

"Paris, 8th August, 1815.

"I have received your letter of the 2nd, regarding the Battle "of Waterloo. The object which you propose to yourself is very "difficult of attainment, and, if really obtained, is not a little "invidious. The history of a battle is not unlike the history of "a ball. Some individuals may recollect all the little events, of "which the great result is the battle lost or won; but no indi-"vidual can recollect the order in which, or the exact moment "at which they occurred, which makes all the difference as to "their value and importance."

To another person he writes, in 1816:—"The Battle of Water-"loo is undoubtedly one of the most interesting events of modern "times, but the Duke entertains no hopes of ever seeing an "account of all its details, which shall be true." Again in 1816 he says:—"The people of England may be entitled to a detailed "and accurate account of the Battle of Waterloo, and I have no "objection to their having it; but I do object to their being mis-"informed and misled by those novels called 'Relations,' 'Im-"'partial Accounts,' &c., &c., of that transaction, containing the "stories which curious travellers have picked up from peasants, "private soldiers, individual officers, &c., &c., and have published "to the world as the truth. . . . . I am really disgusted with "and ashamed of all that I have seen of the Battle of Waterloo. "The number of writings upon it would lead the world to sup-"pose that the British army had never fought a battle before; "and there is not one which contains a true representation, or "even an idea, of the transaction; and this is because the writers "have referred as above quoted, instead of to the official sources "and reports."

Alas! the official reports are very meagre, and the Duke's own despatch is particularly so, and I must say, and every 52nd officer who fought at Waterloo, from the gallant Colborne (Lord Seaton) to the youngest ensign, always felt that that despatch was most unjust towards that man and that regiment, which very probably had saved himself and his army from an ignominious defeat. The Duke surely knew the great exploit which had been performed by Lord Seaton and the 52nd, when he rode down with Sir Colin Campbell to the rear of the centre of the 52nd line, near the Charleroi road, eight hundred yards from their original position on the right of the 1st Guards, and found them there by themselves preparing to attack the three battalions of the grenadiers of the Old Guard, and when he exclaimed, as he rode up to us, " Well done, Colborne ! Well done ! Don't give them time " to rally."

In after years the Duke's recollections of what took place at the crisis of Waterloo were most confused, as will be seen from a memorandum written by him in October, 1836, one-and-twenty years after the battle, which I shall take the liberty of extracting from the despatches and memoranda published by his son. I shall also number the several paragraphs, and give my commentary upon some of them in brackets :—

Memorandum upon the plan of the Battle of Waterloo, written in October, 1836.

1. "I have looked over the plan of the ground of the " Battle of Waterloo, which appears to me to be accurately " drawn."

2. "It is very difficult for me to judge of the particular posi-"tion of each body of the troops under my command, much less " of the Prussian army, at any particular hour."

3. " I was informed that the smoke of the fire of cannon was " seen occasionally from our line, behind Hougomont, at a dis-"tance, in front of our left, about an hour before the *British* "*army advanced to the attack of the enemy's line.*" [The Italics are mine here, and in the succeeding paragraph.]

4. " The attack was ordered possibly at about half-past seven, " *when I saw the confusion in their position* upon *the result of the* " *last attack of their infantry,*" and when I rallied and brought "up again into the first line the Brunswick infantry."

[The hour was much later than " half-past seven," at which

the Duke of Wellington ordered the whole of his troops, then in position, to move forward, "when he saw the confusion on the " French position upon the repulse of the last attack of their in- "fantry." It must have been a quarter past eight o'clock when the 52nd repulsed this last attack of infantry, which was made by the 10,000 men of the Imperial Guard. It will here be seen that the Duke himself makes a distinction between the repulse of this last attack of the French Guard by the 52nd, followed by the advance of the 71st and of the Osnabruck battalion on the right, and the subsequent advance of his cavalry and infantry from the British position. He calls this last advance an "attack," but it will have been seen that after the return of the 3rd battalion of the 1st Guards from driving off the Imperial Guard skirmishers, and the defeat of the columns of the Imperial Guard by the 52nd, and the flight of the French army, there were no remaining French infantry to be attacked, except the three or four battalions of the Old Guard, who had retired hastily, without breaking, from the rear of the columns repulsed by the 52nd, and had brought up, 500 yards to their proper right and rear, on the rising ground situated about midway between the lower end of the inclosures of La Haye Sainte and La Belle Alliance, and which is crossed by the Charleroi road; and these battalions were attacked and driven off by the 52nd; and it would appear from Sir Colin Campbell's and Sir Hussey Vivian's statements that one, if not two of them, was afterwards followed and fired into by Halkett's Osnabruck battalion, and that one of them was that charged by Major Howard and a small party of the 10th Hussars. Vivian's and Vandeleur's brigades of cavalry found and "attacked" the retiring French on and beyond the French position.]

5. "The whole of the British and Allied cavalry of our army " was then in the rear of our infantry. I desired that it might " be collected in rear of our centre; that is, between Hougomont " and La Haye Sainte."

6. "The infantry was advanced in line. I halted them for a " moment in the bottom, that they might be in order to attack " some battalions of the enemy still on the heights."

[There is much confusion in the statements made in the

whole of this memorandum, but this 6th paragraph must refer to the 52nd and 71st, who were each in a four-deep *line*, and the Duke says, in the 9th paragraph, "the infantry was formed into "*columns*, and moved in pursuit in *columns* of battalions," which 9th paragraph must therefore refer to the infantry which advanced after the repulse of the Imperial Guard by the 52nd. What the Duke means, when he says these columns advanced in *pursuit*, I do not quite understand; but they probably moved down the British position some distance, and bivouacked on the lower slope of it, when it was ascertained that the whole French army was in utter *déroute* far beyond the French position.

The infantry, which the Duke says he halted for a moment in the bottom, was the 52nd by itself, which *Lord Seaton* had halted for a moment close to the Charleroi road, (*immediately* before the Duke rode up) in order to dress the line before he attacked the battalions of the Old Guard in his front. The Duke never halted the regiment, but on the contrary, found it just halted, and said, "Well done, Colborne! Go on, &c." One does not altogether wonder at mistakes on the part of the Duke when speaking of movements which had been made by portions of his army at Waterloo one-and-twenty years before, but they help to shew that his statements with regard to the events, and with regard even to the *very great events*, of that battle, must be received with caution.]

7. "The cavalry halted likewise. The whole moved forward "again in very few moments. The enemy did not stand the "attack. Some had fled before we halted. The whole abandoned "their position."

8. "The cavalry were then ordered to charge, and moved "round the flanks of the battalions of infantry."

[I believe scarcely any one but myself could possibly discover what movements the Duke had in his mind when he wrote down paragraphs 7 and 8. I think, after some amount of puzzling, I have found the clue to his meaning. No. 8, which should have preceded No. 7 paragraph, must refer to the advance of Sir Hussey Vivian's hussar brigade, from the British position round the flank of the Guards or of the 2nd battalion of the 95th

Rifles,* the left battalion of our brigade, which, if it had not then left the position, would be in line to the right of the 1st Guards. In a note made the day after a conversation I had with Sir Colin Campbell in 1833, I find the following entry:—" Sir Colin " Campbell told me distinctly that he did not go with the order " to Sir Hussey Vivian *until twenty minutes after our advance* " *against the Imperial Guard;* that he went before the three " squares of the Old Guard and the cuirassiers gave way before " us; that he met Sir Hussey coming down the hill, who said " his brigade was close at hand in his rear." " The cavalry halt- " ing likewise," in paragraph 7, refers to Vivian's disposition of his brigade on the rise of the French position, before they made their charge on the intermingled French cavalry of all arms, somewhere in a line with La Belle Alliance, away to our right.]

9. "The infantry was formed into columns, and moved in " pursuit in columns of battalions."

"WELLINGTON."

[This 9th paragraph I have endeavoured to explain under paragraph 6.]

What the Duke has said of the inaccuracies and mistakes of others, and of the confusion they would be sure to fall into, in attempting to give a history of the Battle of Waterloo, I have found, to my very great disgust and annoyance, to be perfectly and painfully true; but I think my readers will agree with me, that the Duke, in his memorandum of 1836, which I have just quoted and commented on, has shewn himself not to be a whit behind the writers of the " Relations," " Impartial Accounts," and "Histories" of Waterloo, whom he so properly denounces, in the inaccuracies, mistakes, and confusion of ideas which he himself has fallen into.

It may be asked, Are the histories of all battles equally in-

* I am exceedingly sorry not to be able to speak of the position or movements of our gallant friends of the 2nd battalion of the 95th Rifles after the 52nd moved down from the British position on the flank of the Imperial Guard. They were, of course, thrown out by our sudden movement, and were not with us when we defeated the 10,000 men of the French Guard; nor when we afterwards drove off the battalions of the grenadiers of the Guard from the height in front of La Belle Alliance. We were alone from the time we left the British position till we halted for the night at Rosomme, at about a quarter past nine.

MISTAKES REFUTED.

correct? Perhaps never were there anything like so many histories of any other battle written, either before or since, as have been written about Waterloo. I must, however, for myself confess that my confidence in the accuracy of history in general, which was never very great, has received the very rudest possible shake from all that I have read, both in English, German, Prussian, Belgian, French, and Spanish accounts concerning this great battle.

I feel that I must not leave the subject I am endeavouring to elucidate, without introducing one or two specimens of the manner in which persons, professing to describe the leading events of the crisis at Waterloo, have made the most egregious mistakes. The following is one in which much credit is given to General Adam's brigade, consisting of the 52nd, the 71st, and the 2nd and 3rd battalions of the 95th Rifles, for repulsing the French Imperial Guard. I will mark those portions of the account, which I know to be incorrect, in italics, and afterwards advert to it within brackets. It is called, *An extract from a letter from an eye witness:—*

"After various hot and desultory attacks of the day, the last "and most dreadful was made by the Old Imperial Guard, grown "grey in an uninterrupted career of victory. In black, massive, "solid columns, supported and covered by the fire of a numerous "artillery, they advanced in spite of the most desperate resist-"ance. Lord Hill, who had seen the approaching storm, *having* "*formed General Adam's brigade a little 'en potence' on the enemy's* "*left, placed himself at its head,* and advanced with dreadful regu-"larity to the assistance of *the Guards.* General Adam's veterans "of the Peninsula, after one terrible volley within a few yards of "the Imperial Guard, cheered and charged. These gallant "troops (the Imperial Guard) for the first time fled, although "encouraged to the last by the conduct of the brave but unfor-"tunate Ney. *Lord Hill* followed with his usual rapidity, *the* "*British Guards supporting him,* and *at the same instant* our great "Duke ordered the general and decisive advance of the whole "army."

[Lord Hill, and the British Guards, and the 71st, and 2nd and 3rd battalions of the 95th, were not engaged in the attack on these "black, massive, solid columns" of the Imperial Guard. It was made by the 52nd alone. The name of Sir John Colborne (Lord Seaton) should be substituted for that of Lord Hill. General Adam came up at the exact moment of the charge, and behaved most gallantly in front of the 52nd line, and was severely wounded, but he did not at all interfere with the command of the 52nd, which was left entirely to Colborne. After the Imperial Guard had fled, we saw no more of him until he rode into our bivouac at Rosomme, towards ten o'clock. With regard to the "general advance of the army," I have shewn a few pages back, under the paragraph in the Duke's memorandum which I have numbered 6, that it could not have taken place till about twenty minutes after the 52nd had routed the French Imperial Guard.]

I have shewn that Siborne, in his account of the crisis of Waterloo, has made most terrible mistakes. Alison, in his history of Europe, has followed him and taken much of his version of the crisis from Siborne. The Chaplain-General, Gleig, whilst following the account of a French writer, has written a work on the Battle of Waterloo, and dedicated it to the Queen, which appears to me to be about as full of errors as it is possible for any work to be. Hooper, in his history of the campaign of 1815, has followed Siborne, and gives the myth of the British Guards having defeated a first *column* of the Imperial Guard, very much in Siborne's own words. Mr. Hooper has evidently taken much pains to give a correct account of the battle and of the defeat of the French Guard; but he not only speaks of a first column of them, but even makes the British Guards, as Siborne does, both on his model and in his history, to assist in the defeat of a *second column*. Mr. Hooper candidly acknowledges in a note appended to his account of the defeat of the Imperial Guard, that "*much* "*confusion exists in the accounts of these columns of attack,* their "*number and formation,*" but adds, "the conclusions in the text "are derived from a study of the best accounts on both sides." *

---

* I would here ask, If the British Guards sent a *column* of the Imperial Guards flying down the slope, how was it that the 52nd, who were at that time 300 yards in a direct line in front of the British Guards, and at right angles with them; how was it that the 52nd never saw this column, but that they did see the skirmishers of the Imperial Guard run in and form 100 yards in front of the

MISTAKES REFUTED. 113

The following account, from Hooper's work, of the advance of the 52nd, may be taken as nearly correct, if it be recollected that the British Guards were not there, but 300 yards away; that the 71st never reached the enemy, but were away to the right, near the inclosures of Hougomont; that the 95th were not in line with the 52nd, and were not seen by them, and that the column said to have been defeated by the 3rd battalion of the 1st Guards still formed a portion of the "black, massive, solid columns," attacked by the 52nd, and that even the Imperial Guard *skirmishers*, driven back from the British position by the advance of the 3rd battalion of the 1st Guards, had returned to swell the numbers of the enemy, which we believe were fairly estimated as amounting to about ten thousand men.* It must also always be borne in mind that the arena, on which this conflict between the 52nd and the 10,000 picked and veteran soldiers of the Imperial Guard took place, was not towards the *crest* of the British position, as has been related by Siborne and others, but 300 yards below it. Lord Seaton calls it "the plain," Sir Thomas Reynell, of the 71st, speaks of it "as the bottom of the "declivity." Hooper writes as follows :—

"At this moment Sir John Colborne, who had steadily ob-

" black, massive, solid columns of the French Guard," which they (the 52nd) took in flank and overthrew, whilst the whole slope of the British position, above and in front of them, was quite clear of troops of any kind for 300 yards?

* Baron Muffling, who was present with the British army, says, respecting the strength of the columns of the French Guard, defeated by the 52nd, "The "enemy's Guard began to move, and with sixteen battalions, leaving La Haye "Sainte a little to the right, at half-past six o'clock advanced towards the plat- "form." [There is a great mistake here about the *time* of their advance; it must have been nearly eight o'clock when they reached the first ascent of the British position.]

Muffling states also, "Some of the enemy's batteries cover, with grape-shot, "the retreat of the four battalions of the Guard." [These battalions were the battalions of the Old Guard which, on the flight of the rest of the Imperial Guard, drew off hastily towards the French position.]

Sixteen battalions of 800 men each give an amount of 12,800 men, besides the officers and the artillery, and some cavalry of the Guard; so that allowing for any casualties or mistakes as to the numbers, there must have been, as it was always stated by the 52nd officers, about 10,000 of the Imperial Guard, when we attacked and defeated them. Ney, in his letter to the Duke of Otranto, speaks of four regiments, that is eight battalions, of the Middle Guard, and four battalions of the Old Guard.

MISTAKES REFUTED.

"served their progress, wheeled the 52nd upon its left company,*
"and brought it nearly parallel to the left flank of the attacking
"column. What was he going to do? was the inquiry of his
"superior officer. 'To make that column feel our fire,' was the
"prompt answer. The Duke and Lord Hill had seen and ap-
"proved of the movement, and the next moment the 52nd was
"over the brow, and its full fire was brought to bear upon the
"heavy masses before it." [The Duke and Lord Hill only saw
the 52nd when it had moved some distance down the slope, and
then sent to desire Sir John Colborne to continue the movement.]
"The Imperial Guardsmen faced this new and terrible foe, and
"began to fire from the flank. For a brief space the combat was
"one of musketry. 'A thick, white smoke enveloped the con-
"'tending parties.' Napier's guns double-shotted, the muskets
"of the British Guards, the rifles of the 95th, and the rapid fire
"of the 52nd, shook the column from front to rear." [The artillery
had ceased to fire on the Imperial Guard, the left of the 52nd
being in their way; and, I think, the French were then rather
sheltered by the ground from Napier's guns. The British Guards
were on the reverse slope of the British position, 300 yards away;
the 95th were not there; the 52nd had it all to themselves, with
the exception, that their truly gallant general of brigade, Adam,
and his staff, arrived in time to get into the thick of the fight in
front of the 52nd four-deep line.†]

Hooper thus continues his account:—"Reduced to an
"unsteady crowd, it yielded and fled, when, at Colborne's
"command, the 52nd brought down their bayonets to the
"charge, cheered and dashed on. This splendid regiment, sup-
"ported on the right by the 71st and on the left by the 95th,

---

* Sir John Colborne had at first, for a moment, the idea of changing in some
degree the direction of the 52nd line, by wheeling back the right companies,
(No. 1 and No. 6 in its rear,) on their right a few paces only, so as to throw back
the left of the regiment before he brought them over the crest of the position,
but it was immediately given up, and they advanced directly to the front, afterwards bringing their right shoulders forward as they moved down the slope, in
the manner before described.

† General Adam's spurs were well won on that glorious occasion. He was made
a Knight Commander of the Bath; and so was Sir Thomas Reynell of the 71st;
Sir John Colborne had obtained that distinction, and several other honours, at
the close of the Peninsular war in 1814.

"did not halt in its career in the track of the fugitives until it had
"swept, from right to left, along the front of the British centre.
"When the regiment halted, its left flank was in the hollow on
"the chaussée to Genappe, in advance of the orchard of La Haye
"Sainte, 800 yards from the ground at which the charge
"commenced. Colborne had led it from the little hollow above
"the north east angle of Hougomont, working through the
"furrowed and muddy ground, trampling amidst the dead and
"the wounded, a bright beam of red light streaking the sombre
"and misty field until the left flank of the brigade [of the 52nd]
"nearly touched the edge of the Charleroi road. Before its steady
"march the broken Imperialists withdrew without a halt; but
"not without looking back fiercely and grimly upon their pur-
"suers, whose bayonets glittered in the yellow glare of the set-
"ting sun."

Hooper continues:—"The battle was won; it was now the
"time to reap in ample measure the fruits of victory.

"The British leader, watchful of the course of the fight, had
"been patient and persevering for nine hours. It was now his
"turn to attack. He had been stricken long. It was now for
"him to break out from his fastness and strike. The charge of
"the 52nd, so magical and so decisive, begun at the right mo-
"ment, and carried forward by the right kind of daring, was
"speedily sustained. At the order of the Duke, Vivian's un-
"touched light horsemen broke from the cloud of thick smoke,
"which hung over the ridge, and wheeling round the right flank
"of the British Guards poured down the slope, through the space
"left vacant by the light infantry brigade, [52nd, 71st, and 95th,]
"and, ably led by its consummate chief, swept onward over the
"field."

Since the foregoing portion of this volume was written, a work
has come out, entitled "Notes on the battle of Waterloo, by the
"late General Sir James Shaw Kennedy, K.C.B." Captain Shaw,
at the time of the battle, was a captain in the 43rd Light Infantry and deputy-assistant quartermaster-general attached to
General Baron Alten's division, the 3rd division of the British
army. He was an old peninsular officer, and was much
distinguished for his gallantry and intelligence. He afterwards

took the name of Kennedy. He appears to have seen nothing of the 52nd during the action, though he speaks most highly of their advance; nor does he appear to have seen the 3rd battalion of the 1st Guards drive in the skirmishers of the Imperial Guard. What he saw himself is very interesting. In almost everything which he did not see he acknowledges that he has followed Siborne's account.

I propose to select some of his observations and to comment freely upon them, for as Captain Siborne was not at Waterloo, and Shaw Kennedy did not leave the British position, they cannot speak of what happened to the 52nd and to the Imperial Guard 300 yards below that position, with the same authority with which I and other 52nd officers can speak, who saw, and participated in, the remarkable encounter which took place between the 52nd, then about 950 strong, and their renowned adversaries. I repeat here again, that the Imperial Guard was in two columns of *equal* length, apparently consisting of, and always mentioned by us as containing, 10,000 men. All that has been said about a first column of the French Guard having been separated from the other column, and having been defeated by Maitland's brigade of Guards, is a myth. And I repeat again, the 2nd battalion of the 1st Guards, never advanced from the British position, when the 3rd battalion drove in the Imperial Guard skirmishers and probably some skirmishers and their supports of Donzelot's division, and then, after following them a short distance down the slope, retired in some confusion, and did not come in contact with the enemy again, though Siborne states erroneously that both battalions did so.

Sir Shaw Kennedy says of Siborne and his history of Waterloo :—" Captain Siborne's history of the campaign has very great
" merit. I doubt if, as to any other battle, there ever were so great
" a number of facts brought together, or more care, industry, and
" fidelity displayed in their collection, so that all other accounts
" of the battle, to be correct, must, for a great portion of the details,
" borrow from Siborne, as he had access to sources of information
" that no historian following him can have."

As regards the 52nd and the French Imperial Guard, my information, derived from Lord Seaton and other 52nd officers, and from my own very accurate recollection of every movement of the 52nd, must be allowed to come from sources very superior to those from which Siborne or Kennedy derived their information. And even as regards the movements of the 2nd and 3rd battalions of the 1st Guards, I know my information is more accurate than that of either of them. Will the surviving officers of the 2nd battalion of the 1st Guards maintain that their battalion advanced against the Imperial Guard skirmishers or against *a first column* of the Imperial Guard when Lord Hill, who was on their right, and Sir John Byng, (afterwards Lord Strafford,) who had succeeded to the command of the whole divison of the Guards, both declare that they did not? And when it is declared, on the part of the 3rd battalion of the Guards, that the 2nd battalion did not advance with them?

In the "Life" of Sir William Napier, we are told that in a matter of dispute as to whether a howitzer was taken from the French by the 43rd or the 52nd at Sabugal, speaking of his informants of the 43rd, he wrote:—"They know what they have written "and said to me, and I expect them to respond to my appeal. "If they do not, the 43rd regiment must bear the stigma of "having accepted from the Duke of Wellington the credit of an "exploit belonging to another regiment."

Awkward as it may be, should not the 1st Guards even at this late period, when more than fifty years have passed away since the famous battle was fought, listen to my appeal, and no longer "accept," I do not say, "from the Duke of Wellington," for he never assigned that credit to them, but from Captain Siborne, Alison who has copied Siborne, and other mistaken historians of Waterloo, a portion of "the credit of an exploit "belonging [entirely] to another regiment?" Should they not even lend their assistance towards rectifying the representation of a column of the Imperial Guard routed by them, and the position of the 1st Guards on Siborne's beautiful model, so that they should no longer be represented as firing into a column of the Imperial Guard which the 52nd single-handed attacked in flank and completely defeated? Some of the officers of the Guards did much towards rescuing the model from being lost to the public, and no doubt have much in their power, respecting the alteration of the position of troops on the model, in any case in which a most glaring injustice has been perpetrated against one gallant regiment, and undeserved honour has been thrust upon another gallant corps. Siborne himself caused a considerable alteration to be made in the positions he had assigned to several of the Prussian corps, on the representation of some of the superior Prussian officers; thus alteration appears to be possible, without injury being done to the model.

A 52nd officer remarks in a letter, written to me in the year 1853, that " in addition to the honour yet due to the regiment, "the crisis and close of the action of Waterloo is a matter of im-"portance, historically, nationally, and professionally."

The French historians of the battle, who have written of late years, have not been at all unwilling to adopt Siborne's (to the 52nd vexatious) account of the *successive* defeat of the columns of the Imperial Guard; because in a national point of view, there is not so much discredit in the rout, first of all of six battalions of the Imperial Guard by Maitland's brigade of the 1st British Guards, supported by the 33rd and 69th regiments, and then ten or twelve minutes afterwards in the defeat of the remaining battalions of the Imperial Guard by the flank attack of the 52nd assisted by Maitland's Guards in front, as in the defeat of the whole of the Imperial Guard of about 10,000 men, as I have before described it, by the 52nd alone at the distance of 300 yards from any other British or Allied regiments. The defeat, by the advance of a single British battalion, of 10,000 or even 8,000 of the finest troops in Europe is an honour to the regiment, and an honour to Lord Seaton who commanded it, and an honour to the British army and nation, which must not be tamely relinquished whilst there is any British blood and old 52nd Waterloo spirit remaining, combined with the possession of sufficient amount of material and detail to justify one in advancing almost single-handed to meet the many shafts, which I must expect to be levelled against me and my attempt to rescue one of the most daring exploits I believe ever performed in war, from the mass of confusion and error with which succeeding historians have, unwittingly I presume, almost ingulfed it.

When I was going into action at Waterloo I was very anxious

to know how I should feel and conduct myself under fire; I perhaps am not less anxious now as to the point of how I may feel, when I and my work are exposed to the very formidable artillery of the Press levelled against all my inflated and presumptuous pretensions, both military and religious, as they may perhaps consider them. Did my readers ever stop to see what would be the fate of a little dog who goes yelping and barking at a great big mastiff? I have often witnessed such a scene, and have invariably observed, that the little cur, directly the large dog comes up to him throws himself upon his back in token of submission, and the large one never hurts him, but stands over him for a second or two and perhaps licks him and wags his tail. Well, my readers, I am the little dog; the mastiff is the Press; and though I don't mean to knock under, unless I am convinced I am wrong in any point, yet I do humbly deprecate any angry feeling or criticism on the part of the Press.

Baron Muffling, who was attached to the British head-quarters by the Prussian Commander-in-Chief, and was present at the battle of Waterloo, says in his history of the campaign of 1815, when speaking of the advance of the Imperial Guard towards the close of the action, that the columns consisted of *sixteen battalions*.

The following statement of the number of men of which the Imperial Guard consisted in each year from its first formation, is taken from a French history of that celebrated corps.

In 1804	.	.	.	9,798	men.
,, 1805	.	.	.	12,187	,,
,, 1806	.	.	.	15,656	,,
,, 1807	.	.	.	15,361	,,
,, 1808	.	.	.	15,392	,,
,, 1809	.	.	.	31,203	,,
,, 1810	.	.	.	32,130	,,
,, 1811	.	.	.	31,960	,,
,, 1812	.	.	.	56,169	,,
,, 1813	.	.	.	92,472	,,
,. 1814	.	.	.	112,482	,,
,, 1815	.	.	.	25,870	,,

The following table, taken from the same work, gives the composition and amount of the Imperial Guard in 1815.

HEAD QUARTERS	. . . .		20
STAFF	. . . . .		200

INFANTRY.

Grenadiers .	. . .	3 Regiments	3,000
Chasseurs	. . .	3 Regiments	3,000
Tirailleurs .	. . .	6 Regiments	7,200
Voltigeurs	. . .	6 Regiments	7,200
			20,400 20,400

CAVALRY.

Grenadiers .	. .	1 Regiment	800
Chasseurs	. . .	1 Regiment	800
Dragoons .	. . .	1 Regiment	800
Gendarmerie .	. .	1 Company	100
Light Dragoons, Lancers .		1 Regiment	800
			3,300 3,300

ARTILLERY.

Old Guard, 6 Foot Batteries . . .	⎫
Old Guard, 4 Horse Batteries . . .	⎬ 1,500
1 Company of labourers, 1 squadron of the Military Train	⎭
Engineers and Sappers	250
Waggon Train, 1 squadron	200
Total . .	25,870

Mr. George Hooper, in his history of the campaign of 1815, a pleasing and well written book in which the author follows Siborne's mistakes as to the 1st Guards, makes out that altogether there were twelve battalions of the Imperial Guard brought forward by Napoleon to make his last attack on the British right centre, and that two of them were formed in reserve midway between La Belle Alliance and the southern end of Hougomont. This last statement of the two battalions being left in reserve I doubt, because the two columns of *equal* length having not an interval of 30 paces between them, both gave way before the 52nd, but whilst the leading column of the two fled in utter confusion, and a portion of the rear column also, leaving some of the guns of the Old Guard with the horses harnessed to them, yet it is said that some of the rear battalions of the rear column fell back hastily but in comparative order to the French position; their immediate rear, at the time they gave way before the 52nd, being the spot indicated by Hooper as that at which Napoleon

MISTAKES REFUTED. 121

left two battalions of his Guard in reserve—I am inclined to think therefore that these two battalions of the fine Old Guard advanced with, and retired from, the rear column of the two.

Hooper observes in a note:—"Much confusion exists in the "accounts of these columns of attack, their number and formation. "The conclusions in the text are derived from a study of the best "accounts on both sides." I wish Hooper and Siborne and Alison had been with the 52nd at Waterloo, and they would have understood plainly that no column of the Imperial Guard could possibly have advanced upon, or have been defeated by, any portion of the British Guards without their seeing it; and that all three of them, Siborne at their head, have been robbing the 52nd of a portion of the honour belonging to them, by advancing this "column in buckram," or this mythical column, up the British position to the attack of the Guards.

Colonel Gawler, as I have before observed, from being on the extreme right of the 52nd line, and from seeing the dead bodies of Imperial Guardsmen on the summit of the British position the next morning, not reflecting that they might be those of their skirmishers only, fell into the mistake of supposing that the head of the column of the Imperial Guard had reached that point, when in reality it was 300 yards or thereabouts from the position. But Colonel Gawler speaks of the 52nd when it cleared the ascent being "under a furious fire [this however was further "down the position than he supposed] *from the long flank of the* "*columns*," and his book, "The Crisis of Waterloo," was written in 1833 on purpose to maintain "that the attack of the Imperial "Guard was repulsed, and the French army thrown into conse-"quent irretrievable confusion, by a charge of the 52nd covered "by the 71st regiment without the direct co-operation of any "other portion of the Allied army." Colonel Gawler reckoned the columns attacked and defeated by the 52nd at 10,000 men, and he had as good a view of them as any other 52nd man had.

Siborne says in his first preface, dated March, 1844:—" One "of my Waterloo correspondents has humorously remarked, that, "'if ever truth lies at the bottom of a well, she does so immedi-"'ately after a great battle, and it takes an amazingly long time "'before she can be lugged out.'"

I have good reason to believe that the following is the truth with regard both to the advance of the 3rd battalion of the Guards, and to the defeat of the two columns of the Imperial Guard by the 52nd :—That the mass of skirmishers of the Imperial Guard and their supports were joined by the skirmishers and their supports from the French troops massed to the left of La Haye Sainte, and that the whole of the intermingled skirmishers and their supports were still further supported by the advance of the battalions themselves of Donzelot's division, which, with many other divisions of the French army, is spoken of, as moving forward at this time in support of the advancing columns of the Imperial Guard. These skirmishers extended along the front of both the battalions of the Guards who are stated by Kennedy to have been lying down in square, though I do not feel sure of this as regards the right or 2nd battalion; the skirmishers extended also along the front of Sir Colin Halkett's brigade, which was on the British left of Maitland's brigade of Guards, for both these brigades maintain that they were opposed to troops wearing the bear skin caps of the Imperial Guard. And the 2nd battalion of the Guards declared that they were attacked by a "column" of twelve or fourteen hundred men, and that these troops opened fire upon them at a distance of fifty or sixty paces; that the Duke coming along from their left, observed how this 3rd battalion of the 1st Guards was suffering from the heavy fire of the mass of troops in their front, and desired the commanding officer to form line on the front face of the square, and "drive those fellows off," which they did in very gallant style, and followed them for some eighty or a hundred yards down the slope; then there was an alarm of cavalry and the 3rd battalion of the Guards, some of them thinking they were to form square, got into confusion and retired hastily over the crest of the position and beyond it on the reverse slope, to where the 10th Hussars and all Vivian's brigade were, on their way from the extreme left of the position to the interval made by the advance of the 52nd from the position. The 2nd battalion of the 1st Guards took no part in this charge, but was stationary. The only conclusion I can come to is that the mass of troops seen and defeated by the 3rd battalion of the Guards, were, as I have before observed, the skirmishers of the Imperial Guard and of Donzelot's division and their supports; and that when the Guards passed over the top of the position they saw also, away to their left, some of Donzelot's battalions. Any other troops than skirmishers, whom they saw, must have been other than troops of the Imperial Guard.

The skirmishers of the Imperial Guard came down the slope running towards the leading battalion of the French Guard, and formed about 100 yards or rather more in front of it, just as the 52nd was completing its right-shoulder-forward movement and becoming parallel to the left flank of the Imperial columns. There was no smoke, there was a gleam of sunshine on the skirmishers, as they were forming, and I could see them most completely, and 200 yards or more beyond them up the British position. Of any other troops driven in by the 3rd battalion of the 1st Guards we could see nothing, nor of the Guards themselves, therefore they could not have come far down the position in pursuit. Donzelot's skirmishers and their supports, when they gave way, must have run towards their own division in the direction of La Haye Sainte. This formation of the retiring Imperial Guard skirmishers was afterwards spoken of in mistake, by some writers, as an attempt at deployment on the part of their leading battalion.

The 52nd fired into and charged the Imperial Guard, as I have before related, and it gave way and fled in utter confusion, with the exception, it was said, of two or three of the rear battalions of the rear column, who gained the French position hastily and in comparative order.

The 52nd never met with or saw any British troops from the time they left their position till they halted for the night at Rosomme, excepting the English and German cavalry—beforementioned, as having ridden at speed round the flanks and through the centre of the 52nd, when retiring before the cuirassiers—and with the exception also of those whom I suppose to have been engaged in poor Howard's charge.

If there was a second column of the Imperial Guard defeated, as the historians try to make out, partly by the 52nd, and partly by Maitland's brigade of Guards, how came it that Maitland allowed the 52nd *to go on by themselves to, and over, and a mile beyond, the French position, in pursuit of the enemy, when there were tens of thousands of French infantry, and thousands of cavalry still in the field !*

Sir John Byng, who said "we saw the 52nd advancing glori-"ously, as they always do," and who thought it necessary to say to Sir John Colborne, "I could not advance when you did, for "our ammunition was exhausted," would he, if he had been near the 52nd, and been engaged with them in defeating the same column, would he, ammunition or no ammunition, have allowed them to be exposed, single-handed, to all the dangers to which, by their isolation from the rest of the army, they were really exposed ? Must he not, if he had been so near them as is represented, have brought down Maitland's brigade of Guards to their support, instead of keeping them in rear of the crest of the British position until the Duke, long after, made a sort of forward movement from the position of some portion of his troops, which was called an advance of his whole line ?

I wish not, nor do I mean, to say one word in disparagement of any individual or of any regiment, but as I feel certain the 52nd came in contact just below the British position with all the remainder of the Imperial Guard, after the half of it had been sent to Planchenoit to hold the Prussians at bay, that is, that they engaged and defeated two heavy columns of *equal length*, apparently containing 10,000 men, and as this was always the opinion of the 52nd officers who were present, and as the greater portion of these officers have passed away, and I am almost the only person left who could take this matter in hand, I think it right not to shrink from doing so, though I may conjecture that much unpleasantness and annoyance to myself may possibly be the result of my undertaking it.

Another idea occurs to me, and I think it will approve itself to the minds of all military men. "A column" of twelve or fourteen hundred men or more of the Imperial Guard bent on penetrating the British line, and especially if they were backed up by other advancing troops, would never have contented themselves with reaching the crest of the position, and then halting that their front company might fire on a British square, lying down at sixty or eighty yards distance from them on the reverse slope of the position. It is exactly what a swarm of daring French skirmishers *would do*, especially if the Imperial Guard skirmishers and Donzelot's were intermixed and vying with each other. It must be remembered that the square of the 3rd battalion of the 1st Guards, was about 150 yards to the left of the 2nd battalion, and probably at nearly double that distance from the nearest square of Halkett's brigade on its left, so that the skirmishers, intended to occupy ground 300 yards or more in length, would as a matter of course close more and more to the points from which they might fire into the front and flank faces of the square of the 3rd battalion of the Guards. It is most probable also that their supports had joined them. Hence, I suggest, there were enough of skirmishers congregated in a space perhaps not exceeding fifty yards in length, to give them the appearance through the smoke of being a formed body of men.

Although Kennedy, following in Siborne's wake, makes the vexatious mistakes about the defeat of a first column of four battalions of the Imperial Guard by Maitland's brigade of Guards, and about the head of a second column of the Imperial Guard being fired into by Maitland's brigade at the same time that Colborne charged it in flank, (all which is a regular myth,) yet he gives the 52nd as much honour and credit for their share in the rout of the 2nd column of four battalions, *as would have quite satisfied them, for what they really did do, for the defeat of the whole of the ten or twelve battalions of the French Guard, without* any other British regiment being within 300 yards of them. Kennedy says, "The French column, feeling the severity of the "fire of the 52nd, wheeled up its left sections and commenced "firing, but the fire from the 52nd threw it into great disorder, "and the combined fire and formidable advance in line of the "52nd caused the entire rout and dispersion of the four [twelve] "battalions of the French Guard which were opposed to it."

Again, Sir Shaw Kennedy says, "The march of the 52nd "has thus been traced continuously, without referring to other "incidents of the battle during its advance; for its progress was "the leading and distinctive feature of the action during that "period; and it will thus be more easy, by reference to the pro-

"gress of the 52nd, to understand what was done by the rest of
" the Anglo-Allied army, and the Prussian army, during this most
" highly interesting part of the action."

Again, he says, "It is perhaps impossible to point out in history
" any other instance in which so small a force as that with which
" Colborne acted, had so powerful an influence on the result of a
" great battle, in which the numbers engaged on each side were so
" large." Now there is great truth in this last observation, if
applied to the real exploit of the 52nd at the crisis and close of
the Battle of Waterloo, but for which exploit, Sir John Colborne
thought, the columns of the Imperial Guard would be likely to
penetrate the British line of battle.

In consequence of the sad mistake of La Haye Sainte being
allowed to fall into the hands of the enemy,* Donzelot was
enabled to establish himself in force, within 100 yards of the
centre of the British and Allied army, and exceedingly to harass
Alten's division, which occupied the British position for a quarter
of a mile or more, between the centre of the position and the left
of Maitland's brigade of Guards. Had Napoleon sent his
Imperial Guard to attack the British centre by La Haye Sainte
it has been thought by some that he would have succeeded in
defeating the troops at that point, harassed and reduced in
numbers as they were.

When the Imperial Guard was ordered to advance towards
the right centre of the British line, opposite to the spot where
the 3rd battalion of the 1st Guards was lying down in square,
orders were at the same time given that all the French infantry
should advance in support of their attack. Sir Shaw Kennedy,
who be it remembered was with Alten's division during the
whole of the engagement, says, "the attack of Donzelot's division
" from La Haye Sainte preceded that by the Imperial Guard, as
" that attack had never ceased from the taking of that farm, and
" increased in intensity as the grand general attack progressed.

* This took place only at six o'clock in the evening, according to Kennedy, at about the same time that the last of the great cavalry attacks was repulsed. Major Baring, who commanded the 2nd light battalion of the King's German Legion at La Haye Sainte, and the reinforcements subsequently sent there, slept on the ground with Kennedy, on the night of the action, close to the Wellington Tree.

"... . The attack was preceded along the whole line by a "furious cannonade; and the whole front of attack was covered "by a swarm of skirmishers."

Farther on in his work Kennedy adds :—" The effect of the "defeat of the ten battalions of the Imperial Guard, and of "Colborne's diagonal march, was electrical on Donzelot's division, "which was in fact compromised by the advance of Adam's "brigade.* Its attack, which had up to that time been violently "severe on Alten's division, was at once slackened and very soon "suspended, and a retreat commenced."

The loss of the 2nd battalion of the 1st Guards at Waterloo was as follows :—

Killed.			Wounded.			Total.
Officers.	Serjts.	Rank & File.	Officers.	Serjts.	Rank & File.	
1	—	50	5	7	80	143

Of the 3rd battalion as follows :—

3	2	79	6	7	238	335

If we deduct 143, the total loss in killed and wounded of the 2nd battalion, from 335, the total loss of the 3rd battalion, we find that the loss of the 3rd battalion exceeded that of the 2nd battalion by 192. This excess of loss on the part of the 3rd battalion, perhaps helps to prove the truth of what I have advanced, that the 2nd battalion was not engaged to the extent that the 3rd battalion was, and that it was stationary when the latter, by the Duke's order, formed line on the front face of its square, and drove off the mass of skirmishers assembled on the crest of the position before it.

I have already, in a quotation from a work printed and circulated by a very intelligent Peninsular and Waterloo 52nd officer, mentioned that the 1st Guards were made grenadiers, and that the ensigns of all the three regiments of Guards were given precedence over all the ensigns of the line by lieutenant's rank, for their good conduct at Waterloo. All the regiments of the Guards did good service at Quatre Bras and Waterloo, as I have observed before, but the singling those regiments out for these

* Kennedy is wrong, the 52nd were alone ; the 71st were far away, not far from the inclosures of Hougomont and advancing towards the French position ; the other part of the brigade, six companies of the 2nd battalion of the Rifles and two of the 3rd battalion, were not with the 52nd during their advance.

particular rewards was unfair towards the rest of the army. And it was particularly awkward that the 1st Guards should be made grenadiers for defeating the grenadiers of the French Imperial Guard, when all they really did, *as regards the Imperial Guard*, was to drive in their *skirmishers*. There was no harm in their being made a regiment of grenadiers, but it was an awkward mistake that the thing should have been mismanaged as it was.

The giving to the ensigns of the three regiments of Guards the brevet rank of lieutenant, was afterwards followed up by depriving several of the regiments of the Line of little distinctions, some of which were an advantage to them, others merely prized by them as distinctions, probably conferred upon them for services rendered, or supposed to have been rendered to their country, and the being deprived of which occasioned perhaps in some cases only a little annoyance at the time, but in others very considerable hardships. Still if it was an advantage to the service, that there should be no invidious distinctions, then of course the change might be necessary; but why should it not be equally necessary that there should be no invidious distinction in favour of the three regiments of Foot Guards?

It was not till the year 1854, that the Fusileer regiments, the 5th, 7th, 21st, 23rd, and 87th, and the 60th Rifles and the Rifle Brigade had the rank of ensign given to their junior officers instead of that of 2nd lieutenant. In the case of the 7th Fusileers all their subalterns were, till that time, full lieutenants. All this appears to have been fairly done, and without infliction of hardship on individual officers; but still the only reason for it appears to have arisen from a desire to make all the infantry regiments, except the guards, alike, as to the appellation of their junior subalterns.

In the light infantry regiments, it appears, from the following document addressed to the lamented Sir John Moore, that an additional lieutenant was appointed for each company as far back as 1803:—

"War Office, 18th October, 1803.

"Sir,—In pursuance of a communication from His Royal "Highness the Commander-in-Chief, I have the honour to acquaint "you, that as the 52nd Regiment of Foot under your command,

"being a light infantry corps, requires a greater proportion of
"officers and non-commissioned officers than a battalion of the
"Line, His Majesty has been pleased to order that an augmenta-
"tion of one lieutenant, one serjeant, and one corporal per
"company, shall be made to the establishment thereof from the
"25th instant inclusive.

"I have the honour, &c.,

"(Signed)   C. BRAGG.

"Major-General Moore, 52nd Regiment."

I cannot trace the whole detail of circumstances which led to the injustice and hardship perpetuated on some of the officers of the 52nd, and of the other light infantry regiments, in connexion with some of the reductions which took place after Waterloo and the return of the army of occupation from France. There were ten captains with the 52nd at Waterloo (besides Lord March and Yorke who were on the staff) thirty-five lieutenants including the adjutant, and eight ensigns. On the return of the 52nd, then only consisting of one battalion, from France, the establishment of subalterns was reduced to ten lieutenants and ten ensigns, and on the 25th of August, 1822, it was reduced to eight lieutenants and eight ensigns. On the first of these reductions taking place, the junior lieutenants beyond the ten remained on the list of lieutenants, receiving only ensign's pay, until by death-vacancies the two supernumerary lieutenants were absorbed, and in the mean time the ensigns could only become lieutenants by purchase. The grievance created by this paltry and shabby arrangement was very great in the 52nd, and ought to be a lesson to all admirers of Mr. Joseph Hume's views of economy, to consider well the amount of annoyance and disgust which they may occasion to many deserving officers, before they proceed, for the sake of saving the veriest trifle of expense to the country, to recommend and carry out reductions which interfere, in so great a degree as those I speak of did, with the feelings and prospects of individuals. The hardship inflicted upon one of the officers of the 52nd, the late Lieutenant Yonge, was that he was put on ensign's pay, after having received the extra pay of a seven years' lieutenant. In mentioning this in a letter to the Secretary of War some

K

years ago, he also spoke of the injustice it was, "that while the "ensigns of the Guards were made lieutenants on the pretence of "the 1st Guards having repulsed the Imperial Guard, the lieu- "tenants of the regiment that actually did that work were made "ensigns."

In a subsequent letter to the same Secretary of War, he wrote thus:—"But I was led to speak more particularly of the "43rd, 52nd, and Rifle Brigade, because being the originally-formed "light corps, and constituting as they did the light division, to "them especially fell the outpost duties of the Peninsular army, "and the practice of the system, of which they had acquired the "theory from Sir John Moore. How they acquitted themselves "is sufficiently known. Their losses were proportionately severe. "The merit of their services had been continually acknowledged, "and to my own regiment, the 52nd, the Commander-in-Chief "had repeatedly accorded a quite unusual amount of promotion, "professedly on account of the high character it sustained. It "was a strange turn of affairs that, as soon as the war was over, "they should have thus been placed in a more disadvantageous "position than any of the ordinary regiments of the Line, and "this on the miserable pretext that they had no flank companies, "whereas it should rather have been held, that theirs were all "flank companies. The detached services required of them had "been tenfold more numerous than could ever be required of "the flank companies of any Line regiment. . . . . . No one who "is made aware of it can, I am sure, refuse to acknowledge that "the light regiments have not been fairly treated, and it appears "still more glaring, when we look at the Fusileers, differing in "no respect but in name only from the other Line regiments— "yet in these, in the place of the ten lieutenants and ten ensigns "of the light corps, the subalterns of the 7th are all 1st lieute- "nants and the establishment of the 21st and 23rd is twelve "1st lieutenants and eight 2nd lieutenants." Mr. Yonge, who received ensign's pay as a supernumerary lieutenant, after having received extra pay as a seven years' lieutenant, was a very intelligent and good officer. His services are enumerated as follows, in the 52nd record:—"Lieutenant William Crawley "Yonge entered the 52nd in 1810, served with the regiment at

"the Nivelle, the Nive, Orthes, Toulouse, and the intervening
"affairs. He also served in the campaign and Battle of Waterloo.
"He has received the Peninsular war medal with four
"clasps."

These supernumerary lieutenancies, which were to be absorbed by death vacancies, interfered very much with the promotion of the ensigns. The only hardship besides my own which I recollect was that of Ensign Bentham, who stood next to me on the list and remained an ensign twelve years. My own case was a very trying one. My money was lodged all along for the purchase of my lieutenancy, and yet, very much owing to this treatment of the light regiments, I was more than eight years and a half an ensign. And when in November, 1823, I purchased my lieutenancy, the delay that had been occasioned by the falling in of the supernumerary lieutenancy, which had not been filled up when Brevet-Major Shedden died in 1821, was the means of my tardy promotion coming just too late to enable me to avoid the very great mortification of having an ensign four years my junior, by the purchase of a half-pay lieutenancy, and by a subsequent exchange, pass into the regiment again as my senior in the list of lieutenants.

I perhaps should just mention that all the ensigns of the Guards who were at Waterloo, and who remained long enough in their regiments, were lieutenants and *brevet-captains* before I obtained my lieutenancy.

Just as I had written so far, one of my family interrupted me by coming to have an accustomed reading of the scripture with me and prayer, and in the reading these words occurred, appropriate to the subject I am writing on:—"Lift not up "your horn on high, speak not with a stiff neck. For promotion "cometh neither from the east, nor from the west, nor from the "south. But God is the judge, he putteth down one and setteth "up another:" Psalm lxxv, 5—7. I am sure that all these events have been directed by unerring wisdom and in infinite mercy and loving-kindness; and yet I think these mistakes, and injustice, and hardships should be recorded.

I have always felt that the favour and distinctions accorded to the three regiments of Foot Guards in the way of a step in advance of the officers of the other infantry regiments, in the several ranks of ensign, lieutenant, and captain, so that all the ensigns are brevet-lieutenants, the lieutenants captains, and the captains lieutenant-colonels, is not only very annoying and galling to the other officers of the army, but also exceedingly injurious to the service. And so much did I feel this, that, in December, 1855, when the Guards were making some stir about a disadvantage which they considered their senior officers were labouring under, and expressed a desire to be placed on an " equality with their more fortunate brethren of the Line," I went out of my way as a clergyman and took some trouble in drawing up the following letter and explanatory columns, which were published by "The Times," and I think led our friends of the Guards to see that, with regard to the further agitation of the point they aimed at, " the better part of valour was discretion."

THE GUARDS.

" To the Editor of ' The Times.'

"SIR,—The accompanying columns are taken from the 'Army
"' Lists' for April, 1824, and January, 1841, which are the oldest
"' Army Lists' I have at hand. If you think well to publish them
" in 'The Times' they will help to point out what the officers of
" the Guards will obtain if they really are placed on an ' equality
" ' with their more fortunate brethren of the line.'

"I have taken the names and the dates of the commissions
" of the ensigns of the Guards mentioned in the ' Army List' of
" 1824, who subsequently obtained the rank of lieutenant-colonel,
" and have shown from the 'Army List' of 1841 when they arrived
" at that rank. I have also taken from the same ' Army Lists' the
" names of the officers of the first thirty regiments of the Line
" and of the light infantry and rifle regiments, which occur in
" both these lists, and have shown the rank which they respec-
" tively held in 1824 and in 1841. The average time, from their
" first entrance into the army, in which the 19 officers of the
" Guards have obtained their lieutenant-colonelcies, is as nearly as
" possible fifteen years. Of the 76 officers of the Line, men-
" tioned in the two ' Army Lists,' only 16 had arrived at the rank

"of lieutenant-colonel in 1841, and of these not less than 12 were
"on an average 20 years and six months after they got their
"companies in obtaining their lieutenant-colonelcies. If we
"make the moderate calculation that, on an average, they were
"10 years in getting their companies, then it appears that all
"the officers of these Line regiments who reached the rank of
"lieutenant-colonel were, on an average, 30 years in doing so—
"just twice the average time that it took the officers of the
"Guards to attain the same rank. But if your readers will look
"at the columns, they will perceive greater hardships than
"these. For instance, Ensigns Muller and Richardson, of the
"1st Royals, were still only subalterns in 1841, after 21 years'
"service.

"These peculiar privileges of the officers of the Guards have
"always been obnoxious to the other officers of the army, and in
"the opinion of many are not only unjust, but also injurious to
"the best interests of the service. If the brevet rank in each grade
"is a desirable thing, let it be extended to the whole army; if
"not, then let it be abolished as quickly as possible in the regi-
"ments of the Guards. But the present system pushes forward
"many men in the Guards to the rank of major-general who
"know but little of the handling of a battalion, or of its internal
"economy and requirements. If it is to be retained and
"extended, then some plan must be devised by which no
"man shall pass on to the rank of major-general without
"having an adequate acquaintance with the whole regimental
"system.

"The Guards did their duty as well as other regiments at
"Quatre Bras and Waterloo, but they have never done anything
"to entitle them to peculiar privileges, and, unfortunately for
"one of these truly gallant regiments, it was by mistake rewarded
"for that which was actually performed at Waterloo by regiments
"of the Line. I write advisedly, and allude to the defeat of the
"heavy columns of the French Imperial Guard by the 52nd
"Light Infantry, supported by the 71st Light Infantry, and
"by the 2nd and part of the 3rd battalions of the 95th
"Rifles.

"QUÆQUE IPSE MISERRIMA VIDI."

134   MISTAKES REFUTED.

Grenadier Guards.	Date of first Commission.	When made Captain and Lt.-Colonel.	How many years in attaining rank of Lieut.-Colonel.
W. Greenwood	April 18, 1816	May 9, 1834	18 yrs.
J. W. Angerstein	April 9, 1818	Sep. 12, 1834	16¼ yrs.
Sir J. M. Burgoyne	Oct. 1, 1818	June 6, 1835	16¾ yrs.
G. W. Eyres	Dec. 3, 1818	July 1, 1836	17¼ yrs.
W. Fludyer	Oct. 25, 1821	Dec. 2, 1836	15 yrs. 5 weeks
P. J. Perceval	May 23, 1822	Jan. 10, 1837	14 yrs. 8 months
J. R. Cranfurd	Aug. 29, 1822	Feb. 18, 1837	14½ yrs.
Frederick Clinton	Nov. 19, 1823	Jan. 12, 1833	14 yrs. 2 months
R. W. Astell	Nov. 20, 1823	July 7, 1838	14 yrs. 4½ ditto
Coldstream Guards.			
W. H. Cornwall*			
B Broadhead*			
C. M. Hay	Nov. 1, 1821	June 22, 1832	10 yrs. 8 months
J. D. Rawdon	Jan. 30, 1823	Nov. 15, 1833	10 yrs. 10 ditto
Hon. T. Ashburnham	Jan. 30, 1823	Mar. 27, 1835	12 yrs. 2 ditto
W. J. Codrington	April 4, 1823	July 8, 1836	13 yrs. 3 ditto
Ely D. Wigram	May 29, 1823	Jan. 13, 1837	13 yrs. 8 ditto
Fusileer Guards.			
Hon. T. C. Westenra	May 4, 1814	Aug. 9, 1833	19 yrs. 3 months
P. J. Yorke	May 5, 1814	Aug. 7, 1835	21 yrs. 3 ditto
G. Dillon	Jan. 20, 1820	May 20, 1836	16 yrs. 4 ditto
Hon. C. B. Phipps	Aug. 17, 1820	May 26, 1837	16 yrs. 9 ditto
J. G. Robinson	Jan. 23, 1817	Aug. 12, 1837	20 yrs. 6 ditto

* Appear not to have got their first commissions in the Coldstream.

Regiments of the Line.	Rank in Army List of 1824.	Rank in Army List of 1841.
1st Foot—		
Edward Muller	Ensign, 1820	Still Sen. Lieutenant only, 1841
J. Richardson	Ensign, 1820	2nd Lieutenant, 1841
2nd Foot—		
O. Robinson	Ensign, 1820	6th Capt. and Brev.-Major, 1841
G. D. J. Raitt	Ensign, 1823	Senior Captain and Brevet-Major, 1841
3rd Foot—		
R. N. Everard	Ensign, 1817	Senior Captain, 1841
G. L. Christie	Ensign, 1822	2nd Captain, 1841
4th Foot—		
T. Williams	Ensign, 1822	2nd Captain, 1841
5th Foot—		
C. Wood	Ensign, 1820	3rd Captain, 1841
6th Foot—		
J. T. Griffiths	Lieutenant, 1821	3rd Captain, 1841
7th Fusileers*—		
F. Farquharson	Captain, 1819	Lieut.-Colonel, 1832
8th Foot—		
Thomas G. Ball	Captain, 1814	Lieut.-Colonel, 1835
9th Foot—		
G. L. Davis	Lieutenant, 1811	Junior Major, 1841
10th Foot—		
Saville Broom	Lieutenant, 1820	2nd Major, 1841
T. L. L. Galloway	Lieutenant, 1822	Senior Captain, 1841
11th Foot—		
B. V. Derinzy	Captain, 1814	Lieut.-Colonel, 1833
W. Chambre	Captain, 1822	Sen. Capt. and Brev.-Major, 1841

* No subalterns in Army List of 1824 remaining in 1841.

MISTAKES REFUTED. 135

Regiments of the Line.	Rank in Army List of 1824.	Rank in Army List of 1841.
12th Foot—		
Joseph Jones	Captain, 1823	Lieut.-Colonel, 1835
S. F. Glover	Lieutenant, 1813	2nd Captain, 1841
Julius Stirke	Lieutenant, 1823	5th Captain, 1841
13th Light Infantry—		
T. C. Squire	Captain, 1821	2nd Major, 1841
James Kershawe	Ensign, 1817	Senior Captain and Brevet-Major, 1841
A. Wilkinson	Ensign, 1823	8th Captain, 1841
14th Foot—		
M. Everard	Captain, 1807	Lieut.-Colonel, 1831
James Watson	Lieutenant, 1822	Major, 1841
15th Foot—		
T. A. Drought	Captain, 1822	Only Senior Major, 1841
16th Foot—		
H. Clements	Captain, 1813	Junior Major, 1841
R. Browne	Lieutenant, 1809	Senior Captain and Brevet-Major, 1841
J. Dalzell	Lieutenant, 1812	2nd Capt. and Brev.-Major, 1841
H. M'Manus	Lieutenant, 1820	3rd Captain, 1841
J. Brand	Lieutenant, 1820	4th Captain, 1841
C. F. Thompson	Ensign, 1820	Junior Captain, 1841
17th Foot—		
W. Croker	Captain, 1806	Lieut.-Colonel, 1836
J. T. Nagel	Lieutenant, 1820	8th Captain, 1841
18th Foot—		
R. N. Tomlinson	Ensign, 1821	2nd Major, 1841
19th Foot—		
Thomas Hamilton	Lieutenant, 1814	Lieut.-Colonel, 1838
20th Foot—		
Frederick Croad	Lieutenant, 1818	2nd Major, 1841
1st Fusileers—		
J. P. Beete	Ensign, 1820	1st Major, 1841
2nd Foot—		
John Poole	Lieutenant, 1819	1st Major, 1841
3rd Fusileers—		
W. Ross (Waterloo)	Captain, 1813	Lieut.-Colonel, 1837
R. P. Holmes (ditto)	Captain, 1823	Major, 1841
Thomas Matheson	1st Lieutenant, 1823	2nd Major, 1841
J. Enoch (Waterloo)	1st Lieutenant, 1811	2nd Captain, 1841
4th Foot—		
C. Hughes	Captain, 1804	Lieut.-Colonel, 1835
H. D. Townshend	Captain, 1821	Brevet-Lieut.-Colonel, 1839
Robert Marsh	Lieutenant, 1817	3rd Captain, 1841
5th Foot—		
J. J. Hollis	Captain, 1809	Senior Captain and Brevet-Major, 1841
6th Foot—		
W. Johnstone	Captain, 1820	Senior Captain and Brevet-Major, 1841
H. F. Strange	Ensign, 1815	3rd Captain, 1841
James Piggott	Ensign, 1823	6th Captain, 1841
27th Foot—		
D. M'Pherson	Lieutenant, 1806	Lieut.-Colonel, 1840
M. C. Johnstone	Ensign, 1823	Senior Major, 1841
28th Foot—		
Thomas Wheeler	Lieutenant, 1817	Senior Captain, 1841
J. A. Messiter	Ensign, 1823	Senior Major, 1841
29th Foot—		
R. P. Douglas	Lieutenant, 1824	Senior Captain, 1841
30th Foot—		
John Tongue	Captain, 1811	Junior Major, 1841
J. Poyntz	Lieutenant, 1815	3rd Captain, 1841

MISTAKES REFUTED.

REMAINING LIGHT INFANTRY AND RIFLE REGIMENTS.

Regiments of the Line.	Rank in Army List of 1824.	Rank in Army List of 1841.
43rd Light Infantry—		
J. B. B. Estcourt	Ensign, 1820	Brevet Lieut.-Colonel, 1839
Samuel Tryon	Ensign, 1823	3rd Captain, 1841
51st Light Infantry—		
W. H. Elliott (Waterloo)	Captain, 1820	Lieut.-Colonel, 1838
Edward St. Maur	Captain, 1823	Still senior Major only, 1841
O. Ainsworth (Waterloo)	Lieutenant, 1810	Senior Captain, 1841
F. Mainwaring (Waterloo)	Lieutenant, 1813	2nd Major, 1841
52nd Light Infantry—		
William Blois	Ensign, 1815	Lieut.-Colonel, 1839
60th Rifles—		
Ambrose Spong	Lieutenant, 1814	2nd Capt. and Brev.-Major, 1841
68th Light Infantry—		
Harry Smyth	Ensign, 1823	Senior Captain, 1841
71st Light Infantry—		
J. Impett (Waterloo)	Lieutenant, 1820	Senior Captain, 1841
A. R. L'Estrange (Waterloo)	Lieutenant, 1821	2nd Captain, 1841
85th Light Infantry—		
F. Maunsell	Captain, 1819	Lieut.-Colonel, 1836
Henry J. French	Captain, 1823	Senior Major, 1841
William T. Hunt	Lieutenant, 1814	Junior Major, 1841
Manley Power	Lieutenant, 1823	Senior Captain and Brevet-Major, 1841
Herbert E. Taylor	Ensign, 1824	2nd Captain, 1841
90th Light Infantry—		
T. W. Eyles	Ensign, 1820	Senior Major, 1841
John Wilson	Lieutenant, 1824	2nd Captain, 1841
Rifle Brigade—		
J. C. Hope (Waterloo)	Captain, 1820	Lieut.-Colonel, 1837
Richard Irton	2nd Lieutenant, 1815	2nd Major, 1841
Hon. J. St. V. Saumarez	2nd Lieutenant, 1824	4th Major, 1841

It would probably be better for the officers of the Guards themselves, and certainly more pleasant to the officers of the rest of the army, and for the benefit of the service generally, if these distinctions were abolished, perhaps not by taking away the rank which the officers of the Guards hold, but by giving exactly the same rank to the officers of all the other corps in the army. There would not be any very tremendous difficulty in finding out appropriate titles if the present titles for the several grades were considered unsuitable; and the army rank of those who became brevet-lieutenant-colonels, might be so adjusted by antedate (and why should this not be done?) as no longer to allow the regimental captains of the Guards to be of higher standing in the army than captains of other regiments, whose regimental commissions might be of an older date. I suspect, if it should be once conceded that it was injurious to the service that the officers of the Guards should as a rule arrive at the higher ranks of the army at a much earlier age than that at which the officers of the rest of the army should arrive at the same ranks—then some of the various difficulties, which may now appear to loom in the distance, would soon be got over.

One obvious disadvantage of the present system, of the officers of the Guards having invariably a step of army rank in advance of their regimental rank, is this that, both in garrison and camp, and on active service, it may be often happening that considerably younger men will take the command of their seniors and of men of many years' more experience than themselves. The system may probably foster a spirit of pride and conceit in the guardsmen, and a feeling of disgust and annoyance in the minds of the other officers of the army, who suffer from the invidious distinctions heaped upon the Guards. I should suppose it must frequently happen that officers of the latter service, really feel pained, when called upon to command those older and more experienced than themselves.

It may be desirable that there should be a body of men, accustomed to the duties required from the troops usually stationed in London or at Windsor, but their position should be rendered as little invidious in the eyes of the rest of the army as possible. They should be let off taking their turn of duty in the East and West Indies, and in China, and in other distant places; no one would begrudge them those little distinctions:—gallant fellows as they are, and as they have ever shewn themselves, they would always wish to take their turn of *active* service.

CHAPTER VII.

1815.

MARCH TO PARIS.

Nivelles—Letters to England—News of battle—Lists of killed and wounded—Mother ill—Alarm of sisters—March to Binche—Coal pit—Enter France—Le Cateau—Loss of baggage—Claim for remuneration—Other claims rejected—Fate of the baggage—Officers on baggage-guard—Marshal Monçey's Chateau—Distant view of Paris—Montmartre—52nd alone at Argenteuil—Pontoon bridge—Convention—Bridge and graveyard of Neuilly—Enter Paris—Encamp in the Champs Elysées.

IN 1859 I drew up, for the regimental record, a very short account of the march of the 52nd from Waterloo to Paris. I will, in introducing it into this work, endeavour to mention several details, which may possibly add to its interest.

I believe it was between twelve and one o'clock on the 19th, when we left our ground near Maison du Roi, and marched to Nivelles, which, by the road we took, was about nine miles off. We had now fairly started on our triumphant march to the French capital, and all were in the highest state of delight at our glorious victory, in the gaining which the 52nd had been fortunate enough to take such a leading part, and in our glorious prospect of immediately entering France, and eventually Paris itself. We bivouacked about a mile beyond Nivelles, on the left of the chaussée, and about a hundred yards from a beautiful little stream, at which we washed our hands and faces, not having been able even to wash our hands since the morning of the 16th.

Hearing that there was an opportunity of sending letters to England, I got some paper from the colour-serjeant of the company, and wrote two short notes, one to my mother and sisters, the other to a kind friend much interested in the 52nd. My letters, which I am sorry to say, have been long ago lost, though short, were to the point, and very astounding no doubt. I well recollect telling them that we had gained a glorious victory, and that the 52nd had "defeated the Imperial Guard of France, led "on by the Emperor Napoleon Bonaparte in person," using the same words which I had heard Sir John Colborne use in the morning.

My letter did not reach my mother for several days. She was very ill, and confined to her bed with rheumatic fever. The news, that a great battle had been fought, and that there had been great numbers of killed and wounded on both sides, reached every corner of the land some days before the long list of killed and wounded made its appearance. These were days of great suspense and anxiety to my young sisters, who had kept all mention of the battle from their poor mother. They have often given me the account of their proceedings. At last they got the newspaper containing the fearful list. They tremblingly spread it out on the sideboard, that all three might read it together. As every one knows, there was first of all a long list of those who had been killed. They looked down it to the 52nd, and there they read Ensign William ———, and they had time for a moment of agony, before they found that the surname was not mine, but that of my poor brother-ensign. The longer list of the wounded was then examined with almost equal anxiety, and when my name did not appear there, the eldest exclaimed, "Thank God, he's safe;" and they went to my mother, and after telling her quietly that I was safe, they told her of the "bloody "battle and glorious victory of Waterloo," and then they all cried together, and felt very thankful for God's great kindness to us. My brother, who arrived from the Cape a few days after, as a young commander, first heard the news of the victory at Spithead, or on landing at Portsmouth, and first heard that I was in the army, by being told that I had been in the action and was safe. I recollect he wrote me a letter on the occasion, in which he said he always thought that I had "a great desire to smell "powder," which I suppose somewhat flattered my vanity.

On the 20th of June we reached the neighbourhood of Binche, and I think it was not far from our halting-place that I went down a coal-pit of considerable depth. I had to put off *all* my own clothes and to dress myself in the very thick flannel shirt and trowsers which the colliers use; and thus clothed, and with one of their old felt caps on my head, into which a short iron spike was run, with a socket at the end for the lighted candle, I followed my guide down the ladder fixed to the side of the pit, to the depth of, I think they told me, 1100 feet. All the way down there were wooden platforms, at about every forty yards, completely filling up the whole area of the pit, with the exception of the hole which we had to pass through, in our descent from each platform, so that there was some comfort in thinking that if I got giddy I could not fall to the bottom of the pit. After descending some not very considerable distance, the water began to trickle down the sides of the pit, and my candle was frequently put out before we reached the bottom. My guide, whenever this happened, was very attentive in relighting my candle or starting me with a fresh one. When I got amongst the colliers at the bottom of the pit, they were very curious to know who I was, and made many inquiries about me of my guide, some suggesting that I was a deserter, endeavouring to conceal myself from those in pursuit of me. One advantage of my expedition was that I had to wash from head to foot before I could get into my own clothes again. The officers of the company were rather surprised at my little adventure, for they had not missed me.

On the 21st of June, between Binche and Bavay, we passed the frontier, and entered France from Belgium. We bivouacked in a very pleasant orchard, within half-a-mile of Bavay, and an order was given that no one was to enter the town. However, I was soon despatched with a havre-sac, as caterer for the company's officers' mess; they all insisting upon it, when I pleaded the order, that it was not intended to apply to the officers. On getting into Bavay, I tied up my horse and got into a cabaret, the lower rooms of which were filled with English and German soldiers, all intent on getting anything they could meet with in the shape of eatables. I considered myself very fortunate, when

I managed to purchase some small loaves, and two or three very small cheeses, about six inches by four, and one-and-a-half thick; and also a dozen of eggs, which I boiled for a good quarter of an hour. Having put all into my havre-sac, I started off for the bivouac; but whom should I fall in with, as I rode out of the town, but Sir John Colborne, who, however, as he rode by my side, to my great relief did not mention the order, either because it was not intended for the officers, or from a very kind feeling which all persons in authority find it desirable to exercise at times, and which leads them to appear not to notice things, which if noticed at all, would render it necessary that they should speak or act in a way which would be more productive of harm than good. I rode rather fast over part of the way from the auberge to the bivouac, and the consequence was that all my eggs, which I thought were hard-boiled, were smashed, and made a regular mess of the cheese and the bread in the havre-sac, to the no small annoyance of my mess friends and myself. Knowing nothing about egg-boiling, I had neglected to make the water boil before I put the eggs into it.

On the 22nd we marched from Bavay to Le Cateau Cambresis. I think it was on this march, at one of our halts, that I found one of our men washing a nasty-looking wound on his breast-bone, at least half-a-foot square; on my inquiring how he had got it, he told me that it was occasioned by a musket ball striking his breastplate, as we advanced on the Imperial Guard; and that he had determined not to mention it, as he did not wish to be left behind in hospital. But for the breastplate, he would have been a dead man.

We remained at Le Cateau till the morning of the 25th, and the regiment had a very agreeable bivouac in a large, square grass-field, which, as I recollect it, had on two or three sides the ruins of old walls, partly covered with grass. It was close to the town.

Louis XVIII arrived at Le Cateau on the 24th, and was received by the Duke of Wellington.

The Duke halted his advanced troops at this place for several purposes. Some of the French fortresses near the frontier were to be taken possession of. Cambrai was taken on the 24th, and its citadel on the 25th, and Louis the XVIII entered the town on the 26th. Peronne was taken on the 26th. On all these occasions there was but trifling loss.

The Duke wrote as follows, two days afterwards, to Lord Bathurst:—"The armies under Marshal Blucher and myself "have continued their operations since I last wrote to your "Lordship. The necessity which I was under of halting at Le "Cateau, to allow the pontoons and certain stores to reach me, "and to take Cambrai and Peronne, had placed the Marshal one "march before me; but I conceive there is no danger in this "separation between the two armies."

He wrote to Lord Liverpool on the same day:—"You will see "in my letter to Lord Bathurst the account of the state of things "here, which I hope we shall bring to the conclusion we wish for, "without firing another shot. I hope to be in Paris on the 1st "of July."

On the same day the Duke, in writing to the Duke of York, the Commander-in-Chief, made the following recommendation relative to the Companionship of the Bath, and to the gold medal, and to a medal for Waterloo:—

"I confess that I do not concur in the limitation of the order "to field-officers. Many captains in the army conducted them-"selves in a very meritorious manner, and deserve it; and I "never could see the reason for excluding them, either from the "order or from the medal. I would also like to suggest to your "Royal Highness the expediency of giving to the non-commis-"sioned officers and soldiers, engaged in the Battle of Waterloo, "a medal. I am convinced it would have the best effect in the "army; and, if that battle should settle our concerns, they will "well deserve it."

The medal for Waterloo was given to every officer and man in the field, and was distributed to each some little time before the first anniversary of the battle.

The non-commissioned officers and men were allowed two years' time towards any claim for increase of pension; and the Waterloo subalterns were allowed two years for Waterloo towards getting the additional shilling per day which they before received after seven years' service.

The 1st Guards were made "Grenadier Guards," for defeating the grenadiers of the Imperial Guard of France; and the ensigns of all the three regiments of the Guards, were for the future to be ensigns and lieutenants; the ensigns thus having precedence given them over all the ensigns of the British army.

The following are extracts from a general order, dated Nivelles, 20th June, 1815 :—

"The Field-Marshal takes this opportunity of returning to "the army his thanks for their conduct in the glorious action "fought on the 18th instant. With a view to preserve order, "and to provide for attendance at the hospitals at Bruxelles, the "commander of the forces desires that one officer, one non-com- "missioned officer, and three private men, for 100 men sent to "the hospital, wounded in the late actions of the 16th and 18th "instant, may be sent from the several regiments to Bruxelles to- "morrow, and place themselves under the orders of the com- "mandant there.

"No regiment need send officers and men for more than 100 "men, and in case any regiment has not sent more than fifty "men to the hospital, such regiment will send only one non- "commissioned officer and two men to take charge of them."

During the two clear days that we remained at Le Cateau, our hope of seeing our baggage come up was greatly diminished. I rode out several times on the Brussels road, and at times thought I had caught sight of it in the distance; but it always turned out to be the baggage of some other corps. The baggage of half the officers of the 52nd was entirely lost, and it was reported that it was plundered on the 18th, on the road to Brussels, by some foreign cavalry, who were running away from the action. Some time after Waterloo, but I cannot recollect the exact time, I determined on sending in a claim for remuneration for the loss of my baggage; and this I did, notwithstanding that all the officers told me it was perfectly useless for me to prefer such a claim, as remuneration was never allowed unless the baggage had been taken by the enemy. I thought it was a gross piece of injustice that officers should be fighting the battles of their country and risking their lives in its service, and incur such a serious loss without any fault of their own, and that the country should not bear them harmless from it. My claim was accordingly made out; and Colonel Charles Rowan certified that it was correctly and justly stated, and forwarded it to the proper quarter. It included the value of my baggage-horse and saddle, a bearskin bed, and a canteen, and all the clothes, regimentals, &c., &c., which I had not on my back and in a small valise fastened behind the saddle of my riding-horse. The things were all new since the 1st of May, and my outfit had cost me about £200. However, I could only recollect the articles and their prices, which had to be specified, sufficiently to enable me to make out a claim for £77 14s. 0d. I believe the claim was referred by the Duke of Wellington to the proper board in England. After some time the commanding officer received information that the claim was allowed to a certain extent, and that the sum of, I think it was, £63 was to be paid to me. Then, of course, all the other officers of the regiment who had lost their baggage sent in claims for remuneration; but, notwithstanding my success, all their claims were rejected. I, of course, was rather proud of having displayed more generalship than any of them. However, the matter did not quite end there, for Colonel Rowan wrote a letter of expostulation on the subject, in which he stated that some of the officers claiming were in the same company with me, and their horses in the same string of horses with mine; that I had received remuneration for my loss, and that it would, of course, be considered a very great hardship if they should not be remunerated also. I was rather joked and twitted about the probability of my having to refund the money which I had received; but, as I thought it well to have some answer to this threatened and very probable disaster, I used to say, " Oh! that's impossible, for I have spent it all." In due time a reply came to Colonel Rowan's letter, and then I had a regular crow over all my friends. The reply was, that " if Ensign Leeke "had received remuneration for the baggage which he lost at " Waterloo, all the Duke of Wellington could say was, that he "knew nothing at all about it." And thus it all ended. We heard at the time that one other officer in the army had obtained remuneration for loss of baggage.

We afterwards learnt the true fate of the baggage of some of the officers. Two of the bâtmen, of which the man having charge of the string of horses belonging to McNair's company was one, reached Brussels, and had the rascality to pass themselves off as wounded English officers, having managed to rig themselves out with the officers' clothes which had been entrusted to them; they managed to obtain billets from the proper authorities. This was not likely to last long, when there were upwards of 170 wounded officers and men of their own regiment in Brussels, besides the officers and men who had been sent there to look after the wounded; so in the course of three or four weeks they were denounced to the officers, and I recollect our man was sent up to the regiment, and tried by a general regimental court-martial, and was sentenced to be transported for seven years.

Amongst the clothes which this man had not got rid of—and he had sold the greater part of the things—there were articles of clothing discovered belonging to all the other officers of Mc Nair's company except myself. After the court-marshal I asked him how this happened to be the case, and he told me that in the great confusion which there was amongst the baggage, it was almost impossible for one man to take care of a string of four or five horses, and that much baggage was lost in consequence; that my horse was the last, and that he saw a Belgian peasant cut the rope which fastened him to the horse before him; that he could not leave the leading horse, and that whilst he was loading his firelock to have a shot at the Belgian, some increased confusion took place, and the man succeeded in getting off with my horse and baggage. Very possibly this account was correct. I forget what became of the other delinquent, but he was not tried at the same time with our bâtman.

I believe it was not unfrequently the case in the Peninsula, that officers on baggage-guard at the time of a general action, ran the risk of getting into a scrape, and left their guard and went up to the front, to their regiments, to see the fun, as it was termed. I think I understood that our subaltern on the baggage-guard did this at Waterloo; and probably, had he not done so, much of the confusion and loss I have described would have been avoided. But I dare say there was not an officer, who sustained the loss of his baggage on that occasion, who would not rather have done so than that this poor fellow should have missed the pleasure of being present with his regiment at Waterloo. And yet the practice cannot be defended, and I do not mean to defend it, but merely to describe the feeling on the subject.

It is related in the 52nd regimental record that the late Duke of Richmond, The Prince of Orange, and Lord Fitzroy Somerset (afterwards Lord Raglan) entered the breach at Ciudad Rodrigo with the 52nd storming party, and that on the following morning, when taking their places at breakfast in Lord Wellington's tent, "they received a gentle reproof for adventuring into a posi-"tion which, being officers of the staff, they were not called upon "to undertake by the customs of the service."

I believe it was at Le Cateau that we had notice that there was a sale of the effects of some of the German officers who had been killed at Waterloo. I went to it, as some of us were very much in want of a change of linen; somehow or other I only succeeded in securing two shirts, the best of which fell to the lot of one of my brother-officers. It was either when we were at Le Cateau or a day or two afterwards, that Sir John Colborne, on finding that my boots were in a most dilapidated state, very kindly made me a present of a new pair of his own.

On the 25th of June the 52nd marched from Le Cateau to the neighbourhood of Joncour; on the 26th they were near Beauvoir and Lanchy; on the 27th close to Roye; on the 28th at Petit Crevecœur, on the road to St. Just; on the 29th near Clermont; on the 30th near La Chapelle. On the 30th I think it was that Captain McNair's company (No. 9) was sent, in consequence of an application from Marshal Monçey, Duke of Cornegliano, to occupy for the night and protect his chateau, about a mile from the bivouac of the regiment. The grounds of this chateau, and the chateau itself, were in excellent taste, and we considered ourselves very fortunate in being quartered there for the night. The servants provided us with a very nice dinner, but the greatest luxury was to be able for the first time since the 16th to undress ourselves and sleep in a bed. They told me that the room selected for me was Mademoiselle Monçey's.

I must not neglect to mention, that one of the officers of the company having met with an accident and injured his shin, some time before we arrived at Waterloo, the wound became so troublesome that his trowsers stuck to it, and got into such a state on the outside that, when the battle was over, he sent back his servant to search for another pair for him, and he succeeded in bringing him a pair drawn from the body of a dead Frenchman. It happened that the Frenchman was what is termed "Dutch-"built," and the officer was taller and thinner than his predecessor in the property; and so, after bearing for twelve days with the inconvenience arising from the unfitness of the trowsers for him, and finding that there was no chance of the baggage turning up, he took advantage of our occupying the chateau to lie in his cloak for some hours, whilst a tailor belonging to the company reduced the trowsers to dimensions suited to the wants and taste of their new proprietor.

Sir John Colborne also took up his quarters at this chateau, but I did not come across him. The next morning, when the company had marched about a hundred yards from the gates, we met a very gentlemanly-looking elderly man on a handsome long-tailed grey horse, whom we supposed to be the duke, but he passed us without taking any notice of us, or we of him. He might have thanked us for taking care of his property, but we could not well take any notice of him, as we were not sure that he was the duke.

Some days before this it was currently reported in the army that Marshal Blucher had declared most positively, that if the Prussians got hold of Bonaparte, he would hang him. And he was equally determined to destroy any monuments in Paris which recorded any of the victories gained by the French over the Prussians in former years. Some days after our arrival at Paris, I saw the Prussian engineers very busy under one of the arches of the bridge of Jena, which received its name to commemorate a victory gained by the French in 1806. There was also a strong report that Blucher would destroy the splendid column in the Place Vendôme formed out of the brass cannon taken by the French from their enemies during their long course of victories in former years. He intended also to impose a heavy contribution on the city of Paris. The Duke of Wellington had some difficulty in restraining Blucher's angry impetuosity until the course of action as to these and other matters should be decided by all the Allied powers.

The following letter from Lord Castlereagh to Lord Liverpool, written June 25th, will give some idea of the state of affairs at this time:—

"The papers of the 23rd just arrived.

"Bonaparte has abdicated in favour of his son. The assem-
"blies have accepted the abdication unconditionally. They have
"nominated a provisional government of five, of which Fouché,
"Carnot, and Caulaincourt are three, and determined to send
"commissioners to the Allies to negotiate.

"The Minister of War states in the House of Peers, that they
"have still an army of 60,000 men to cover the north; Ney con-
"tradicts this, and says it does not exceed 25,000; and that
"there is nothing that can prevent the advance of the enemy to
"Paris. He tells them they have no choice but to negotiate
"with the Allies. The French army is admitted to have been en-
"tirely dissolved in the battle of the 18th. Vandamme seems to
"have got with 10,000 men in the rear of the Allies, and to be
"thus cut off.

"Sir C. Stuart writes from Mons, the 23rd, to which place
"Louis XVIII had removed:—'Wellington at Cateau Cambresis;
"'Blucher at Avesnes. We have parked 172 cannon; the Prus-
"'sians 62.' I have called a cabinet council. Ever yours,

"CASTLEREAGH."

On the 1st of July, when we were not many miles from Marshal Monçey's chateau, the 52nd first saw Paris, and the splendid dome of the hospital of the Invalides in the distance. It was a beautiful day. The regiment moved off the road to the right to a rising ground, called the Jardin de Paris, finding large quantities of fruit-trees covering an immense extent of ground. Here they looked down on St. Denis, rather towards the left, and the hill of Montmartre, between them and the French capital. Montmartre appeared very rugged and to be strongly fortified, and our feelings got on to the war establishment again, as we fancied we might very probably have to storm this not very pleasant-looking fortified hill on the morrow. It was when we arrived at the Jardin de Paris that we first saw the French troops again after their defeat at Waterloo, they having sent out from St. Denis along the high road a few skirmishers to fire at one of the English videttes. It was not a very pleasant post for him to be on sentry in, as he had some thirty or forty fellows blazing away at him for some considerable time at a distance of about 250 yards. As he walked his horse up and down on his post, he occasionally returned the fire of the skirmishers by giving them a shot from his carbine. Sir John Colborne, who had commanded the brigade since the action, Adam and Reynell being wounded, sent down a party of the 71st, who drove the French skirmishers off.

I remember we very much enjoyed the ripe currants and cherries on the slope to the right below our bivouac. At the bottom of the slope, about half-a-mile off, I found a deserted village, in which there were a great number of gentlemen's houses completely plundered, and every atom of furniture destroyed in the most wanton manner by the Prussians. Mirrors and chests of drawers, &c., &c., were smashed to atoms. This was the first time that we had come across the Prussian line of march. They were determined to retaliate upon the French civilians all the suffering and cruelty they had experienced at the hands of the French soldiers in by-gone years.

On the 2nd of July the 52nd were alone at Argenteuil on the Seine. Here we found the village had been plundered by the Prussians. Three of them who had to turn out of the village, when we arrived there, not being well pleased at being interfered with, did us the favour, when they had proceeded about two or three hundred yards on the road, to send three musket-balls whistling through our bivouac; they rather astonished us, but did no harm; and I think the fellows were not followed and punished.

In the afternoon of the 2nd McNair's company crossed the Seine in boats, and took possession of and loopholed a gentleman's house on the other side, to protect the formation of a pontoon bridge across the Seine; the French troops being about a mile off, but not shewing themselves. The next morning another company of the 52nd joined us, and pushed on an officer and some men to a village in front, from which a few French soldiers hastily retired as they entered it. On the 2nd and 3rd of July the Prussians were twice attacked by the French under Davoust, and the latter were defeated, the Prussians following them nearly to the walls of Paris.

On the same day a convention was signed, Napoleon having abdicated and fled, by which, amongst other arrangements, it was agreed that there should be a suspension of arms, that the French army opposed to us should evacuate Paris in three days, and retire behind the Loire, and that, within the same space of time, all the barriers of Paris and also Montmartre should be given up. The English and Prussian commissioners, Colonel Hervey and Baron Muffling, were fired at in the streets of Paris, shortly after entering it by the barrier of Villette; which might have led to very disastrous consequences, but an ample apology was made by the Prince of Eckmühl and the French commissioners charged with the execution of the convention, and the affair was passed over.

On the afternoon of the 3rd of July the 52nd crossed the Seine on the pontoon bridge, and proceeded to the bridge of Neuilly. We observed places along the side of the road where the Prussians and French were buried who had been killed there, I think, the day before. Sir John Colborne had received orders to cross the bridge of Neuilly; but the French refused to retire from the strong barricade, which had been built across the centre of it. The two front companies of the 52nd (10 and 9) were advanced a very short distance in front of the column of companies, on the road by the side of the river, with fixed bayonets. Sir John Colborne coolly took out his watch and allowed five minutes to the French commander in which to give up the bridge or to have it stormed; in two or three minutes it was given up, some few men coming over and shouting "Vive le Roi!" The village of Neuilly, within a short distance of one of the barriers of Paris, was occupied, and the 52nd passed the night in the walled graveyard of that place. The only things I recollect as occurring on that night were the getting some bread and cheese in a cabaret; and, with the assistance of one of the officers, getting late at night a truss of hay for our horses out of the hayloft belonging to a gentleman's house, which was either deserted, or the inhabitants declined to "shew up."

On the morning of the 4th of July we saw the last of the French troops, two videttes close to the gate of the graveyard, having two English videttes within twenty paces of them, and a French infantry picket about half-a-mile off on the road to Paris. They soon retired, and the French army began to evacuate Paris that day, and, I think, it was on the same day, that the National Guard of Paris relieved the guard of the troops of the Line at the Barrière de l'Etoile. The 52nd proceeded to the Bois de Boulogne, to the right of the road from Neuilly to Paris, and remained there till the 7th. On the 5th Montmartre was given up to the English, and on the 6th, I believe, some of our brigade took possession of the Barrière de l'Etoile.

On the morning of the 7th of July General Adam's brigade (52nd, 71st, and 95th) had the honour of entering Paris by the Barrière de l'Etoile. They marched down the centre of the road leading through the Champs Elysées, to the Place Louis Quinze, (now the Place de la Concorde) and the Tuileries. A brigade of artillery, with lighted matches, was posted close to the barrier on either side of the chaussée. It was a proud and happy moment, when, with bands and bugles playing, we thus took possession of, and entered, the capital of France. At least I am sure it was the proudest moment of my life, when I found myself riding down the centre of the avenue of the Champs Elysées, bearing in triumph, into the enemy's capital, that same 52nd regimental colour which I had the honour of carrying to victory on the eventful and glorious day of Waterloo.

The whole brigade halted and piled arms in the Champs Elysées, to the right of the main road and between it and the Seine, and not far from the Place Louis Quinze. These were the British troops which occupied the French capital; almost the whole of the rest of the Allied army remained in the Bois de Boulogne, although some were at Montmartre. Before the 52nd band was dismissed, Sir John Colborne ordered it to play " Vive Henri "Quatre," one of the principal royalist tunes, but it did not appear to attract any number of people. Indeed, there were not many more persons stirring at that hour—it was between eight and nine—than one would see at the same hour in Hyde Park, between Apsley House and the Marble Arch. Mr. Hollond, an

English gentleman, who had a house in Paris, had ridden out to see the arrival of his compatriots, and having entered into conversation with me, invited me to go and breakfast with him in the Rue de Mont Blanc. I willingly accepted his invitation, and having deposited my colour, I rode with him into Paris and along the beautiful boulevards to his residence. With the exception of Colonel Hervey, the commissioner, I suspect I was the first individual of the British army who entered the *streets* of Paris.* Mr. Hollond was exceedingly kind, and I remember that, amongst other things, when on inquiry he found I had only a few ducats in my pocket, he insisted on becoming my banker and on lending me ten napoleons till I should get a bill on England cashed. McNair begged of me, directly I got back to the Champs Elysées, not to lose a day in getting a bill cashed by the paymaster and in repaying the money. This I did the very next day. I was not aware, till he told me, that I had done anything wrong, or *infra dig*, in thus allowing a stranger to become my banker for a few days. Just as we had finished breakfast, a Prussian general and his aide-de-camp arrived with a billet on Mr. Hollond's house, which must have been a considerable nuisance to him, but not so great a one as it would have been, had he not been a bachelor. The Prussian officers were remarkably quiet and gentlemanly in their demeanour.

On my way back, as I walked my horse along the boulevards, some boys did me the favour of throwing stones at me, but as I thought that, on that occasion at least, "the better part of valour "was discretion," I contented myself with quietly cantering away from them.

The 52nd, in the course of the morning, crossed the main road and encamped on the other side of the Champs Elysées, leaving the 71st and 95th on the side nearest to the river, and

* I at one time used rather to boast of three things, that *very probably* I had the honour of being the youngest officer at Waterloo, of being the nearest British officer to the Emperor Napoleon in that battle, (I mean when the 52nd colour was in front of the 52nd line with the covering serjeants, at the moment that the Duke and Lord Uxbridge were in our rear, and Bonaparte was, as it was afterwards reported, with the Old Guard in our front,) and thirdly, as I have mentioned, that I was the first officer who entered Paris. I lately heard of a Waterloo officer, who was my junior by about six weeks.

throwing its sentries forward about 140 yards to the low rail separating the Champs Elysées from the Place Louis Quinze, where the unfortunate Louis XVI and Marie Antoinette were executed in 1783. For a day or two the whole regiment was together, encamped in a large open square place bordered on the four sides by rows of trees. The Champs Elysées consisted of a series of these large square openings; there was the main road from the Arc de Triomphe and the Barrière de l'Etoile in the direction of the Tuileries, down which we had marched, and about half-way up it was crossed at right angles by another main road, leading from the Rue du Faubourg St. Honoré, and the palace called the Elysée Bourbon, to the Seine. On the other side of the river were the Champs de Mars, the Ecole Militaire, and the hospital of the Invalides facing the Champs Elysées. The bridge of Jena, which was near the barrier, and which Blucher wished to destroy, led from the Champ de Mars towards the Champs Elysées.

Close to the large open space in which the 52nd encamped there was a decent *restaurateur's*. There were several of these places, and also dancing houses, in different parts of the Champs Elysées.

CHAPTER VIII.

1815.

PARIS. THE 52ND ENCAMPED IN THE CHAMPS ELYSÉES.

Two companies a guard to the duke's house—Colonel W. Rowan commandant—Bonaparte finds refuge on board the Bellerophon—Entry of Louis XVIII into Paris—The Imperial Guard—Position of 52nd in Paris—Cricket and drill—Dine with Sir John Colborne—Restoration of pictures, &c., taken by the French—Review of Russian Guards—Accident—Cossacks of the Don—Ecole de Natation—Practical jokes—Row in the Palais Royal—Row at St. Cloud—Gaming-houses—Observations on the evil of letting children play at games for money—Soldier condemned to be shot—Caricatures of English—"Les Anglaises pour rire"—"Monsieur Calico"—Playhouses to be avoided.

EITHER the day after we entered Paris, or on the following day, No. 9 and No. 10 companies of the 52nd were ordered to encamp nearer to the Place Louis Quinze, and near to where the quarter-guard already was, close to the wall of the Duke of Wellington's garden. The cords of the officers' tents were close to the short palings, which fenced off about ten feet of garden-ground between them and the wall. My tent was against the little gate in the palings which led to the garden-door, and close up to it, so close that one day, about a week or fortnight after we arrived, I heard somebody floundering about and stumbling over the cords, and, on looking out, found it was the duke himself, who sometimes, but not often, came out that way. He desired that the tent might be moved a few feet forward. The whole brigade remained encamped in the manner I have mentioned till the 2nd of November, a period of nearly four months.

Lieut.-Colonel W. Rowan of the 52nd was made commandant of the first arrondissement of Paris. We, who belonged to No. 9 and No. 10, considered ourselves as an especial guard to the Duke. There was a serjeant's guard at the entrance to the courtyard of his residence, in a short street leading out of the Place Louis Quinze. I think it was on the afternoon of the 8th, that two of the King's Garde du Corps took refuge with this guard, having been pursued by a street mob.

Bonaparte, after lingering at the Elysée and then for several days at Malmaison, in the vain hope that something might occur, which would afford him a chance of retrieving his broken fortunes, was persuaded, if not forced, by the provisional government, to take the road to Rochefort, where they had placed two French frigates at his disposal, with the view of his escaping to America. He embarked in the Saale on the 8th of July, but in vain did some of his devoted friends endeavour to obtain a promise from Captain Maitland of the Bellerophon, the blockading English ship, that he would allow the French frigates to pass with Napoleon on board. In a few days he found it necessary to take refuge in the Bellerophon, and before he reached the quarter-deck of that ship, the French frigates had both hoisted the white flag. The Bellerophon, on her way to Torbay, which she reached on the 15th, astonished the captain and crew of an English frigate on their way to Spithead from the Adriatic, who were quite unacquainted with recent events in France, by signalling "Napoleon on board." The Bellerophon was ordered to Plymouth, where Bonaparte was transferred to the Northumberland. He was not permitted to land either at Torbay or Plymouth. It was decided, after some little time, that he should be sent as a prisoner of war to St. Helena, for which island the Northumberland sailed on the 8th of August.

The King, Louis XVIII, reached Paris on the 8th of July, the day after we entered the city. I was present in the Tuileries on the afternoon of the day of his arrival, and I think no one could have desired to have a greater display of enthusiasm and loyalty than was manifested on the occasion of his presenting himself to the people on one of the balconies of the Tuileries looking towards the Champs Elysées. There must have been from fifteen to twenty thousand persons assembled. When the King came forward there was a cry for the people to take their hats off, which almost all appeared to do, and, being tall, I had a good view over the whole assembled people. I was in the midst of the crowd, and whilst they knocked off the hats of one or two obstinate fellows near me, they treated me with marked civility, one patting me on the back, as the Prussian officer did on the night of the Battle of Waterloo, and calling me " Brave Anglais." As an officer in uniform I of course kept my cap on. I saw two other English officers at a distance in the crowd.

I must now record something more about the proceedings of the Imperial Guard. It must be remembered that it consisted in 1815 of 25,870 men. There were 20,400 infantry, 3300 cavalry, and 2170 artillery, sappers, waggon train, &c. Of these 25,870 men, after deducting for casualties on the 16th and 17th, probably nearly the half were engaged with the Prussians at Planchenoit. After the defeat of the whole of the Imperial Guard at Waterloo, " Generals "Morand and Colbert succeeded in rallying some remnants of com- "panies of them at Beaumont," about five-and-twenty miles from Waterloo, and from thence they proceeded towards Paris, and made a considerable stand against the Prussians at the village of Vertus, near St. Denis, and afterwards made good their retreat from that place when forced out of it by very superior numbers. The French historian of the Imperial Guard states that this affair of the 30th of June was the last in which they were engaged. During the 4th, 5th, and 6th of July, the whole French army marched from the neighbourhood of Paris on the road to Orleans, and retired behind the Loire. Great numbers retired to their homes. On the breaking up of the army, many of the officers of the Imperial Guard emigrated, some to Turkey, others to Greece, others again to America. Several of the chief officers, Marshal Grouchy, and the Generals Clausel, Vandamme, Lefèvre-Desnouettes, Rigaud, and a great many officers of rank, were at New York and Philadelphia in 1817, and a large portion of them, under the direction of General Lallemand, attempted to found a colony in Texas, but it did not prosper, and after losing three-fourths of their numbers, the remainder of these poor fellows returned to New Orleans and settled there.

IN THE CHAMPS ELYSÉES. 157

The encampment of Adam's brigade in the Champs Elysées was about the same thing, as regarded Paris and its inhabitants, as would be the encampment of 2500 men in Hyde Park, between the entrance gate near Apsley house and the statue of Achilles, to London and its inhabitants; or the same number in the Green Park, near Piccadilly; or in St. James's park, between the Horse Guards and Dartmouth street; it was also the same sort of thing to us. We were not troubled with any orders about not appearing in the streets except in uniform. We generally wore the blue surtout coat, when in undress, and had but to exchange a foraging-cap for a round hat, and spring over the low rails in front of our quarter-guard near the Café Ledoyen, and we found ourselves in Paris, *en bourgeois*, in less than two minutes after we had made up our minds to go there. We were within four or five minutes' walk of the principal entrance to the Tuileries, which was just across the Place Louis Quinze. The men could only pass the cordon of sentries under certain regulations. There was no regular officers' mess whilst we were in Paris, but the officers of each company messed together in one of their tents, and I remember that I continued to be the caterer, and a very inexpensive mess it was, for we none of us cared much about eating and drinking.

A considerable number of the Parisians visited our camp from the first, and some of them I know were ladies belonging to superior Bonapartist families; such confidence had they in the discipline and good behaviour of the British soldiers. Crowds of persons came to see us play at cricket, which we sometimes did in the 52nd. It was a game to which the French were unaccustomed, and one speech which was overheard was that, "no " wonder the English were not afraid of cannon-balls, when " they could so fearlessly meet and stop those dreadful cricket- " balls coming towards them with such terrific force." It was a current report at Paris, that the Emperor had said, that "at " Waterloo the English squares had stood like walls, and the " French cannon-balls could make no impression on them."

Out on the same open place on which we played at cricket, beyond the 52nd encampment, our regular drill was carried on, and as I had done very little in the way of drill before the campaign commenced, I had much to learn after we reached Paris. I perhaps was the only British officer who had the honour of finishing his drill in the French capital. We had many spectators who, of course, were much interested in the light infantry movements, and the bugle sounds. We had some forty men who had to go through the same amount of drill that I had. The 52nd drill instructors were always required to be most particular in the marching drill, from the goose-step upwards; and it was to this great attention paid to the balancing of the body in marching, and the avoiding of all flourishing of the foot as it came to the ground, that we used to attribute the good marching of the 52nd, and especially their beautiful advances in line, for which they were very remarkable in my 52nd days, and for years afterwards; I hope they are so still.

About ten days after our arrival in Paris, Sir John Colborne (Lord Seaton) very kindly invited me to dine with him at his lodgings, or billet, somewhere to the left, in a line with the principal entrance of the Tuileries from the Place Louis Quinze, and in the street leading down past the end of the Rue de la Paix. I met there only three or four of the senior officers of the regiment, and I well recollect his telling me, before them, that I might consider myself one of the most fortunate fellows in the whole army; for I had only been in it two months, and had, in that short space of time, not only taken part in the glorious action at Waterloo, but had also been present at the taking of the capital of France.

I kept no journal at that time, and not till about four years afterwards, and then only occasionally during the next four or five years, so that in describing the circumstances that occurred at Paris and elsewhere, I have to trust to my memory, which I have good reason to think is particularly retentive and accurate.

The French commanders, as is well known, had during a long course of years, wherever their arms were successful, brought away from the museums of the several countries, and from other places where they were to be found, great numbers of the choicest paintings and statues. Vast numbers of these paintings, etc., were found in the Louvre when the Allies took possession of Paris. The French ministers, and also the King, were very unwilling to restore these improperly acquired treasures of art to their rightful owners, more especially perhaps as they knew such restitution would be very unpalatable to the French people. The following extracts from a letter from the Duke of Wellington to Lord Castlereagh will show how the affair ended :—

"PARIS, 23rd September, 1815.

"Shortly after the arrival of the sovereigns at Paris, the "minister of the King of the Netherlands claimed the pictures, "etc., belonging to his sovereign equally with those of other "powers; and, as far as I could learn, never could get any "satisfactory reply from the French government. After several "conversations with me he addressed your lordship in an "official note, which was laid before the ministers of the Allied "sovereigns assembled in conference, and the subject was "taken into consideration repeatedly, with a view to discover a "mode of doing justice to the claimants of the specimens of "the arts in the museums, without hurting the feelings of the "King of France. In the mean time the Prussians had obtained "from his majesty not only all the really Prussian pictures, "but those belonging to the Prussian territories on the left of "the Rhine, and the pictures, etc., belonging to all the allies of his "Prussian majesty; and the subject pressed for an early decision ; "and your lordship wrote your note of the 11th instant, in "which it was fully discussed.

"The minister of the King of the Netherlands, still having "no satisfactory answer from the French government, applied to "me, as the Commander-in-Chief of the army of the King of "the Netherlands, to know if I had any objection to employ "his majesty's troops to obtain possession of what was his "undoubted property. I referred this application again to the "ministers of the Allied courts, and no objection having been "stated, I considered it my duty to take the necessary measures "to obtain what was his right.

"I spoke to Prince de Talleyrand on the subject . . . . and "begged him to state the case to the King, (of France,) and to

"ask his majesty to do me the favour to point out the mode of
"effecting the object of the King of the Netherlands, which
"which should be least offensive to his majesty.

"The Prince de Talleyrand promised me an answer on the
"following evening; which not having received, I called upon
"him at night, and had another discussion with him on the
"subject, in which he informed me that the King could give no
"orders upon it; that I might act as I thought proper, and
"that I might communicate with M. Denon.

"I sent my aide-de-camp, Lieut.-Colonel Fremantle, to
"M. Denon in the morning, who informed him that he had no
"orders to give any pictures out of the gallery, and that he
"could give none without the use of force.

"I then sent Colonel Fremantle to the Prince de Talleyrand
"to inform him of this answer, and to acquaint him that the
"troops would go the next morning at twelve o'clock to take
"possession of the King of the Netherland's pictures; and to
"point out, that if any disturbance resulted from this measure,
"the King's ministers, and not I, were responsible. Colonel
"Fremantle also informed M. Denon that the same measure
"would be adopted.

"It was not necessary however to send the troops, as a
"Prussian guard had always remained in possession of the
"gallery, and the pictures were taken without the necessity of
"calling for those under my command, excepting as a working
"party to assist in taking them down and packing them.

. . . .

"The Allies, having the contents of the museum justly in
"their possession, could not do otherwise than restore them to
"the countries from which, contrary to the practice of civilized
"warfare, they had been torn during the disastrous period of the
"French revolution and the tyranny of Bonaparte.

"It has never appeared to me to be necessary that the Allied
"sovereigns should omit this opportunity to do justice and to
"gratify their own subjects, in order to gratify the people of
"France.

"It is on many accounts desirable, as well for their own
"happiness as that of the world, that the people of France, if

"they do not already feel that Europe is too strong for them, "should be made sensible of it."

The Duke argues, in conclusion, that it would not only be unjust in the sovereigns to give way in this matter, but also "impolitic, as it would deprive them of the opportunity of "giving the people of France a great moral lesson."

I was at the Louvre once or twice when this taking down and packing the pictures was going on; whether or not I was there on duty I do not recollect, but I remember seeing a fatigue-party of the 52nd there. There was no particular excitement observable amongst the French on that occasion.

But about that time the 52nd remained fully accoutred and ready to fall in at a moment's notice, for eight-and-forty hours, and on one of those two days, we were marched up, and remained for two or three hours on the Place Louis Quinze, in front of the gates of the Tuileries; I think it was when the Austrians were taking down the horses dedicated to the sun from the top of the gateway leading into the Place du Carrousel. They had been taken from Venice. It was expected that much discontent would be manifested by the French, and perhaps some violence on that occasion. Each horse was taken away separately, and was escorted by a whole regiment of Austrian dragoons. I was the orderly-officer on the day that the last horse was removed and was sent that evening by Sir John Colborne to report to General Adam, who had recovered from his wound and taken command of the brigade again, that all had passed off quietly.

We had one or two reviews on rather a large scale on an extensive plain near Paris, in which we passed over immense quantities of beet-root, which is grown there in order to produce sugar from it. I fear a large amount of damage was done to the crops, as we could scarcely take a step without each person treading on, and breaking in two, one of the roots; but the reviews were especially memorable for the clouds of black dust in which the troops were enveloped during nearly the whole time they were marching and manœuvring. We must have been terrible warriors to look at, as on our return to camp we marched through the streets of Paris covered from head to foot with this dust, and with our clothes and accoutrements, our faces, eyes, and ears, and our hair and whiskers, (at least of those who had any of the latter,) completely blackened by it. A considerable amount of time was consumed in getting all right again, to say nothing of the possible injury done to the clothing and appointments of both officers and men.

Sir John Colborne took the 52nd several times to the Champ de Mars, which was a very extensive and good exercising-ground. There we first practised the half-face movement in column, which I think was taken up from the Prussians, and was afterwards found to be a most useful movement. One day we came across the Emperor of Russia and his staff, in the Champ de Mars, and Sir John very neatly threw the regiment into close column just as the Emperor was arriving in front of the flank company, and saluted him with carried arms. As the Emperor was merely riding across the Champ de Mars, and as we were only there for drill, the salute with carried arms in close column was the only available method, under the circumstances, of shewing him any attention. It was the Emperor Alexander who received and acknowledged this salute.

I think it was not many weeks after our arrival in Paris that there was a review of several thousands of the Russian Guards in the Champs Elysées, on the road leading from the Barrière de l'Etoile to the Tuileries. They were a very fine body of picked men. The Russian soldiers of the Line appeared to me to be shorter and smaller men than the ordinary soldiers of any of the other armies who were in the neigbourhood of Paris at that time. On returning from this review I met with a rather severe fall, when galloping round one of the sunk plantations inclosed by balustrades in the Place Louis Quinze. My horse's legs flew from under him and he came down heavily on his side on my left leg, by which my knee and shoulder were cut. It was rather a nuisance, too, to be thus sent sprawling in uniform on the paved square in the presence of a good number of spectators; and I was very glad to slink off into our camp, which was close at hand.

Two or three hundred yards from the 52nd encampment towards the barrier there was stationed a troop of Cossacks of the Don, whom we occasionally used to visit. They were fine men and very orderly. Their horses were tied to the trees in the Champs Elysées, four or five round the same tree. Whenever there was any disturbance amongst them in the shape of biting or kicking, the Cossacks reduced them to order by thrashing them severely with the flat part of their naked swords. It was no uncommon thing among the Cossacks, though we saw nothing of the kind at Paris, for the officers to order their men to receive the same description of punishment for not very grave offences. One of the members of an English family which was thrown very much among the Cossacks, when the Russians marched on Paris in 1814, told me that on complaints being made to the officers of any infringement of the rules laid down, they would tell them in French that the delinquent should forthwith receive "vingt-cinq coups de plat de sabre."

When I was in Paris in 1817, I observed that great numbers of the trees which the Cossack horses had barked in 1815 had been thereby destroyed and that fresh trees had been planted in their place.

There was a very good swimming-bath on the Seine, not far from our camp, called in French the "Ecole de Natation." I learnt to swim there, and used it very frequently during the whole time of our occupation of Paris. I think it was on the first occasion of my visiting it, that I was in some danger of being drowned, by foolishly jumping into deep water, about six feet from the nettings, to try and solve the question, "Why, as "every other animal will swim, if thrown into water, should not "man do the same?" My attempts to swim were abortive, and I had gone under water twice, when six or eight of the bathers jumped in, and one of them saved me from going down again by pushing me against the netting at the side. Before we left Paris, I could swim and float very fairly.

There was always plenty of excitement for us, encamped as we were so far within the barrier of Paris, and so close to the Tuileries and other public places; the Champs Elysées were a favourite resort of the Parisians, and, although scarcely any of us had any opportunity of entering into French society, yet the meeting with numbers of the better classes in the public walks, and in the various places of public amusement, and the numbers of things we had to see, always prevented the time from hanging heavily on our hands. Besides which, some of us had friends from England staying there, who helped to make our occupation of Paris very pleasant to us.

I recollect only a few of the tricks which we used to play each other; a very approved one, now and then practised, was the quietly loosening the cords and loops of a tent from their stakes on a very wet night, and then letting the wet tent down on the helpless and infuriated occupier; the perpetrator generally managing not to be discovered. I did hear of one man, who undertook to take a portmanteau from under the walls, or lower canvass of a tent, but the occupant heard him and attacked him with his sword, very reasonably taking him for a thief, when the attacking party after seizing the sword, and getting his hands cut, found it necessary to beat a retreat.

The only practical joke I remember to have played at Paris, occurred as follows; and as far as the joke went it was a very innocent one:—Two of us came into camp from Paris one very dark night, and, after replying to the sentry's challenge, we passed the tent of the officer of the quarter-guard, whom we saw fully accoutred lying on his back on his guard-bed, very fast asleep with his mouth open: there were eight or ten rather large books on the table, and going into the tent I piled them up on a chair, one above another, till the top one touched the tent just over our friend's head. I then went round to the back of the tent, where, by the light of the candle inside, I could easily see the upper book, and giving it a push I sent the pile on to our victim's face, having done which I quietly and quickly got round to the darkness, pervading the trees of the Champs Elysées, at a very short distance, opposite to the tent door; from this we saw the officer coming out of his tent, hardly aware of what had exactly happened, and we heard the following short dialogue between him and the sentry. *Officer calls out:*—"Sentry!" *The Sentry replies:*—"Yes, Sir!" "*Officer:*—"Has "any one just come into camp?" *Sentry:*—"No, Sir!" We then made off, leaving the officer of the guard to renew his slumbers. This was the officer who, when the 52nd were pursuing the French at Vera, about two years before, went over a short mountain path with Sir John Colborne and four soldiers, and rushed down on to the road, into the middle of the 9th French light infantry, and summoned them to surrender, which those who were thus cut off did, to the number of two or three hundred. This officer, Lieutenant Cargill, received on the spot, and tucked under his arm, the swords of fourteen of the French officers. I have frequently heard it mentioned as a fact, that one of these officers having hesitated to deliver up *his* sword, Cargill struck him a blow in his face with his fist which made his mouth bleed, and had the effect of making him tractable. In these days such acts of daring would be deservedly rewarded by the grant of the Victoria Cross.

The anecdote just related brings to my remembrance an occurrence which took place at Paris a few weeks after we had left it. Some detachments sent out from England, just at the time that the army was about to proceed to take up its cantonments in the north of France, arrived in the neighbourhood of Paris, and several of the officers, amongst whom were two of the 52nd, availed themselves of the opportunity of seeing something of the French capital. One of the places they visited was the Palais Royal. As they were walking along the covered pavement, near the shops, they met several persons, who had all the appearance of being half-pay French officers; one of these, as they passed them, kicked against the foot of one of the 52nd officers with the evident design of insulting him; the 52nd officer immediately started round and inquired what he meant, but he not knowing much of French, the other 52nd man began to interpose, when the Frenchman gave him a smart box on the ear, asking him at the same time, what *he* had to do with it? This of course was responded to in the shape of a heavy blow planted on the Frenchman's mouth, which made his teeth both rattle and bleed: before the row had proceeded to any greater length, the guard appeared, and marched off both parties to the Prefecture, where the whole case was gone into. The Frenchmen were adjudged to be the aggressors, and the English officers were freed from all blame in the transaction. Insults offered to the English were seldom heard of during the three years of our occupation of France.

I went with three or four artillery officers, whom I knew, to the fair of St. Cloud, and we rather enjoyed it, and got on very well, till we were just coming away, when we got into a considerable unpleasantness through the stupidity, and possibly also the rascality, of the driver of the carriage which we had hired for the occasion. When we were about to return, he insisted upon it that he should be paid before we started: possibly somebody had done him out of what he considered his fare on some former occasion. However that may have been, he positively refused to drive us back to Paris, unless we first settled with him; this we considered very impertinent on his part, and determined not to give way to it. A crowd of eighty or a hundred persons were gathered round us, and on our attempting to take possession of the carriage, an altercation ensued with some of them, and then, without its actually coming to a fight, they began to interrupt our proceeding. A friend of mine, a very nice fellow, by the name of Heisse, belonging to one of the Hanoverian Jäger Corps, to whom I had been speaking during the day, happening to pass, saw our difficulty, and ran down to the bridge of St. Cloud, where a German picket was stationed, and brought up a few men to our assistance just at the right moment. They very unceremoniously made the mob stand back by striking at their legs with the butt ends of their muskets. The Prussians were to leave the neighbourhood of Paris the next morning, and our driver, who appeared to have a very wholesome fear of them, was considerably alarmed by hearing some of our party say, that it would serve him right, and do him good, if we could manage to get him pressed into their service, on the occasion of their march northwards.

Paris, of course, had many temptations for the officers of the British army. One was that arising from the gaming-houses, of which there were many, especially in the Palais Royal. I never heard, whilst we were there, of any body having suffered very severely from them; but yet I have no doubt that many were inconveniently fleeced, to say the least of it, by occasionally visiting them. I do not think it will be injurious to my readers, if I briefly mention what I saw of them. I had been to one of the theatres with a captain of the 52nd, and when it was over I found he was not going back to camp, but going to look into one of these gaming-houses at the Palais Royal. I had never seen a gaming-house, and begged that I might accompany him; but he said, Colborne would never forgive him, if he took me to such a place; however, on my pressing him, and shewing him that I had not above two napoleons in my pocket, so that I could not lose much, he gave way, and I went with him. The way to the first and second floors of these houses was up a very wide and substantial staircase, lighted with one gloomy lamp on each landing, the whole appearance of which led one's mind to associate with these places scenes of violence and assassination. There were about forty or fifty persons standing, and several of them playing at a roulette table in one room, and about as many more at a rouge-et-noir table in another. If I recollect rightly, I won a few napoleons that night by playing with two-franc pieces, which I think was the lowest sum which by the rules of the place was allowed to be hazarded. On a subsequent evening I took with me about seven napoleons, thinking that if I had been able to win a tolerable sum by playing with two-franc pieces, I might perhaps gain ten times as much by playing with napoleons. On this second night I seemed to have what is termed, a great run of luck, and at last I found my two waistcoat pockets to be so full of napoleons that it was not safe to put any more into them, and I began to stow away my winnings in my trowsers pockets. I could make no proper calculation of the amount of my "ill gotten wealth," but I observed at last that I had attracted the attention of most of the persons present, and especially that of the croupiers who received and handed out the money.

I now began to think of making good my retreat, but how to do it decently I did not know. However, having made up my mind to leave the place, I very quietly, though unexpectedly to them, walked to the door, and went tolerably quickly down the stairs, but, quick as I was in my movements, a man who followed me was on the landing-place at the bottom of the first flight of stairs before I had quitted it. He begged me to give him some money, as he was a person in distress; this I declined to do, not only because I thought it was not quite safe to be parleying with him under all the circumstances, but also because I felt annoyed that a person should pursue the degraded course of watching the gaming-tables for the purpose of demanding charity from the successful players.

As I crossed the Palais Royal, I roughly calculated that I had two or three hundred napoleons in my pocket, and thought that these would soon be gone and would do me no permanent good, whereas, if I could make the sum up to a thousand, I could, in some way, make it do me some more lasting benefit. With this idea in my head I went into another house on the opposite side of the Palais Royal, and played away as largely as I had done before; my pockets were very nearly emptied again. I determined, however, not to return to camp without taking back with me a small roll of napoleons which I felt were still remaining in my pocket, and which I judged to amount to about the sum I had started with. I was surprised, on reaching my tent, and counting over my remaining napoleons, that I had thirty-nine, instead of seven, remaining. This led me to think that I had been greatly mistaken as to the sum which I had at first gained, and that it must have amounted to three or four times as much as I had roughly calculated it to be.

This was a great ordeal for a boy under eighteen years of age to go through; but it was a very great mercy that I lost the money which I had gained. As it was, my taste for play continued, to an extent, for some years, (until I saw that it was decidedly wrong and sinful, and evidently a breach of the tenth commandment, to desire to win another person's money,) and if I had carried away with me the large sum above mentioned, it would probably have been more injurious to me than one can well imagine. I went three or four times after that to these *maisons de jeu*, but I was careful not to lose my money to any great extent; yet I did lose it, I am now thankful to say.

I have hesitated to write down the foregoing account, lest it should possibly do harm, in the way of exciting in any one an "itch for gambling." I may possibly not publish it; if I do so, I wish it to be accompanied by my protest against a practice which I believe is not so prevalent now in the houses of our gentry as it was fifty or sixty years ago; I mean the allowing children to play at cards or other games of chance, by which they may win money. I trace much evil that arises in the way of ruinous betting at races, or in playing at cards or billiards, for large sums of money, to this practice. I recollect it was the custom to set a dozen or more of children to play at commerce, when each put down a shilling, and the winner of the game took the whole of the money. It was this sort of thing, which led to an immense deal of gambling in a small way at schools, where the boys played at marbles and with tops, and at other things, for money; this easily paved the way for attendance and betting at public billiard-tables and races. I never but once made a bet at a race, but I knew a youth most respectably connected, who was utterly ruined both in character and fortune, who told me that his evil courses commenced when a near relative took him to a racecourse, and encouraged him to bet there. Many years ago, when I little thought of publishing a book, I used to say, half in joke, "If ever I publish a book, it "shall be against allowing boys at school, or in the streets, to "play at marbles for money," so convinced was I of the importance of endeavouring to check any disposition to gamble at an early age, or, what is still better, as far as possible not to let children or young people be at places, or amongst persons, where anything of the sort is practised. I have always enjoined on my children never to play at any game for money, and never on any account to make even the smallest bet, and I have never had a card in my house. I consider myself to be fully justified in stating, that all desire to win anything belonging to another, at a game of chance or skill, is contrary to that which God enjoins upon His people in the tenth commandment. I must apologize to my readers for this digression from the account of the various occurrences which took place whilst we were at Paris; but I do sincerely hope that all parents, and heads of schools, and others who may read it, will use their best efforts to nip in the bud that taste for gambling, which is yet so prevalent amongst both rich and poor, and which I believe, in nine cases out of ten, commences in early youth. It is obvious that every thing in the shape of a lottery or raffle is of evil tendency.

I must not attempt to speak of the execution of Marshal

Ney and Colonel Labédoyère, which all of us were much grieved at; nor of the remarkable escape of Lavalette from prison, by putting on some of his wife's clothes, she remaining behind whilst he passed out of the prison, nor of his escape from Paris, disguised as an English general, by the help of Sir Robert Wilson and two other Englishmen. These things took place whilst we were at Paris, and the accounts of them may easily be obtained.

A very sad and exciting business occurred, whilst we were at Paris, in connexion with the mutinous behaviour of one of our own men, when coming to join the army with detachments under the command of a captain and other officers belonging to other regiments; I think I recollect the circumstances very clearly, they were these:—Several of the men of these detachments had got drunk, and this man, when ordered by Captain —— to be silent, or to perform some duty, refused to obey, as he was not a 52nd officer, and swore at him, calling him a d——d ——; the officer drew his sword, and cut the drunken mutineer very severely across the shoulder. For this the officer was afterwards brought to a court-martial and honourably acquitted. The Duke of Wellington, on reading the proceedings of the court-martial, ordered the 52nd soldier to be brought to a general court-martial for mutinous conduct towards his superior officer; he was accordingly tried, found guilty, and condemned to be shot. The Duke, who always felt the vast importance of upholding the discipline of the army, determined that the sentence should be executed. I saw at a little distance, not far from my tent, an interview between the Duke and Sir John Colborne, which I had reason to believe was connected with this man's execution. The Duke had come into our camp from his garden door, and as Colborne almost immediately joined him, I fancy the interview had been arranged before. The Duke, who generally appeared to be a person of very quiet demeanour, seemed on this occasion to speak with some considerable earnestness, and Colborne, who was most anxious, as we all were, that the man's life should be spared, was equally energetic. The conversation did not last more than seven or eight minutes, and I did not learn the result, until the order for the execution appeared in orders. I think the next morning, the regiments of the brigade marched to some ground near the walls of Paris, to see the sentence carried into effect.

The regiments were drawn up so that each occupied one side of a large square, the man to be executed being placed in the middle of the fourth side of the square with his coffin behind him, and the firing party, consisting I think, of a serjeant and twelve rank and file, a few paces in his front. The brigade-major, or some other staff-officer, then rode forward and read the charge against the soldier, the finding of the court-martial, and the sentence. When this was done, an aide-de-camp, the bearer of a reprieve, rode into the square; I think it was an order from the Duke, granting the man a pardon, and stating, amongst other reasons for doing so, that it was partly in consideration of the high character of the regiment to which he belonged, that the Duke was induced to take this course.

I have an idea that some of us were aware the night before that the man would be pardoned, but the man himself, and the men of the regiment and of the brigade generally, expected the execution to take place. I met him close to the camp, in the course of the afternoon, walking with one of the men, and I recollect that the poor fellow sobbed as he passed and saluted me. I cannot quite bear in mind whether I spoke to him or not; but I am sure I must have shewn him, in some way, how much I felt for him.

Two or three other recollections which I have of Paris at the time of our encampment there, are of a much lighter character than the occurrences I have just mentioned. Great numbers of English families came out to Paris during the summer and autumn of 1815, and the costumes of many of the women, who, according to the most approved English fashion of that day, wore very short waists and very long bonnets, appeared very odd and ridiculous, even to us who were their countrymen, when contrasted with the neat and elegant style of dress of the Parisian ladies. We used to think that our fair countrywomen, as a general rule, greatly excelled the French females in beauty, whilst the latter carried away the palm with regard to dress.

The caricatures of the English visitors, exhibited in the shop windows, were very good, and did not go far beyond the reality. A large stout John Bull, weighing from sixteen to eighteen stone, was generally the principal figure, and there were generally Mrs. and some Misses Bull with their short waists, &c., and sometimes a Master Bull or two, staring about, as one saw them do every day, at everything they came across. Sometimes the whole party were represented as standing out in the middle of the street, curiously examining the tops of the tall houses, at other times walking along the streets, staring at everything and everybody. But the French were not satisfied with exhibiting caricatures of our females, dressed in the inelegant national costume of that day, but they brought forward a comedy at one of the theatres, called "*Les Anglaises pour rire*,' in which the same sort of characters and costumes were represented on the stage. I once saw the play acted, and could not but join in the general laugh at the ludicrous exhibitions made of the curiosity, and want of taste in dress, of our fair countrywomen.

One evening some English officers determined to oppose the acting of the play, and there was some skirmishing between them and the police before the opposition ceased; shortly afterwards the piece was given up.

There was also another very laughable piece, which was brought forward at one of the theatres, and which met with great success. It was intended as a burlesque on the drapers' and other shopkeepers' assistants, many of whom were in the habit, on Sundays and fête-days, of dressing, and passing themselves off, as military men. The farce was called "Monsieur Calico."

Monsieur Calico himself was represented, in the caricatures and on the stage, as a young man of three or four-and-twenty, about five feet high, dressed, I think, in a tailed coat and round hat, and manifesting considerable pretensions also, as regards the hair, whiskers, front of shirt, and stock. But the most remarkable appendage was a pair of steel spurs, about four inches in length, attached to the heels of his boots. The linen drapers' assistants, and numerous other young men, who felt themselves aggrieved, were furious at the representation, and at the success which it met with, and for several nights they endeavoured to take possession of the theatre, and to put down the obnoxious piece. I believe it was withdrawn after some little time.

It would not be right that I should leave the subject of attending theatres, without stating my very decided opinion, that parents should keep their children from such places, as being calculated to do them the greatest injury. It is well known that they are often frequented by the very worst characters of both sexes; indeed, I have heard it stated, fifty years ago, that if such characters were excluded, some of the largest theatres in London would become regular failures. Then it was notorious in those days that many of the actors and actresses were not persons of good moral character. I know not how far there has been any improvement of late years. I know that respectable persons do still take their children to such scenes, but I always wonder how they can do so. Supposing the attending the theatre to be free from the above objections, which it is not, many of the representations which take place are not calculated to improve the moral and religious tone of society. When I was a very little child I went to see a play at a country theatre, in which a man rushed on the stage with a child in his arms, in the midst of a storm of thunder and lightning, and, dropping on one knee, offered up earnest words of prayer to God for protection. Notwithstanding all that may be advanced about its being a proper representation of what those who fear God are encouraged to do in all times of danger, I consider that such addresses, pretended to be offered up in theatrical representations, must be highly offensive to the Almighty. I am glad to think that increasing numbers of respectable persons, of all classes of society, now avoid the theatre. My rule will well apply here:— "Never allow yourself, for purposes of 'amusement, to be in any company or place in which God is 'dishonoured."

CHAPTER IX.

1815, 1816.

THE 52ND QUARTERED AT VERSAILLES, ST. GERMAIN, AND CLERMONT.

Quarter at Versailles—Palace—St. Germain—Sir John Colborne goes on leave—His good advice—Clermont—Anniversary of the death of Louis XVI—A guard of honour in the church—Atchison and Dawson of the artillery.

ON the 2nd of November, 1815, we broke up our agreeable encampment in the Champs Elysées, and went into quarters at Versailles, which is about fourteen miles from Paris. Versailles is a beautifully built town, and I was quartered in a very good house belonging to Madame Courtin, a very nice old lady, who was very kind to me, and gave me three neatly-bound volumes, containing Voltaire's Histories of Peter the Great, of Russia, and of Charles XII, of Sweden; they now lie before me, as I write this, fifty years after I received them. We had not much to do at Versailles, where we remained about six weeks, and I spent much of my time in the palace, and in the adjoining beautiful gardens and grounds. In this palace of Versailles Louis XVI and Marie Antoinette were attacked five-and-twenty years before, by the Parisian mob, accompanied by soldiers under La Fayette, and treated with great indignity; they were forced to accompany them the next day to Paris, and I believe never returned again to Versailles.

About the middle of December the 52nd marched from Versailles to St. Germain. The men were in the palace, and the officers were quartered on the inhabitants. I was on guard the first night, and passed one of the most wretched nights I ever passed in my life. By some accident there was no proper officers' guard-room, and when it was too late, I found myself with a whole suite of magnificent rooms, on the first floor of the palace, for my guard-rooms, without one single article of furniture in them; there were some logs of wood, but no other means had I of igniting them, or of keeping any heat in my body during that very cold night, than by collecting from time to time, and burning, quantities of straw, which had been swept out on to the balconies extending along the whole of the suite of apartments.

Sir John Colborne went on leave, during the short time that the 52nd was at St. Germain. On my calling upon him shortly before I started, he gave me some good advice on the subject of the importance of my improving myself by reading, &c., &c., and kindly told me he might very probably have it in his power to be of use to me in the service, but that of course my getting on well in the army must depend chiefly on my own attention to the reading and studies necessary in order to my becoming a good and useful officer. He was travelling in Germany during most of the time that he was absent from the regiment, and I think he joined us again about June or July, 1818, at the camp near St. Omer, when I was much pleased by his saying that Colonel Charles Rowan had given him a good account of my endeavours to improve myself during his absence.

In order to strengthen the government of Louis XVIII, and to give him time to reconstruct his army, and to feel increasing security against any attempts which might be made again to overthrow the newly established order of things in France, it had been determined by the Allied sovereigns that an army of 150,000 should remain in the north of France for three years, and that certain fortresses should be held and garrisoned by them during that period. The troops were to be paid,* clothed, and provisioned at the expence of France. The leading powers of Europe sent their several quotas of troops, and the whole Allied army of

* Will it be believed, that under these circumstances the officers of the British portion of the army of occupation had to pay an income-tax of ten per cent.? I well recollect that it was deducted from my ensign's pay of about £95 a year. There must have been some meanness or rascality somewhere. The amount thus deducted from the British officers, certainly would not find its way into the French Treasury.

occupation was placed under the command of the Duke of Wellington.

The 52nd marched from St. Germain, I think, on Christmas-day, towards the cantonments which they were to occupy in the Pas de Calais. All the necessary arrangements appear not to have been completed at that time, for we were quartered in the town of Clermont, about thirty miles from Paris, and in some of the neighbouring villages, for about a month before we proceeded to our destination. I have very little recollection of Clermont and of the village about a mile and a half from it, which I occupied with about forty or fifty men. I well remember that I first tried to smoke a cigar as I walked out from the town one night, and that it made me dreadfully ill; I also remember that on the 21st of January, the anniversary of the death of Louis the XVI, in 1793, a guard of honour, accompanied by the King's colour, was allowed to be present in the church at Clermont: at a particular moment, I suppose on the elevation of the host, the colour was lowered, and the guard presented arms, at the same time each man coming down on one knee. The whole scene appeared to me to be exceedingly ludicrous, and this arose especially from the awkward business the men made of saluting in a posture which they were of course unaccustomed to. We thought nothing at the time of the sin of thus joining in an idolatrous ceremony. I trust the practice, which prevailed so many years, of requiring our officers and soldiers to take part in the idolatrous ceremonies of the Roman Catholic and Greek churches, has now been entirely given up.

In the year 1824 Captain Atchison and Lieutenant Dawson, two officers of the Royal Artillery stationed at Malta, were cashiered by sentence of a court-martial, the president of which was the Roman Catholic colonel of the Maltese Fencibles, for requesting to be excused from superintending the tolling of a bell and the firing of a petteraro salute in honour of the procession of St. ; the petteraroes were small pieces of cannon, used by the priests for such purposes. Mr. Dawson was first put in orders for the performance of this unmilitary duty; but he, feeling the irksomeness of having anything to do with what he had religious and conscientious scruples against, requested the officer commanding the artillery at Malta, to excuse him from it; this request he very kindly acceded to, and Captain Atchison was put in orders for it; but Captain Atchison also had his strong objections to the performance of the obnoxious duty, and requested the commanding officer to let him off: this he readily did, and very good-naturedly superintended the tolling of the bell and the firing of the salute himself.

The affair was supposed to have been settled, but of course it was talked of in the garrison, and after a considerable time the thing was referred to the Horse Guards by Sir Thomas Maitland, and orders eventually came out for Atchison and Dawson to be brought to a court-martial for disobedience of orders. In their defence they not only pleaded that they had not disobeyed orders, and that it was not a military duty from which they had requested to be excused, but they wished also to shew from Scripture that the service required of them was idolatrous and profane, and contrary to what was laid down in the articles and homilies of the Church of England. In this last mentioned line of defence they were not allowed to proceed; they consequently declined to continue their defence. The proceedings of the court-martial were sent to England, and the judge-advocate returned them to Malta, observing that the officers must be permitted to shew, as they desired to do, that the duty they were ordered to perform, was opposed to what was contained in the Word of God and in the Prayer Book; the court reassembled, and its proceedings were resumed, and Captain Atchison and Mr. Dawson were found guilty of disobedience of orders. In promulgating, in a general order, the sentence of dismissal from the service, the Duke of York, who was then Commander-in-Chief, laid down the monstrous dogma, that a "lawful order was any order given by a lawful "superior;" so that if a superior officer were to order an officer junior to him to clean his boots, or should he desire any officer or man to kill an innocent person or persons, he must be obeyed, although it might be strongly suspected that he was intoxicated, or labouring under some aberration of intellect. I myself knew the case of an officer, belonging to the army of occupation in France, who, under a delusion of mind, after firing away his servant's ammunition at every living person or thing he could see, without doing any damage, ordered the corporal's guard to turn out and fire at every person who might shew himself in any of the village streets. According to the Duke of York's idea, this order should have been obeyed, as it was "the order of a lawful "superior." It was, however, not obeyed, and the officer was immediately sent in charge of another officer to England, and placed under the care of his friends.

Many years ago I wrote to the Hon. John Forbes, who had been in the 52nd, and who, at the time I wrote, was aide-de-camp to General Sir A. Woodford, at Corfu; and at my request he gave me an account of the procession of the Greek Church, in which the British officers were expected to take part, carrying long lighted candles, in honour of St. Spiridione. I have, I am sorry to say, lost his letter.

Some time after the court-martial on Captain Atchison and Mr. Dawson, I took considerable pains to induce persons, who felt strongly the injustice which had been done to these officers, to get up petitions to parliament, and addresses to the Crown, on the subject. Many petitions, &c., were consequently sent up from Derbyshire. I drew out a petition, in which a few clergymen, formerly in the army, joined, stating we knew the necessity that existed for prompt obedience to military commands, but that, had we been required to perform the service required of Captain Atchison and Lieutenant Dawson, we must have refused to obey the order, even had we known that death would be the consequence of such refusal. This petition, with the others, made some stir. Dr. Blomfield, Bishop of London, undertook to present it in the House of Lords, and called on Lord Hill, the then Commander-in-Chief, and wrote to the Duke of Wellington on the subject. The Duke had not replied to his letter when I called on the Bishop the second time, and he felt annoyed at his apparent inattention. When the petition was presented in the House of Commons, amongst others Daniel O'Connell stood up and spoke warmly on the subject, saying, that if the state of the case, with regard to Protestant officers and soldiers being required to join in the ceremonies of the Roman Catholic and Greek churches, was as the petition represented it to be, the objectionable practice should at once be done away with.

Mr. Dawson became a clergyman of the church of England, and resided at Jersey for some considerable time. He has been dead now for many years. Captain Atchison was, after several years, restored to his rank and pay as a captain of artillery, and he has been for many years, and still is, colonel-commandant of the Royal Lancashire Artillery Militia.*

On our way from Clermont to our cantonments, we halted for two days at Amiens. On the first day I was on guard. When relieved from guard the next day, I went to the house I was quartered on; it was occupied by a very quiet, gentlemanly man and his wife; but in finding me accommodation they shewed an extreme ignorance of the relative positions of officer and soldier in the British army, for I found at night that they had actually made up a stretcher-bed for my servant in the small room which I was to occupy; I had the greatest difficulty in getting them to understand that this arrangement would never do. After some considerable parley, it ended in my servant and I carrying the stretcher-bed into a sitting room on the other side of the passage; they all the time thinking me a most unreasonable person, and maintaining that as the arrangement was only for one night, we might as well submit to it.

* Colonel Atchison has kindly promised to give me the particulars of his restoration to the service, and I hope they will reach me in sufficient time to enable me to place them in Chapter XLV of this work.

CHAPTER X.

1816.

CANTONMENTS IN THE NORTH OF FRANCE.

Villages around Thérouenne—Henry VIII—Siege of Thérouenne and Battle of Spurs three hundred years before—Honours gained by ancestors—Alarming occurrence—Periodical encampment and march to Valenciennes—Kind feeling between the villagers and our men—Meadow at Thérouenne—Bathing in the river Lys—Sir Denis Pack's inspection—Brigade orders—Curious occurrence—Remarkable case of one of the men becoming religious.

ABOUT the beginning of February, 1816, we reached our cantonments in the north of France. The regiment occupied six-and-twenty villages. They were within a circle of which the ancient town (now only a village) of Thérouenne might be considered as the centre; the diameter of the circle would be about seven miles. Thérouenne was besieged and taken by our Henry VIII, in 1514; it is situated about seven miles south of St. Omer, and is on the Lys, a very small river, fordable in many places below the town, but not above it. The first village we arrived at was Estréeblanche, which was my quarter during the greater part of our occupation of France; but I was stationed first of all, for several months, at Enguinegatte or Guinegatte, a village about two miles from Estréeblanche, and the same distance from Thérouenne, a quarter of a mile to the left of the road, the Chaussée Brunehaut. Here the Battle of Spurs was fought, during the siege of Thérouenne, between the French and English. The garrison was in great want of provisions, and Louis XI, the French king, sent all his cavalry, to the number of 8000, to try and convey succours to them. King Henry, it is said, by the advice of the emperor Maximilian, who was serving as a private soldier under him, threw several bridges over the Lys, which I know above the town, abreast of Enguinegatte, is deep and rapid, and for a long distance from fifteen to twenty feet broad; by following this advice, the English king was enabled to pass his troops over, so as to meet the enemy on the side by which they were most likely to approach the town. The French were totally defeated with great loss, " and fled so fast, that thar from it was "called the Battel of Spurs, for that they used more their spurs in "running away, than their launces in fighting." The Duke of Longueville, who commanded, and several superior officers, were made prisoners. The town of Thérouenne shortly after surrendered, and the fortifications were levelled.

Enguinegatte, close to which the Battle of Spurs was fought, is two miles from Thérouenne; but that which makes these places and these events particularly interesting, in connexion with their forming part of the cantonments of the 52nd, is this—that there is good ground for thinking it probable that the ancestors of two of the 52nd officers who occupied them, fought and obtained honours at the Battle of Spurs, and at the siege of Thérouenne, three hundred years before.

Sir William Henry Clerke, Bart., was a lieutenant in the 52nd in the Peninsula, and at Waterloo. From 1816 to 1818 he was quartered about two miles from the ground on which the Battle of Spurs was fought. The services of his ancestor on that occasion are thus mentioned in the peerage :—" Sir John Clerke, "Knt., of Weston, a military man of great valour, had the fortune "to make Louis d'Orleans, Duke of Longueville, prisoner, at Borny, "near Thérouenne, 14th August, in the fifth year of Henry VIII, "and was, for that signal service, rewarded by the king with an "honorary addition to his arms." I presume the addition was that of the two fleur-de-lis, which I see form part of the Clerke arms.

Sir John Leke, who died in 1522, " was knighted by Henry "VIII at the siege of Lisle; the king gave him for his crest two "eagles as supporters to a peacock's tail." Now there appears to have been no siege of Lisle; but Tournay, near Lisle, was besieged immediately after the fall of Thérouenne; so that the addition of the eagles to his crest must have been given for his good conduct at and near Thérouenne, or at Tournay, near Lisle. Henry VIII. visited Lisle during the siege of Tournay, and on his march from Thérouenne; hence probably the mistake about the siege of Lisle. My family have the crest of a peacock's tail, with eagles as supporters, handed down to them on very old seals. When quartered at Enguinegatte, on my inquiring of the people if they had any tradition as to where the famous Battle of the Spurs was fought, they told me that the house in which I was then quartered was built on the very ground. It was on the western extremity of the village. I often to this day think with what pleasure, and with what proud, martial feelings, I frequently on a moonlight night used to walk up and down the few pasture fields of that part of the village, whistling bugle tunes, or listening to the tattoo, sounded so well and so clearly by the two buglers of my detachment. Until our arrival, no sound of British martial music had been heard there since the Battle of Spurs three hundred years before. And *we* had something to be proud of, as well as our forefathers of the tenth generation back, who had fought and conquered on that very ground.

The house I was first quartered in at Enguinegatte, was not the same as that above-mentioned, to which I had to remove on one of our assistant surgeons, who had a choice of quarters before me, being ordered to that village. My first quarter was at the house of the principal man of the village, a most respectable farmer, by the name of Ledoux, I think. He was one of the finest men I ever saw; his son and daughter also were fine, handsome young people, of about twenty-one and nineteen. I had a large square room, the principal room in the house, which served me both as a sitting and a bed room; the windows were towards the garden, and the lower part of them, where there was a ledge of nearly the breadth of the wall, was about four feet from the ground; I should say they were four feet square. I have been thus particular in describing the room on account of a somewhat alarming occurrence which took place on the very first night of my arrival at Enguinegatte. I must premise that I am rather ashamed of relating the occurrence, but I do so more particularly for the benefit of my younger readers.

My narrow iron bedstead was placed in one corner of the room, close under one of the windows, and there was just room for a chair between the bedstead and an old fashioned fireplace, which was on the same side of the room with the head of my bed and the chair; the fireplace projected about twenty inches from the wall. As I was in a strange place and amongst strangers, I thought it desirable before I went to bed to examine the fastenings of my doors before I retired to rest. As usual, there was no fastening to the main door communicating with the farm-house kitchen, and the other door was locked or bolted on the other side. On going to bed, I laid my sword, in the scabbard, along the sill of the window, which was above my bed to the left. I soon fell asleep, and slept soundly for some hours; in the middle of the night I awoke, and was conscious that I had been awakened by some noise in the room. I listened for some seconds, and quietly taking my sword from the window, I drew it, and having a good hold of it so that I could use it, if necessary, I laid it along the outside of the bed clothes, and listened very anxiously for any sound which might discover to me who or what it was that had disturbed me. I could hear no footstep or other sound for a minute or two, but after a little time, I distinctly heard what appeared to be the breathing of a person standing by the side of my bed, with his head a foot or two above my face. Without any consideration, I immediately made a horizontal cut, with all the force I could use in my horizontal position, in the direction of the fire-place: to my great astonishment, I only cut through the air, and my sword made a tremendous clatter against the projecting wall of the fire-place. I lay quietly for a minute or two, and then heard the breathing again, but closer to me; and then I thought it possibly proceeded from a rat either on my bed or on the chair; in order to dislodge this enemy, I took the pillow, and making a dash at him with it, upset the chair, and altogether made so much noise, that it disturbed my host and hostess, who, I then found, from a peculiar cough of one of them, were my neighbours, in the room the door of which was fastened on the other side. They probably began to wonder what the young English officer, who had just taken up his residence with them, was up to, in making all these terrible noises in the middle of the night. I did not hear any rat scamper away, but wishing to find out, if I could, what had led to all this disturbance, and recollecting that possibly there might yet be some small remains of fire in the wood ashes on the hearth, I felt my way to the fireplace, and found the bellows, a long iron tube about two feet and a half long, and more than half an inch in diameter in the inside, and blowing through this tube, I produced enough light from the dying embers to shew me, not a fairy, but a poor quiet tabby cat sitting and warming herself in the chimney corner.

I had about seventy men of No. 9 company with me at Enguinegatte; the remainder of them were at Estréeblanche with the two other officers: when the weather permitted, the two parties met about ten o'clock each day, two or three times a week, on the company's parade ground, which was between the two villages, and about a mile from each; the whole regiment was occasionally assembled at Thérouenne, but the frequent assembling of the regiment during the winter was not necessary, as in the summer months the whole division was encamped at Racquingham, not far from St. Omer, and each autumn we marched to Valenciennes, and its neighbourhood, and joined the rest of the British and German troops for the purpose of engaging in sham fights and other field movements. In 1816 and in 1817, towards the end of October, the 52nd returned from Valenciennes to their old cantonments, but after proceeding to Valenciennes in 1818, and being encamped on the glacis there for some time, they occupied the citadel of that place for several weeks, till they marched on the 19th of November to Calais, to embark for England, being the last remaining regiment of the British army of occupation.

The kind feeling which existed between the inhabitants of the villages in which we were quartered and ourselves, both officers and men, is described in the following extract from a letter I received from Colonel Hall, on my mentioning to him my idea of publishing my reminiscences of the 52nd at Waterloo, &c., &c.:—" You might, I think, make some mention of the " excellent people amongst whom we passed nearly three years. " The public statistics show that the population of this part is the " most moral, the most intelligent, and the best behaved of all

"France. You must remember the peasants; how sober, steady,
" and industrious they were—how obliging and respectful, without
" the least taint of servility—and the women, how gentle, good,
" and kind. You must remember the quiet and comfortable habits
" of life in the farm-houses, where, as in England of old, the un-
" married labourers dwelt under the same roof with their masters—
" the prayers morning and evening—the little patches of land,
" leased in part payment of labour, a strong incentive to industry,
" and which created in the fields a variety agreeable and novel to
" our eyes. I recall, with grateful feelings, the friendly feeling
" which we strangers experienced from the people who were com-
" pelled to endure us. Our men, as you know, became domesticated
" in their billets, and, as it were, members of the cottage families;
" they partook of the household fare, and their rations went into
" the common stock; even the tobacco which the French govern-
" ment issued to them, they shared with their hosts. It was the
" same in the towns of the neighbourhood, where all were kindly
" disposed towards us. The banker at St. Omer cashed our bills
" at once without any endorsement; he asked for no reference
" nor recommendation, and the sole security he had was the uniform
" we wore. It is gratifying to reflect that his generous confidence
" was not misplaced: after the army of occupation had been with-
" drawn, he declared he had not lost a franc by the British officers."

I think few of the families of the French gentry remained at their residences in our cantonments; but there were many such families in St. Omer, Aire, and Bethune, which were fortified towns, with French garrisons in them; we were, however, very little mixed up with them. When at Estréeblanche, two of us were quartered in the house of a very respectable miller by the name of Campagne, who was also the mayor of the commune; Captain McNair was quartered at the chateau of Monsieur Robichez, a kind old man; he was scarcely ever resident there, but left his establishment in the care of a very faithful housekeeper, named Angelique. As it was within two or three hundred yards of our quarters, we usually messed there, and M. Robichez very kindly supplied us with most excellent wine at the cost price: I particularly well recollect some beautiful red champagne at fifteenpence a bottle. In the spring we got up a mess at

Thérouenne for several weeks, from sixteen to twenty officers usually dining at it; no one could be there every day, but it was a pleasant change for us, when we could get there. I think I was the only one of the Estréeblanche party who managed it, for it was a ride of eight miles there and back: then sometimes we went earlier in the day, and spent several hours together. Poor Jock Anderson, who lost his leg at Waterloo, was at Thérouenne, and usually had some friends who visited him, and tried to amuse him.

In the long meadow of Thérouenne, as it was called, we had our regimental drills and the general's inspections. The Lys formed its southern boundary, and some of us used to bathe there. I particularly well remember the pleasure I felt at having learnt to swim so well at Paris, that I could make head against the rapid stream of the Lys; sometimes I used to fold my arms and allow it to carry me down, in four or five seconds, a distance of twenty yards, which it had taken me as many minutes to make good when swimming against the stream. I have often been reminded, in after years, of this little feat connected with my bathing in the Lys, when thinking of the difficulties which a child of God, one who trusts in the death of Christ as the satisfaction made for sin, and whose heart is turned from the love and practice of sin to the love of God and His commands, has to contend with in his course through this world. So long as he strives to live near to God, diligently using all the appointed means of grace, and seeking especially to grow in knowledge, faith, holiness, and peace, by means of God's word, under the teaching of the Holy Spirit (1 Peter ii, 1—3), so long as he thus seeks help from God, so long shall he be enabled successfully to make head against the temptations of his powerful, but not all-powerful, enemies—the world, the flesh, and the devil; but let him cease to meditate daily in the Word of God, and to watch, and to pray for strength to do what is right, and to give up what is wrong in thought, word, and deed—let him fold his arms and cease to strive, and almost before he has time to think of what has happened to him, he may find that he has been most fearfully carried down the stream of worldliness and sin by the force of those temptations which he has not taken the appointed means to overcome. That a child of God, one born of the Spirit, may fearfully fall into sin, is evident from the case of David. His new nature, although it cannot perish, will be greatly enfeebled, and he will lose the comfort of knowing that he is one of God's children, as David did; and he can only recover it in the same way of humiliation and prayer and watchfulness and diligence that David had recourse to, as we read in Psalm li, 7—11.

I will not pursue this subject except to observe the following is the most satisfactory definition of the word "world," as used in 1 John v, 4, 5, which I have met with, I forget whose it is:—
" By the world is meant everything around us, which tends to
" draw or keep our hearts from God, including all persons,
" whether neighbours, relatives, or acquaintances; superiors,
" equals, or inferiors; friends or enemies; or all objects or cir-
" cumstances (whatever they may be) which, by the power they
" exert over our bodies or our minds, prevent our loving or
" serving God as we ought to do." The flesh is our old corrupt nature, which, as the 9th article of the Church of England states, " doth remain, yea in them that are regenerate." It is made up of all the sinful desires and propensities of the mind and body (Gal. v, 19—21), which the devil (Eph. vi, 12) stirs up to make a sinful use of the world. These are subdued, but not eradicated, in the hearts of those whose hearts are changed and turned to God, who have put on the new man, (the image, or character, or likeness of Christ,) " which after God is created in righteousness " and true holiness." This new nature is formed in every believer (2 Cor. v, 17), though it is in an infant state at first. It is made up of the fruits of the Spirit (Gal. v, 22, 23); and to put on Christ, or to put on the new man, *i.e.* to increase in all the fruits of the Spirit, and to put off the old man, or the old corrupt nature, that is, to have the fruits of the flesh subdued in him, is the daily prayer and aim and desire of every child of God: 1 Peter ii, 1—3. When a man is endeavouring, looking for that "strength which is made perfect in weakness," to do what is right with regard to persons, things, and circumstances, he is trying to make a right use of the world; he is "using the " world as not abusing it:" 1 Cor. vii, 31. In connexion with

this subject, let us well consider those two important verses in 1 John v, 4, 5: "Whatsoever is born of God overcometh the "world, even our faith. Who is he that overcometh the world "but he that believeth that Jesus is the Son of God?" I should add, that I believe these three enemies never act separately; that the devil always makes use of some person, object, or circumstance, in acting upon the corrupt nature of man. I trust many of my readers may derive benefit from the consideration of this subject.

When the alterations were made in the various brigades and divisions after the battle of Waterloo, and before the army of occupation marched to the north of France, the 52nd was placed in Major-General Sir Denis Pack's brigade with the 4th regiment and 79th highlanders; and in the division commanded by Lieut.-General Sir Charles Colville. Pack inspected us in the long meadow near Thérouenne early in June, 1816, and afterwards issued the following:—

"*Extract from Brigade Orders, June 11th, 1816.*

"Major-General Sir Denis Pack feels much pleasure in re-"cording his opinion that the appearance of the 52nd regiment, "on his late inspection, justified all he heard in praise of the "system established in that corps. He thinks particular praise "is due to the officers for the good example they set by their "strict uniformity of dress and officer-like appearance in every "respect."

I believe it was on this occasion that he halted the regiment, and inquired of one of the officers "where was the place for the "covering-serjeant of a company, when the battalion was in "open column of sections, left in front?" The 52nd practice was not exactly in accordance with his view of what was correct, and after asking the same question from a second officer and not getting the right answer, he told us "that the place for the covering-"serjeant, under the circumstances, was on the right of the rear "section, that, when the company wheeled into line, he might be "in his proper place." After the movements, &c., were ended, the general and the officers proceeded to the paymaster's quarter at, I think, the north-eastern extremity of the meadow. While we were there, bearing in mind what had occurred about the covering-serjeant's post, he desired an officer, who I think was on his staff or acting on the staff for the day, to look the thing out in Dundas; and when he had turned over the pages for some time, the general said "how can you be so stupid, Major "———?" and took the book himself. He was quite as unable to find the place as the other officer had been, and had to relinquish his task with rather a bad grace.

As my plan is to record my recollections of most of the things which can be properly recorded without giving annoyance to any one, I must mention a circumstance which occurred either then or at some other time in the garden of the paymaster's quarter. Two of us were amusing ourselves, and whiling the time away by playing at pitch-and-toss with five-franc pieces, when one of the pieces, which had been pitched not more than five yards, on to the centre of the gravel walk, disappeared in a most remarkable manner. We had both seen it pitched to the mark, and had then lost sight of it, to our very great astonishment. We hunted for it and searched everywhere and everything for it, within several feet of the mark, for a good quarter of an hour or more, but it was all in vain; and we seriously, and not at all laughingly or in a joke, felt constrained to come to the conclusion that it had disappeared through the agency of Satan himself. It made a great impression on me at the moment, and the thoughts passed my mind, that it had possibly been permitted on account of our sins, or that it foreboded some impending evil. After we had given up every idea of finding the five-franc piece, on turning up a leaf, which appeared to be flat on the ground and to be no larger than the piece itself, there it was, to our very great surprise.

I believe there was scarcely anything that could be considered religion, or even the appearance of religion, amongst us at that time. Some years afterwards I heard that, whilst we were in those cantonments, an agent from some Bible Society, I believe it was the Naval and Military Bible Society, had sold or given bibles to a few of our men. Long afterwards one of the soldiers, who had become quite a religious man, said that this great change had taken place in him, solely through his having read one of these bibles, whilst he was quartered on a Roman Catholic family near Thérouenne, without his having had any communication with them on the subject of religion. It was the only means of grace he had at the time; chaplains' visits to the regiments were almost unknown in those scattered quarters. I have no doubt but that God in His mercy does sometimes, perhaps frequently, bring the truths of His word home to the hearts and consciences of persons whilst they are studying it alone and without the intervention of others, although His usual mode of proceeding, in effecting a change of heart in a poor sinner, is by his becoming acquainted with the truths of His word through their being taught to him by His ministers or by others, or through their being brought before him in some of those useful religious publications which are now so abundant, but were rarely met with fifty years ago. It must always be borne in mind that, whoever may be the instrument of leading a fellow-sinner to feel his sins and his need of a Saviour, it is His own Word by which God converts the soul, and also builds up the believer's soul in faith and holiness and peace. We are said by the inspired apostle St. Peter, "to be born again, not of cor- "ruptible seed, but of incorruptible, by the word of God which "liveth and abideth for ever:" 1 Peter i, 23, 25; James i, 18; Psalm xix, 7. It is the Holy Spirit which makes the Word effectual; so we are said to be "born again of the Spirit." May we pray that He may effect this change in every heart.

When we were in these separate villages, I do not recollect that any attention was paid to the observance of the Lord's Day, either as regarded ourselves or the men. There was no instruction for them in anything of a religious nature; nor indeed did it occur to us to endeavour to employ and amuse them by giving them any other kind of instruction. When encamped at Valenciennes, service was performed by the chaplain, but whether he was attached to the brigade or to the division I forget.

CHAPTER XI.

1816.

AMUSEMENTS IN CANTONMENTS.

The regiment start a pack of fox-hounds—Anecdotes connected with our hunting—Accident—Go over to the cavalry quarters—Commandant of St. Omer and his staff—Lord Combermere joins the party—His regret at not having been at Waterloo—Dissertation on cruelty to the animals hunted—A singular argument on the subject—Extinction of poaching—A trumpeter-boy of the Life Guards.

OUR amusements were not much varied, yet we managed to pass our days very pleasantly. I think it was after our return from Valenciennes, in the autumn of 1816, that we started a pack of fox-hounds in the regiment; they were a very nice pack, and were well managed under the superintendence of one or two of the officers. When we returned to England at the end of November, 1818, ten couples were sold at Tattersall's at a high price. I was very fond of hunting, and will mention a few anecdotes connected with our proceedings in that direction. Almost the whole of the country was uninclosed; the woods and villages being the exceptions. When we were clear of them, the chief impediments to a straightforward gallop were deep hollow roads, and steep banks. There was a long bank, some miles from my quarters, which, on more than one occasion, was a sore trouble to a sailor friend of mine, by the name of Charles English, who was staying with me and others of the 52nd for some time. I mounted him; and as he was not a first-rate horseman, the difficulties he frequently got into, afforded his friends much amusement; and after he had got safely back to our quarters, the recounting them afforded him also much gratification. This high bank was perhaps about seventeen feet deep, and certainly very steep, but still it was what those who were used to such things would take their horses down on their haunches, yet it was a real trouble to our friend, and I recollect looking back for him several times, in the space of about two miles that we had ridden away from him, and still seeing him riding backwards and forwards on the top of the bank, doing what we termed " life-guardsman's duty," searching for some more promising-looking place of descent than he had hitherto discovered.

One day, when I was the officer of the day, I had to go to make a report to Colonel Charles Rowan, who was quartered at the Chateau d'Uppen, about a mile from Thérouenne. On coming away, after making my report, I found that our hounds had just run a fox into the adjoining wood, and, as my duty was performed, I at once joined them, although, as I was in full regimentals and had my sword hanging by my side, I was not very suitably equipped for hunting. As soon as the fox had broken cover again, a greyhound joined in the chase, and threatened to spoil our sport, so as I was well mounted, and could, when I chose, ride from the rear to the front of the hounds, I rode ahead to drive him off. Having done this, I kept my place at the head of the party, as we entered the inclosures of a village, with the hounds well up to the fox. After passing two or three fields, in taking a fence, my cap was knocked off my head by the bough of a tree. Of course, as I was before everybody, I could not stop to pick it up, but, noting the place, I rode on till in a short time we killed our fox. This being accomplished, I began to think of recovering my cap, and returned to the fence, at which I felt quite sure I had lost it. The cap, however, was no where to be seen. Our caps or shakoes were at that time ornamented, or rather disfigured, by a very broad band of silver round the top, a very unsuitable appendage to the cap of a light infantry officer. I thought I could not have made a mistake about the fence, and became convinced that somebody, tempted by the silver lace on the cap, had walked off with it. On raising myself in my stirrups and taking a survey, as well as I could, of the fences of the adjoining fields, I saw the head of a woman through the higher branches of one of them, about two fields distant from me. On riding up to her and inquiring if she had seen my cap, she strenuously denied knowing anything about it; however, notwithstanding that she endeavoured to keep in a position to prevent my discovering that she had something bulky under her clothing, I at once perceived that such was the case; and on my accusing her of having my unfortunate cap there, she was forced to hand it out, and I was only too glad to recover and ride off with it, after giving her a good scolding for her dishonesty.

I have forgotten to mention an occurrence which took place at the first meet of our hounds. My recollection of the ground leads me to think that we met abreast of Enguinegatte, near to the south-eastern corner of that long village, nearly on the reverse side of it from that on which the Battle of Spurs was fought. I am not quite sure that this was the place, but I mention it, as perhaps some of the surviving officers of the 52nd may recollect it. I believe almost all the officers of the regiment, and no others, were present on the occasion. The thought crosses my mind as I write, and I feel disposed to give my readers the benefit of it—If these recent warriors and heroes of Waterloo could have met at this place the warriors and heroes who had fought and conquered at the Battle of the Spurs, what an astonishing interview it would have been. But let me for a moment follow on with the idea—They will assuredly one day meet together—the day is coming, when all who have ever lived, or ever shall live, upon this earth, shall stand together "before the judgment "seat of Christ," "when the Lord Jesus shall be revealed from "heaven with his mighty angels, in flaming fire taking ven- "geance on them that know not God, and that obey not the "gospel of the Lord Jesus Christ: who shall be punished with "everlasting destruction from the presence of the Lord and "from the glory of his power; when he shall come to be glori- "fied in his saints, and to be admired in all them that believe." May we all prepare daily and diligently for that solemn, and awful, and most glorious day! Then at least will all our foolish "pride of human glory be stained."

How, after this digression, I am to get back to the trifling anecdote I was about to mention, I know not :—The officers of the 52nd were all assembled to see their new hounds throw off. The hounds had never hunted together, and were of course very wild. As we were all sitting very carelessly on our horses, one of the horses got loose and galloped away. This was a great deal too much for the sobriety of the new hounds, and they set off in full cry after the horse; and this sudden start made many of the horses set off also. I was sitting in my saddle, with my bridle lying on my horse's neck, and my horse, "Norman," (not the one before mentioned,) a horse well known in the regiment as something very superior to a baggage-horse, and whom I saw last in the stables of the posting-house at Calais, this horse made a sudden start away, which threw me quite backwards before I could touch the bridle, and from his back I fell off on the left side without being able to disengage my foot from the left stirrup; I was consequently dragged a short distance, and, either accidently in his gallop, or purposely by a kick, he gave me a heavy blow on my jaw, close to my chin, which covered me with blood, and the mark of which I carry to this day. I was desperately afraid that my jaw was broken, and sought out our assistant-surgeon, who was on the ground. It seems but yesterday, so vividly do I recollect the scene, although it took place as nearly as possible fifty years ago from the day on which I am writing this. The following short dialogue took place:— "Macartney! I fear my jaw is broken." He then took hold of my chin and giving it a slight shake, said, "Oh, your jaw is not "broken." I think no other person was thrown. I forget what sort of a run we had that day, but I remember my horse got planted in some ploughed land, and that I thought he was at last paid off for all his ill behaviour at the start.

I don't know if any other regiment in the army of occupation kept a pack of hounds, though I think the brigade in which the 29th was kept a pack. We once by arrangement took our hounds to the cavalry quarters to the north of St. Omer, to give the cavalry officers a day's sport. Lord Combermere,* who had

---

* The great disappointment of the gallant Sir Stapleton Cotton, (Lord Combermere,) at not being allowed to proceed to Flanders in 1815, as Commander-in-Chief of the cavalry, is mentioned in very strong terms in his "Life," which has just

taken the command of the cavalry, after Lord Uxbridge (the Marquis of Anglesea) had lost his leg at Waterloo, went out with us, and many other cavalry officers. The French general and his staff came out from St. Omer, in full uniform, to see the fun. In order to avoid disappointment, a bag-fox had been provided, which was turned out about a mile or more to the northward of St. Omer, on the chaussée, along which it went for perhaps half a mile. When it had had sufficient "law," the hounds were laid on. It was a brilliant day, and there was a good and well-mounted field. As we galloped after the hounds, none appeared to enjoy the sport or to ride faster than the French general and his staff; but as they were not at all used to hunting after our English fashion, their pleasure soon came to an end. The fox after a time was headed, and crossing a tolerably wide ditch to the left of the road, took to the open country. The ditch was altogether too much for our French friends, as it would have been for my sailor friend of whom I wrote before, but all the rest of the party thought nothing of it. Before I had gone half a mile from it, I had the misfortune, when I was well placed, to break one of my stirrup-leathers, and I thought the best plan was to pull up and see what I could do to remedy the disaster. Fortunately it had broken exactly at the buckle, so that by shortening my stirrups one hole, which I could well afford to do, I avoided the, to me, great annoyance of riding the rest of the day without stirrups. I was not very long in getting all to-rights, and at once began to fetch up my lee-way in pretty good style ; and it certainly was a considerable pleasure when I found myself steadily advancing upon, and then passing, Lord Combermere, who of course was well mounted. After some time I found myself ahead of everybody, and I rode for several minutes nearly abreast of the two leading hounds, being about thirty yards on

---

been published by Lady Combermere :—" All was of no avail. Both his personal
" claims and the representations of the Duke of Wellington failed to induce the
" Prince Regent to forego his revenge or partiality for the sake of the public
" service, and at Waterloo Stapleton Cotton's sword flashed not in the van as it
" was wont to be. The disappointment was grievous, and to the end of his days
" he never could bear to speak on the subject of the Battle of Waterloo. On
" the 15th of July, 1815, in a letter from Paris, he wrote :—'I regret more than
" ' ever not having been at the famous battle which decided the fate of Europe.'"

their right, and they gradually gaining on the fox, which I had in full view all the time, till we came to the inclosures of a village. There we had to gallop at speed up the most muddy lane I ever galloped through in my life. One of the 52nd came next to me and rode within about eight yards, and got his face and the whole front of his body regularly plastered with thick mud, after a fashion which I never saw equalled either before or since. The fox took to a large piece of water in the village, and was caught by our huntsman in a boat, and given to the hounds, after having afforded us a very excellent run. I think it was recollecting, several years afterwards, the miserable plight in which I had seen this poor wretched fox, that first determined me to give up hunting, of which amusement I was exceedingly fond. There may be other reasons why a man who fears God might avoid hunting—for instance, he might think it calculated to lead him on other occasions into the society of persons not of congenial habits and feelings with himself; but it appeared to me (I have never forced these opinions on others) that I had no right to inflict pain on any of God's creatures—my fellow-creatures, for such they are—merely for my amusement. The same argument may be made use of I think with regard to shooting and fishing, and some other amusements of a similar kind. It is true we may freely destroy noxious animals, and we may kill game or any other animals which we may require for food, but then, in both cases, we are certainly bound to kill the animals in the most humane manner possible. The snaring birds and hares, and then killing them as quickly as possible, must surely be a more humane practice than that of shooting them, with the great chance, particularly in the case of bad shots, of leaving a considerable portion of them in a wounded state to linger in great pain, perhaps for a week or two—or more, before they die. I have found wounded hares, with broken legs, several days or a week after there had been any shooting in the neighbourhood; and whenever there is a shooting party and plenty of game, how many birds have the feathers knocked out of them, which shews they are severely wounded, and yet get away. What should we say of a man, who, instead of letting his sheep be killed as quickly and humanely as it could be done by the butcher, should, for his amusement and that of his friends, fire at them with ball from behind the fence walls, or mountain crags, killing and taking away some, but leaving others to get away wounded, and to die after languishing, for days perhaps, in misery and pain? Should we not say of such a man that he was brutal and cruel? And yet the very thing must constantly occur in deer-stalking. How careful owners of hounds and others are to preserve foxes, in order (may I say?) to torment them for their own amusement, when, if the plea of their being noxious animals is urged as an excuse, it would be so easy, particularly when they are young, to put several of them together to a ten times more humane death, by suffocating them in their holes. I recollect a case in which an owner of hounds imported fifty foxes from France; so the excuse for destroying them by hunting, because they are destroyers of poultry, &c., falls to the ground.

But now I come, if my readers have not already tossed the book aside, and will bear with me a little longer, to a very specious plea for hunting and shooting for mere amusement, although the engaging in these sports is attended, as has been shewn, with very great cruelty to the animals hunted or shot; I do not speak of cruelty to the dogs and horses, for I believe they enjoy the sport; but no one will persuade me that the fox likes to be hunted, or the hares and birds to be shot and wounded.

The specious plea I have just alluded to, in favour of hunting and shooting for mere amusement, notwithstanding the cruelty inflicted, is this:—These sports help to raise up amongst us a bold and hardy race of gentlemen, many of whom, having been thus inured to danger and fatigue from their early youth, become most effective, valuable, and daring officers in our army and navy. Not that I think many of our sailor friends have acquired their dash in the hunting field. I quite agree that the same men who will ride straight across a country at a gallop, taking their fences generally as they come, without pulling up, will be likely to do anything or everything which may be required of them in action, be it the leading a charge of cavalry, the mounting a rampart or breach, or (in order that I may include our gallant sailors) storming a battery or boarding an enemy's frigate. No doubt, these manly exercises, engaged in by our gentry, are of much benefit to them, and through them, of benefit to the country. And these sports also help to give us, what is also a great advantage, a number of resident gentlemen in the various localities, who, but for these amusements, would spend a much greater portion of their lives than they now do, either in London or in travelling abroad, to the neglect of those various duties of a country life, the engaging in which may render their residence amongst them so beneficial, in various ways, to those who come within their sphere of influence.

But there is much to be said in answer to all this. First of all, we have had many as gallant an officer as ever stepped, who never rode hunting in his life. Then, our common soldiers and sailors—equally brave with their officers, ready to go anywhere, and into any danger—did they acquire their hardihood and courage in the hunting field, and in amusing themselves by exercising cruelty on foxes and hares? Surely the British soldier or the British sailor has plenty of pluck, innate or acquired, without its having been so engendered.

But again, let it be granted that the manly amusement of hunting is of national benefit, or that great numbers are not willing to give it up, merely because there is great cruelty attending the present mode of carrying on the sport: is there no plan of proceeding by which the various benefits and desires above-mentioned may be as fully met and realized without the attendant cruelty, as with it? From what I know of hunting, I am inclined to maintain that as good sport may be had by hunting a drag, as by hunting a fox, or a hare, or a wild boar. Let a good rider and the best horse be started with a drag, and let them have a start of a quarter of an hour, less or more according to circumstances, and there is no reason why they should not give a well mounted field a good twenty miles' run on any day when the scent will lie; and if twenty miles should not be sufficient for our modern Nimrods, the run might easily be extended, with, or even without, a fresh drag, horse, and rider, to double that distance. A second drag might always be carried, in case of any accident happening to the first.

But I am inclined, from some experience in such matters, to maintain that as good sport may be obtained not only without an animal or a drag to hunt, but also even *without hounds*, as can be met with in the best hunts of the present day. In the beginning of 1819, when I was quartered at Chester, on one occasion when hunting with the Cheshire hounds, we had had very little sport, and being about seven miles from Chester, several of us determined to ride there across the country. The horses were quite as eager as they would have been had they been following the hounds. I found by measurement a few days afterwards that my mare, in taking a hedge about three feet high at a fair gallop on level turf, had cleared two-and-twenty feet.

One advantage which I hereby propose to my hunting friends is, the saving all the expence of keeping a pack of hounds, of earth-stopping, of huntsmen and whippers-in, &c., &c. Then this mode of riding across a country would help to supersede the present mode of steeple-chasing, which certainly is frequently attended with cruelty, witness the broken backs of the horses, and the broken limbs and necks of the riders which we sometimes read of. Then, again, it certainly would be a great boon to the community if it might be allowed by our sporting friends to supersede the present system of horse-racing, with all its attendant evils—cruelty to the horses, gambling, the rascality practised in racing stables, drinking, and the assembling together of the very worst characters. In many places they are mainly got up by the public-house keepers for their own benefit, and it would be of very great benefit to the youth of both sexes, if races and the race course could be altogether abolished. It is a fact which should have its weight with all frequenters of races, plays, and pleasure fairs, that whenever persons become really religious, and, consequently, sincerely desirous that God should be honoured in all things, generally one of their first resolves is that they will avoid, and try to lead others to avoid, all places, and companies, and practices which in any way tend to promote that which is sinful and hateful in His sight.

If the seeking our amusement in that which is attended with cruelty to animals is wrong, then any proposal to do away with such a system should, to say the least, receive attention and consideration on the part of those to whom it is made. Now what substitute can be proposed for, I presume I may call it, the cruel amusement of shooting? Before, however, I proceed to answer my own question, I would observe that a very small proportion of the community have the opportunity of following this amusement; I must also mention that were half the inhumanity which is practised towards hunted foxes, and wounded hares, pheasants, and partridges, to be displayed by the owners or drivers of our London cabs towards their horses, or by our drovers with regard to the animals entrusted to their care, I suspect they would very likely be at once committed to durance vile for a month or six weeks, without the option of paying a fine.

I have proposed a substitute for hunting animals, and now I will say something about a substitute for the cruel amusement of shooting at, and maiming, hares and partridges; though, if the thing is wrong, the upright man should give up the amusement without requiring that a substitute for it should be discovered for him. All will be of opinion that the enrolment of our noble corps of volunteers, and the rifle competition which has everywhere been engaged in by them, affords to great numbers of our young men, of all classes of society, an exciting, healthy, and, at the same time, a most useful employment; great numbers of individuals have devoted, no doubt, much of the time which they used to employ in shooting, in endeavouring to perfect themselves in rifle-shooting. Much might be done in the way of increasing the amusement of rifle-shooting; perhaps by constructing moveable inanimate objects to be fired at; but this, on account of the danger, could only be done on or near the sea, or on the mountain side, or on a very extensive level. Common shooting, in lieu of killing and maiming partridges and hares, might take place somewhat after the popinjay fashion; or that might be improved upon by clever inventors who, by means of simple machinery, might make to move rapidly, along high wires, figures of birds or anything else, which might be so constructed as to be knocked down when fairly struck, and they might contain that which should constitute as great a prize as a head of game would be. But what would then become of all the game in the country? In reply to that I would say, abolish the game laws, give, under certain restrictions, the general right of pursuing and snaring game for a certain time, and probably in two years there would scarcely be a head of game in our island. Attend more closely to the rearing of domestic fowls; but I would do away with pigeons, which not only tempt poaching-people to try and kill them in the fields, but which also, it is computed, consume yearly grain, not generally belonging to their owners, to the value of a million and a half sterling. I confess that I find it difficult to propose anything which would be a substitute for the healthy and exciting walk of miles either on enclosed or open land, on the moor or mountain, which the amusement of shooting induces; and yet I think I could myself enjoy, and benefit by, the long and varied walk equally well if I had neither dogs nor gun with me, particularly if I was accompanied by a pleasant companion. And then what a great blessing it would be to the country to do away with all temptation to poaching, by destroying the game. If, as I believe it might be fairly calculated, there are two occasional or regular poachers, on an average, in every parish in our land, and, in addition, fifty regular poachers in every town containing 50,000 inhabitants and upwards, then, at a rough estimate, we may say there are some 30,000 poachers in the country. What an improvement it would be if there were no temptation to these men to continue their demoralizing pursuit of game, and consequently no temptation to those, who come after them, to tread in their steps.

The most difficult objection to answer to the giving up hunting and shooting on the ground that we have no right to inflict cruelty and pain on any portion of God's animal creation is, I think, the following:—God Himself has allowed numbers of animals to prey on others, and to inflict a certain amount of pain on them, and almost all kinds of animals, &c., die a death of suffering and pain; and people might argue, if a kind and merciful God permits this, why need we be so particular about inflicting pain in killing animals, &c., for our food, or in the pursuit of amusement? I should have no difficulty as to the propriety of inflicting any amount of pain by bad shooting, or in any other way, if I could not procure food in any other way, but it appears to me to be contrary to the Scripture injunctions to be "gentle" and "tender-hearted," that we should be careless about inflicting pain on animals. God has, no doubt for wise purposes, permitted animals, birds, fishes, and insects to prey on each other; He has left numbers of them to die the most painful deaths; but surely that must not be made an excuse by man for revelling in cruelty, and inflicting pain on animals, &c., for mere amusement. How contrary, also, such an idea is to all those lessons of kindness to animals, and birds, and insects, and even worms, which have been instilled into most of us by our tender mothers amongst the first ideas which our infant minds received.

I must, having gone so far, venture to pursue the subject still further. When God first gave *permission* to man to eat animal food, (perhaps man did so before,) and said, Genesis ix, 3, "every moving thing that liveth shall be meat for you; even as "the green herb have I given you all things," the permission was accompanied by this restriction, as we read in the next verse, "but flesh with the life thereof, which is the blood thereof, shall "ye not eat." Thomas Scott, in his Commentary, says on this passage, "The grant here given fully warrants our use of the "animals for food, but not the abuse of them by intemperance or "cruelty. The restriction might be intended as a check to "cruelty, lest men, inured to shed and feed upon the blood of "animals, should grow unfeeling, and be the less shocked at "shedding human blood."

I have begun to think that it may not be really unfair, if men pursue the sports of hunting, shooting, &c., for pleasure, regardless of the pain and misery inflicted upon the animals, that they have no right to complain, if they should find themselves classed with such men as Nero, or any other cruel monster of former or more recent ages.

In Hooper's Waterloo is the following anecdote, which I venture to borrow from him; I omitted to do so in the more suitable part of my work:—"A trumpeter-boy of the 2nd Life "Guards, Thomas Beamond, was riding through the field when a "cuirassier rushed at him, with his sword's point levelled at the "boy's breast. Discovering he was a mere lad, the gallant "Frenchman dropped his point, spared him, and passed on. Sad "to relate, in sight of the poor boy, a comrade, who had not "witnessed the noble act of the cuirassier, fell upon him and "slew him. When the boy, grown a man, told the story to my "informant, he was, even after years had passed by, affected even "to tears."

May such gentle and generous feelings be cultivated, as far as possible, by all contending armies, until God shall "make "wars to cease unto the end of the earth."

CHAPTER XII.

1816.

AMUSEMENTS AND INCIDENTS IN THE NORTH OF FRANCE.

Hunting at Callone—Captain English—Duke of Wellington's boar-hounds—Lord Hill and his brother—Gymnastic club near St. Pol—52nd play the rest of Colville's division at cricket—Fatal accident—Mess at Thérouenne in the summer—Accident to a friend in the 71st—Medals for Waterloo served out—Two of us wear them on going to Aire—Death of a poor woman in the Grande Place—Curious anecdote about the 18th of June, 1816, by a corporal of the 23rd Fusileers—Ball given by the English officers at St. Omer—My servant drowned—Remarkable dreams—Holman's servant shot—A corporal stabbed by a French officer—Capture of thieves—Winterbottom and his former comrade—Anecdote of the master tailor.

WE had not a very great variety of amusements during the time of our occupation of the North of France. I received from time to time during several weeks, as a present, from our regimental pack, those hounds which, from their being rather small or for any other reason, our managing committee wished to part with; and thus I collected, I think, seven hounds, for my kind friend Captain Frederick English, of the Engineers, who was quartered with his family at the chateau of Callone, near St. Pol, about seventeen miles from us. Whilst I was collecting them, two or three of us got a little private hunting of our own occasionally. At Callone they were considered a great acquisition, and I several times went there for two or three days, and enjoyed hunting with them very much. On one occasion I remember riding ahead with a drag, which afforded us very good sport. There was in existence at one time, several years after our return from

France, a very spirited sketch, by Captain English, of the officers, horses, and hounds of that hunt; I think he never mustered more than five horsemen, even when I made one of the party. Captain English and his horse, and I and my mare, were amongst the figures; and I should have liked to have brought away with me the sketch, if they could have parted with it, when I last saw my kind friends in England some thirty years ago.

The Duke of Wellington, whose head-quarters were at Cambrai, between fifty and sixty miles distant from our cantonments, on one occasion sent his boar-hounds for a day's hunting in our direction, and four of the 52nd officers went between twenty and thirty miles the day before in order to hunt with them. They threw off not very far from the inn at which we slept, in a forest, the name of which I have forgotten, but we had scarcely any sport. The hounds found a boar, and hunted him for a considerable time, and we rode up and down the rides of the forest; at last he broke cover, but merely to run about half a mile across an open space to another part of the forest. There was a tremendous and awkward leap out of the forest, which my mare managed very cleverly. The boar is said to be a fast runner when hunted, but I had not the pleasure of seeing him during the whole day. Lord Hill and his brother, Colonel Hill, of the Blues, were out, and I think not more than half a dozen other people, besides ourselves, one of whom was Colonel Fremantle. Lord Hill and his brother carried boar-spears, as did one or two of the others. Soon after we got into the forest, as I was walking my horse along, about 150 yards behind the other 52nd men, Lord Hill overtook me, and coming up alongside, asked me "How are Sir John Colborne and the 52nd, Sir?" He *might* have heard that some 52nd officers were to be out that day, but I remember my impression then was, that he had not had the opportunity of hearing that we were to be there, and that it was a case of remembering, after having only once or at the most twice, seen me before; the one occasion being when he rode very close upon me in the standing corn, half an hour or an hour before the commencement of the Battle of Waterloo; the other, in passing along the front at a review, when the troops were standing in contiguous close columns, and when I think I carried one of the colours.

Some of our officers got some good coursing; I only occasionally joined them. The shooting was very bad, the birds being very wild on the extensive cultivated lands between the villages. Sometimes, for want of something else to do, I recollect firing ball from my double-barrelled gun at partridges, which I could often see running on the rise of the ground 200 yards off, when I could not get within half that distance of them. I need scarcely add, that this ball-practice of mine did not inflict any serious injury on the enemy in my front.

Some spirited officers, quartered in the neighbourhood of St. Pol, belonging to our division, proposed, in the spring of 1816, I think, the establishment of a gymnastic club, at which those of the officers of the division who were so disposed, might meet at stated times to play at cricket and other games. The meetings were to take place some few miles to the northward of St. Pol. This was at a great distance from our brigade, but two of us from the 52nd attended the first meeting. The 71st, belonging to another brigade, were close to us at Estréeblanche to the eastward; and inclining towards the south, and in the direction of St. Pol, were the 6th regiment, I think, at or near Lillers, and beyond them the 29th regiment; and nearer to St. Pol, and beyond it, there was another brigade and some artillery. These being nearer to the place of meeting than Pack's brigade, were enabled to contribute a goodly number of members to the institution. I forget what games were played at the first meeting, but after dinner, Captain McDonald, the hon. secretary, came to where I was sitting, and said it was proposed that our brigade should play the rest of the division at cricket, at the next meeting of the club, and asked if I would undertake, on the part of the brigade, to accept the challenge; I was foolish enough to reply, that I could not answer for the rest of the brigade, as I knew nothing of them, but that I would undertake that the 52nd should play the rest of the division. I dare say I should just as readily have said that they would play "All England." I have no doubt it created some smiles when this was announced, as it immediately was.

On my giving an account, on my return to the regiment, of all that had taken place, they told me that I had acted very foolishly in what I had done, but that as the thing was considered as fixed, they would endeavour to turn out in sufficient force to try and do some credit to the expectations which I might have raised of their prowess as cricketers. We did not take any men with us, but eight of the officers including myself went, and some of them must have ridden upwards of forty miles there and back; for I was the nearest to the place of meeting, and I reckoned that my quarters were about sixteen miles from it.

We found a numerous assemblage of the officers of the division there. It was arranged that there should be only eight on a side. We were not overmatched, and had a most excellent game. They paid us the compliment of saying, that they never saw better fielding in their lives. They had a major in the artillery on the other side, who got fifty-two runs. We consoled ourselves with saying, that had he been an ordinary batter, and had not made more than half that score, we should have carried away the laurels. But I have a sad addition to make to this account. We heard a few days afterwards, that this poor major of artillery, I am sorry I cannot recollect his name, who had been full of health and spirits, and who was the hero of the day, was killed on his return to his quarters that evening, by the upsetting of the gig, in which he and another officer were riding, at the turn of a road. How often do the solemn warnings come to us—" memento mori!" and, " there is but a step between me " and death!"

One moonlight evening, as four of us, including a young acquaintance of mine, a fine young fellow by the name of Barnett, of the 71st Highland Light Infantry, were returning along the Chaussée Brunehaut, from our mess at Thérouenne, to Estréeblanche, four miles distant, the 71st officer and another of the party determined to ride a race, from the top of the ascent from Thérouenne, in the direction of Estréeblanche. I always thought those races on roads extremely dangerous and disagreeable, and being mounted on a small Galloway, contented myself with trotting smartly along the road. When I had proceeded about a mile, I heard a voice crying out, "Hold hard, "hold hard!" The first object which I saw was one of the horses fixed in a ditch to the right of the road, two feet wide and two feet deep, with his back at the bottom of it, and the four feet up in the air. The two racing horses, in some curious way, had got their fore feet entangled and had both fallen. The 52nd officer and his horse had not taken much harm; but my poor 71st friend was insensible, having fallen most heavily on his head; his horse was in the ditch, as I have described. The 52nd officer was sitting down with the head of the other on his lap. The fourth man of the party was up immediately after me; they left me with poor Barnett, and one of the other two rode off to a village two miles off, for an assistant-surgeon, and the second, after giving notice to some of our men at Enguinegatte, a third of a mile off, to come to my assistance, went in another direction. As I sat supporting our injured friend, I desired the last officer, as he was moving off, if he had a knife in his pocket, to leave it with me, intending to get some blood from his temples or some other part, if Barnett should appear to cease to breathe. I was often joked afterwards about this. It was not a very pleasant position to be in, for I thought it most probable that my companion would die before assistance came. When we had been there about twenty minutes, I was for a moment startled by four of our men rushing down some broken ground behind us, with drawn bayonets, one exclaiming, as he saw our figures, "Where's Mr. Leeke?" They were the men quartered at the first farm house, and had misunderstood the hasty notice given by the officer, that they should lose no time in going to my assistance. They gathered that there was a dying man on the Thérouenne road, and that I was there, and probably thought that we had been attacked by some party. Two or three others came to our assistance, and we placed Barnett, still insensible, upright on one of the horses; and, two men holding him on and I leading the horse by the bridle, we proceeded to my quarters at Estréeblanche. A small river, called the Laquele, flowed along the road of the village for eighty or a hundred yards, completely filling it and being nearly knee deep, the footpath going along the bank on the right. On our arriving at this water,

Barnett astonished me by taking hold of the bridle and pulling the
horse up, and saying that I must not go through the water. Here
was a momentary consciousness. Of course, however, I did this.
He was put into a bed at my quarters, and our assistant-surgeon
attended him. The day after, the surgeon and the assistant-
surgeon of the 71st arrived, and said he had received a severe
concussion of the brain; they were anxious to get him into their
neighbourhood, and he was removed to his own quarters on the
third day, where he gradually recovered. I wonder whether he
is still living. Perhaps one fourth of the officers who fought at
Waterloo, still survive at this date, December 8, 1865; at
least that is about the proportion of survivors of the 52nd
Waterloo officers. There were sixty-three officers present on
that occasion, including the surgeons and two aides-de-camp, of
whom it is ascertained that about forty-five are dead. I only
know of fourteen that survive, now at the end of fifty years.
Three of these were captains at Waterloo; William Rowan, James
Frederick Love, and Charles Yorke, now lieutenant-generals and
G.C.B.'s. Ten of them were then lieutenants: George Hall,
(now lieutenant-colonel,) George Gawler, (now colonel,) George
Whichcote, (major-general,) Hon. William Ogilvy, (captain,)
E. R. Northey, (lieutenant-colonel,) Hon. W. Browne, Edward
Scoones, (major,) W. Austin, (major,) Charles Holman, (captain,)
G. E. Scott. One only was then an ensign, William Leeke.

Just before the 18th of June, 1816, the medals for Waterloo
were served out to all those who had been present, and on the
anniversary of the victory two of us thought well to ride into
Aire, which was about six miles from Estréeblanche; it was the
nearest fortified place to our village, and was garrisoned by the
French. None of our non-commissioned officers or soldiers
were admitted into St. Omer or Aire without a pass from the
officers commanding the company to which each belonged, but
officers in uniform might enter without any pass. It must
be recollected that there were very few soldiers remaining in the
French army who had been at Waterloo, and that they were
now the soldiers of our ally Louis XVIII, for whom we had
fought and some thousands of our comrades had shed their
blood, but, nevertheless, our riding into one of the French

garrisons on the first anniversary of a victory gained over French troops, would perhaps have been better avoided. My companion, on the occasion, thus speaks of it in a letter which I received from him not very long ago. "Do you remember how "you and I rode into Aire, on the first anniversary of Waterloo, "wearing the medals just issued, and laurel in our shakos. The "guards at the gate scowled, but we met with no adventure. "Kenny, a very correct and rather censorious person, thought we "had been extremely unwise—it was all your doing too—I, so "many years older, ought to have tried to dissuade you, instead "of being led away by you as I was." In reply, I told him that I perfectly well recollected the whole affair, and that it certainly was much more like me than like him to engage in such an adventure. I felt rather confident that it was on this occasion that the following, in some little measure redeeming, occurrence took place, but my friend says he has not the least recollection of it, so it is probable that it happened when I rode into Aire on some other occasion with some other officer. As we rode across the large square of the town, an old woman, carrying one of those small tin boxes with lighted charcoal, which the older French women are so constantly seen with, suddenly fell down in what appeared to be a fainting fit; we immediately jumped off our horses, and letting them loose, carried the poor woman into the nearest house: on our seating her in a chair, her lower clothes were found to be slightly on fire from the charcoal-box, and she was quite dead.

A fine old soldier, a corporal in the 23rd Fusileers, recently told me that their grenadier company, in which he was, adopted a singular method of parading their medals on the first anniversary of Waterloo. Two of their comrades were, for some not very serious offence, confined in the guard-house at headquarters, not very far distant from their colonel's quarters; so they made one of their number put on his red jacket and all his regimentals, and having fastened the whole of their medals all over the front of his jacket, they borrowed an ass, on which he rode to their head-quarters, accompanied by the whole of the grenadier company. When they arrived, they asked permission to see the colonel, and he immediately came out to them, and on his asking what they wanted, they told him that they had come to ask him to do them a great favor on the anniversary of the great victory, and it was that he would have the kindness to forgive their two comrades, who were in disgrace. He smiled at their gallant cavalier bedizened with medals, and good naturedly told them that their comrades should be at the village they were quartered at, before the company could get there themselves. The two men joined them in a very few minutes after they left the colonel's quarters.

Monsieur Robichez, the owner of the chateau, at Estrée-blanche, at which Captain McNair was quartered, on one occasion pressed me very much to go with him to a ball, at Betune, a French fortress, about ten miles from Aire. I was the only Englishman there; indeed, all the rest were French, and many of them French officers in uniform, and although there was nothing uncivil in their conduct, yet there was a certain constraint, which was almost sure to arise under the circumstances, and which made me feel I had been very foolish in allowing myself to be placed in such a position.

Although I was too far from St. Omer to have any acquaintances amongst either the inhabitants or the few English residents there; yet, on one occasion I, with many 52nd officers, joined the other regiments of Pack's brigade, and the cavalry quartered to the north of St. Omer, in giving a grand ball to the people of the town and neighbourhood, both English and French; which was attended, including the entertainers, by about four hundred people. The supper-tables, it was arranged, were first to accommodate the one half of the assemblage, and when they had been duly feasted, then the other half were to be admitted, and the only thing I now remember of that ball is, that when the second detachment of supper-eaters arived, every bonbon, and every other pocketable eatable, had been carried off by those who had been invited to make the first attack upon the abundant provision, which had been intended to be more than sufficient for the whole party.

As I was returning from the ball-room to the hotel at which I was to sleep, at a very badly lighted spot I made some wrong turn, and lost my way for a minute or two; I heard some one coming, but could not, as it was very dark, see more than the figure of a man approaching. I took him to be a Frenchman, and asked him which was the way to the hotel. He answered in French, and gave me some directions, which, although I had in some degree lost my way, I felt very confident were incorrect, and, as I thought he was leading me wrong on purpose, I gave him somewhat of a scolding for his conduct in my best French, which he took very quietly, and then said good naturedly in English, "Oh come with me and I'll shew you the way à l'ancienne poste." I walked with him twenty or thirty yards, when he put me into the right direction, for which I thanked him. I could not see his face, but I discovered from his voice that it was the commanding officer of the 4th English regiment. I cannot at all understand how it was that, in a fortified place of some extent, the streets, or at least some of them, were left in such a state of darkness.

I think the army was very healthy during the time of the occupation of France. We had two sad accidents at Estrée-blanche, and whilst we were there one of our men was mortally wounded by a retired French officer, who lodged in the village.

I have mentioned that at one time we regularly dined at the chateau at which Captain McNair was quartered. It was surrounded by a moat about thirty feet broad, over which there was a bridge about five or six feet wide, formed of planks, resting on four or five walls built up from the bottom of the moat; there was no railing on either side of the wooden bridge. It communicated with a vaulted passage, which passed under some of the rooms to a small open court within, surrounded by the buildings on three sides, whilst on that side which was opposite to the passage to the bridge, we looked over the moat to the field beyond it. There was a massive door between the end of the passage and the bridge. We often crossed this bridge on the darkest nights without the least apprehension of danger, although the water was deep all round the chateau except at the edge.

One dark night my servant, whose name was George Soones, with another soldier, was passing through the doorway close to the bridge, and, as it was blowing hard through the passage from the opposite direction, he found some difficulty in keeping the door open, and at the same time in keeping alight a piece of candle which he was carrying between his fingers. The other man was nearly across the bridge, and heard Soones say, "If "this light goes out I'm done." At that moment the door was blown heavily to upon him, and the light went out, and before he had reached the middle of the bridge he fell over, striking his neck, it was supposed, against one of the buttresses on which the bridge was built; he was a good swimmer, and, notwithstanding the hurt he received, which was shown by an extensive bruise on the side of the neck, he swam about five-and-thirty yards, but not towards the shore of the moat. His body was not found until about two hours afterwards, under the walls of the chateau.

I was away from Estréeblanche on that evening, and was very much grieved to hear of poor Soones's fate. He and his two brothers had volunteered into the 52nd from the South Hants Militia, and his friends, I found, lived within two miles of my home, though I had never known them; and possibly this made me feel his death all the more. It was truly melancholy for me to enter my bedroom at night. He had been the last person there, and had turned down my bed, and laid out my things. It was impossible to get to sleep, and I felt very wretched. Divided from my room by a thin lath and plaster partition was the servants' room, in which they kept their firelocks and accoutrements, and slept. Holman's servant, a nice fellow by the name of Blackman, slept, or rather dozed there on the night in question. I heard him all night tumbling about on his bed, and more than once I heard him say, "I'm coming, "George, I'm coming!"

The next morning, in good time, I sent a man to the next village, about a mile and a half off, occupied by Shedden's company, in which Soones's brothers were, to break the melancholy intelligence to them. On his return, he told me that he had met one of them before he reached the village, and on his saying that he was come to look for him, he at once exclaimed, "You "have no occasion to tell me what you are come for, I dreamt "last night that my brother was drowned." Now I am sure, so much did every one feel the melancholy death which had occurred, that the man would tell me exactly what passed between him and the brother, and I perfectly remember it all. However, I should probably not have thought so much about this dream, had it not been for the additional circumstance which I am going to mention. I wrote home to my mother to request her to inform George Soones's family of his death. She could not go to their house, and therefore sent to request that one of them would come and speak to her; the poor mother came, and on being informed that her son was dead, immediately said, "Was he drowned, Ma'am?" and on being told that he was, she replied, "I thought so, for I dreamt several nights ago, "that he was drowned." These things made considerable impression on our minds at the time, but I do not think they produced any *religious* feeling. As I write, the words of the 73rd Psalm occur to me, though they are there used in a different way by the Psalmist, to that in which they would have been applicable to us—"So foolish was I, and ignorant; I was as a beast "before thee." I do not place any confidence in dreams, although there are many well authenticated instances of remarkable dreams turning out to be true, but we must allow that dreams, as all other circumstances, are under the control of God, therefore they may lead us to reflexion. I well remember how melancholy I felt, as we marched along a long pathway, by the side of a high hedge, following poor Soones's remains from the chateau to the Roman Catholic church at Estréeblanche, on the north side of which he was buried. The "Dead March in Saul," which I had never heard before, was sounded very nicely, by our two buglers, who preceded the corpse, and had a very solemn effect. I have no recollection of the service being read over his remains, though I suppose it was read by McNair or Holman; nor do I recollect the firing the three volleys over his grave, though that must have been done. So curious is memory! Some very trifling words or circumstances we remember with the greatest accuracy, when somewhat more important things, which happened at the same time, we entirely forget.

But I have another very sad event to relate, which happened a week only after poor Soones's death. The whole company, or the Estréeblanche portion of it, I forget which, were at ball-practice, about half a mile above the village, under the command of Holman. I was not present, and I have some idea I was at Enguinegatte. One of the men's firelocks would not go off, (it was the same man who was just in front of Soones when he fell off the bridge,) he went to the rear of the firing-party to hammer the flint with his turnscrew, but instead of pointing his musket to the rear, he thoughtlessly pointed it towards the men standing in line in front of him. It went off, and the ball went through the arm (breaking it) and through the lungs of a corporal in the rear rank, and lodged in the body of poor Blackman, Holman's servant, who was in the front rank. The corporal recovered, but Blackman was mortally wounded. He was taken to the nearest cottage, and placed on a chair, and lived about three-quarters of an hour. I think no surgeon could get to him before his death. They told me, he was quite aware that he had not long to live, and said he should "soon be with poor George;" and again, immediately before his death, "I'm going to poor George." He was buried by the side of poor Soones, and I often think of their last resting-place. Blackman also was a Hampshire man, and I think the man who accidentally shot him, also came out of the South Hants Militia. This man afterwards became my servant, somewhat I believe to the astonishment of people, as they thought "he was so unlucky." I do not think I took him as a servant out of bravado, but out of compassion in some measure, for he felt how unfortunate he had been in the matter of these deaths, and how blameable for his great carelessness as regarded that of poor Blackman. He was a clean, smart soldier, and one likely to make a good servant.

We were sitting at our mess one evening after dinner, and Brisbane, one of our assistant-surgeons, was with us, when a messenger came from the village, to say that Corporal Gilpin had been stabbed by a Frenchman. We found, on going to the public house, that the intestines being wounded there was scarcely any hope of his recovery. His wound was dressed and sewn up, and he was the next day sent to the hospital, where he died within the week. Gilpin and this retired French officer were great friends, and they studied a little together; the Frenchman assisting Gilpin, I think, in French and arithmetic; but they also drank together, and on this occasion they were both in liquor, and a quarrel arose between them, when Gilpin struck the other severely with his fists. The French officer took up a chair to protect himself with it, at the same time opening his knife, and when Gilpin again advanced upon him, he stabbed him under the chair. Corporal Gilpin was one of our finest men, and was the right hand man of the company.

The Frenchman made his escape into Belgium, and was afterwards, if I recollect right, condemned to death, "par con-"tumace," I think they call it. He was very nearly taken, for he jumped out of a window with his double-barrelled gun in his hand, just as our village guard, of a corporal and three, came to the other side of the house in which he lodged, and they pursued him down the garden, but lost sight of him. I remember his once being examined as a witness at a court-martial, at Estrée-blanche, and I met him once afterwards as I was returning from shooting, where, as he passed me at about sixty yards distance, he saluted me by taking off his hat, which of course I returned. Captain McNair had to attend with some others at the trial, when he was found guilty.

McNair also had to give evidence on another occasion. The circumstances were these, and although there was nothing very particular in what occurred, they were well remembered because they afforded us some little excitement for the moment in the midst of our rather monotonous life:—We were sitting quietly one moonlight evening after dinner, when Angelique, M. Robichez's housekeeper, came into the room, and told us she had just watched some men who had gone into her master's barn, about eighty yards from the chateau, no doubt for the purpose of stealing the wheat, and requested us to come and try and secure them. We did not at first pay much attention to what she said, but presently she returned in a very excited state, saying she had seen people going into the barn, and reproached us with being unwilling to take any trouble to prevent her master from being robbed. On this we sallied out, and one or two of the servants came also. McNair stopped to take a pistol with him, so that I got downstairs and over the bridge the first, and picked up a switch, for want of something more suitable, as I ran along. Just as I came to the barn door it was partly opened, and then shut to again hastily; so, giving it a smart cut with the switch, I ran round to a door, which I knew was on the other side; on my arriving at it, the persons within had got it half open for the purpose of getting away, but on seeing me they closed it again, and I could not move it when I pushed heavily against it, nor could all our party together make any impression on the doors; so one of the men was sent to the village, a quarter of a mile off, for the corporal's guard. Just then we heard voices about fifty yards off, and recognised amongst them the voice of one of our own men, who was a drinking, troublesome fellow, and we immediately feared that he and his companions were in some way mixed up with the proceedings in the barn. Leaving two of our party, one of them with his musket in his hand, to look after the barn doors, and to prevent the escape of the men within, McNair and I proceeded to reconnoitre the party whom we heard talking at a little distance. They turned out to be the man, whose voice we had recognised, and six soldiers of the 71st. They were on the footpath leading from Estréeblanche to the nearest 71st village, which was rather more than a mile off, and they were all out after hours. On our coming up to them they made no attempt to run off, and at once obeyed McNair's order to follow each other in single file. He told me to keep by the rear man and bring them all along. I was greatly afraid that finding themselves brought along by only two persons, they might be tempted to break away from us, for I knew, if they did so, that McNair would certainly shoot one of them, he being a most determined man. However they walked quietly along till we came abreast of the gable end of the barn, and a little beyond, when they were ordered to halt and remain there. They then saw that something was up at the barn.

The guard had by this time arrived, and we proceeded to force open the principal door, which had been barricaded with beams by those within. Angelique bravely volunteered so to hold the lantern that we might see those within, when the door gave way. It opened inwards, and was about four feet wide; and it shut to against a sill at the bottom, about fourteen inches high. The four men of the guard with their bayonets fixed, with my help added, soon made the props yield a little, and two or three of us got each a foot over the sill, and the butt ends of two or three muskets were in, and the door had opened nearly two feet at my end, when the brave Angelique ran right off with the lantern, leaving the small open space in darkness; so, for a few seconds, we allowed the door to close to upon us again. I took the lantern from Angelique, and we again made good our footing within the sill, and the door went right back on its hinges, all of us going forward almost on our faces; and then, I confess, I felt somewhat ashamed, for we found in the barn only two poor frightened Frenchmen, who fell on their knees, crying "Misericors, Misericors." I think they were afraid that our soldiers would bayonet them. Angelique's courage returned, and, mounting a wheelbarrow which was in the barn, she harangued them vehemently for their ingratitude in robbing so kind a master as M. Robichez. They were afterwards condemned to five years' imprisonment. The seven soldiers, when it was found that they were not mixed up with the attempt to rob the barn, were, I think, allowed to go to their quarters. I believe all our characters rose wonderfully in the estimation of Angelique.

We had a court-marshal on one of our men at Estreéblanche, for being drunk on guard, when he was found guilty, and received one hundred lashes. Winterbottom, our adjutant, who had risen from the ranks, and of whom I have written much in another place,* told me, when the sentence was executed, that the poor fellow had been his comrade when first he entered the regiment, and added, "I feel very sorry for him. He took to drinking-"ways, which has brought him to this degradation and punish-"ment. I avoided drinking, and tried to do my duty, and am "now adjutant, and nearly the senior lieutenant of the regiment."

I had a curious complaint made to me by one of the men, when the new clothing of the company was being fitted on at Thérouenne. He came to me and said, "If you please, Sir, ser-"jeant —— (the master tailor) has cut my chin with his scissors." I told him it must have been done accidently. He replied, "No, "Sir, I believe it was done out of spite. He has always had a

* See Chapter XX.

"spite against me, since I brought up his wife, when I was
"sentry on the quarter-guard at St. Omer camp, and she tried to
"pass into camp without answering, when I challenged her." I
immediately went with the man, who I think was the same man
who had his pouch knocked off at Waterloo by a cannon-shot,
to the master tailor, and told him of the complaint, when he said,
"I was trying on his jacket, Sir, with my scissors in my hand,
"when he fidgetted about so much, that he made me impatient,
"and I said, 'do stand still,' at the same time putting up my
"hand, when the point of the scissors caught him accidentally
"on the chin." There was nothing to be done but to accept this
excuse, and to tell him quietly to be more careful in future.
The master tailor of the regiment was attached to No. 9 company,
and was in the rear of it as a serjeant on inspection and review
days. He tried to have himself looked upon as a privileged
character, on those occasions, with regard to his military bearing,
&c., but this I never permitted. There was no great harm in
him, but he was rather conceited in his undress and in his walk,
and attempted to be a bit of a dandy. I recollect on the occasion of one of the older officers joining at the citadel of Valenciennes, after having been away from the regiment for some very
considerable time, he was shaking hands very cordially with all
the officers who met him, when the master tailor passed along,
dressed in a blue surtout coat which he was allowed to wear,
and an undress cap, somewhat resembling those of the officers,
and before he could salute the major, the latter, knowing his face
and taking him for one of the officers, put out his hand and
gave it a hearty shake, saying, "I'm very glad to see you, my
"good fellow;" which my unmilitary readers must understand
was, under the circumstances, rather contrary to military etiquette.
On finding out his mistake, and getting a little laughed at for it,
the major uttered something in which the words "scoundrel,"
and "put him in the guard-house," were distinguishable.

It is a general feeling, I believe, in the army, that officers
cannot be too particular in their behaviour to sentries, when
challenged by them. The sentry may be placed in very awkward circumstances, particularly with regard to officers, when
enforcing the orders of his post. At the camp near St. Omer,

one night when I was the officer of the guard, as I lay on my guard-bed, I heard one of my sentries challenge some one who was passing near his post without receiving any reply, and the " Halt, who comes there?" was repeated several times without the question being answered. At last he crossed the path of the person, who proved to be an officer of another regiment encamped beyond us, and stopped him, when he gave the answer, "officer," and I heard the sentry say, "Then, Sir, you should have said "that you were an officer." I was just going to the sentry's assistance, when I found that the officer made no further reply, and was allowed to pass on. But I had no idea of allowing sentries to be improperly treated by anyone.

CHAPTER XIII.

1816, 1817, 1818.

LEAVE TO ENGLAND AND PARIS. RETURN OF THE ARMY TO ENGLAND.

Cheltenham — Duke of Wellington — Paris in 1817 — French family — Chef d'escadron—Labédoyère's tomb—Ball at the English Ambassador's —Denain—General Beckwith—Encampment again at St. Omer in 1818— Sir John Colborne joins — Purchases a horse from me — The horse's proceedings on parade— Last visit to Valenciennes—52nd occupy citadel— Review by the Emperor of Russia—52nd the last regiment in France— March to Calais — Embarkation — Arrival in England, November 29, 1818.

In the autumn of 1816, I obtained three months' leave of absence to go to England. We were told afterwards, that on the very night of our departure, there was a very heavy gale with rain; and that great numbers of the tents were blown down. There were two other officers went on leave at the same time, but I forget who they were. We started on a Sunday morning from Dover, in a postchaise, for London. I was voted the paymaster for the journey, and at one of the turnpikes I recollect I had a bad shilling given to me in the change for a pound note, and that it gave us some trouble, as we went along, so to shy it out of the window that no one might be likely to find it. I well remember the delight and pleasure I felt that morning, on finding myself again in our own dear country. I have always felt that one great advantage to be derived from travelling in other parts of the world, was the learning from it to love and value one's own country all the more. As it was Sunday, all the people were very nicely dressed, and in our eyes our fair countrywomen carried off the palm of beauty, when compared with the nice and kind-hearted females on the other side of the channel. I had not then learnt to value the Sunday as a day set apart by Almighty God as a day of rest, and of holy observance, and, consequently, if rightly observed, of spiritual benefit to man.

I recollect nothing more of the journey, than that I found myself on the the afternoon of the next day at Cheltenham, where my family were staying. I was not expected, and was not at first recognized by my mother and sisters, when I was ushered into the drawing room, without being announced. Each looked at the other, as much as to enquire who the stranger was. I was now more than eighteen years and a half old, and fifteen months had made some considerable alteration in my appearance. At last one of them ventured to mention my christian name, and then we enjoyed one of those happy meetings which occur so seldom in the course of our lives.

I have not much to relate about Cheltenham; but one of the first things I discovered was, that the Duke of Wellington and I were still nearer neighbours there, than we were when my tent was close to the garden door of his house at Paris. He was in the next house to us; but all I remember of him was, the seeing him attending to the present Duke, and, I think, his brother, when they were put on a couple of ponies, apparently for the first time, on the other side of the fence which separated the drives up to the two houses. There was a great deal of gaiety going forward at that time at Cheltenham, which we entered into very freely. One of our chief friends, with whom we first became acquainted there, was Captain Sir Edward Tucker,* of the Navy, who early in 1817 married my eldest sister. After spending about a month at Cheltenham, and a very agreeable week at Malvern with a very large party, we went into Hampshire, and I returned to the north of France in the early part of November. One day at Cheltenham an old

---

* Admiral Sir Edward Tucker was one of our most gallant officers, and was made a K.C.B. in 1814, for distinguished services rendered in the capture of several of the Molucca Islands, when in command of H.M. Ship Dover. He died in 1864, at the age of 86, humbly trusting in the righteousness and atonement of the Lord Jesus Christ.

RETURN OF THE ARMY TO ENGLAND. 223

gentleman accosted me, and told me he had been in my regiment at the Battle of Bunker's Hill; but I never fell in with him afterwards. He did not mention his name, but I think it very likely that he was General Hunter, who I know served at Bunker's Hill in 1777, and whose journal of what took place with regard to the services of the 52nd in America and India, is largely quoted in the early part of the regimental record.

Towards the end of the summer of 1817, Colonel Charles Rowan very kindly applied for three months' leave for me to go to Paris, to improve myself in French. I lived in the family of a superior French officer, who had suffered a great reverse of fortune and prospects by the overthrow of Bonaparte, and the restoration of the Bourbons. They were very nice people, and were very kind to me; but they were very strong Bonapartists. I picked up a good deal of French whilst I was there, and tried to make a start in German. I also did something, but very little, in the way of military surveying. Several other persons usually dined with the family with whom I had taken up my quarters; amongst them was a French chef d'escadron, who had served at Waterloo in the cuirassiers. He was now on half-pay. He generally sat at a distant part of the table from me, so that I knew little of him; we were however on very good terms. I only remember two circumstances connected with him, one of which shewed rather strongly his dislike to the English, a dislike very natural, and, I suspect, almost universal amongst Bonaparte's officers and soldiers, many of whom had met with such signal defeats at the hands of the English in the Peninsula and at Waterloo. The circumstance was this:—We were sitting at dinner one day, when I heard some considerable laughing at the other end of the table, and found, from several of the party looking towards me, that they rather wondered if I had heard what had just been said by the French officer. On my requesting that he would repeat it, he did so, and said, good humouredly, "I was saying, 'we dislike "'very much the Russians, the Prussians, and the other dogs, "'[meaning the Austrians] but with regard to these English we "'*detest* them.'" The words "autres chiens," (in English, *other dogs*,) sound very much like the word "Autrichiens," which is the French word for Austrians. I think this play upon the words was common amongst the French at that time. I took the speech very quietly, and merely said, that "there was no "love lost between us."

The other circumstance connected with the proceedings of this French officer was as follows:—We went with a party to the cemetery of Père la Chaise, and as I followed them I found our friend the cuirassier writing something on one of the tombs in pencil. On my asking, if I might read what he had written, he made no difficulty in allowing me to do so. The words were very treasonable, and had he been denounced to the government, no doubt they would have cost him his liberty, if not his life. They were to the following effect:—" Rise, " Frenchmen, and avenge yourselves on this executioner of a " king, [ce bourreau du roi] who has deprived of life the noble " Labédoyère."* I think some few years afterwards I saw an account in the papers of some trouble which this officer had got into, in connexion with a disturbance in front of the Chamber of Deputies.

I had several English friends at Paris, which enabled me to spend my time there very pleasantly, although I did not allow my intercourse with them to interfere with my study of French, for which I had principally gone to Paris. I recollect a very pleasant picnic to Malmaison, with a large party of English and French; and the going to a ball at the English ambassador's. As some of the French royal family were to be there, it was necessary to go in a court dress; I had no regimental court dress with me, and, therefore, as was customary, hired a civilian's dress. It consisted of a chocolate-coloured coat and waistcoat, with cut steel buttons, black satin knee-breeches, with buckles, white silk stockings, shoes and buckles, sword, and cocked hat.

* On the return of Napoleon from Elba, Colonel Labédoyère was one of the first sent, at the head of his regiment, to oppose his progress towards Paris; but instead of doing so, he, and the troops he commanded, went over to the late Emperor. After serving at Fleurus and at Waterloo, he retired, at the capitulation of Paris, with the French army behind the Loire. He was soon afterwards arrested, brought to Paris, tried by a court-martial, and condemned to death. He was shot on the plains of Grenoble, on the 19th of August, 1815, when he was not yet thirty years of age.

On my return from Paris, I found the 52nd at Valenciennes. On my way thither with the mail courier, I encountered, near Denain, the most tremendous thunder-storm I was ever exposed to. We were afterwards encamped for two or three weeks, and the army was reviewed, on the plains of Denain. Two of us put one of our tents over the other, which helped to keep out the cold. We had a brother-officer in the next tent to us, whose horse's name was "Chance," and having, on two or three mornings, heard him ask his servant, when he called him, "How "is old Chance?" (he pronounced the name in a peculiar manner) we, during the remainder of our encampment there, made a point, the first thing every morning, of inquiring after the health of his horse, in the same words, and with the same peculiarity in pronouncing the animal's name. Every morning, for a fortnight, might be heard the following colloquy; for although after a few days it was very difficult to get him to answer when we called to him by name, yet we always persisted, sometimes in a coaxing way, till we made him do so, which latterly he did, by saying, somewhat impatiently, "Well, "what do *you* want?" when we immediately replied by asking, "How is old Chance?" I fear I have not been able to make the anecdote so amusing to my readers, as the little daily inquiry after the horse's welfare was to us. The words are often quoted by my sons; when at cricket or any other game, I have made some lucky stroke, or have had some lucky escape, they to this day often exclaim, "How is old Chance?"

Lieut.-Colonel Beckwith, whom I have mentioned in my account of the battle of Waterloo,* dined with us one day in our large-mess marquée in the neighbourhood of Denain, and kept the whole mess in roars of laughter when talking over, with his old Peninsula friends many of their adventures of former days. He was a great favourite in the light division. We returned to Estreelaville and Therouenne late in October, 1817, and I think I have nothing to remark of the ensuing winter and spring, which has not been already mentioned.

* See page 37. He afterwards became a very religious man, and took a great interest in the Vaudois, amongst whom he lived for many years, and to whom he rendered many services, by his influence with the Sardinian government.

Early in June, 1818, we occupied our old encampment-ground to the south of St. Omer. Sir John Colborne joined us there, and I remember his telling me, he was glad to hear from Colonel Rowan, that I had not been idling away my time, during his absence from the regiment, but had been trying to improve myself. His establishment of horses was not complete, and some one mentioned that I had a horse to part with, which it was thought might suit him. On the first day on which he appeared on parade, mounted on his new purchase, the horse behaved very well for a time. But on our forming square, and Sir John Colborne, who was on the outside, giving the word of command, "Prepare to receive cavalry," the horse bolted, and carried him off the common, and down the hill to his quarters a mile and a half away; and we saw no more of him till the next morning. His right arm had been disabled at Ciudad Rodrigo, and he had consequently no proper command of the horse.

About the middle of August we marched to Valenciennes, and encamped on the glacis and in the ditch; one officer per company having to remain in camp, and the others being quartered in the town. In October the 52nd marched into the citadel. On the 23rd of October the army was reviewed by the Emperor of Russia, the King of Prussia, and their chief commanders, and I was left on guard in the hornwork of the citadel, with some thirty or forty men, for eight-and-forty hours. I think there were no other troops in the town; I had some particular orders, but I forget now what they were, but no one was likely to endeavour to gain possession of a fortress, which, in less than a month, was to be handed over to the French. After the review the 52nd returned to the citadel, and held possession of it till the rest of the British army had embarked.

The following came out in general orders, just as the army was breaking up :—

"Cambrai, 10th November, 1818.

"Upon the return to England of the troops which have so "long served under the command of the Field-Marshal, he again "returns his thanks for their uniform good conduct, during the "period in which they have formed part of the army of "occupation.

"The Field-Marshal has in another order, addressed to the "army of occupation at large, expressed his sentiments regarding "the conduct of, and his obligation to, the general-officers and "officers of that army. These are especially due to the general-"officers and officers of the British contingent, and he begs them "to accept of his best acknowledgments, for the example they "have given to others, by their own good conduct, and for the "support and assistance they have invariably afforded him, to "maintain the discipline of the army.

"After a service of ten years' duration, almost without "interruption, with the same officers and troops, the Field-"Marshal separates from them with regret; but he trusts that "they will believe that he will never cease to feel a concern for "their honour and interest."

I think it desirable to insert here what the Duke said of the British army when leaving Spain and France in 1814. It is extracted from his evidence given before the royal commission for inquiring into military punishments:—"I always thought "I could have gone anywhere, or done anything with that "army. It was impossible to have a machine more highly "mounted and in better order, and in a better state of discipline "than that army was. When I quitted that army upon the "Garonne, I do not think it was possible to see anything in a "higher state of discipline; and I believe there was a total "discontinuance of all punishment."

I do not know the exact order in which the British troops were withdrawn from France, or the exact time of the embarkation of each corps at Calais. Sir Robert Arbuthnot of the Guards, who was commandant of Valenciennes, left the place some little time before we did. I went to make some report to him one morning, and found him in his shirt sleeves, very hard at work packing some wine, which he was starting for England. Two or three hundred Sappers and Miners, with the Engineer officers, were the last troops to leave us. When they had fairly started, I recollect a passing thought of loneliness passed over my mind, at the idea of the 52nd being the only English regiment left in France.

The night before the Sappers left Valenciennes, the Engineer officers dined at our mess. I was president or vice-president, and I well remember having a very long and interesting conversation with the officer on my left, about the truth of the Christian religion. I was not very capable of arguing correctly on the subject, and I now wonder how I managed at all, in attempting to combat his sceptical ideas. He was quartered in the town, and I went with him to see him safely out of the citadel and over the esplanade into the first street. I never read the last sentence but one in Acts xii, 10, without thinking of him. When we were about to separate, I said, "I wonder when we "two shall meet again?" He replied "*Perhaps* in heaven." I understood, several years afterwards, that he had accompanied Mr. Owen, of Lanark, to America.

Colonel Hall has given me the following account of our giving over the town and citadel of Valenciennes to the French civil authorities, which I think we did on the 22nd of November, 1818:—

"The authorities wished to embody some of the National "Guard to receive over the place, but Colborne would allow no "Frenchmen in arms until we had quitted it. The regiment "marched out, and halted on the glacis, leaving the main-guard "under Clerke, in the Grande Place. When the citadel had been "given over to the civil authorities, the town was also formally "surrendered. Clerke and his guard joined us on the glacis, "and we marched to Auberchicourt, a coaling village, for that "night. Some hours after we left Valenciennes, a French garrison "of the line entered the town. I forget for what reason, Clerke "returned to pass the night there. We heard from him that the "town had been illuminated on the occasion of our departure. "He remarked, either in lamps, or on a transparency, the words, "'The more we see of strangers, the more we like our own "'countrymen:' base, if only to curry favour with the new "garrison; and ungrateful, if a true sentiment. The English had "been great benefactors to Valenciennes, and we never ex- "perienced the smallest symptom of dislike from the inhabitants. "The tradesmen, I am sure, regretted us. A good woman who "kept a shop of pastry and comestibles, seemed inconsolable at "our departure. She made it known that she wished we would

"all come and take leave of her the day before we left, and
"help ourselves *gratis* to the best she had. So we did all go
"in the course of the day, and ate some little thing to please
"her, of course without offering payment. The poor woman
"was sitting with her handkerchief to her eyes all day, in the
"greatest distress. This was something more than interested
"sorrow for the loss of custom."

The mention of the main-guard in the foregoing account reminds me that shortly before our departure from Valenciennes the Emperor of Russia slept there one night. We had notice that it was his intention to do so, and that he wished that no attention should be shewn to him beyond that of placing a couple of sentries at the gate of the house in which he took up his quarters, and, to supply these sentries, a few more men were sent to join the guard some little time before the Emperor (Alexander) was expected. I commanded the main-guard that day, and determined to give him a salute, if he did not pass through the Grande Place too quickly. Although the Place was rather crowded and noisy, (I think it was about eight o'clock at night on the market day,) and he passed along the other side of it, at a distance of about fifty yards from us, we managed to turn out and salute him in time. He was travelling in an open caleche, drawn by four post horses, and had three other persons in the carriage with him, and two attendants on the seat behind. He did not at first, on account of the noise of the carriage and people, observe the salute, or hear the accompanying bugle sound; but I observed that one of the officers with him pointed out the guard to him, when he immediately acknowledged the salute in the usual foreign style, by placing the two first fingers of his right hand against the forward point of his cocked hat. Soon after the Emperor's arrival, Sir John Colborne saw General Winzingerode for a minute or two to see if the arrangement made was what was desired, and I visited the sentries as a part of my guard. The Emperor went away early, having left a small but handsome sum of money to be given to those who had been actually sentries at his house.

We made seven days' march from Valenciennes to Calais. I think it was after we had halted on the third day, that I heard

Sir John Colborne telling some one that he was just going to write to the commandant of St. Omer to request that the regiment, or a portion of it might, when it arrived in his district, be quartered within the *territoires de la place,* so as to avoid the fatigue and annoyance to the men of being taken two or three miles from the line of march to the several villages from which they would have to return the same distance the next morning. On the 26th I was ordered to go forward to see that proper arrangements had been made with respect to the quarters, and found that no orders had been given that we should be quartered within the territories, but that the old plan was adhered to, which involved much additional fatigue to the men; I therefore took upon myself to ride into St. Omer, and to see the commandant. (I could not recognize him as our fox-hunting friend.) I told him that I came on the part of the Chevalier Colborne, who, I understood, had written to him to request that he would allow the regiment, or a portion of it, to be quartered for the night within the *territoires de la place.* He said he had not received any letter from Colborne, but immediately granted the permission requested, and issued the necessary orders. When I reached the column of march, I found that one or two companies had already branched off from the main road to occupy the distant quarters intended for them; they were greatly pleased when I quickly overtook them, and thus saved them some considerable extra fatigue, and Sir John Colborne was pleased with my having taken upon myself to call on the commandant of St. Omer.

We embarked at Calais on the afternoon of the 28th of November in about thirty small sailing craft, and reached England the next morning. There are some strange mistakes about some of these points in the 52nd record: it makes us to have been only five days on the march from Valenciennes to Calais, and three nights and two days between Calais and Dover. The wind was contrary, but there was not much of it till the next morning, and the night was tolerably clear. We had about half the company in the vessel in which I was with another officer. As each vessel of the flotilla sailed independently of the others, they soon got well separated; but as we tacked about, we occasionally came near enough to some of them to give them a hail

With the help of the master's speaking-trumpet we contrived to give ourselves some considerable amusement, by keeping up a little talk with them in the following fashion. *Self:*—"What "ship is that?" *Reply:*—"The Harriet, of Ramsgate." *Self:*—"What have you on board?" *Reply:*—"Troops." *Self:*—"What troops?" *Reply:*—"Part of Captain ——'s company, of "the 52nd Light Infantry." *Self:*—"Ar'nt you ashamed of "yourselves, you lubberly set of fellows?" In the morning the breeze freshened a good deal; almost all the vessels got into Ramsgate; two were on the Goodwin sands for some hours, and the one I was in, and another, put into Dover. Thus the last portion of the army of occupation reached England on the 29th of November, 1818.

CHAPTER XIV.

1818, 1819.

THE 52ND MARCH TO CHESTER AND ARE STATIONED THERE.

Dover—Deal—Ramsgate—Custom-house—Scene at Canterbury—Start for Sheerness—Short visit to friends—Sir John Moore's mother—Various incidents—Balls—Races—Hunting—The Bishop and Archdeacon—Special assize—Lord Lyndhurst commandant of the garrison—Fire, and amusing incident—52nd ball given to the town and county—Several incidents—Visit to Bold Hall—Obtain leave to go to Germany—Proceed to Plymouth—Ball at General Brown's—Sail in Myrmidon to Spithead—Bishop Crowther rescued from slavery by Myrmidon—Incidents connected with his deliverance.

ACCORDING to my arrangement, I found letters in the post office at Dover from my brother, and found that his ship, the Alert, was to be in the downs that day from Sheerness, so leaving my men to proceed to Canterbury the next morning under the command of the other officer, I posted off to Deal, where I could hear no tidings of the Alert, but, I afterwards learnt that my brother had sent a boat on shore that evening, on his arrival, to enquire for me; I therefore proceeded to Ramsgate, where my baggage and my horse were landed, and where I found the rest of the regiment. Either that night or the next morning, I discovered, that, in the absence of my keys, the custom-house officers had broken open my trunks and chests to see if they contained any contraband articles. It was somewhat curious, that I had brought, from Valenciennes, a tolerable quantity of handkerchiefs and other things intended for my friends, which I meant to pay for, and which the custom-house officers had overlooked. Under the circumstances, the matter certainly does not

weigh so heavily on my conscience as to lead me to offer to
repay to the revenue what it lost by the transaction. As my locks
were injured, it is possible that *I* may have been the loser by it.
It would have been but a proper compliment to their victorious
troops on their return from France, if an order had been sent
down by the government to let all their baggage be landed,
without being subjected to the, at all times, unpleasant ordeal
of undergoing an examination. But what we looked upon as a
real grievance, and as a very shabby transaction, was the requiring the officers of the army of occupation, who were paid and
provisioned by the French government, to pay ten per cent.
income-tax on the amount of their pay. I suspect it did not
find its way back to the coffers of the French treasury.

We marched the next morning to Canterbury. Some of
the officers had relatives there, and the regiment had been
frequently stationed there. It was known also that it was the
last regiment to arrive from the army of occupation in France,
and there was consequently an unusual scene when it halted in
the main street. It appeared as if all the principal families of
that ancient city had assembled to greet its arrival. It certainly
was a very pleasing scene and "a proud moment." I had
obtained leave from Sir John Colborne to proceed to Sheerness
to look after my brother; as I proceeded, I found the road in
one place so exceedingly muddy that I turned my horse on to
the footpath for a short distance, and came in for a greeting
and a specimen of English manners and civility which stood in
rather unfavourable contrast with the scene which I had just
before witnessed at *Canterbury*. A young fellow, of about my
own age, who might have been the son of a farmer, or of rather
a lower grade, was a few yards before me, with a gun in his
hand, and I suppose thinking that my riding on the footpath
was an undue interference with his liberty and rights as an
Englishman, had the hardihood to tell me, that if I did not get
off the footpath he should take my horse off for me. Mine was
almost a case of necessity; but, however that might be, and as
I was not in his way at all, I was not going to let him take the
law into his own hands. After telling him that he had better
not attempt to put his threat into execution, I attacked him

about his carrying a gun without a qualification, and it was curious to observe how the consciousness that he was doing an illegal thing completely silenced him.

A few miles from Canterbury, I met two sailors, who had come from Sheerness that morning, and who told me the Alert had sailed for *Portsmouth*. I immediately determined to go to my home, near Portsmouth, and got on as fast as I could to Sittingbourne in the hope of falling in with some coach to London, which would be in time for the Portsmouth mail. I left my horse at Sittingbourne, at which place a detachment of the 52nd was to halt the next day, and left a note for one of the officers to take the horse on, and proceeded in a post-chaise to overtake a coach which had started only a very short time before I arrived. I overtook it, I think, at Rochester, and reached London, and the Angel at the back of St. Clements, in very good time for the Portsmouth mail. I reached Horndean very early in the morning, and slept there for a few hours, and got home about ten o'clock, to the great delight of the whole party, who had not the least expectation of seeing me. It does not now appear to be more than four or five years ago, but five-and-forty years have passed since then. I recollect very well that as I went up to the drawing-room, I purposely let my sword dangle against the stairs, rather to astonish whoever might be there. I heard them rush to the door, one of them saying, "If it should be William." That was one of the truly happy days of my life. There was no Alert at Portsmouth. It was a mistake of the sailors. After spending a clear day or two at home, and seeing several of my old friends in the neighbourhood, I returned to London, and from thence in a day or two went to Uxbridge, where the regiment had orders to remain for about a week. At this time I went with some valued relations, who were as fond of the 52nd as I was, (they being also near relatives of Sir John Colborne,) to call on Mrs. and Miss Moore, the aged mother and sister of that great and gallant commander, Sir John Moore, who was killed at Corunna, in 1809, and who had been colonel of the 52nd, and had introduced into it and into the 43rd and the old 95th Rifles (now the Rifle Brigade) that system of drill, &c., which helped to make them such splendid and efficient regiments, when with two battalions of Portuguese caçadores they formed the famous light division in the Peninsula. Mrs. Moore, whom I had before seen when I was starting for Flanders in 1815, asked me, "Where the 52nd were now?" when I told her that the last detachment of them had marched through London that morning on their way to Uxbridge, she said, she should have liked to have seen them, adding " I would go some distance to see the 52nd."

During the time the 52nd were at Uxbridge, I had permission to be at Hillingdon with some kind friends and connexions, Dr. Hodgson, the Dean of Carlisle, and his family. I recollect on my arrival, the Dean and Mrs. Hodgson were at a dinner party and had desired their two pretty little daughters to entertain me, if I should arrive that evening. When eight o'clock arrived, the elder one, who was nearly fourteen, said to her sister who was a year younger; " I think, Mary, as it is "eight o'clock you had better go to bed," which she accordingly did. Their mother told me that the next morning, in relating what had passed, one of them observed, " He talked so sensibly, just "like you, mamma."

It had been intended that the 52nd, on its return from France, should be stationed at Plymouth, but their destination was altered, and they were sent, the head-quarters and five companies to Chester, three companies to Liverpool, one to Warrington, and one to the Isle of Man. We enjoyed the march from Uxbridge to Chester very much. One way in which some of us at times beguiled the weariness of the march was by getting into the fields and taking in succession every fence which ran at right angles from the line of march; these were generally taken, as in hunting, at a gallop, and of course without knowing what kind of a landing there was on the other side; consequently now and then we came down, horse and all, but usually recovered ourselves without parting company from our horses. It was a great amusement to the men, and helped them to look upon our marches as anything but tedious. Then the enlivening and martial airs played alternately by the band, and our corps of more than thirty buglers, as we passed through the various towns on our route, of course brought the whole population, male and female, either into the streets or to their doors and windows, and we were not a little proud of ourselves and of our fine 52nd fellows, the vast majority of whom were decorated with the medal, which was the first which had ever been given to a British soldier. We passed through Aylesbury, Coventry, where we saw peeping Tom, and Birmingham, where thousands thronged us as we marched away, so that we could hardly get along, and every soldier seemed to have some dear friend who pressed into the ranks to try and get the last shake of the hand. I think it was at Wellington beyond Shiffnall, or at a village full of colliers, called Oakenwood Gates, that I was billetted by myself for the Saturday and Sunday with the whole or a portion of Captain McNair's company, and the daughter of the landlord, on being requested to supply me with some books, brought me a volume of Mrs. Opie's tales, in which I found the story of "White Lies," which I was much pleased with. It called my attention to an important point which I had never thought of before.

We arrived at Chester about the 20th of December, and were very much pleased with our quarters, the only quarter I ever was in in England. We met with great attention and kindness from the various families of the town and neighbourhood. The men and two officers were in the barracks in the castle, the other officers in lodgings in the town. Our mess-room was in the castle on a rock looking over the city walls underneath, on to the river Dee. The 20th Roman legion was stationed at Chester after the defeat of Caractacus. The old rows or galleries in front of the houses in two or three of the streets, and which serve as covered footpaths, are supposed by some to be of Roman origin. Here the 52nd remained for more than six months. I should think it could not have been surpassed, as an agreeable quarter, by any other place in England or elsewhere. Our walks on the Rhoodee and along the bank of the Dee, on the walls, which are nearly two miles in circumference, and in the rows, with our kind and fair Chester friends, have often been looked back to in after years with pleasure and regret. It would be bad taste to mention the families by name, though they are all well and gratefully remembered. During the races, which took place on the Rhoodee, and lasted nearly a week, the dinner engagements were two for each day at different houses. The races commenced at two; and the first dinner was at one, and the second at seven. It was the gayest time of the year at Chester. There were also balls and other amusements. Some of us hunted occasionally. I well recollect the first time we went out with the Cheshire hounds; I enquired who were the most forward riders, and some of my acquaintance pointed out two persons, one of them on a white horse, as those who would shew the way to the whole field. Being well mounted, I determined to keep my eye on them. The country was what was called a stiff one. Directly the fox and hounds had got away I was much pleased at seeing at least a dozen fellows, of whom I was one, take the first fence together at a gallop. They took no more fences *together*. My friend on the white horse soared rather ahead, and took his fences at a first-rate pace and in first-rate style. After we had gone about a quarter of a mile, I gave him the go-by, and maintained my position afterwards. I recollect a curious scene, in the course of our nine miles' run, which occurred amongst some inundations, occasioned by the overflowing of a brook. The two or three first horses got through the brook very well, it was impossible to leap it; but the opposite bank, which was somewhat steep and only passable in two or three places, became very slippery after the first few had passed, and as I trotted on to take a low fence with the water on both sides of it, I looked back and counted seventeen of our friends some on and some off their horses in the brook. The horses had slipped and fallen back from the slippery bank. The next time I went out with the hounds, I found nearly the whole field reconnoitred and admired my horse: she had been bought in France from an officer of the 12th Light Dragoons, and was up to any pace or any practicable fence. The last time I ever hunted, in taking a severe fence and ditch out of a wood on to lower ground, she met with an over-reach, which laid her up for many weeks.

When the 52nd were ordered to Chester, one of my relatives wrote to the good Bishop to request him to shew me some attention; but immediately after our arrival he experienced a severe domestic affliction, and shortly he went away, and did not return whilst I remained there. He deputed one of the dignitaries of the church to call upon me, and to express his sorrow that he could not see me himself. Something led me on one occasion to ask this gentleman if he ever played at whist, and if he would come to my lodgings on a certain evening and play a rubber with some of my brother officers. This he assented to, and came accordingly. We always dined very late, and we never thought of tea afterwards; so that, strange as it may appear, it did not cross my mind that our friend had come to *drink tea* with us, until quite late he very modestly inquired if he "might ask for a glass of water." Frequently in after years was I told by my brother-officers of my inhospitable behaviour to the kind Archdeacon.

Whilst we were at Chester, Lord Lyndhurst, then Sir John Copley, came there to hold a special assize for the trial of some prisoners accused of high treason. The custom then with regard to the military was that they should not be removed during the assizes, but that the Judge should be considered as the commandant of the garrison, and the officer on duty should receive the watchword and countersign from him. Accordingly on the first day, when the court had adjourned, I proceeded to his lodgings and explained to him the custom, at which he seemed amused, and gave me two of the Peninsula battles, I think Vimiero and Busaco, as the watchword and countersign.

One night there was an alarm given that the Dee mills were on fire. They were very extensive and lofty mills, which were the property of a gentleman in the town. The progress of the fire could not be arrested, and they were burnt down. I worked hard in various ways, as I usually did on such occasions, and had a most narrow escape of being run over by one of the engines, which the people were moving without being aware that I was just in front of it, and unable to extricate myself from my position. It was one of my most narrow escapes, as the engine touched me when it was stopped. It was considered necessary to convey the hose of the engine across the stream, which was then running out with great rapidity. I undertook to do this, but had not proceeded two yards, when to my astonishment I was swept off my legs, and four or five of our men, who made a dash to lay hold of me, were also swept down. We were, however, all brought to the bank, without receiving any injury. During the progress of the fire, the following somewhat ludicrous occurrence took place. A servant in livery came up to me and addressing me somewhat in the heroic style, said, "I have "mentioned your conduct, Mr. Leeke, to the Miss ——s, (ladies "to whose family the buildings belonged,) and they desired me "to present their compliments, and to thank you, and to beg you, "to continue your exertions." It was my turn for duty of that sort, therefore I had to take charge of the guard which was necessary to keep the crowds of people from going near the dangerous ruins. At my request, however, the adjutant remained in charge himself, whilst I went to change my wet clothes. I recollect the master of the house, in which my lodgings were, begged me not to delay for a moment changing my things; he told me that on a similar occasion, some months before, he had got very wet, and had neglected himself, and was then in a hopeless state of consumption.

In return for all the civilities and kindness we had received from the gentry of the city and county of Chester, we determined to invite them to a grand ball and supper. I had the chief arrangement and management of it, and it was said that it gave universal satisfaction. I came across the bill of costs very lately, amongst some old papers. I recollect two or three incidents connected with this ball. We read a long and flaming account of it in a Chester paper before we left the room, in which I was described as the *Hon.* Mr. L. On proceeding to leave the hotel, we found a gentleman lying very drunk on the floor of the entrance hall; the hotel people knew nothing of him, and said that he had not secured any bed there. My impression is that he had not been at our ball, but that he was in hunting costume. Although he was quite a stranger to all of us, we did not like to leave him. On arousing him, we could just make out that he had a lodging in some other street in the town : so we got him out, and found that with some help he could manage to walk. He pointed out the direction in which the street was, and we asked him, when we came to the first turn, if that was it, and on his saying it was not, we went on to the next street, which he thought was the right one, so we took him along it, although it seemed quite hopeless that we should discover the lodging. At last, in a window at the top of one house, we saw a light, and rapping loudly, inquired of a woman, who put her head out of the window, if a gentleman was expected who had taken a lodging there: she replied in the affirmative, and told us to open the door, which was not fastened, and how to find a light and the room. On getting him into the room he objected strongly, and for some time, to get into bed; when asked his reason, he refused to tell us. At last I proposed that he should whisper it to me, which he consented to do, and the poor fellow said he "could not "go to bed without saying his prayers." We persuaded him at last to go to bed, and then we left him, though we were not at all assured that he was the person for whom the bed was intended, the woman of the house not having taken the trouble to ascertain the fact.

One Sunday afternoon, towards the close of my stay at Chester, I rode out a short distance into the country, and seeing a gate rather sloping, so as to make it not a high leap, I put my horse, a new one, at it; he managed the leap very clumsily, and came down on the other side, falling on my leg, without, however, hurting me in the least. I had no religious feeling at that time, but as I rode back to Chester, I remember that I thought it was a judgment, and a warning to me that I should not so profane the Sabbath day.

On one occasion four of us accepted an invitation to go to Bold Hall, in Lancashire, where we spent one or two clear days very pleasantly, and made the acquaintance of the pleasing daughters of the house, the eldest of whom, who was heiress to the immense property of her father, afterwards married Prince Saphie, and did not long survive her marriage. The second married Sir Henry Houghton. I sat next to the eldest daughter at dinner, and in the course of conversation on the subject of engagements, she made the following very true remark:—That she thought young persons with very large fortunes were very much to be pitied, on two grounds—the first, that men paid them attention, and made offers of marriage to them, who were not really attached to them, and only sought them for the sake of their money—the second, that they themselves were very liable to miss the opportunities of becoming better acquainted with men who might be very suitable husbands for them, and who might have shewn them some attention, from the fear or suspicion that these men also were attracted by their money, and not by a personal regard for themselves. I find it very difficult, in writing my various recollections of bygone days, to adhere to my determination to avoid all such subjects as the above, and the mention of anything which, by any possibility, may occasion annoyance to any one. I have reason, however, to believe that the relation of the above conversation cannot now give the least pain to any person.

I had here committed to paper the relation of a circumstance which I thought might be both useful and amusing, but, just on the point of printing it, I think it better to withdraw the anecdote, and merely to give the useful portion of it, by stating that I have *often* observed that many people do not seem to be aware that, by the light of a fire, or a candle by night, or from the morning sun shining strongly into their rooms, they can sometimes be seen into very clearly, even from a distance of fifty or sixty yards or more.

Some little time before the regiment left Chester, I thought one evening, as I was hastily preparing for mess, that I was leading a very idle life; and I began to consider what I could do, in the shape of setting to work, to improve myself; and I decided, certainly in less than ten minutes, that I would try and get leave of absence to proceed to Germany, for the purpose of learning German. At mess I happened to sit next to the commanding officer, Sir John Tylden, and told him what I had been thinking of:—he replied, "and a very good thing too, I will "apply for leave for you at once, if you like." This I assented to, and in less than a week I received six months' leave. Another officer, a nobleman, for whom application was made at the same time for leave to go and see his friends, was refused his leave. The authorities, it appeared from this, were desirous of encouraging officers to acquire a knowledge of foreign languages. I was very sorry to leave Chester.

My brother was fitting out the Myrmidon at Plymouth, so I

went there to take leave of him. I went with him to call on General Brown, who commanded that district; on our way we came across the 85th Light Infantry, one of the finest body of men I ever saw; they were advancing in line, which movement they made exceedingly well, even in my eyes, who had seen such wonderful advances in line, even over broken ground, by the 52nd. General Brown enquired about my regiment, saying that he had never seen a regiment move so well as the 85th, but that he was told they were not equal to the 52nd. He then asked me what I thought about it, and I replied that I could not say anything about the relative merits of the regiments with regard to their movements, but that I believed the 52nd were in as high a state of efficiency at that moment as they had ever been in. Some of General Brown's family asked me why the 52nd had not come to Plymouth, as was at first intended, and said that they understood Colonel C. Rowan had got our destination changed. There was an amusing story which had been told to us first by Lord Seaton. It was this: that there was some grass not very far from the Government-house, and the orders of one of the sentries were, that nothing was to be allowed to go on it, except the general's cow. One day Lady Thornborough, the port admiral's wife, who was walking there, got on to the turf, and was immediately ordered off by the sentry, who, on her remonstrating with him, was very peremptory in carrying out his orders. At last Lady Thornborough said, "Do you know who I am?" When he answered, "No, but I know you are not General Brown's cow." She went into General Brown's directly, and was delighted to tell them the story.

During my short stay at Plymouth, we went to Puslinch, and met Lord and Lady Seaton there; and we went also with a large party to Soltrum to a picnic. I dined at the mess of the 85th, and was particularly pleased with two men there, one of whom was Vandeleur; the names of all the other officers I forget. We had a ball on board the Myrmidon, and, immediately after, another, which the Browns gave more particularly on our account; at four in the morning we went from the ball on board the Myrmidon, sailed immediately for Portsmouth, and, after a pleasant run, anchored at Spithead, at twelve at night.

The Myrmidon shortly after sailed for the coast of Africa, where she was stationed for three years, and did some good service there, for which my brother obtained the honour of knighthood. The Myrmidon took and destroyed numbers of slave vessels, and, on one occasion, when in company with the Iphigenia, took the vessel in which Samuel Crowther was. He was then a boy of twelve years of age. He was transferred to the Myrmidon, and remained in that ship for some weeks. He is now Bishop of the Niger.

I have twice met this truly good and sensible man—once several years ago—and more recently, just as he was about to be consecrated as Bishop of the Niger. He gave me the whole account of the village in which he lived being attacked, of his father being killed in resisting the attack, and of his mother and her children being sold into slavery. He was on his way in a slave-ship to the West Indies, when the Myrmidon and the Iphigenia fell in with the ship. He told me how frightened he was at the serjeant of marines, who was pacing the deck of the slaver, as the slaves were being transferred to the British ships; for the Spanish slave-dealers had told them how cruel the English were, and that they were in the habit of killing the slaves, and dyeing their soldiers' jackets with their blood. He and five other boys agreed to keep back as much as they could, so that they might be the last to be taken on board the English man-of-war. In speaking of the serjeant, he said, "I assure you I was very "much afraid of that gentleman." These six boys were taken on board the Myrmidon, and their alarm was greatly increased as they stepped on the quarter-deck of the corvette, by seeing, as they thought, the body of one of their companions hanging in the rigging, and the heads of many of them ranged in a row all round the deck of the ship, between the guns. They were greatly relieved when they found out that what they took to be the body of a man was that of a pig, which was about to be cut up, and served out to the crew, and the supposed heads were cannon-balls painted black, and ranged round the ship on a rack. He assured me that his feelings at first were exactly as I have here described them. My lamented sister-in-law, the late Lady Leeke, made him his first clothes; whether or not she attempted to teach him anything I am not quite sure. Not very long after his release from slavery, he was taken to Sierra Leone, and placed under the care and instruction of the missionaries of that excellent society, the Church Missionary Society, and soon became one of their most promising scholars. How wonderful are the ways of God! How wonderfully has He overruled the cruel and iniquitous slave-trade for taking persons from several of the tribes of Western Africa, bringing them to Sierra Leone for instruction in the great truths of Christianity, and then returning many of them, as preachers of salvation through Christ, to the persons amongst whom they have lived, and whose language and habits they are acquainted with! After the lapse of many years Bishop Crowther's mother was restored to him again, and became a convert to Christianity. I think it was about the beginning of 1852 that my brother sent out a nice Bible, and that I sent to him a copy of Simeon's "Life." He told us afterwards that he lost both these presents when his house was burnt to the ground. My brother presented him in 1864 with another Bible, with the following inscription written in it:—" To the Right Reverend Samuel Edjai "Crowther, Bishop of the region of the Niger river, in Western "Africa, this copy of God's holy Word is presented, on the occa- "sion of his consecration as Bishop, at Canterbury, on the 29th "of June, 1864, by his friend Admiral Sir Henry John Leeke, "who, when commanding His Majesty's ship Myrmidon on the "coast of Africa in the year 1821, captured the slave vessel in "which S. E. Crowther, then a boy of about twelve years of age, "was being conveyed to the West Indies to a life of slavery. "Isaiah lv; Acts xx, 28; John xxi, 15—17."

CHAPTER XV.

1819, 1820.

GERMANY, ENGLAND, PARIS, NICE.

Calais to Brussels—Murder of English gentlemen—How discovered—Tradition about the fight at Cheriton in the time of Charles I.—Visit the field of Waterloo—Corn rank where we defeated the Imperial Guard—The Rhine—Ehrenbreitstein, beautiful scenery—University of Gottingen—Curious funeral ceremonies—Hanover—The Jäger Guards—Colonel Reynett—Leave Hanover for Bottrum—Arrangements for learning German—Alarming illness—Religious feeling—Return to Hanover—Difficulty in speaking English properly—Advised to return to England—Paper written on my 22nd birthday—Ludicrous difficulty at Yarmouth—Thames frozen over—Anecdote connected with the loss of the Royal George—Unpleasant occurrence at races—Think of going on half pay—Kind remonstrance from the regiment—Proceed to Nice—Bonaparte at Frejus in 1814—Religious friends, &c.—Adventure with a mosquito—The climate of the south of France and Italy.

I EMBARKED at Dover and arrived at Calais, on my way into Germany, on the 19th of July, 1819. A journal which I commenced at that time states that I "met in the packet Mr. Rogers, Beauclerc, and a Frenchman, a very entertaining fellow, who was quite in raptures about England," and that I "dined with them at Quillac's, and went to the play, and very stupid it was. My friend, the Frenchman, insisted on my breakfasting with him in the morning." I have not now the least idea of who these agreeable fellows were. The next morning I started in the *diligence*, by way of Dunkirk, Lille, and Tournay, for Brussels, which place I reached only on the third day. It is by that route sixty leagues from Calais.

Between Calais and Dunkirk the following tragedy occurred, not many miles from the former place. It is thus stated in Burke's "Peerage and Baronetage," in the pedigree of the Sebrights:—" Edward, second son of the third baronet, was "murdered in 1723, near Calais, as he was travelling with some " English gentlemen. A monument to his memory was erected " on the spot where the foul deed was committed." My mother, several times in former years, mentioned this murder to me, and stated that Mr. Locke, a relative of her grandfather, who was a Locke, (they both were from the same stem as John Locke, who wrote on the human understanding,) was the only friend who was with Mr. Sebright at the time. They were murdered by the innkeeper and his son, belonging to the inn at which they had been staying at Calais. Mr. Locke was alive when he was found with his throat cut, but life was instantly destroyed by a woman pouring brandy into the wound. The murderers were discovered about six months afterwards, when the innkeeper sent some of the linen to the same washerwoman, who observed that "she "had seen none so fine, since she washed that of the English "gentlemen, who were murdered." My mother had this account from her mother, who was a Locke, and was born two or three years after the murder.

The above tradition is not very striking as regards the time which has elapsed since the event took place. The following, however, which has come down to us, through the same family, is remarkable. My mother told me that her aunt, Miss Locke, whom I also recollect very well, stated to her that her grandmother told her, that when she was a girl, she stood at a certain gate, on or near a farm now belonging to my brother, Admiral Sir Henry Leeke, and saw the fight at Cheriton, between three and four miles off, in the time of Charles I.

At Lille I went to see the citadel, into which I was allowed to pass without interruption. The esplanade is pretty, as is also its bridge. Left Lille at four o'clock in the morning, breakfasted at Tournay, and a little way from it saw the ground on which the Battle of Fontenoy was fought. Passed through Ath, Enghien, and Hal, and arrived at the Hotel d'Angleterre, at Brussels, at eight in the evening.

On the 24th of July I went from Brussels to visit the field of Waterloo, and went over a great deal of the same ground which the 52nd had gone over four years before. Numbers had been buried where we remained so long in squares, and where we were charged by the French cavalry. But many hundreds had been buried more towards La Haye Sainte, about three hundred yards below the British position, where the 52nd had defeated the French Imperial Guard. The corn was rank and nearly rotten in these places. The people said the soil was still too rich. I dined at La Belle Alliance on bread and cheese, and returned to Brussels in time to start that evening for Aix La Chapelle, which I reached the next day. In the evening I went to the *maison de jeu*, or salon, where all the gentry of the place seemed to have assembled. There, for the last time, I risked and lost a few napoleons at roulette, or rouge-et-noir.

On the 26th I started for Cologne, and the next day went up the left bank of the Rhine to Coblentz. On the 28th I started for Hesse Cassel, in a *chaise de poste* with a merchant of Brunswick, passing over the Rhine on a bridge of boats to Ehrenbreitstein, a fortress on the opposite height. Between this place and Limburg the scenery was most beautiful; scores of wooded hills shewing their summits in front, and to the right and left, as far as the eye could reach. We forded the river Lahn twice, and passed through Weisbourg, Wetzlar, and Giessen, all in the duchy of Nassau. The travelling was exceedingly slow; the postillion, I think, did not once touch the horses with his whip; and consequently they might well look fat and sleek. He appeared very fond of them. He played nicely on his horn several times, especially as the horses trotted quickly up the paved streets of Cassel, after midnight, when he thought it desirable that the inhabitants should be aroused from their slumbers to learn the important fact, that travellers of distinction had come amongst them. On the evening of the 30th I arrived at the University of Gottingen, where I proposed to take up my residence for some time. I find the following entry made in my journal:—" Arrived at Gottingen at seven o'clock. All anxiety to know how I am to get on. Speak scarcely a word of German and don't know a soul. Dined (or rather supped) at the table d'hote, and never opened my lips except to ask for bread." The next day I dined at the table d'hote at one o'clock, and met several Hanoverian officers and four young Englishmen, three of whom were in the army. I find I forthwith applied myself with much diligence to the study of German, taking two lessons a day, of an hour each, and working hard at it also by myself, but the being acquainted with so many Englishmen, and with Hanoverians who spoke English very fluently, was a great hindrance to me; I therefore soon began to make enquiries about some respectable German family into which I could be received, and who would be able to assist me in learning their language. I soon heard of a clergyman's family, living in a village between Bremen and Hamburg, who would be willing to receive me; and, after remaining altogether a month at Gottingen, I started for Hanover, which had been my original destination. I had been informed that purer German was spoken in the kingdoms of Hanover and Saxony than in any other part of Germany.

Whilst I was at Gottingen I saw two funerals. At one of them, from a house opposite to my lodging, the coffin was brought out by twelve men, in plain blue dresses, Hessian boots, and cocked hats with crape streamers, and was placed on a low car, about nine or ten feet long and six broad, drawn by four horses and covered with black cloth. The coffin was not made to the shape of the body, but was three feet high, and appeared to shut down like a trunk. The postillions walked by the side of their horses, and a woman, who seemed to be the mistress of the ceremonies, went in front, and the twelve men, headed by a sort of commanding officer with a sword, followed the car, the procession moving as slowly as possible. On another occasion I attended the funeral of a rich merchant, who was followed to the grave by about forty or fifty of the principal people of the town, some on foot, some in miserable carriages. The grave was about eight feet deep. There was no funeral service, but when the coffin was in the grave, all the people said a short prayer in their hats; and then, looking into the grave, each said "guten "morgen," after which they went away.

Professor Blumenbach had a large collection of the sculls of all nations, which I went to see. He told me he wanted very much to get the scull of a Scotchman. There were between thirty and forty professors at Gottingen, who gave lectures which the students might attend on paying a moderate fee. Herr Blumenbach gave lectures on natural history, comparative anatomy, and physiology.

Some of our English friends got into a scrape for painting some of the doors white, and kicking up a row, and were imprisoned by the authorities for two nights and a day; rooms, however, were fitted up for them on the occasion. The day before I left Hanover, I met at dinner the *grand maitre des forets*, who offered me as much shooting as I pleased. I left Gottingen in the evening of the 29th of August, after taking coffee with many of my friends, who again met me at the post-house. When I had proceeded some miles, I was exceedingly annoyed to find that I had omitted to pay my small account at the hotel, where they had the table d'hote, amounting, perhaps, to half a louis. However, when we changed horses, I went to the post-office, and, by the postmaster's advice, sent a louis in a letter to one of my English friends, requesting him to pay my debt. As the Germans are generally honest fellows, I trust the money reached him, though I never heard from him about it. The journey from Gottingen to Hanover in one of the public conveyances was not performed in those days under one-and-twenty hours, so that we only made good three English miles an hour.

At Hanover I found Colonel Reynett, of the 52nd, who was on the Duke of Cambridge's staff. Colonel Rowan had written to him about me. He was exceedingly kind, and had arranged, if I remained at Hanover, that I should mess with the officers of the Jäger Guards, but as they had many of them served with the English army, and could speak English, he agreed with me, that I was not so likely to improve so much in German amongst them, as I should be if I followed out the before-mentioned plan. He shewed me over the Duke of Cambridge's house, and offered to take charge of my letters, which were to be directed to him at Cambridge house, London, and must be there on "Tuesdays and "Fridays." I saw the king's stables, with about two hundred horses; there were thirty away with the Duke of Cambridge, and about two hundred mares and colts in the country. There were eight cream-coloured horses, and six white ones. I made an arrangement with the bugle-major of the Jäger Guards to write out for me about two hundred bugle tunes, such as he felt tolerably sure the 52nd could not have. These he was to send to England, and I paid him, I think, ten louis for them. Colonel Charles Rowan wrote afterwards to thank me for my handsome present to the regiment. I also received a letter to the same effect, in French, from Kirwan Hill of the 52nd.*

I left Hanover for Sottrum, between Bremen and Hamburg, on the first of September, at half-past four in the morning, and, passing through Nieustadt, reached Hoya about eight at night. As there was a ball at the principal inn, and I could not secure a bed, I determined to go on to Verden, which place I reached about twelve o'clock. This proceeding from Hoya to sleep at Verden that night had, as will presently appear, a most remarkable influence on the whole of my future course of life. The night was bitterly cold, and I had foolishly not brought a great coat with me, and on arriving at Verden the people of the inn had all retired to rest. There was no fire, and, regularly chilled through as I was, I had nothing left for it but to turn into a cold bed, in which I slept soundly for several hours. When, however, I awoke in the morning I was surprised to find that my legs and feet were as wretchedly cold as they were when I went to bed. I did not think much about it, and having got my breakfast I felt as well as usual. I had a letter for General Victor Alten, who lived at Verden, from his son, but, as he was from home, I proceeded at once to Sottrum, which was about fifteen English miles off. Here I met with a kind welcome from the clergyman, Herr Büttner, and his mother and sisters, and also from a Hanoverian Waterloo officer who was staying with them, by the name of Schleppegrell. They were a very happy party, though they often spoke of a severe affliction which had befallen them some years before, when Bonaparte had taken possession of the kingdom of Hanover, and their two brothers had been taken from their home as conscripts. One perished in the retreat from Moscow; what became of the other they had never known.

* See Appendix No. 6.

The terms for board and lodging and instruction were soon arranged; they were most moderate. The whole party helped to teach me their language, so that I had the benefit of reading or conversing with one or another of them, during the greater part of the day. Even when we walked out our chief business was attended to, and my German and English dictionary accompanied us. French was now and then spoken by us, in order to explain a German word or sentence, but very seldom for any other purpose. English was almost entirely banished from our conversation, although they knew a little of it. In this way I of course made rapid progress, both in understanding and speaking German.

When I had been at Sottrum a fortnight, I went with some of the family to Bremen, distant about twenty-five miles. It is a neat, pleasant place, with beautiful walks. We visited the Bley Keller or Lead Cellar, the atmosphere of which has the peculiar property of preserving from decay the human and other bodies which are placed in it. We saw there the body of a Countess Stanhope, who died at Bremen about the year 1565, and also the bodies of Count Brake and his aide-de-camp, who were killed in the thirty years' war. Bremen is on the Weser, and contained at that time 40,000 inhabitants. We saw Madame Reichard ascend in a balloon. We were from eight in the evening till half-past two in the morning in getting back to Sottrum. It was a cold night, and I was on the box. When we stopped at the inn to give the horses some hay and water, I took a wine glass full of brandy "to keep the cold out." As we pursued our journey, I found that I had constantly to clear my throat and mouth, but when I reached Sottrum I found, to my dismay, that I was coughing up a quantity of blood. No doubt my exposure on the journey, and my cold sleep at Verden, a fortnight before, had laid the foundation for this; and the exposure on the road from Bremen, together with the strong stimulant, which I was not at all accustomed to take, brought matters to a climax. I was alarmed at first, but as I did not feel ill, and as the blood very much decreased in quantity, I remained quietly at Sottrum, and pursued my studies. About a year afterwards it was clearly ascertained that the blood proceeded from the throat, and not from the lungs as I at first feared.

I had been confirmed and had received the sacrament when I was about fifteen or sixteen, and, at the time, felt very serious; but the impression soon passed away, and when I went to Sottrum I had for years been very careless, negligent, and ignorant about religion. It was at this time that I recollect forming some very strong resolutions, that I would make a determined effort to serve God in everything, and give up whatever I might discover to be wrong in His sight. I remained very ignorant about real religion for nearly a year after this. Still I believe I was sincerely desiring to do what was right. I have a clear recollection that in one of the few walks, which I took by myself during my stay at Sottrum, I went to the "Fir Wood," as they called it, and that all at once the question presented itself to me: —Is it right that a person, who wishes to honour God and to benefit his fellow-creatures, should follow the profession of a soldier, whose chief employment, when he is actively engaged, is to take away, or help to take away, the lives of his fellow-men? This idea had never crossed my mind before, and it startled me exceedingly, for I was devotedly attached to my regiment, and to a soldier's life, and I thought I would more willingly part with my right arm than leave the army; yet I determined that I would endeavour to examine the matter thoroughly, and if I found that I could not conscientiously remain in the army I would at once leave it. I, however, soon convinced myself, by a very short process of reasoning, that it was right for a nation to have an army for its own defence, and for the defence of a weak ally; otherwise it might soon be overrun, and be oppressed by even a very small number of its neighbours; and that sometimes the best mode of defence would be to carry the war into the enemy's country. I have merely gone into this matter in order to shew that here was a decided intention to give up what was wrong and to do what was right.

I remained with my kind friends at Sottrum nearly two months and a half, when, finding that my health was not in a satisfactory state, I thought it better to go to Hanover to consult the principal physician there. I left Sottrum with great regret, on the 12th of November. A curious fact was, that on reaching Hanover and going to see Colonel Reynett, I found that for some little time I could not speak English properly. I had been talking nothing but German for so long a time, that when first I began to speak in English, I found myself disposed to construct many of the sentences as I should have done in German. On going to consult the court physician, (I forget his name, but he was a most kind old man,) I found him sitting with his pipe in a regular cloud of smoke. After hearing what I had to say, and after my pressing him to let me know if he thought I was likely to recover, all I could get out of him was, that I had better return at once to my friends in England. I left Hanover for Cuxhaven at the mouth of the Elbe about the 22nd of December. I think the packet was detained two or three days by contrary winds; and these days I passed very wretchedly, as will appear from the following note which was written at that time, and which, as I am writing, I have just taken from an old writing-desk. On the outside are written the following words:—

"To be opened on the 27th of November, 1820."

It is dated, "Ritzebüttel near Cuxhaven, 27th of November, 1819.

"My birth-day, 22 years old, here in this *blessed* [meaning
" *miserable*] place, waiting to go to England, with *terrible* pains
" in the breast, and difficulty of breathing. Convinced that my
" lungs are dangerously affected, I have little hope of reaching
" my 23rd birthday. This, however, is to be opened on the 27th
" of November, 1820. If I do not open it myself, some of my
" dear friends will do so. God bless them. Time will shew how
" things are to turn out. W. L."

The following memorandum is written on the same paper:—

"Read this forty years afterwards, November 27th, 1859,
" having by God's mercy been so long spared, and having a
" humble expectation that, through the blood of Jesus, I shall,
" whenever I am taken hence, go to be with Him in glory.
" When, forty years ago, the first part of this was written, I
" knew nothing aright of the things belonging to my everlasting
" peace, but I had determined to try and do right at all cost;
" having been much struck at Sottrum with a paper, I think in
" 'The Idler' or 'The Rambler,'* beginning about some one

* It is in the 2nd volume of "The Rambler," No. 65, and is well suited, by God's blessing, to arrest the attention of any careless young man.

"having left the caravansary early in the morning, and forsaking the "main road for a flowery path, &c. God bless my dear wife and "nine children. WM. LEEKE."

My journal closes as follows:—"Left Hanover about the 22nd, embarked at Cuxhaven on the 29th, and landed at Yarmouth on the 1st of December, 1819, very ill."

I made up my mind, before landing at Yarmouth, that I was too ill to proceed to London in the coach, and that I would post it; but on looking at the money which I had left, I found that I had not sufficient for my purpose. This led to a series of ludicrous adventures, which were very annoying to me at the time. As we were in the boat between the packet and the shore, I mentioned my difficulty to the captain, and said I was afraid I should have to remain at Yarmouth till I got a remittance from London. He immediately replied that he would put his name to a draft on my agents, and that I should find no difficulty in getting it cashed when we landed. I told him I was very much obliged to him, though I rather wondered, in my own mind, that he should venture thus to accommodate one whom he had only known for six-and-thirty hours. After landing, and getting my things through the Custom-house, I met my friend, the captain of the packet, in the passage of the hotel, when he said to me:— "I have been thinking, Sir, that I shall not be doing right to put "my name to your bill, for I don't know more about you than "anybody else does." This was not very pleasant, but I felt it was very natural that he should, on second thoughts, take this view of the matter. On my asking him what I could do, as I was very unwilling to be detained at Yarmouth, he said he thought the landlord of the hotel could manage the thing for me. On my speaking to the landlord he very readily undertook to give me the ten pounds I required, and said he had often accommodated gentlemen with money under similar circumstances, but that it was customary for them to leave some of their luggage as a security for the repayment of the sum advanced. This, I told him, I could do without any inconvenience, as I had one case containing articles of value, which I should not want for some little time. When I went to Germany I had been supplied with letters of introduction for some of the ambassadors, and thought it desirable to take my 52nd court dress with me, which consisted of a coat with epaulettes instead of wings, a waistcoat, breeches with silver buckles, white silk stockings, and shoes with silver buckles; there were also a cocked hat, a dress-sword, and various other articles. On my opening the case and shewing him the various things which it contained, he observed, in a very off-hand way, that he thought the whole lot of them was not worth five pounds. So I closed the case, and had no more to say to the landlord. As a last resource I went to one of the banks and stated my difficulty, and who I was, and what I wanted. Here I met with very great civility; they had no doubt about my being the gentleman I represented myself to be, but it was not at all consistent with their usual way of doing business, that they should advance money on the draft of one who was quite a stranger to them. I found that I had just money enough to pay for a postchaise, &c., for two stages on the road to London, and that by going so far I should only be detained one clear day on the road, and could easily reach town the day after. So I ordered a postchaise, having first written to Cox and Greenwood, to request them to send me a letter of credit for twenty pounds, on the banker of the town which I intended to reach that night. On my arrival, I do not think I had a single shilling left, after paying for the postchaise and driver. On the morning of the next day but one, the letter of credit arrived, and on my inquiring for the banker, I was directed to the house of, I think, a large linen draper or mercer. He read my letter of credit from Cox and Greenwood, and said it was quite correct, but that he was not a banker, but only agent for a bank at the county town, and he doubted whether he ought to cash my draft. However, on my telling him how I had been annoyed, and asking him what his bankers would say, if he refused to give me the money, he consented to let me have it.

Shortly after my arrival in London my family joined me, and we remained there for some time, that I might have the advantage of getting the best medical advice. All along I was treated for an affection of the chest, and was a good deal lowered. After a few weeks we went home; on our journey into Hampshire we saw, just as we passed out of town, that the Thames was completely frozen over. We were very well acquainted with some of the near relatives of Admiral Sir Digby Dent, and I have often heard that when he first went into the navy, I think it was in 1840, there was such a great frost, that his things were wheeled on board the guard-ship, in Portsmouth harbour, in a wheelbarrow. And this leads me to mention a singular fact connected with my family, which I think I ought to record somewhere in this work:—My grandfather, my mother's father, who was an old naval officer, lived at Fareham, in Hampshire. It is about seven miles in a direct line from Spithead, and he was in the habit of going on to the leads of his house every day, when the weather was clear, to take a look with his glass at the shipping in Portsmouth harbour and at Spithead. On looking one day at the various ships, he saw no particular change amongst them, and that the admiral's flag was flying at Spithead as usual. Before he left the top of the house he thought he would take another look at Spithead, when to his surprise and dismay, the flag ship was not to be seen. On going downstairs he observed to some of his family that he thought that something strange had happened to the ship; and in two or three hours the melancholy intelligence arrived that the Royal George had gone down at her moorings; and that Admiral Kempenfelt and eight hundred officers and men had perished.

After I returned home in January, 1820, I had a great deal of time for reading, and amongst other books, which came in my way, I was led to read Paley's "Theology," which interested me much, and paved the way for my reading his "Evidences of "Christianity," which I have no doubt was a great blessing to me, inasmuch as it overturned all my sceptical ideas, and convinced me that the Bible was the inspired Word of the Most High God. Yet, strange to say, it was not till many months afterwards, that I was led to see that it was my duty to read some portion of it daily, with prayer that I might become acquainted with the will of God, and endeavour to have my conduct conformed to it. At this time I certainly began to try and pray from the heart to God, but I had very confused ideas of religion. I remember that about this time I was so ignorant, that on finding, in a prayer I was using, a petition that the Holy Spirit might be given me, I asked my mother if she thought it was a proper petition for me to offer up to God. On her telling me that it was, I continued to use it, and certainly after some little time I had much increased seriousness of feeling. About this time a kind friend lent me Bowdler's "Remains," which was also of much service to me; still I had no clear views of the leading truths of religion. During the spring and summer of 1820, I was not at all well, and probably the living upon a diet of milk and fruit, and vegetables without any meat, did not tend to increase my strength. I had spitting of blood from time to time, but not in large quantities. I took riding exercise to some extent, and I recollect that one day my spirits were considerably raised by my being caught in a smart shower, as it put me in mind of old times.

On one occasion, some country races, I think, for farmers' horses, were got up about five or six miles from our residence, to which I subscribed, and to which we went in some force. I rode to the ground, and then, for fear of overtaxing my strength, joined the party in the carriage, lending my horse to my brother-in-law. After some of the heats had been run, the steward of the course, or some other persons, (they were strangers to me,) wishing to prevent people from riding up and down the course, passed a rope across it, about sixty or seventy yards from where we were; the consequence was, that a considerable number of horsemen were brought up on each side of it, and as none of them could exactly understand the necessity for their being thus prevented from passing, they were inclined to do so, if they could, in some way or other. Seeing my relative trying to make my horse leap over the rope, which was held by a number of men at each end near the ropes of the course, and seeing that the horse would not rise at the rope, I walked towards him for the purpose of telling him that if he liked to risk his neck, I was quite willing to risk the horse, if he chose to force him at it. This nearly led several other gentlemen into a very disagreeable row. On coming to the rope and seeing how matters stood, I felt a very strong disposition to solve the difficulty, by cutting the rope, which I did in sailor fashion, by giving three cuts on the upper surface at intervals of about an inch from each other.

I had no right to do this, and certainly richly deserved some abuse, if not rough treatment, for my performance ; but the effect of it was very magical—the rope gave way, and eight or ten strong fellows at either end, who were pulling with all their might, went down rather heavily over each other. The horsemen, seeing that the rope had given way, pursued their respective courses, and scarcely anybody, besides two or three of my friends who were near me, knew how the thing had been accomplished. But I was not to get off so quietly. In three or four seconds a very tall elderly man rushed out from one side of the course, exclaiming, "Where's the blackguard who cut the rope." I did not feel inclined to sneak off, and therefore called out, "*I* cut the rope ;" and then commenced a sort of row and altercation, and I thought we should have had a regular melée, when another man, a yeoman, strode forth to our help, and called upon our assailant for fair play, and that gentlemen should not be so treated, when perhaps they had done nothing wrong. Then there was some bandying of words between the other party and my brother-in-law, our opponent inquiring what business I had to cut the rope, which the subscribers to the races had desired to be placed there? He was told that I also was a subscriber, and had as much right to cut the rope, as others had to place it there to the annoyance of everybody. He knew my brother-in-law, at least by name, and said, "I am surprised at "*you*, Sir Edward," and received the following reply, " We all "see it's after dinner with you, my friend," which raised a laugh against him from everybody around, and he was glad to slink away ; and thus we came off with flying colours, from an affair which at one moment promised to be anything but pleasant.

It was arranged that I should spend the ensuing winter in the south of France or Italy, and as I had already twice sent in a sick certificate for three months' leave, and had been altogether a twelvemonth absent from the regiment, I began to think it was hardly fair to send in any more sick certificates, without first proposing to go on half pay. I wrote to Colonel Charles Rowan to this effect, and received a most kind reply, begging that I would not think of leaving the 52nd, and saying how glad they should be to see me back again with restored health.

On the 16th of August, 1820, I went to France with my brother-in-law and sister. We were to remain together till we reached Paris, when I was to go forward without them to Nice. We went from Calais to Cassel, from which in clear weather no less than seventeen fortresses may be counted, and then to Lille, Enghien, and Brussels. We visited the Field of Waterloo, and then proceeded by Mons, Valenciennes, Ham, and Compiegne to Paris. At Compiegne we saw the palace, with its superb furniture. During my stay at Paris, two of the old Marshals of France died, Lefebre, Duke of Dantzic; and Kellerman, Duke of Valmy. They both served at Waterloo, in command of cavalry divisions. Kellerman, just before his death, told his brother-in-law to make known, in the proper quarter, his request that his heart might be buried on the field of battle of Valmy, and that a monument might be erected to the memory of the "braves" who fell there on the 19th of September, 1792, when he defeated the Duke of Brunswick. He was originally a private hussar in the legion of Conflans.

At this time I became acquainted with a remarkably intelligent Frenchman by the name of Cherval, with whom I had at times a great deal of useful conversation. He was a devoted admirer of the Bourbons, and a most enthusiastic defender of the old system of government which obtained in France before the revolution. He told us that in the commencement of the revolution, he had travelled from Normandy to Franche Comté in different disguises, and that some little time after his escape, he read, to his great horror, in the Moniteur, that the mayor and twelve or thirteen individuals of a certain village, through which he had passed, having suffered themselves to be corrupted by the Queen's emissary, Monsieur Cherval, had been brought to Paris, and had been guillotined.

The weather at Paris during the month of September in this year was most beautiful, and the climate most suitable for persons suffering from complaints of the chest. Towards the end of the month I left Paris for the South of France, having first provided myself with a *chaise de poste*, and having engaged as a servant a very nice fellow, who had served in Bonaparte's Horse Grenadiers. I passed through Fontainbleau, Nevers, Moulins, and Roanne to Lyons; and from Lyons down the left bank of the Rhone, by Vienne, Valence, Montelimart, and Orange to Avignon, where I left the Rhone and proceeded by Aix and Orgou to Marseilles, and from thence by Toulon, Frejus, and Antibes to Nice, at which place I arrived on the 6th or 7th of October.

The following extracts from my journal, of this eleven days' journey from Paris to Nice, may not be without interest to some of my readers:—

"My sleep was interrupted rather early this morning by the drums of a French regiment which is on its march to Paris. The getting up by candle-light, and the noise of drums and bugles at the same time, made me think of old times, when I was with my regiment, stout and strong.

"October 2nd. This evening was ushered in by the dreaded north-east wind, the *mistral;* a person who had not seen it, could not imagine the violence with which it blows. This wind only commences below Valence, so I should think the Alps must occasion it. It lasts generally three or four days, and troubles the natives, on an average, three times a month. Numbers of the people we met on the road had fortified their eyes against it with glasses fixed in crape. Travelled this day in twelve hours more than eighty-five English miles; pretty well for French postboys and an invalid.

"Just before we entered Orange we saw a triumphal arch erected in memory of the victory of Marius over the Cimbri, at a place called Aquæ Sextiæ, near where the town of Aix now stands. It is in high preservation, the middle arch is for carriages, the two outer ones are smaller. The *mistral* as we passed was putting its strength to a severe test, and enveloping it in clouds of dust. How many *mistrals* has this monument witnessed? How many generations from Marius to the present day have fluttered for a time about the surface of the earth, and then have passed away and shortly after fallen into oblivion, making room for others to play the same butterfly game?

"The *coup d'œil* from the top of a hill three miles from Marseilles is most delightful. On the right is the sea in a handsome bay, in the opening are two or three rocky islands; on the left of the road are some hundreds of little country-houses scattered amongst olive trees. The plain is bounded by a chain of mountains to the south which form a curve, and under it to the north is seen the town. The rain had prevented me hitherto from seeing anything of the town, which seems all alive; what Portsmouth was in time of war.

"The country almost the whole way from Marseilles to Toulon is covered with vines. The vintage has commenced. In every house are to be seen presses, barrels, sieves, &c.; and in every direction we met donkeys with panniers of grapes. A great many tread the grapes instead of using the press; the seeing the dirty shoes and naked legs, shows one how useless it is to be over nice with regard to what we eat and drink. The people of this country do not pretend to give the pure juice of the grape; they showed me a dust which they mixed with the wine, and which was of the same material as the plaster of the walls of their houses; they think it gives a flavour to the wine, and some of them put it into the cask unmixed.

"October 5th. I did not like to quit Toulon without seeing the harbour. There are two harbours, the old and the new; I only saw the latter, which was constructed by Louis XIV, for ships of war, of which I only saw two or three. It is a fine spacious concern, bounded on three sides by broad wharfs. It has an arsenal, and everything complete for building and fitting out ships. The heights, from which the French bombarded the town, almost hang over it, and completely command every part of it. At Toulon, Bonaparte distinguished himself as an officer of artillery, in the early part of the war of the revolution, when it was retaken from the English; here also at Frejus, in the room in which I am writing, he slept in 1814, on his way to Elba; he was very ill, suffering from severe indigestion after eating crab; this, together with the loss of his crown, must have made him pass a deplorably uncomfortable night. I must now to roost, in Napoleon's bed.

"Saw the place where Bonaparte landed on the 1st of March, 1815, a league to the eastward of Cannes. He sent an officer to that place to order rations to be provided for 6000 men; but his party at the utmost did not exceed 1100."

I passed the Var into Piedmont from France, I think, on the 7th of October. I entered Nice, which is only a mile or two from the frontier, during very heavy rain, which did not give me a very favourable impression of the place. Here I remained more than three months, and, although I thought several times that I should probably die at Nice, it pleased God not only that my illness should take a favourable turn before I left it, but that the serious feelings, which I had already in some measure experienced, should be greatly deepened and strengthened during my residence there. On looking back five-and-forty years, to the time of my first becoming ill near Bremen, I wonder at the mercy and goodness of God, who led me, step by step, to be prepared to receive religious information and benefit from several friends into whose society He brought me at Nice. The propriety of this observation will appear, when it is recollected, that, had I been brought into contact with these same persons a twelvemonth earlier, I should most probably have avoided them at once, as being too strict and too precise. Surely God leads us in a way that we know not.

A physician whom I consulted at Paris, on hearing that I thought of passing the winter at Nice, had given me a letter to a friend of his, who was residing there. It is not pleasant to go to a place for any time, and not to know a single person there; I was therefore glad to have this letter; but, although this gentleman was exceedingly civil and kind to me, it will be seen that he was not exactly the sort of person to be of service to me in a religious point of view; yet was he the instrument, without intending it, indeed whilst he intended quite the reverse, of leading me to become acquainted with those very persons who in God's providence were to be made religiously useful to me. He kindly accompanied me in my search for lodgings, and on my pointing out the Maison Ferdinand, in the Croix de Marbre, which he was passing by, as a large pleasant-looking house, he said, it would not at all suit me, as he knew an "infernal Methodist" who had been there the winter before, and had gone up to Switzerland for the summer months, had taken rooms there for the ensuing season. This would have been quite sufficient twelve months before to decide me not to think of the house for

one moment; but now the thought immediately occurred to me :—
Probably this man is only called a Methodist, because he
wishes to do what is right in the sight of God, and is more
strictly religious than most of those around him!

I think I secured rooms in this house the very next day, and,
in the course of two or three days more, my fellow-lodger made
his appearance. We soon became acquainted, and, after a little
time, arranged to take our meals together. I found that he was
well acquainted with the Scriptures, and that in our conversations
on religious subjects, he always referred to them to prove the
truth of any opinion he advanced; this I was unable to do. We
had other friends who frequently dined and spent the evening
with us, especially a Norwich clergyman by the name of Day, a
truly good man, and a nice young man, a Mr. Ward, who had
been in the army; he was seriously disposed, but, like myself,
had only confused views of religion. I look back with feelings
of great thankfulness to God for having brought me into the
society of these good men, and also that He disposed me to converse with them on religious subjects. I recollect on one occasion,
soon after we began to discuss religious questions, that I made
the following ignorant speech—" you will never make me believe
"that I shall not be saved if I do as well as I can!" I was
immediately shewn, from the Word of God, that this was an
unscriptural assertion. Such passages as the following were
pointed out to me :—Ephesians ii, 8—10: "By grace are ye
"saved, through faith, and that not of yourselves, it is the gift of
"God; not of works, lest any man should boast. For we are
"his workmanship, created in Christ Jesus unto good works,
"which God hath before ordained that we should walk in them:"
and John iii, 16, 36; John i, 12, 13; Romans iii, 20—31; Gal.
iii, 10—13; 2 Cor. v, 17. One important consequence of our
conversation on that evening was, that I made up my mind that
I would, with God's help, and with prayer for His teaching, read
some portion of His Word every day until I should have read it
through. This good practice has never been discontinued. A
feeling strongly impressed upon my mind about that time was,
that if the Bible was the Word of God, I could not possibly
expect to be happy, either here or hereafter, unless I took

it as the rule and guide of all my conduct: John v, 39; 1 Peter ii, 1—3.

I had several very agreeable acquaintances at Nice; amongst them were Captain and Mr. Felix, the latter of the 95th Rifles, Colonel and Mrs. Vincent, Mr. and Mrs. Townsend, of Castle Townsend, near Kinsale, and Colonel and Mrs. Campbell: he was an old Peninsular officer, and, I think, in the light division. I may here insert the following anecdote without fear of giving the least annoyance to any one. Amongst my principal friends were two who stuttered most terribly. They frequently came to see us, and the effect of their conversing with each other was generally too much for my gravity: it was an understood thing, however, that I might laugh as much as I liked, but my friend and fellow-lodger always greatly feared that the convulsive laughter, which I sometimes could not avoid, might be very dangerous to me as regarded my supposed ailment. On one occasion we had the addition to our party of another friend, who also hung fire very much when speaking; and these three several times conversed with each other. Probably such a singular case has never occurred before, that in a party of five persons three should be regular stammerers. At this time Queen Caroline's trial was going on, and everybody was eager for the arrival of the accounts of the proceedings, which we got in Galignani.

My expectation of recovery from my illness varied almost from day to day. Some of the following entries were made in my journal under the impression that I very probably should not live to return to England, and that they would be read by my relatives after my death; they shew that, by degrees, my views had become clearer, and my religious feelings stronger than they had been.

"December 2nd, 1820. This morning I have expectorated a little blood. I am thankful I am not at home, as I know my dear mother would be much alarmed on my account; if it were not for that, how delighted I should be to be with her. The Almighty visits us with these little afflictions for wise and good purposes. Last night I prayed to Him for a return of health; it has pleased Him, however, not to grant my request—His will be done! Manifold are the ways of His providence! Had I never been afflicted with this spitting of blood, I should, most likely, have been still pursuing a thoughtless course of life, regardless of religion, and estranged from my God and Saviour. He, of His infinite goodness, has brought me more than once into the society of religious people, whose discourse has, as it were, awakened me from my apathy, and laid open to my eyes the precipice on the edge of which I have been straying. What helpless, nothingless beings we are of ourselves! Happy is the man who feels his own weakness, and who, at the same time, clings for support to the cross of his Redeemer; and blessed is the Almighty, who awakens in him this feeling.

"December 3rd. This day is so fine, that I have been able to sit with my windows open for two hours; there is a pear-tree in blossom in the garden. How beautiful are the collect and epistle for Advent Sunday! How interesting, also, is the 14th chapter of St. John!

"December 10th. The thoughts of leaving this world are only painful when I think of the dear friends I must leave behind. If ever this should meet the eyes of any of them, may it induce them to think of the short, short time they may have to live. The eye that reads this, as well as the hand which traces it, must, ere many years, perhaps weeks, be closed and chilled by death. We should always bear in mind how inevitable death is—a few years, and the present generation will have passed away. The thoughts of death, instead of being terrible, are grateful to the person who looks forward to a better world, through the merits of a gracious Redeemer. I pray God that, in health and in sickness, He will not withdraw His Holy Comforter from me. My dear friends are what the world calls religious, but are they sufficiently so, and have they proper ideas on the subject? Are they aware of the total insufficiency of the best of their own works to save them? I have received great pleasure and instruction from Mr. Wilberforce's 'Treatise on Christianity,' and from Serle's 'Christian Remembrancer.' I humbly trust that I am a partaker of the grace of the Almighty. I consider myself to-day in a worse state of health than I have ever yet been in, but I do not feel particularly annoyed at it; the will of God be done, and may He ever give to me and mine, and to all poor sinners, the same feeling.

"December 12th. Dr. B. found a vessel open in my throat.

"December 13th. Dr. B. and Dr. T. held a consultation, and decided on the propriety of my getting farther away from the sea. They discovered the vessel from which I had had the discharge of blood, and the mucus formed on the wound. Dr. T. told me my case was a straightforward one, if I was only careful. Dec. 14th. Dr. B. was able to apply something to the wound in my throat by means of a quill with a sponge at the end of it. Dec. 24th. Gained strength at a great rate. Dec. 25th. Fine day, but cold; received the sacrament. Ate my Christmas dinner at Colonel Vincent's, and met a Mr. and Mrs. Wills, of the County Roscommon."

Soon after I got to Nice, I met with the following adventure. I had desired my servant to be always most particular in taking care that there were no mosquitoes under the mosquito curtain, when it was let down for the night. One night, however, after I had been in bed for some time, I found, to my horror, that one of these animals was under the curtain. I thought I would almost as soon have heard the roar of a tiger, for there was very little prospect of getting any sleep that night. After catching at it for a long time, whenever I heard it buzzing near my face, I at last thought I had killed it, as I heard nothing more of it; in the morning, however, whilst I was dressing, I was seized with a most violent fit of coughing, which lasted for a good half-hour, and I began to fear that it would end in death, or in my becoming most seriously ill, when, to my astonishment, I coughed up the leg of a mosquito, and, by degrees, the other parts of the animal made their appearance. The doctor thought I had had a very narrow escape.

It is foreign to my purpose to lengthen out this work by describing the beautiful scenery on all sides of Nice; nor do I wish to say much about the climate. From what I read and observed on that subject, I came to the conclusion, that no place close to the sea is a fit place of residence for an invalid at all subject to spitting of blood; and that, after the very beginning of January, Nice is not a suitable place for any persons suffering from affection of the chest. After Christmas, Pisa and Rome are recommended, as being more inland. Sir James Clarke, many years ago, wrote a very clever work on the "Climate and "Diseases of the South of France and Italy," and, if I do not mistake, he takes the above-mentioned view of the subject.

CHAPTER XVI

1821.

ITALY.

Proceed by water to Genoa—From Genoa to Pisa—Cross a portion of the Apennines—Misunderstanding with a *vetturino*—Bridge over the Serchio carried away—The leaning tower at Pisa, etc.—The death of a student—The Carnival, etc.—Florence to Rome—Austrians bivouacked around Terni-St. Peter's at Rome—Curious scene—From Rome to Naples—Appii Forum —Cicero's villa and tomb—Naples—Portici, Pompeii—Go up Vesuvius— English squadron—Sir Graham Moore—Return by Rome, Florence, Milan, Turin, and Geneva to England—Dr. Malan at Geneva—Narrow escape at the mortar-practice there.

I LEFT Nice for Genoa about the second or third of January, 1821, in company with Mr. Ward, in the Italian mail felucca. We had a not very disagreeable voyage of 120 miles. The accommodations of the felucca were not "first class," as we more particularly discovered when we had to turn in at night. The views of the coast, and of the maritime Alps, were most splendid. We did not remain long at Genoa, and my principal recollection of it is, that the streets were remarkably narrow, and the houses, or, rather palaces, very lofty and well built.

I find myself very much puzzled as to the inflicting, or not, on my readers, an account of my travels to Pisa, Florence, Rome, and Naples; and my return to England by Rome, Florence, Bologna, Milan, Turin, Geneva, and Paris. I am unwilling to swell this work to too large a size; and, on the other hand, there are many things of considerable interest which I think I ought not to omit. I will therefore, with the assistance of my journal, which was tolerably well kept at that time, endeavour to give as concise an account as I can of this period of about five months; and I can cut it down, or leave it out afterwards, if I find it necessary. I took with me into Italy, Eustace's "Classical Tour," in four octavo volumes, and four small volumes of Reichard's "Guide des Voyageurs en Europe." Both these works were very useful; I should think no traveller in Italy should be without Eustace, even in the present day. And now I will begin with my journal:—

"1821. Made a bargain with a man to take us (Mr. Ward, myself, and servant) from Genoa to Pisa, for thirteen napoleons, and started on Saturday, the 6th of January, in a coach drawn by three horses. The road runs along the coast as far as Recco, and the Apennines rise nearly perpendicularly from it on the left. Sometimes we were separated from the sea by small groves of olives and orange-trees, and as we looked down upon it through them it had a most beautiful appearance. The wildness of the Apennines was heightened by the rain, as numerous cascades, rolling from the very top of them to the bottom, added to the effect. We had bargained to go as far as Sestri, but the badness of the weather prevented our getting farther than Rapalo. A little beyond Recco the postillion pulled up, and told us we could not proceed, owing to the swelling of a river; however, by threatening that we would not pay him, if he did not push on, we induced him to do so. We passed the river on men's shoulders, and slept at a miserable inn at Rapalo. The dashing of the sea against the house under my window, prevented my sleeping very well. From my room, in the morning, I had a very pretty view of the coast of the gulf of Rapalo as far as Porto Fino, formerly Portus Delphini.

"January 7th. From Rapalo to Chiavari the road is along the seashore, and winds along the side of the mountains; in some places there are perpendicular precipices more than 500 feet deep. In one place a part of the hill had given way, and the road was almost blocked up. We were lucky in finding some men who helped to clear the way for us. I thought the scenery for six or seven miles on this side (the south) of Rapalo, most beautiful.

The road runs through the rock in two places. Chiavari is situated in a small plain almost surrounded on every side, except towards the sea, by mountains. The cultivated land around it looks like a large garden divided into beds; all along the coast is a row of large aloes. The orange-trees at this place were looking most beautiful; in one little garden of about half an acre there were at least 200 trees, and on an average there must have been 400 oranges on each. Last winter the orange-trees at Nice were terribly cut up by the frost, but all along this coast they appear in a most thriving condition. Half a mile before we came to Sestri, we passed along a road formed nearly at the bottom of the rock. The sea was high, and at times beat over it, and we narrowly escaped a wave, which completely ducked, and almost carried away, a man who was only three or four yards behind the carriage. We stopped an hour or two at Sestri, and then set forward to cross a ridge of the Apennines; I in a sedan chair, borne by six stout fellows, and the others and the baggage on mules and horses. There was an Italian merchant of Brescia in company. My bearers kept up pretty well with the cavalcade, and at about four o'clock we arrived at the post of Braco. Everybody wished to go on to the next village, about eight miles forward, so I did not object, although it was getting dark. It rained very hard at times, and I thought the scene was really sublime when I saw the lightning flashing horizontally below me. We got a light about five o'clock at a solitary house, and proceeded on our mountain excursion. The road was very narrow, and in some places there were frightful precipices, down which I was terribly afraid some of the mules would slip. Ward's mule slipped only twice, although the road was very steep at times, and in many places lay over the naked rock; he observed that the poor animal trembled very much both times after it. When he was in front it annoyed him every now and then, by turning round to look at the light; this was not very pleasant, considering the narrowness of the path, and the precipice below. My men lost the path once, and before they could find it again the candle went out, and we were in a pretty predicament. They hallooed to the party in front, who came to our aid. Three or four sulphur boxes were produced, and, as the wind was high, they were forced to light the matches in my chair; it was a long time before we could succeed in lighting the candle, and in the meantime I was almost suffocated with brimstone. We slept at a horrible place called Carrotta. There was no fireplace in the village, and we were ushered into a small room with a fire lighted on the floor, in the centre, the smoke escaping out of the door. There were benches fixed against the walls round the fire, and all hands, to the amount of thirteen, set to work to warm and dry themselves. I almost fancied myself in a robber's cave, such was the appearance of the people and place. We could get nothing to eat but bread and eggs. Ward and I were accommodated with the bed of the host and hostess, on which we lay down in our clothes; there were only shutters, and no windows, but I was so used to rough it, by that time, that I had no apprehension of taking cold."

On the 8th we started from Carrotta about half-past seven. The road was better, and my men tripped along at a famous rate. We arrived at Spezia about two o'clock. I fancy I cut rather an odd figure in my cloak and large brown nightcap, as many people asked if I were a *Spagnuolo* (Spaniard.) We got away from Spezia about three o'clock, in a carriage. The Gulf of Spezia looked very beautiful; the English erected some forts here in 1814. There is a fountain of fresh water rising in the midst of the salt water, a long way out at sea. We passed part of the Magra in a boat. I mounted a post-horse, which came over with us, and, after fording the other part, rode to Sarzana, where we lodged, at a very good inn, called the Aquila Nigra, kept by a Frenchman.

"January 9th. At Sarzana we permitted our Genoese conductor to hand us over to a *vetturino*; his carriage, however, was so bad that we wished to stop at Massa, to get another. The road runs past the town, which he refused to enter, and, notwithstanding all we could say, he persisted in driving on. My servant, Frederick, stopped him, and Ward and I went into the town to see if we could not get redress by applying to the police. I managed to express myself very tolerably in Italian, and the head man sent a police-officer to bring the man to him; but the bird had flown; he had followed us into the town, and, hearing me say I should go to the police, he returned to the carriage and told Frederick that we wished him to proceed with the baggage, and that we intended to follow in a post-carriage. The *commissaire* gave us a letter, stating the case, to the *commissaire* at Pietra Santa, and after eating a good dinner at the hotel, we followed in a *caleche*, with post-horses. We obtained full redress at Pietra Santa. This part of the business was managed very well by Frederick, who took the letter to the police office. The man narrowly escaped being put in prison, and was forced to pay all the extra expenses we had incurred."

On the 10th we left Pietra Santa, in a return Pisa carriage; the *vetturini* always hand people over to each other in this way when they can, and we were not sorry to change. Both this day and yesterday the country we passed through was much inundated. The vines hang most beautifully in festoons from tree to tree. The country looks like a large garden, and we passed several large groves of olives. About four miles after passing Viareggio, we were stopped for more than three hours, in consequence of the bridge over the Serchio having given way. We walked down to the place, and found that not only the bridge, but also part of the river bank had been washed away. The bridge had been tottering all the morning, and about half an hour before our arrival, not five seconds after the courier had passed, a large tree carried it away. The country was inundated on all sides, as far as the eye could reach. The people were striving to pick up the planks and posts which were floating along, and three or four fellows were swimming for the same purpose. After quarrelling a great deal with the postillion about the payment, we agreed to give him the whole fare to Pisa, provided he would cross the water with us, proceed to Lucca, and bring us out a carriage to the other bank of the river. We crossed in a boat, making a round of about a mile among the trees, which were beautifully festooned with long branches of the vine, hanging from one to the other. When we were in the carriage on the other side, the driver refused to go to Pisa, as he said the road was dangerous from the inundations, but we induced him to proceed by threatening not to pay the other postillion if he did not.

We passed through some lanes full of water, with a man before to try the depth of it; the horses were in some places up to their bellies, but we soon gained the high road from Lucca. At Ripafratta, a name suggestive of the breaking of the left bank of the Serchio in former days, our passports were examined, on our entrance into the Tuscan territory. The night was very fine, and the moon shone in great splendour, and before entering Pisa we had a distant view of the leaning tower; its deviation from the perpendicular was very visible at the distance of a mile by moonlight. We were kept some time at the gate of Pisa, in consequence of the people not being able to make out my name. There is an order that no carriage is to be in the town at night without a light, so they gave us a candle which we held up at the window. We brought up at the hotel of "The Three Damsels."

As was to be expected, after the rather trying journey which I had encountered, I did not feel quite so well on my arrival at Pisa as I was when I left Nice. Mr. Fitzgibbon had kindly given me a letter to Mr. Blizard, an eminent London surgeon who was staying at Pisa, and he was most kind and attentive to me. I gave him the whole history of my case, which he thought very favourably of, but recommended me to be careful not to expose myself again. He prescribed a ride to the baths of Pisa, which are about four miles from the town, every forenoon when the day was fine, to drink the waters; but I presume the giving me daily riding exercise was his principal object. I found at Pisa some old friends, Mr. and Mrs. Poore, and when the weather was not fine enough for horse exercise I frequently went with them in their carriage to the *caschina*, or cow park, of the Grand Duke of Tuscany, where we could generally get a walk, well sheltered from the wind. There we saw the descendants of camels brought from the Holy Land in the time of the Crusades.

I remained at Pisa between six and seven weeks, and, during that time, not only gained much strength from being enabled, owing to the mildness of the climate, to ride and walk out almost every day, but I managed also to pick up some considerable knowledge of Italian and of Italian history. I will here again introduce a few extracts from my journal.

" January 13th. Went to see the hanging tower, (which is the clock tower, hanging twenty-two feet over the perpendicular,) the cathedral, the baptistery, and the *campo santo*, or burial-ground. These four buildings stand rather separated from the town, but I am inclined to differ with our friend Eustace, as I think it is the green turf in front of them which is so peculiarly pleasing to the English eye, and not their isolated situation. I felt quite gratified at the sight of the turf, for I think I have not seen any before since I left Paris. In the south of France, in Piedmont, and in Italy, every crook and corner is cultivated. 19th. Rode out towards the hills; the peasants of the Val d'Arno seem not to be so poor and wretched as those of Piedmont; they are remarkably civil; some of them who were working in the fields, at least a hundred yards from the road, I observed looking till they engaged my attention in order to shew the civility of taking off their hats. A student died about a fortnight ago, and to-day he was buried, all the students attending; they subscribed so much each in order that they might have a splendid funeral. Out of the six hundred students I did not see one who might be called a fine young man. 25th. My Italian master, who is a student, requested me to take some other book rather than Pignotti's "Storia della Toscana," as he could not accompany me in reading that, it having been forbidden to all Catholics by the Pope. 27th. Rode on the Leghorn road. The poor people here seem to make it a rule to attack every Englishman they see for money; I gave a lad two paoli (about a shilling) for the sake of making him happy. He knelt down to thank me, and then went away jumping and shouting, and fully as much gratified as I should have been with a present of £500. It was at their return from the Holy Land, in the time of the Crusades, that the Pisan gallies brought cargoes of the famous earth, with which the *campo* is filled; it is said to have the property of destroying bodies buried in it in a very short space of time; now, however, it is not permitted to bury there; for the last thirty-five years there has been a law in force which forbids the burial of people within the walls of Pisa.

"January 30th. Visited the *campo santo*, the *duomo* (cathedral) and baptistery for a few minutes. The *duomo* is most splendid in the interior. I only took a peep at it, the air was so cold. There are many paintings by the first masters; the granite pillars are very fine. The *campo santo* requires more time than I could venture to give it, considering its dampness. There are numbers of tombs, monuments and sarcophagi. The monument erected by Frederick the Great of Prussia, to Algorotti, attracted my attention; the inscription is "Algorotto Ovidii œmulo, Newtonii discipulo Friedericus magnus," underneath there is "Algorottus non omnis." The baptistery has some very fine sculpture in it, particularly the pulpit; on the outside on the top is the figure of John the Baptist. Here is the only font in Pisa.

"February 1st. Read the Life of Colonel Gardiner, which pleased me very much; the latter part of his life seems to have been passed in that fulness of happiness which only the advanced Christian must expect. May such be the lot of many. Those who place not their affections on the corruptible things of this world, are certainly the people who pass through it with the greatest comfort; all the little ups and downs of life they look upon as trifles, their great aim is heaven, and the confident hope of enjoying a blessed eternity makes them, in a degree, callous to what the world calls adversity." I have copied the above from my journal to shew that there was an increasing religious feeling at the time it was written. I should write it somewhat differently now.

The next entry in my journal refers to the history of Italy, and I should not introduce it here, but for the curious circumstance it relates :—"The new Pope Gregory was neither a Guelf nor a Ghibelline; he wished to reconcile these two parties. Florence having opposed his desire, was excommunicated. Rather an odd circumstance occurred on his return from the council of Lyons in 1276; he wished to avoid Florence, but the Arno had overflown its banks and prevented his passing by Pisa, therefore he was forced to go by way of Florence. It would not have been proper for him to have entered an accursed city, so he blessed it on going in, and after he had passed through, turned round and excommunicated it. He died on his journey at Arezzo. He had made a law, that if the Pope should die away from Rome, his successor should be chosen immediately on the spot. Innocent V was elected in his stead."

"February 4th. There is a young Englishman here who is going to be married to a Miss ——, she is a tall girl and he rather short; they are constantly walking about together and looking very loving. This being the first day of the Carnival, on which masks have appeared on the Lung' Arno, two young men, I fancy students, were dressed as an English gentleman and lady; the lady was tall, her companion a little man. I am told they took off the lovers admirably. A Miss ——, going to dine at the house of a friend on Saturday last, the day before that appointed for the first appearance of the masks, had the misfortune to walk up the Lung' Arno alone, in her English evening low dress; she had a veil on, and, although the sun was down, a parasol, for the purpose I suppose of hiding her face. The people took her, or pretended to take her, for a masked character, and numbers of them followed her; indeed, some proposed stopping her, as being out of order in appearing in such trim a day too soon. The poor lady was in a sad fright, and took refuge in a friend's house; some say she was forced to appear on the balcony before the people would go away.

"In almost all the towns of Italy there is a *Societa della misericordia*, the members of which make it their business to find out the poor and those in need of assistance, and to minister to their necessities. The members of the society here belong, some of them, to the first families in Pisa. If a poor man is sick, they either attend him at his own house or carry him to the hospital, as the case may be. They wear masks and black cloaks, partly that they may not be known, and partly that there may be no difference in the dress of the rich and poor members. I met twelve or fourteen of them the other day, going out on their work of mercy. I am told that any person who is unfortunate is sure to meet with assistance from this society."

On the 27th of February I went from Pisa to Florence, on my way to Rome, much improved in health, but still being advised to pass the winter and spring in Italy. I only remained in Florence five or six days, during which I saw all that was particularly worth seeing, including the Palazzo Pitti, and the famous Medicean gallery, with all its beautiful statues and paintings, some of both of which had travelled many hundreds of miles since I had seen them at Paris in 1815. The museum at Florence was chiefly remarkable for its wax anatomical specimens, which were contained in nearly or quite thirty rooms.

I left Florence on the 5th of March and got to Rome on the 8th, having travelled by Arezzo, Perugia, Foligno, Spoleto, Terni, Narni, and Civita Castellana. After leaving Spoleto, we drove along the side of a torrent for some four or five miles between high hills, and then ascended Monte Somma, the most elevated mountain of that range of the Apennines; the mountain and woody scenery were very beautiful. The ascent of the Somma, on its eastern side, is rather more than a mile in length. The road is excellent the whole way from Foligno to Rome, and particularly so over the Somma. We began to descend as it was getting dark. We changed horses at the hamlet of Strettura, about four miles down. The descent continues for six or seven miles beyond Strettura, indeed almost as far as Terni. In one of the darkest parts of the winding descent, where we were almost entirely shut in by mountains, to add to the effect we saw a squadron of Austrian dragoons, on their march towards Loretto. We found about 18,000 men in bivouac around Terni. The blaze of the fires among the olive groves, and the almost savage appearance of the Hungarian and Austrian soldiers, made me fancy the scene a very romantic one. I found Terni so full of officers that I could get no accommodation there, and so, relinquishing my plan of visiting the waterfall, I proceeded to Narni for the night. As we approached Rome the next day we met hundreds of carriages; the people had come out to see the Germans, ten thousand of whom they heard were coming in. We entered Rome by the Porta del Popolo, and drove to the Piazza di Spagna, in which two or three of the hotels were quite full; but I at last found room at the Locanda di Parigi.

I must be understood as not professing to give any regular account of the places I visited in Italy, or of the circumstances in which I was placed; I purpose only to select, from what I recollect and from my journal, a very few points which perhaps may interest the reader.

Part of the entry made in my journal the day after my arrival at Rome is as follows:—

"March 9th. I was rather disappointed with the outside of St. Peter's, but highly delighted with the interior. On entering, I was much amused at seeing two ladies kneeling before an altar at the respectful distance of fifty yards from it, with two livery servants kneeling behind them, at a considerable distance; one of the servants was just reaching over to give the other a pinch of snuff. In one part of the church is a statue of St. Peter, the toe of which it is the fashion to kiss; I saw numbers of people doing this, and also rubbing their eyes against it. As one young man was kissing it, his companion pushed his head against it by way of joke. When people of distinction kiss the saint's toe, it is customary for a servant first of all to wipe it with a cambric handkerchief.

"March 14th. Went last night to a party at Lady Ellenborough's, and was much gratified by hearing an *improvisatore*, who, as far as I could judge, acquitted himself extremely well. He was not at all aware of what the subjects would be until they were given to him, when he immediately commenced. The subjects were Dante, Eurydice and Orpheus, another which he treated in verse, and the last was Alexander at the tomb of Achilles, in prose. I could not follow him in his poetry, but I understood the whole of the prose."

The tomb of Cecilia Metella, about two miles out of Rome on the Appian way, has its walls exceedingly thick, and is in a state of good preservation; there is, or was, a large space in the inside, into which I rode. I found there, also on horseback, a Mr. ———, who had known some of my family, and we soon became acquainted. We returned to Rome together, and about a mile from the city saw a large cavalcade approaching. It was the Pope, who was attended by a guard and a suite of several persons. He had left his carriage, and was walking on the footpath. An officer of the guard rode forward to us and said he should be very much obliged if, just before we met the Pope, we would dismount and take off our hats. Although there was at first some disinclination on my part to go through this ceremony, yet a moment's reflection shewed me that the customary mark of respect should be rendered to the Pope as sovereign of the country. We dismounted and stood with our hats off as he passed, which much pleased the body-guard, who thanked us for our courtesy. The Pope also and all his suite saluted us. It was amusing to see the common people throw down their burdens and run across the road to kiss his foot. He seemed to treat them with very great kindness, and dispensed his blessings very bountifully.

On the 30th of March, after being at Rome three weeks, I decided on paying a short visit to Naples, with two friends. We travelled in a carriage which I had purchased at Florence. We passed along the Appian way and over the Pomptine Marshes, so called from Pometium, an ancient town of the Volsci, and saw the "Three Taverns" and Appii Forum, at which places the Roman Christians met St. Paul when he was journeying to Rome. Terracina, the ancient Auxur, is about half-way between Rome and Naples. It is prettily situated on the sea.

We arrived at Mola di Gaeta before nine o'clock. The Locanda di Cicerone, situated on the ruins of Cicero's lower villa, is a very excellent inn. In the morning I walked back a mile on the road we came, in order to visit Cicero's tomb, which is almost close to the road. He had a villa on the hill above, the ruins of which I saw. It is supposed that he was murdered just on the spot where his tomb is erected, which answers to the description of the historian, who says he was murdered in a grove between his villa and the sea. We had a fine view of the promontory, town, and bay of Gaeta, rendered celebrated by Homer and Virgil. The ancient town was founded by the Lœstrygons, and it took its name from the nurse of Æneas, who died on the coast :—

"Tu quoque littoribus nostris, Æneia nutrix,
Æternam, moriens, famam Cajeta dedisti."

We left Mola about ten o'clock, and soon arrived at
" The rich fields that Liris laves,
Where silent roll his deep'ning waves."—
" Rura quæ Liris quietâ
Mordet aquâ, taciturnus amnis."

This river was the southern boundary of Latium. Just before we arrived at this river, now called the Garigliano, we saw the ruins of the ancient Minturnæ. It was in the marshes to the left of this, that Caius Marius hid himself. He was discovered, dragged out, and imprisoned at Minturnæ. A Gaulish soldier was sent to kill him, but the countenance of Marius disarmed him; the dagger fell from his hand. The people of Minturnæ rose and rescued Marius. Close to this is the hill of Falernum, so famous for its wine. We passed the Volturno and entered Capua, which is one of the few fortified places of the kingdom of Naples: it is a wretched poor place. Here we paid a barrier duty on the carriage of two scudi. We arrived at Naples about seven o'clock, and drove to the Grande Bretagna, where we found General Frimont and a guard of eighty grenadiers. There are three English ships here, the Rochfort, Iphigenia, and Cambrian, the latter in quarantine. There are also seven or eight sail of ships belonging to other powers. The guard turns out at least every quarter of an hour; we have had nothing but drumming all day long; it seems to be turned out to everybody with an outrider. Went to the grotto of Pausilippo, which is nearly half a mile long, about eighteen feet broad, and generally about twenty-four feet high, though in some places more. It was probably at first nothing more than a quarry, as close to it there are many other excavations of that sort, made for the sake of the sandstone. After passing through the grotto and returning, we made a tour up and round the hill of about a mile, and came to Virgil's tomb, which hangs directly over the entrance of the grotto of Pausilippo. There was formerly a little urn in the centre, supported by white pillars, but it has long been removed, and is now lost. The following inscription was on it:—

"Mantua me genuit, Calabri rapuere, tenet nunc
Parthenope, cecini pascua, rura, duces."
"At Mantua I first saw the day,
Calabrians snatched me away,
My bones lie now 'midst Naples' rocks,
I've sung of leaders, fields, and flocks."

The above spirited translation by Mr. Gage and Mr. Leeke!!! There is no laurel now growing spontaneously on Virgil's tomb. Near it the Duchess of Devonshire has raised a monument in memory of a favourite dog, and I think Her Grace has thereby shewn a deplorable want of taste.

The Grande Bretagna has the royal garden and the sea before it. In the garden is the famous Toro Farnese, supposed to be the best sculptured quadruped in existence, though I myself could not discover anything very super-excellent in it, and indeed at first took it for a horse.

"April 3rd. Went to the museum and saw numbers of copper utensils which had been dug out of Pompeii and Herculaneum, and various Greek vases discovered in tombs. It was often the custom to put into the tombs whatever the dead person had liked most when living, and I have heard that pots of rouge were put into the tombs of some of the ladies. We saw the rolls of papyrus extracted from Herculaneum, and were present whilst part of one was unrolled: they use what we call goldbeater's skin in this process. The papyrus very much resembles burnt paper, and appears to have scarcely any more consistency; the characters are not plain, but it is possible to make them out. The collection of pictures is not good; there are plenty of medals and some good models of temples. The Farnese Hercules is, to my mind, too clumsy to be pleasing, but it is finely sculptured. I was to have dined with Sir Graham Moore, but one of the midshipmen was taken dangerously ill at his house, and they were forced to postpone their party.

"The Gages and Mr. and Mrs. Wills went to the Grotto del Cane, and saw a poor dog put to a temporary death; in a few seconds he became insensible, but this mephitic air had no effect on some frogs they put in, which jumped about in it at a great rate.

"April 4th. Went with the Gages and Mr. Wills to Pompeii, which is about thirteen miles from Naples. The day was fine, though at times hazy, and we had a good sight of Vesuvius. Beyond Portici we saw a great deal of lava; in some places it was five or six feet deep. In the year 63 there was an earthquake which nearly overturned Pompeii, and in 79 it was completely covered by showers of ashes from Vesuvius. We saw the walls of many buildings in a tolerable state of preservation. The colours of the fresco were in very bright and good preservation. The little theatre is well preserved; it would contain about 1800 people. It is a great pity that all the cooking utensils and articles of furniture have been removed from the places where they were found, to the museums, to be stuck up in stupid rows. How pleasing it would have been to have seen the cooking utensils, surgical instruments, &c., in the cooks' and surgeons' shops. Some of the best paintings were found in the temple of Isis, and were sawn off the walls with great trouble.

"The tomb of the gladiators, so called I fancy because there was a representation of a show of gladiators on it, is in a good state of preservation. This, and all the tombs, are outside the town, and on either side of the road. There are two or three little monuments raised to the Diomedes, and nearly opposite to them was a large house, belonging to the same family. In the cellar of this house, close to the doorway, were found seventeen skeletons. We saw the mask of one of them against the wall; it is supposed that they took shelter there from the ashes. In another part of the town were found, in what was supposed to be a prison, two skeletons, with irons about the bones of the legs.

"The streets are very narrow, so much so that two of our modern carriages could hardly pass each other in them; the marks of the wheels on the pavement are very visible. On either side are footways, not quite a foot and a half in breadth, and about ten inches above the level of the street. Almost all the rooms we saw were very small—seven or eight feet square, but they were, I conceive, mostly shops. On the outside they had their signs painted on the wall. There was a goat with a full udder painted on the outside of the shop of a milkman, where we saw a number of earthen jars, in which it is supposed the milk was kept. On the cooks' shops were painted game, hams, &c. There are still more than three-fourths of the town unexcavated.

"April 5th. Mr. Wills, the Gages, and I, started about three o'clock for Vesuvius. Portici is six or seven miles from Naples, and about seven or eight from the summit of the mountain. On our arrival here we were surrounded by some fifteen or twenty men leading as many asses, each vehemently soliciting us to favour him with the care of our carcasses to the top of Vesuvius. They wanted a piastre for each; however, we at last bargained with them to take one guide and four donkies, paying two piastres for the whole. We had not proceeded far out of the town, when the other three fellows came and said they must have more than three carlini for each of the steeds, so we dismounted and sent them back, rather angry with themselves, I fancy, for 'quarrelling with their own bread and butter.' I rode on the remaining donkey more than half way to the hermitage, where we arrived in about an hour after leaving Portici: the ascent is not very steep. There are a great many rooms at the hermitage. The hermit was glad to see us, and produced four bottles of Lachrymæ Christi, which we got through pretty soon; thus fortified, we resumed our journey with fresh courage. After going forward about half a mile we turned to the left and crossed the lava which flowed in 1810; it was about eight or nine hundred yards in breadth. After passing it, we came to some which had only ceased to flow three days before; it was quite warm, and I observed it had furrowed up the sand in its course. Hundreds of different forms and figures appear on all sides, produced as the lava cooled in the act of running and bubbling. Through the different clefts we had views of the fiery furnace underneath. A few weeks ago a Frenchman threw himself into the running lava, and was consumed immediately. We saw the place where this happened; it was close to the mouth of a small crater at the bottom of the cone, from which lava has been flowing since Christmas. From the mouth of the crater I broke off some fine specimens of lava, covered with incrustations of saltpetre, alum, &c. The cone did not appear very high, but we were more than an hour in ascending it; by the time we got half way up, it was nine o'clock and very dark. Our guide took us to the leeward side of the crater, and the consequence was that we were almost smothered. He was very unwilling to proceed to the mouth of it, but of course we could not go so far without looking into it. Mr. Wills and I crawled on our hands and knees, the guide having discovered, by throwing up cinders till they did not return, that we were within a few feet of the edge. We could not see, but succeeded in putting our heads over it, and were nearly suffocated. We neither heard any rumbling noises nor saw any flames.

"We came down the cone of Vesuvius much faster than we had climbed up. The descent on the cinders took us about ten minutes. We revisited the lava, and by descending into a hole formed by the cooled lava, I had a famous view of the vast burning furnace beneath. It was rather dangerous work walking on the lava at night, but we escaped without hurting ourselves. There was something very gratifying in walking on the hardened part of it, and in being able to light a stick by thrusting it through the fissures under our feet. We observed that our guide walked with a pistol in his hand, and we found out that, since the Neapolitan army had been disbanded, and since the Austrians had entered the country, this mountain had been infested with robbers. The hermit's wine and three other bottles the party had got through when climbing, had made them very valiant, although it was scarcely stronger than small beer. We regained the hermitage in safety, that is to say, with some broken shins, cut boots, and burnt trowsers. Another Englishman, with two boys as guides, had gone up the cone with us. The whole party got through four more bottles of the good father's wine, and having written our names in his album, which contains the effusions of the genius of most of the visitants to Vesuvius, and having paid him three piastres for his wine, eggs, and civility, we set out to descend to Portici, where we arrived about eleven o'clock, and returned in our carriage to Naples.

"April 6th. Went on board the Rochfort with Mr. Eden, flag-lieutenant, Mr. and Mrs. Wills, and Mr. Gage. Walked in the afternoon with Mr. Wills nearly as far as Portici. Dined with Admiral Sir Graham Moore, who very kindly promised to take me to Malta, if I liked to go, and, if possible, to get me a passage home from thence in a man-of-war. He was Sir John Moore's brother. Captain Schomberg dined there, Captain Hamilton of the Cambrian, and Bacon of the 10th Hussars, also a Swedish count doing duty on board the Iphigenia.

"April 7th. Went to the museum at Portici; it contains walls, painted *al fresco*, taken from Herculaneum, Pompeii, and Strabia; the colouring was very fresh, though the paintings are clumsy, but we cannot suppose that the fresco paintings of the ancients were their best performances. I mentioned before, that on our visit to Pompeii, in a house outside the walls, we had seen the mark of a person's figure against the wall. In the Portici museum we saw a large crust of hardened ashes, in which was the print of one of her breasts. Her scull is preserved here, and there is also one arm-bone, round which was found a gold bracelet. Mr. Massey, son of Mr. Massey of Chester, dined with us.

"April 8th. Went with Mr. Wills on board the Rochfort, to hear divine service. Lunched with the admiral. Went from the Rochfort to the Cambrian, and called on Lord G. Paulet. Mr. Hart of the Rochfort, brother to Hart of the 86th, formerly in the 52nd, dined with us.

"April 9. This being our last day at Naples, we very much wished to go to Baiæ, but the weather being very wet in the morning, we gave it up. Stephen Poyntz breakfasted and spent the day with us. A Neapolitan frigate got on shore in the night, and we drove about three miles on the Portici road to the place. Our boats were all there getting her stores out, as it was found impossible to save her. In the course of the afternoon one of the Iphigenia's boats, which was riding at anchor about a hundred yards from the shore, was swamped, and two men who were in her were unfortunately drowned. Poyntz and I walked up to the Fort of St. Elmo, but the Austrian commandant refused to let us in. The view of Naples from this elevated spot is extremely magnificent. Poyntz and I paid a second visit to the stranded frigate with Captain Schomberg, and after walking through the arsenal, where we saw the remains of the seventy-four burnt some time before, went and dined at a *trattoria* in the Toledo.

"April 10. Left Naples a little after five in the morning, and arrived at Terracina about eight in the evening. Six of the robbers had returned to their old pursuits in the mountains, but their companions, to shew their earnest repentance, had pursued, taken, and lodged them in the prison of Fondi. We started for Rome at five o'clock on the 11th. Over the Pomptine marshes we were driven at the rate of a post in thirty-five minutes: almost all the postillions are mere boys. We breakfasted at Velletri about twelve o'clock, and got to Rome at four. Went to a party at Mr. Vesey's. 12th. Went in the evening to Torlonia's. 13th. Saw the collection of pictures in the Palazzo Borghese; some of them are very good, particularly those of Titian. I afterwards visited Thorwaldsen's studio, and was much pleased with observing the artists at work. In the evening I went to a concert at the Palazzo Caferelli on the Campidoglio. There were about thirty singers; the music was sacred, and I was delighted with it, notwithstanding our being bored by the noise of one of our countrymen, who seemed to take no more delight in it than a cow would have done.

"April 14th. Rode with Hope, Hesketh, Levinge, and a Polish count, to Frascati. From the hill there is an extensive view of the Campagna, but the day was rather too hazy for it. We proceeded, some walking and some on donkies, to Tusculum, to see the remains of Cicero's villa. We fell in with the Prince of Saxony and his daughter, and visited, *en passant*, a villa, where we saw some fine water-works, and heard a horn sounded by the statue of a centaur, by means of the running water. We saw a few ruins lying here and there on the hill of Tusculum. On returning to Frascati, Hope and I started off to see the Alban Lake. At some distance before reaching the lake I thought the scenery more beautiful than any scenery I had seen in Italy or France. We almost fancied ourselves in an English wood on a summer's day! The lake is supposed to be in the crater of an ancient volcano. In very early times a subterraneous passage, a mile in length, was dug from it through the hill, to let off its waters and to prevent sudden and dangerous swells, to which it was formerly subject. This day I rode upwards of thirty miles, without being the worse for it. The day was very hot and sultry.

"April 15th. This being Palm Sunday, the Pope performed divine service, at his own chapel, at the Quirinal. We were too late to see him officiate, but we saw him carried in procession round the large hall, preceded by choristers, cardinals, &c. We afterwards went into the chapel, where there were many English ladies, and some English officers in uniform. Went to Sir Walter Synot's, where I met the Veseys, and heard two good sermons.

"Have been so engaged lately, that my journal has been totally neglected. I regret not having kept it regularly during the holy week, but that would have been almost impossible. The Pope blessed, amongst others who were assembled in front of St. Peter's on Easter Sunday, 10,000 Austrian soldiers; I was in uniform, and there were about sixty English officers in uniform there. When the multitude knelt to receive the Pope's blessing, I looked over the whole assembly, and saw that only two English officers, besides myself, were standing. I could not have knelt, but I think we should have kept away altogether.

"April 30th. Rode to Tivoli, where I joined Mr. and the Misses Wolfe, and Mr. and Mrs. Wills. The gentlemen paid three visits to the grotto of Neptune, and one to that of the sibyl. In the morning of the 1st of May we visited Adrian's villa, which I thought very pleasing; the number and variety of the ruins, the luxuriant evergreens growing on and about them in all directions, the delightful season of the year, the solitary appearance of the place—all united to make the effect delightful. We afterwards went to the Solfatura, and then returned to Rome.

"May 3rd. Left Rome in the morning at half-past one, and reached Radicofani at nine at night. Left Radicofani a little before five, and arrived at Florence at midnight. Just as I was about to start from Rome, about eight o'clock at night on the 2nd, I found I had forgotten to procure permission to take post-horses. A friend, however, wrote to Baron Reden, the Hanoverian ambassador, who wrote to Cardinal Consalvi, and, after midnight, I got the permission. May 8th. Just starting for Milan. I suspect Florence is not a good spring climate, for all my acquaintances here are looking much paler than when I last saw them."

I left my carriage at Florence, with directions that it should be sold, and started, in the afternoon of the 8th of May, 1821, with the Milanese courier. The evening was fine, and the country looking very beautiful. Near Pietramala, which is about half-way between Florence and Bologna, at some distance to the right of the road, there is a small volcano, which constantly throws out fire; its crater is about fifteen feet in circumference; we were all asleep, and did not see it. I walked up the road over the Ciogo, which is five miles long; it is the highest mountain of the Apennines. From sitting down to rest myself, I caught a violent cold. We arrived at Bologna about nine in the morning. The museum of the institute contains many interesting things; in a room containing anatomical specimens there is a complete young Cyclops. We arrived at Modena about four in the afternoon, having left Bologna in the middle of the day. Some miles before we came to Mantua, we passed the Po on a superb bridge of boats, at least it looked very superb by moonlight, and afterwards the Mincio. From the top of the Campanile of Cremona I had a fine view of the adjacent country, and of the windings of the Po; opposite to Cremona there are some large islands, apparently well cultivated. To the westward I saw Piacenza, and beyond it the Apennines, and to the eastward I had a fine view of the snowy Alps; I could not see the Lago di Garda. They have commenced hay-making here, although they have not done so in Tuscany.

"May 10th. Pizzighitone is a small, but strong fortress, and is washed by the Adda, which is a fine large river. Francis I was conducted here when he was made a prisoner at Pavia. We arrived at Lodi about ten o'clock at night, and I walked about a mile to the bridge over the Adda, which Bonaparte forced in such gallant style in 1795. The bridge is more than a quarter of a mile long, and was defended by 10,000 Austrians, and lots of artillery. The French must have lost a great many men, and it must have been a gallant exploit, but I do not think it was a very difficult one, for when once the French were on the bridge, their best plan was to advance as rapidly as possible; had they turned, they must have experienced a much greater loss than they did in advancing. We arrived at Milan at three o'clock on the morning of the 11th, and I felt completely knocked up, and resolved never again to travel two days and three nights without stopping, if I can avoid it.

"Milan, May 11th. Went to the Scala; thought the opera stupid, and the singing very bad. The ballet was got up in a most splendid manner, and two or three of the performers danced exceedingly well. In the evening of the 12th I went to Signor Girolomo's puppet exhibition, and was much entertained. The title of the piece was 'Samson and the Philistines,' and Samson certainly knocked out the brains of four or five of his enemies in very great style. The figure of Samson himself was very good. All the speaking is by one person; the action is uncommonly good; the hands, feet, and head have strings fixed to them from above. I went again to see this performance; the imitation of part of the ballet at the Scala is super-excellent; it only astonishes me that it is possible to make the figures dance so well."

Blencowe arrived from Florence, and we agreed to travel together to Turin, where Sir E. and my sister, and Fitzgibbon, had arranged to meet me from Nice. Having purchased an old *chaise de poste* between us, we left Milan in the afternoon of the 17th of May. The following is written across my journal:—

"N. B. Tossed up for the *chaise de poste* at Turin, when I lost it. Blencowe desires I will add this by way of postscript, so that in case anything should happen to me, my friends may not accuse him of stealing my share of the produce of the carriage."

About a mile beyond Bufalora, we passed the Ticino, which, taking its rise in the Simplon, flows through the Lago Maggiore, and runs into the Po a mile or two below Pavia. We drank coffee at Novara, and reached Vercelli about the middle of the night; the place is on the Sesia. During the night we saw immense quantities of fireflies; some of the meadows seemed to be quite on fire with them. The morning was foggy; as it dawned, we descended from the upper plain into the lower one, in which Turin is situated. We passed many rivers—the Dora Baltea, the Orco, Stura, and Dora; over many of these are pontoon bridges, which must be highly necessary in the great floods, but at present most of the boats are dry. We reached Turin about half-past seven on the morning of the 19th.

I travelled from Turin, with my friend Fitzgibbon, through Geneva and Paris to Havre de Grace, and arrived at Southampton on the 17th of June. The having passed the winter and spring in Italy had been of great service to my health; and my religious feelings had been strengthened, and my views of religion had become clearer during this period. At Geneva I was introduced, by my friend Fitzgibbon, to that good man, Dr. Cæsar Malan, a name since so well known in England, and we passed the greater part of two clear days in his society. I do not now agree with all his views of religion, but I have always since felt great respect and veneration for him as a holy and devoted minister of the gospel. My friend Fitzgibbon had been much concerned to find that, with all my religious feeling, I could not see that it was wrong, for one who feared God, to go to the opera and theatre, and to other places of amusement which he very much disapproved of. He was not satisfied with my assurance that, whenever I should see these things to be sinful and wrong in the sight of God, I would have nothing more to do with them. I have often been surprised, in after years, that I did not at once see the vanity and sin of some of these things, especially of theatres, which are generally attended by numbers of the worst characters of both sexes, and where, in the representations, amongst many other things which militate against religion and morality, it often happens that the name of God is grievously profaned.

My friend was most anxious that I should converse with Dr. Malan upon these matters, and I being not at all unwilling to do so, we were left together, in one of our walks, for that purpose. I knew that Dr. Malan was aware of our friend's object in leaving us together, and I was rather expecting that he would introduce the subject; this, however, he did not do, so I told him that Mr. Fitzgibbon was very desirous that I should have some conversation with him upon the point of whether or not it was wrong, for one who desired to do what was pleasing in the sight of God in all things, to go to plays, and races, and balls; that I could not at present see the evil of them, but was prepared to renounce them whenever I should be convinced that it was my duty to do so. I was particularly struck with Dr. Malan's judicious conduct on the occasion. Instead of entering into any argument with me, or on any statement of his views on the subject, he merely replied as follows :—" My dear Sir, if you really love our dear Saviour, "you will very soon have no inclination for these amusements "which you have been speaking of."

I believe it was on our return from this walk, that we had a very narrow escape of being killed, or seriously wounded, whilst we were looking on at some mortar-practice which was taking place from the walls of Geneva. The mark they were firing at was placed in the middle of a large open square, some hundreds of yards from the town, and inclosed on each side by rows of high trees, on the outside of which the spectators were standing. The artillerymen were firing very badly, and I had just observed that the barrel, I think it was, which they were firing at, was lently the safest spot, when a shell came over the trees into midst of our party of five or six, who were all standing close ther. In coming to the ground it knocked off the hat of one he party, and just grazed the arm of another, without doing er of them the least injury: of course the shells were not led. At his family prayers, that night, Dr. Malan offered up ise and thanksgiving for our merciful deliverance.

CHAPTER XVII.

1821.

AT HOME, AND THEN REJOIN THE 52ND AT DUBLIN.

Feelings of my relatives with regard to my religious views—Family prayers—Testimony of some now gone—Sir John Colborne—Coronation of George IV—Queen Caroline—Feelings of the people—Rejoin the 52nd at Dublin—My altered feelings with regard to religion—Found Gawler a religious man—Several incidents connected with his change—First intimation to the other officers of my altered views—Attendance at mess—The King's visit to Dublin—Incidents on his landing—Levee at the castle—A judge awkwardly circumstanced—43rd and 52nd reviewed by the King—In command of McNair's company that day—A ramrod accidentally discharged—Charge of cavalry, shewing that the horses would be willing to go on to the bayonets—The King's visit to St. Patrick's Cathedral—Mr. Guinness.

ON my return home for a short time before I rejoined my regiment, my poor dear mother, who had been somewhat alarmed by the earnestness and frequency of my observations on religion, displayed in my letters from Italy, was quite delighted to find me so changed for the better. My ideas about religion had undergone an entire revolution since I had last been at home, and I believe this was very apparent from my outward conduct. The subject of religion was much discussed in the family, and I have reason to know that, from that time, there was more anxious inquiry about it than there had ever been before amongst us. Family prayers, and reading of the Scriptures, which had only been attended to in former times on the Sunday evening, were now introduced, and afterwards were always regularly observed on every morning and evening; and this same observance was carried out, in succeeding years, in the families and households of the children. Some, who are now gone, have often referred to this period, and have told me how they thanked God that He had led me to think about these things as He had done, and had thus conferred such a benefit and blessing on the whole family.

Shortly after my return home, an important ball came off in the neighbourhood, and although I pleaded great disinclination to attend it, it was very fairly argued by some of the family that, as I did not see any harm in balls, I was bound out of kindness to my mother and sisters to accompany them on this occasion, as they particularly wished it; I accordingly went, and met at the ball great numbers of my old friends; I did not feel disposed to dance, but had much conversation with two or three of them on that subject which was uppermost in my mind. This, of course, very much astonished those who had known me before as quite a different sort of person. I got very tired of the ball, and went away, at the end of two hours, to the friend's house in which we were to sleep: this was the last ball I ever attended. In the course of this work I shall endeavour to state, as fully and clearly as I can, the views which I gradually arrived at, with regard to what is usually called "intercourse with the world."

My leave expired on the 24th of July, 1821; and on my way to join the 52nd in Dublin, I spent some days in London, where I called on Sir John and Lady Colborne; he was there for the coronation of George IV. He asked me if I would walk with him to the Horse Guards, and said, as we were going along, " I have " always made it a rule not to ask for anything for myself, but I " have just heard that Sir Robert Arbuthnot, on applying for the " command at Guernsey, has been told by the Duke of York that " he intended to offer it to Sir John Colborne, so I am just going " to the Horse Guards to tell the Duke that I shall be very happy " to accept it:" he added, " I do not consider this the same thing " as making an application for it, which I should not do." I have always, from that time, acted upon the same plan, and have never asked for anything in the way of advancement for myself; I probably have not lost anything by adhering to it, but I have, at all events, thereby avoided much unpleasantness which the meeting with refusals might have occasioned.

Sir John Colborne was entitled, as King's aide-de-camp, to tickets of admission for two friends, to see the ceremony of the coronation, and, on hearing that I intended to see what I could of it, said he was sorry his tickets had been given away before he was aware of my being in town. I worked my way through the immense crowd in Parliament Street, and, by paying a guinea, obtained a seat which afforded me an excellent view of the procession. In Parliament street, whilst standing on a door-step, I saw poor Queen Caroline, attended by three gentlemen, proceeding in an open barouche and four to Westminster Abbey. She soon returned, looking extremely mortified. Both on going and returning, she was tremendously cheered by the people. A few soldiers, under the command of a corporal, who were making their way along the pavement in single file, were greeted with hisses, and cries of "God save the Queen" were dinned into their ears. By way of taking their part, and keeping them in countenance, I cried out, "God save the King," when a woman near me said to me, very savagely, "You had better hold your tongue, young man, "or you will get your nose slit."

There was something very formidable in going back to my regiment, and to my brother-officers, after a long absence, with my views on the subject of religion so changed, and with a determination, with God's help, to give up my old careless and sinful ways. No one in the regiment had any idea of what had taken place in my mind. I had some considerable hope that I might find one of my old companions to be of a congenial disposition with myself, for one of the officers, in writing to me about a horse which I had left with him, had written the following sentence :—"Gawler is making a great cake of himself, converting "the men." And a few months after, in another letter, he wrote :—"Gawler is about to be married to a lady as religious as himself." When I saw Sir John Colborne in London, I thought I would try and learn something more on this point, and asked, "Gawler "has become very religious, has he not, Sir ?" But he was not inclined to be very communicative on the subject, and all the reply I received was, "Yes, I believe he has."

The following is extracted from my journal :—"I proceeded to Dublin, viâ Liverpool, and joined my regiment at the Richmond barracks on the 25th of July, 1821. This was, of course, a season of trial to me, when meeting my old companions, with whom I had in former days entered into all kinds of folly and dissipation, but an all-merciful God had shewn me the error and folly of my former course of life, and now enabled me boldly to declare my sentiments."

I think it was on the afternoon of the day of my arrival, that Gawler, who was a married man, and living at some distance from the barracks, rode into the barrack square, and thus I had at once the opportunity of making known to him my religious sentiments. I feel it desirable, in relating this and several other circumstances which occurred in my intercourse with my brother-officers and others, to relate them in detail, and sometimes to mention, as far as I can, the very words which were used; I think the doing so may, by God's mercy, be made useful to many young persons who may read this work. There was something very remarkable in the meeting of Gawler and myself on this occasion. More than four years before this time he had gone on leave from the regiment, when it was in cantonments in the north of France, and, from ill health, had been unable to rejoin us until the very evening before the day of my starting from Chester, in 1819, to go into Germany. He was in time for mess on that evening, and I recollect just speaking to him in the ante-room before we went into dinner. I did not sit near him, and I had no idea whatever that he had returned to the regiment quite an altered man with regard to religion. He had been, as too many were in those days, sceptical about the Christian religion, and the truth of the Scriptures. His heavenly Father "led him "in a way that he knew not." He was ill and confined to his bed, for some considerable time, in a lodging in London. Whilst he lay there, in his lonely chamber, he began to think over all the arguments which he had read in Paley's "Evidences of Christianity," when he had been forced many years before to get up that work for an examination at the junior department of the Military College. His powerful and clear understanding,[*] and

[*] When I went, as a 52nd officer, ten years after Gawler's time, to study at the senior department at Sandhurst, Colonel Butler, the lieutenant-governor, enquired very earnestly after him, and spoke of him as the best man they had ever had there.

retentive memory, enabled him to succeed in this, and he became most deeply convinced that the Bible was the inspired Word of God. His eyesight very much failed him at that time, and he paid a young man to come for a certain time to read to him every day. He read principally to him out of the New Testament, and when Gawler heard of the spotless character and holy precepts of the Lord Jesus Christ, one immediate effect upon his mind was, that he came to the conclusion that there was not a Christian man in the world; another effect was, which shewed his sincerity, that he determined he would try, from that time forward, to be a true Christian, and to act up to all the commands of his God. It was not until some considerable time had elapsed that, from attending the house of God, and from becoming acquainted with some serious Christian people, he learnt the "way of God more perfectly," and discovered that it was not by his own holiness, but through trusting in the meritorious death of the Son of God that he was to be saved, his faith evidencing itself to be a saving faith by the fruits of holiness which it produced. When, after the recovery of his health, he rejoined his regiment, he was most anxious to be of service, in a religious point of view, both to his brother-officers and to the men. He had served in the Peninsula and at Waterloo, and was then high up in the list of lieutenants, and was considered a very intelligent and good officer;* yet, of course, his altered views and ways very much astonished all his old friends, who were altogether unaccustomed to such anxious and earnest feelings in matters of religion. Almost all of us, I believe, thought very little about it,

* The following is extracted from the 52nd record, published in 1860:— "Colonel Gawler was essentially a 52nd officer. He served in this regiment only, "and was a type of that steady, cool, and gallant set of company officers, whose "attention to regimental duty, and experience in the field, so materially helped "to place the 52nd amid the most distinguished in the service of Britain. En-"tering the 52nd Light Infantry in November, 1811, Colonel Gawler served to "the end of the Peninsular War, in 1814, and was present at the storming of "Badajoz, (when he led the ladder party of the 52nd stormers,) at the battles of "Vittoria, Vera, the Nivelle, the Nive, Orthes, and Toulouse, besides various "minor affairs. At Waterloo, he commanded the right company of the 52nd "after his captain (Diggle) was put *hors de combat*. He was wounded below the "right knee at Badajoz, and in the neck at St. Munos, and has received the war-"medal with seven clasps."

and had very confused and sceptical notions on the subject, one ignorant and prevailing idea being that, through the death of Christ, there was a mitigation of the strictness of the requirements of God's law, and there was a perversion of the truth that "God " is not extreme to mark what is done amiss;" the idea, in fact, resolving itself into this, that people might follow their inclinations, and do pretty much as they liked, and yet that a merciful God would receive and bless them in the end. There was no fear of God's anger against sin, no proper notion of the way of pardon through trusting in the satisfaction made by the death of Christ, or of the necessity of a change of heart, and of holiness of life, as indicative of a true and saving faith. He met with the greatest kindness from Sir John Colborne and Colonel Charles Rowan, the commanding officers of that period. In the summer of 1819, when the regiment was stationed at Weedon, Northampton, and Daventry, he obtained leave from Sir John Colborne to march a very considerable number of the men, who appeared to be seriously disposed, to receive the sacrament of the Lord's Supper at Daventry, I think. At the risk of getting rather too far away from the account of what happened to me on my arrival in Dublin in 1821, I must not omit an anecdote which was afterwards related to me by Gawler, and which helps to show that God does not despise, but that, on the contrary, He often greatly honours the humble and prayerful efforts of His servants, whatever their calling or profession may be, to do good to the souls of their fellow-creatures. In the early part of 1820, he was with some companies of the 52nd at Derby, and after he had been there for some weeks, it occurred to him, one Sunday morning, that he had been some time in the town without having made any attempt to direct the attention of some of his poor ignorant fellow-sinners around him to those truths of Scripture which, by the Holy Spirit's teaching, make men wise unto salvation. With prayer to God for direction and a blessing, he went out, in plain clothes, and turned out of one of the main streets into a narrow street, evidently inhabited by very poor people, and entered the first house he came to, in which he found a woman sweeping the floor. On his speaking to her, she, thinking he was the doctor, immediately said, "Oh, Sir, it's in the next house that the woman lives, who is so ill!" He immediately took the hint, and went into the next house, in which he found a poor, wretched woman, extremely ill, lying on a dirty bed, with everything around her denoting extreme destitution. He discovered afterwards that she had been a woman of very drunken habits. On his speaking to her seriously, and trying to point out to her her danger on account of sin, and the love of God in sending His Son into the world to save sinners, she became very angry and outrageous, and told him that he was a sinner himself, and called him a hypocrite. He bore all this quietly, and told her he had indeed been a great sinner against God, but that he had sought and had found pardon through the blood-shedding of Christ. He did not lose sight of her, and she afterwards became an altered character, and a truly religious woman: she told Gawler that the thing which first touched her feelings was, his saying that he himself had been a great sinner, and had found mercy through the satisfaction made by the death of the Son of God. Many years after this, I went to call upon this poor woman, and found her well versed in the Scriptures, and having clear views of religion. Although she could not read, she had become well acquainted with the Word of God, and with portions of psalms and hymns, by getting friends frequently to read to her; she was also quite a pattern of neatness, and was much respected by all who knew her. She has now been dead for many years.

Before Gawler and I parted, on the first day of my arrival in Dublin, we arranged to meet again the next day. He was much astonished and pleased to hear of my change, but was almost inclined at first to doubt the reality of it. I recollect, on his leaving me, one of the officers who had been standing not very far from us, said to me, "Leeke, are you become a 'New Light?'" I replied, "What do you mean by a 'New Light,' and what makes "you think I am one?" He said, "I heard you say to Gawler, "that you thought your religious views and sentiments were very "much the same as his; he is a regular 'New Light,' and has "been trying to convert the men." Nothing further happened until after mess that day, when I went with my old captain, McNair, and two other officers, to one of their barrack-rooms, to talk over several matters, and, amongst other things, to arrange that McNair should go to Colonel Rowan, and request that I might rejoin my old company, No. 9. And now came my first trial with regard to my desire to do what I considered to be right in the sight of God. After speaking for some little time on various subjects, something was said by one of the party which was decidedly sinful, and painful to me, and which I could not listen to conscientiously. I felt it necessary at once to say to them, " since I have been away from the regiment, I have learnt " that many of these things which we used to think nothing of, " are wrong in the sight of God, and, as I have determined to try " and rule my conduct according to His Word, I must not stay here " to listen to them." One of them replied, at the same time pulling me quietly into my chair, " Oh don't go away, man, we won't " speak in any way which is unpleasant to you;" so I remained for some little time longer, till one of the party inadvertently recurred to the same kind of conversation, when I got up, saying again, " I cannot remain here to listen to this kind of thing, " I must go away," which I at once did, although they were again very kind about it, and wished to detain me. I have always, whenever I have thought of that evening in after years, felt most thankful to God that He enabled me thus decidedly to act upon my religious convictions. I was never afterwards urged by any of my brother-officers to do anything which I told them I thought to be wrong.

An arrangement was made by Colonel Rowan, by which I was appointed to McNair's company, in which I had been since I first joined the regiment in 1815. I expected that my greatest trials might possibly arise at the mess; either from anything in the shape of swearing, or of indelicate conversation taking place near me; and I thought if anything really objectionable should occur, at any time, that the right thing to do, would be quietly to say something to stop it, and if the thing was persisted in, then to get up and leave the room. I only recollect this sort of thing happening once, when I think I said to the offender, " If I were " you, ———— , I would not speak in that way;" and he replied, " Surely it's no business of yours," but the offensive conversation ceased. I have often wondered at, and have been most thankful for, all the kindness I met with from all those kind, noble-hearted fellows, who must have been, many of them, more or less annoyed by the unexpected change in my feelings, and in my way of going on. Before I returned, I had prayed much that I might be the means, under God, of leading them to forsake their careless and sinful ways, and to lead a life of faith and holiness, and, in my simplicity, I expected that, possibly, a large proportion of them might be induced, by my history of my own change, to read their Bibles, and to seek the true knowledge of God, and His salvation. Perhaps I may think it well, before I close this work, to advert to some cases in which I think real benefit arose to some from their attention having been drawn so prominently to the subject of religion. One thing I ought to mention, as it may be an encouragement to some who may read this, "in everything by "prayer and supplication, with thanksgiving, to make their "requests known unto God:" Philippians iv, 6, 7. I never, I think, put my hand on the handle of the mess-room door without offering up a short prayer, that God would bless me, and keep me from that which was wrong and sinful, or calculated in any way to discredit the cause of religion in the sight of others.

It had been arranged between Gawler and myself, that on the day after that on which I arrived, I should drink tea with him and his wife, and accompany them to a weekly evening service and sermon which they were in the habit of attending at one of the churches in Dublin. He told me, some time afterwards, that he could scarcely feel assured at first that I had not been deceiving myself, as to the reality of my religious convictions and feelings; and that he thought, if, instead of going to mess on that evening, I preferred drinking tea quietly with them and accompanying them to a religious service, it would be some proof that I was in earnest. I am not sure whether it was on this occasion that I was first led to see the propriety of saying grace, not only before and after dinner, as is customary with most persons, but also at the commencement of every meal. However, I determined from that time forward to follow the example of our Lord and Master, and to thank God and to pray to Him, at every meal, to give His blessing with what He had graciously provided for me.

About three weeks after his coronation, and shortly after I had returned to the regiment, King George IV visited Ireland, and there was much to enliven us in the shape of reviews, a procession of the King's to St. Patrick's, and a levée which he held at the castle; I will endeavour to give some details of these, which may be found interesting to the reader. The King, on landing, was received by the Irish in a most enthusiastic manner, and many droll things were mentioned at the time, as having occurred; of these I only recollect the two following: the people pressed on the King as he landed, and one of them said "How do ye do, "your majesty?" The King answered, "How do you do, Pat?" at which the man was highly delighted, and exclaimed, "See! "he knows me!" The King shook hands with many of the people as he landed, and one of them much gratified by this act of kindness and condescension, held up his hand and addressed it as follows: "Well! *you* shall never be washed again as long as I live."

The streets of Dublin were lined by the troops as the King passed through them to the castle, and he must have been much pleased at his reception by the citizens. The levée was of course very much crowded, and I should presume that the pressure must have been much worse than even anything of the sort which has taken place in later years at St. James's. I well remember the crush that there was the whole of the way up the staircase, and indeed until each person to be presented was ushered into the King's presence. There were dignitaries of the church, judges, naval and military officers and civilians, all in one confused and heated mass. On the stairs I found myself in very close contact with one of the judges, who certainly was in a most ludicrous and somewhat pitiable condition: I fear I shall scarcely succeed in describing the sad plight in which he was: his wig was twisted round, so that the part which should have been on his ear was brought round so that the edge of the wig came to the middle of his forehead and passed down the bridge of his nose and over the middle of his mouth, covering about one half of his face, whilst down the other half large powdered drops of perspiration were chasing each other in rather quick succession; what made his case the more distressing was, that he was utterly powerless to help himself and to place his wig in its proper position, his arms and hands being down, and fixed to his body by the pressure as closely as if they had been firmly tied by ropes; he must have remained in this predicament for ten minutes at the least, for we proceeded from one stair to another somewhat at the same rate at which the devout Romanists mount on their knees Pontius Pilate's stairs at Rome. The judge was rather short than otherwise, which made matters worse for him, for tall men have always a great advantage in a dense mass of people, as I have frequently experienced, especially in the swaying to and fro of the crowd. On this occasion, as every person tried to make good his footing on each stair, when he got carried forward to it, somebody, whether the judge or not I forget, lost his temper and exclaimed, "Can "these be gentlemen?" This of course produced a general titter, and some one said, "The best thing we can all do is to keep our "tempers." In crossing the ante-room from one door to the other there was a little "opening out" of the closely packed column, and to our right we saw sundry proofs of the disasters which had occurred to those who had preceded us, in the shape of stray shoe-buckles and other articles forming part of a full-dress costume. As every man seemed bent on not losing his place, the crushing and confusion were at their worst at the entrance of the presentation room: as each person came to the doorway he had to make a violent effort to disengage himself from those with whom he was wedged in, and he was extremely fortunate if, after getting himself into the room, he succeeded in taking after him the skirts of his coat. I calculate that on that occasion about eight persons kissed hands and passed on in each minute, which would be at the rate of nearly five hundred in an hour. Directly the person entered the room, the lord-in-waiting took his card and read out his name, which name, as he knelt on one knee and kissed hands, the King repeated, as he addressed him, adding, " I "hope you are very well." On passing on through the room two of us, who had kept pretty well together, got down by some other stairs, and of course in vain tried to find the carriage in which we had come to the levée; indeed there was no getting out and making our way through the castle yard and through the crowd beyond it, so we made our way down into the basement story, and passing through various passages by the side of the extensive kitchens and offices, we got out into a narrow street at some distance from the main entrance, and after passing through two or three streets succeeded in securing an inside Irish car, which took us to the barracks, but we had not proceeded far before we met with a trifling incident, which rather amused us :—A girl of eleven or twelve years of age rushed after the car and succeeded in getting a seat on the step behind, from which we told her to get down; in doing so she fell and rolled on the ground. We desired the driver to pull up, thinking she might be hurt, which was not the case; this brought several women to their doors, and one of them exclaimed, "You rascals! I saw the wheel go over "her." We drove on, leaving them to settle the matter amongst them.

During his visit to Dublin the King reviewed the whole of the garrison in the Phœnix Park, on August the 18th, and on a subsequent day he reviewed, on the same ground, the 43rd and and 52nd Regiments of Light Infantry, which had formed, with the old 95th Rifles and two battalions of Portuguese caçadores, the famous light division of the Peninsular War. The King wished to see the 43rd and 52nd by themselves, without any of the rest of the garrison, except a squadron of hussars to help to show off the movements of the two regiments. On this occasion I commanded Captain McNair's company, and was the only officer with it. The reader must kindly bear with my mentioning this and other circumstances in the course of my narrative, which may tend to show that I was considered a good and efficient officer. It helps to prove that when a man becomes truly anxious to serve his God, he is not thereby the less fitted for the life and duties of a soldier. There was something peculiar in the circumstance of an ensign being left in command of a company on this rather important occasion, for it was the regular custom, on field days, for the adjutant to send one of the senior lieutenants from some other company to supersede a rather junior officer in such command, and there were plenty of subaltern officers with the other companies. He would hardly have ventured to leave me in command of No. 9 on that day, without there being some special reason for it.

In the course of the day my company skirmished a good deal, and on seeing the cavalry preparing to charge us, we formed rallying square and opened fire upon them. On reloading, I heard a ramrod go from a musket close to me, doing the man no injury, except that of stinging his fingers; as the musket was sloped outwards it carried the ramrod away in the direction of the group around the King and the Commander-in-Chief. Very shortly afterwards an aide-de-camp brought it back to the square, and I was glad to find that it had not done any mischief. Whilst No. 9 company was skirmishing, the 43rd and 52nd formed squares in echelon, the right rear angle of the front square being about twelve paces from the left and front angle of the other. The cavalry were ordered to charge through the interval, and the squares to open fire upon them; I saw the charge very plainly, there was no hesitation on the part of the horses, they galloped fairly up to the bayonets in the face of the fire from the rear face of the front square and of the left face of the rear one, and the front of the cavalry being too long for the interval, the men on each flank filed inwards, only diminishing their charging pace sufficiently to enable them to do this. From what I saw on this occasion, and from what I saw of the charges of the French cuirassiers at Waterloo, and from the example of poor Howard of the 10th hussars at Waterloo, I am perfectly convinced that if cavalry do not charge home upon infantry in square, it is not the fault of the horses. Still, from all that I have heard on the subject, I believe that it is useless for cavalry alone, (*i.e.* unattended by infantry or artillery,) however numerous they may be, to attempt to make an impression on steady squares of infantry.

The only other event I recollect in connexion with the King's sojourn at Dublin was his visit to St. Patrick's cathedral, when the streets were lined with troops, and we had a soaking day of it. The inhabitants were very hospitable, and pressed us to take refreshment in their houses. Colonel Rowan, in consideration of my recent recovery from illness, would not allow me to remain exposed to the pouring rain, and very kindly sent me off to the barracks. The mention of St. Patrick's naturally leads me to speak of the munificent gift, by Mr. Benjamin Guinness, of £150,000 for the restoration, &c., of that magnificent building. I recollect him very well, at the period I am writing about, and his excellent father, Mr. Arthur Guinness, the governor of the bank of Ireland, from whom and from other branches of the family, I received much kind attention during our stay in Dublin.

CHAPTER XVIII.

1821.

DUELLING.

Major Oliver of the artillery—Is sent to "Coventry" by the artillery officers of the Dublin district—I become acquainted with him—Discussions on duelling, at the 52nd mess—Colonel Rowan's opinion—Remarkable instance of apology—Recent additions to the articles of war—Roman Catholic officers of the Prussian Guards removed for declaring they would not fight a duel—Severe sentence on officers of the Russian Guards for fighting a duel—Belgian Minister of War sentenced to imprisonment for engaging in a duel.

JUST before I rejoined the 52nd at Dublin, the following circumstance had occurred in the garrison. The field-officer of the day, Major Oliver (afterwards General Oliver) of the artillery, on going his rounds at night, found that a civilian had just been handed over, most improperly, to a serjeant's guard, by a mate or officer of the navy, for some alleged offence. In his report to the general, Major Oliver stated that there was some reason for supposing that the naval officer was not sober. Some little time after, the captain of the man-of-war met Major Oliver in one of the streets, and told him he had heard that, in his report to the general, he had accused his officer of being drunk, and that it was "a ——— lie!" This was also reported to the general, who desired that Major Oliver would not call the naval captain to account for the language which he had used; but he was, of course, prevented from doing that by his religious principles. The officers of the artillery of the Dublin district then addressed the Duke of Wellington, as master-general of the ordnance, on the subject, and agreed to send Major Oliver to "Coventry" for not

X

calling the man out who had insulted him. The Duke, in his reply, refused to take notice of the matter. This was the state of things when I arrived in Dublin, and when I first became acquainted with Major Oliver, whom I met one morning at the house of a mutual friend on whom we happened to call at the same time. I was aware of most of the circumstances above related before I saw him, though he gave me the whole account of the affair some time afterwards. We left the house, at which we were calling, together, and we had not proceeded far, when I fancied that he thought it would be somewhat injurious to me to be seen walking with so notorious a character as he was, and that he was trying to leave me, for he said he wanted to call at one of the houses which we were passing; his friends, however, were not at home, so we continued to walk together along Sackville street, and met two of our 52nd captains, with whom I exchanged nods. At mess that evening, one of them asked me, across the table, if that was Major Oliver with whom he had seen me walking in the morning. On my replying that it was Major Oliver, he said, "you are a young man, so let me give you a piece "of advice—don't you be seen walking with Major Oliver any "more; he is not well thought of in the garrison, and it will be a "disadvantage to you to be seen with him." My reply was, and I felt thankful that I was enabled to make it, " I know all about "Major Oliver, and the affair to which you allude; I consider that " he has acted in it in accordance with the commands of his God, "with the articles of war, and with the laws of his country; I "consider it an honour to be acquainted with Major Oliver, and "I shall certainly not be ashamed to be seen walking with him, "whenever I have the opportunity of doing so." Major Oliver's conduct, and the whole subject of duelling, was frequently discussed at the mess of the 52nd, and I often declared that, whatever might happen to me, I would never fight a duel; and this statement was received without its being ridiculed and scouted. I recollect, on one occasion, Colonel Charles Rowan left the mess-room at the same time that I did, and said, as we were going out, " I believe, Leeke, you are quite right in the views "you have been upholding, but," he added, "I think a man "holding such views should not remain in the army." He would not have added this last sentence at a later period of his life, when it pleased God to lead him, as a poor sinner, to trust in the atoning death of Christ for the pardon of his sins, and to walk, under the influence and guidance of the Spirit and Word of God, in holiness and peace. I became very intimate with Major Oliver, and often walked with him. He told me that some of the artillery officers would take notice of him in passing, when they were alone, but would not do so when walking with any other person; and that he just let them take their course, only speaking to them when they wished it. By degrees the artillery officers began to think themselves wrong, and to be ashamed of the position which they had taken up. When Major Oliver, some time afterwards, went over to Plymouth to give evidence at the court-martial held on the naval officer, he was received and treated with the most marked attention and kindness by the artillery officers in that garrison, and subsequently was received in the same way at Woolwich. The whole affair was a great trial to Major Oliver at the time; I have no doubt, however, but it was one of the chief means, in the providence of God, of leading people to see the folly and wickedness of the whole system of duelling.

It may be well for me to mention the following case, which occurred rather more than a year after Major Oliver's affair, and with the particulars of which I was well acquainted:—A subaltern officer, of some years' standing, had some very offensive expressions addressed to him after dinner in the mess-room by the officer then in command of his regiment, before several other officers. There had been scarcely a glass of wine drunk, and nothing had been said calculated to give offence; indeed, the officer in question had remained after mess at the express request of the commanding officer. I may mention, however, that the latter had received a severe wound in the Peninsula, which was supposed by some to have led to his unaccountable behaviour. The officer insulted immediately left the mess-room, and of course felt himself to be in a most unpleasant predicament. Expressions had been used which he could not pass over, without rendering himself liable to be brought to a court-martial for not having taken proper notice of them. (Samuel, in his book on military law, had mentioned the case of an officer who, under such circumstances, had been cashiered.) He knew that his courage could not be impugned, but he had long before made up his mind that duelling was wrong, and that, whatever might occur, he would never have recourse to it. The next morning one of the other officers undertook to go to the commanding officer to mention the expressions he had used, and to request that he would say he was sorry he had used them. On his refusing to apologize, he told him that, if he persisted in this, charges would be preferred against him, in accordance with one of the articles of war, for acting in an unofficerlike and ungentlemanly manner. The reply was, that there would be no apology, and that the officer aggrieved might do what he liked. On this being reported to him, the officer requested his friend to have the kindness to go once more to the commanding officer, and to say to him that he must know that if ———— positively stated he must prefer charges against him unless he received an apology, he would most certainly do what he said. This second application was successful, and on the officer's going, at his request, to his barrack-room, the commanding officer made a most handsome and kind apology to him, saying, that he had behaved very ill to him on the previous evening, and that he was very sorry for it, and also that he would take an opportunity of stating as much to the officers who had been present.

I have detailed the circumstances of both Major Oliver's case and the other, in order that it may be seen in what difficulties officers have at times been placed with regard to the course they should take, when they have been subject to insult. In almost every case in which differences have arisen between officers, kind friends have managed to heal them, but it has not been always so; though I never recollect, in my time, to have heard of a duel between two officers.

I copy the following from "The Cabinet Lawyer," which shews that, in more recent days than those of which I have written, very strenuous, and I think effectual, means have been taken to put down duelling in the army, and also, consequently, to discourage it amongst other classes:—

"DUELLING IN THE ARMY.—The practice of duelling having

"ceased to be in accordance with the reason and humanity of the
"age, endeavours have been made by the Commander of the
"Forces to check the resort to arms for the settlement of quarrels.
"In 1844 the following three new articles of war were issued,
"with a view to the abatement of duelling in the army.

"'1. Every officer who shall give or send a challenge, or who
"shall accept a challenge to fight a duel with another officer, or
"who, being privy to an intention to fight a duel, shall not take
"active measures to prevent such duel, or who shall upbraid
"another for refusing or for not giving a challenge, or who shall
"reject or advise the rejection of a reasonable proposition made
"for the honourable adjustment of a difference, shall be liable, if
"convicted before a general court-martial, to be cashiered, or suffer
"such other punishment as the court may award.

"'2. In the event of an officer being brought to a court-mar-
"tial for having acted as second in a duel, if it appear that such
"officer exerted himself strenuously to effect an honourable ad-
"justment of the difference, but failed through the unwillingness
"of the adverse parties, then such officer is to suffer such punish-
"ment as the court shall award.

"'3. Approbation is expressed of the conduct of those who,
"having had the misfortune to give offence to, or injure or insult
"others, shall frankly explain, apologise, or offer redress for the
"same, or who, having received offence, shall cordially accept frank
"explanation or apologies for the same; or, if such apologies are
"refused to be made or accepted, shall submit the matter to the
"commanding officer: and, lastly, all officers and soldiers are
"acquitted of disgrace or disadvantage who, being willing to make
"or accept such redress, refuse to accept challenges, as they will
"only have acted as is suitable to the character of honourable
"men, and have done their duty as good soldiers who subject
"themselves to discipline.'"

The following extracts from the public journals, bearing upon the subject of duelling, are very interesting.

"The Times' Correspondent" writes from Berlin, on the 2nd of June, 1864, as follows:—

"Considerable sensation has been excited in the Catholic dis-
"tricts of Prussia, and especially on the Rhine, by the dismissal

"from the army, on very peculiar grounds, of three brothers—the
"Counts of Schmising Kerffenbrock. In the year 1859 they
"joined the 1st Regiment of Foot Guards as officers, and they
"have always passed among their comrades for spirited, joyous
"young men, very frank and honourable. Two or three months
"ago, it appears, the eldest of the three brothers had an unim-
"portant dispute, in which he was in no way to blame, with one
"of his comrades. The affair did not come to a challenge, nor
"was there any occasion that it should do so, consequently young
"Kerffenbrock could in no degree be charged with having declined
"a duel. Nevertheless he found it necessary to inform the officer
"who acted as go-between in the business, and who arranged it
"in a manner perfectly satisfactory for both parties, that the
"Catholic Church forbade duels and all participation in them,
"and denounced excommunication against those of its members
"who should violate this law, a law which he himself, he added,
"was fully determined, under all circumstances, to keep. The me-
"diator thereupon urged him to make the same declaration to the
"commander of the regiment, and declared that if he did not do so,
"he himself should feel bound to report what he had said. He pre-
"ferred the former course, informed his colonel of what had occurred,
"and at the same time urgently entreated that he might be
"allowed to join the army in Schleswig, in order to prove to his
"comrades that it was from no want of personal courage, but from
"Christian feeling and duty towards his Church, that he had
"made up his mind not to fight duels. His prayer was refused.
"After a time the commanding officer of the regiment sent for
"the two younger brothers, and informed them that he felt it his
"duty to ascertain positively whether they shared the views of
"their elder brother with respect to duelling, views which, how-
"ever respectable the motive might be, might sooner or later
"compromise the body of officers intrusted to his charge. The
"two brothers refused to answer the question, declaring that when
"circumstances arose which should place them, according to the
"views of the world, in the necessity of seeking or accepting a
"duel, it then would be time enough for them to show by their
"conduct whether they were more obedient to their religion, or
"to the laws established by men. They added that it was an

"especial duty for a Catholic to avoid whatever could lead to "quarrels, and that they strove constantly to perform that duty. "This did not satisfy the colonel, who laid his commands upon "them to state their views with respect to duels. The three "brothers then declared that their Church forbade duelling, and "that they were firmly resolved to respect the prohibition. Some "time afterwards they were again called before their colonel, and "a Cabinet order was read to them, whereby, without any motive "being assigned, they were dismissed the service. The above is "the substance of the accounts of the affair published by the "*Cologne Gazette* and other papers, and no contradiction of which "has yet reached me."

The following paragraph has been subsequently extracted from one of the papers, and appears to refer to the above-mentioned circumstances:—

"THE PRUSSIAN ARMY AND DUELLING.—A short time ago two "brothers were dismissed the Prussian army, in which they were "officers, for refusing, on account of their scruples as Roman "Catholics, to fight in a duel. All the Prussian bishops have "just addressed a petition to the King on the matter. They ask "if this is really the reason of dismissal, for they cannot believe "that such a conflict exists between the undoubted law of the "Church and the obligations of military service."

The following is from "The Times" of November 26th, 1864:—

"DUELLING IN THE RUSSIAN ARMY.—Since the return of the "Emperor to St Petersburg he has decided on the sentences to "be passed on several officers of the Equestrian Guard who were "concerned in a duel which cost the life of a brother-officer. The "Emperor's anger was justly aroused, for, in opposition to his "known wish to prevent duels, the officers of the regiment "fomented the quarrel between the opponents, instead of endea- "vouring to appease their mutual anger. The original sentence "passed on the offenders by the court-martial was very severe. "The principal and the two seconds were condemned to the loss "of their rank, their orders and medals, and their civil rights. "The principal, a colonel, was also sentenced to twelve years' "forced labour in the mines; and the seconds, a captain and a "lieutenant, to be confined in a fortress for ten years. The

"council of supervision approved these sentences, but, in con-
"sideration that the officers 'had acted under the inspiration of
"'deep-rooted prejudices respecting military honour,' the grace
" of His Majesty was solicited, and it was recommended that the
"colonel should lose his rank and orders, and should serve as a
" private soldier, while the seconds should be confined in a fortress
" for three months. The Emperor was pleased to approve these
" milder sentences."

The next paper is from "The Daily News" of July —, 1865 :—

"THE LATE DUEL IN BELGIUM.—It will be recollected that
"some few months ago a duel took place in Belgium between
" Baron Chazal, the Minister of War, and M. Delaet, a Member
" of the Chamber. Proceedings were taken against the combat-
"ants, and the case came before the Court of Cassation in Brussels
" on Wednesday. It was opened by the reading of a resolution
" of the Chamber authorizing the prosecution, this being necessary,
"as both of the accused were Members of Parliament. M. No-
"thomb, also a Member of Parliament, and who had acted as
"the second of M. Delaet, then gave evidence stating the circum-
"stances under which the hostile meeting had taken place. There
" had been two kinds of provocation, he said—one parliamentary,
" for which Baron Chazal was answerable; the other, extra-
"parliamentary, the responsibility of which rested with M. Delaet.
" Another witness, M. Soudain de Niederweth, deposed as
" follows :—

"' In consequence of a difference between M Delaet and the
"Minister of War a meeting between them was decided upon.
" M. Chazal left the choice of arms to his adversary. M. Delaet
"chose pistols. A riding school at St. Jossæten-Noode was
"selected. The adversaries were placed at twenty paces. Both
" fired, and the Minister of War, who was slightly wounded,
"wished to continue the combat, and was supported in this desire
" by his seconds. Those of M. Delaet would not consent, on the
"ground that the duel had taken place under rigid conditions,
"and at a very short distance, and with liberty to take aim.
"They were, therefore, of opinion that honour was satisfied. The
" Minister of War assented, and declared that there was nothing

"more to be said. M. Delaet thereupon approached the General,
"and said to him, "General, I am happy to repeat to you what
"" my seconds said to you yesterday. I have no personal ani-
"" mosity against you. I have never doubted either your candour
"" or your honour. General, I esteem and honour you."'

"When called upon for their defence, both the accused said
"they had none to offer. They had heard the depositions of the
"witnesses, threw themselves on the court, and had nothing to
"say. The court then retired in order to deliberate, and returned
"in half an hour with the following sentence:—M. Delaet, three
"months' imprisonment and three hundred francs fine; Baron
"Chazal, two months' imprisonment and two hundred francs fine,
"the fine, however, in the latter case, to be commuted, in accord-
"ance with the provisions of the Military Code, into eight days'
"arrest. The *Nord* of yesterday comments upon this sentence
"in the following terms:—'We do not think we exaggerate in
"saying that this sentence will produce a profound sensation far
"beyond the limits of Belgium, both on account of the excep-
"tional character of the accused, and the very remarkable spirit
"of independence which the honourable magistrates of the Court
"of Cassation have manifested in this matter. Long usage, and
"perhaps other and more important reasons, have caused the
"celebrated saying, "We have judges at Berlin!" to fall into
"desuetude. Henceforth it will be more original and quite as
"true to say, " We have judges at Brussels!"'"

CHAPTER XIX.

1821, 1822.

THE 52ND AT DUBLIN.

Meeting of naval and military officers for reading the Scriptures—Lady Grey, Mr. Mathias, Mr. Nixon—Scripture argument against balls—Village dances—Refuse an invitation to a ball at Dublin—Difficulties and plan with regard to intercourse with the families of any neighbourhood.

I HAD introductions to several persons in Dublin; amongst others, to the Commander-in-Chief, General Sir David Baird. Almost all my acquaintances were religious persons. Some of the serious officers of the garrison were in the habit of meeting together to read the Scriptures, and to unite in prayer for God's blessing. I thus became acquainted with Pringle of the artillery; Frazer of the engineers; McGregor of the 78th, and some others. I also knew at the same time Captain White of the 20th, who was staying for some time at Dublin, and Captain Monck Mason of the navy. The two last I became acquainted with through the excellent Lady Grey, who, for so many years, was permitted to exercise such a beneficial influence on the minds of numbers of the officers, both of the army and navy, when she resided at the dockyard at Portsmouth, of which the late Sir George Grey was the commissioner. I had also the great advantage of hearing those excellent clergymen, Mr. Nixon and Mr. Mathias. In a preceding chapter I have spoken of my short conversation with Dr. Malan, of Geneva, on the subject of a religious person's attending balls and plays, and of my going to my last ball immediately after my arrival in England. As I observed before, I found Dr. Malan's prediction to be correct. I soon had no taste for such things. There was no difficulty in arriving at the conclusion that it was right to avoid plays, races, and fairs, at which gambling, profaneness, drunkenness, and other glaring evils abound; for anyone who wishes to do what is right in the sight of God, must never be found, for purposes of amusement and pleasure, as I have before stated, in any company or place where God is dishonoured. There appeared, however, to be a great distinction between a ball, which appeared to be an innocent amusement, and these more gross amusements. It is often asked —" What can be the harm of a ball?" " How are young per"sons to become known to each other and to be married, if they "never go to a ball?" At first I merely had a disinclination for balls, without seeing the harm of them; then I recollected that family prayers must almost necessarily be omitted or slurred over in consequence of the lateness of the hours at which persons returned from a ball, and I was satisfied with this one objection, though I suspected there must be other grounds on which religious parents kept their children away from such amusements. Although I had so much remaining sin to contend with, and now almost daily offer up the first prayer in the Common Prayer Book, that of the confession of sin, and that in Psalm li, 9—11, yet I could not shut my eyes to the fact, that the great proportion of those, whom one met in society in this Christian country, were not really in earnest about the salvation of their souls; were not "seeking first the kingdom of God and his righteousness," and were not truly desirous to walk in strict holiness of life. We are warned in the 2nd Timothy iii, 1—5, that there would be such persons in the latter days of the Christian dispensation, who would fall into some of the grievous sins enumerated in that passage. It is as follows:—" This know also, that in the last " days perilous times shall come. For men shall be lovers of " their own selves, covetous, boasters, proud, blasphemers, dis-" obedient to parents, unthankful, unholy, without natural affec-" tion, truce-breakers, false accusers, incontinent, fierce, *despisers* " *of those that are good*, traitors, heady, highminded, *lovers of plea-* " *sures more than lovers of God, having a form of godliness, but* " *denying the power thereof: from such turn away.*" It seemed to be very clear to me, that those, who were spending their days in vanity and pleasure, going one night to a ball, on another to a rout, on a third to a play or to some other amusement, many of the men spending their days in hunting, shooting, fishing, &c., whilst they appeared to be, and often by their language and conduct shewed that they were, regardless of God's commands, were the sort of persons of whom St. Paul spoke in the above-quoted passage from his second epistle to Timothy. They were " lovers "of pleasures more than lovers of God, having a form of godliness, "but denying the power thereof." The apostle adds the decided and strong injunction, "From such turn away." This passage I consider not only justifies a religious person in abstaining from worldly society, but requires that he should do so. There is also another argument against balls, which I think calculated to have some weight with all religiously-disposed persons. The dances at the village public-houses, which are very much frequented by young persons belonging to the working classes, are anything but innocent amusements; swearing, and drunkenness, and debauchery, abound at them. Of such evil tendency are these dances, that the clergyman of the parish, and all well-disposed persons, do what they can to prevent persons from attending them. It is, however, all the more difficult to persuade them of the evil tendency of these dances, when they know that young persons in the higher ranks of society are constantly in the habit of frequenting balls. The telling them that these balls are scenes of a very different character from the public-house dances may have some weight with them, but what their friends say comes with more power to their minds, when they can add that, on religious grounds, neither they, nor those young persons who are under their influence and controul, allow themselves to be mixed up with these amusements. I was invited to one ball at Dublin, but, of course, with my views and feelings, I did not go to it. The whole subject of "mixing with the world" has been found, by most religious persons, to be one of difficulty. The plan which for many years I have adopted, is to consider God's providential leadings in the matter. On going into a new parish and neighhood, I have always been on friendly and visiting terms with those who have been kind enough to call upon me, although they might not all of them have held exactly the same religious views which I do, and I have afterwards regulated my intercourse, and that of my family, with them according to circumstances, always desiring and praying that God's blessing may rest upon it. I never go to any party except with that view. Sometimes at a dinner party I have been satisfied that I was not out of the path of duty, when, instead of forcing on general religious conversation, I have endeavoured, if only for some little time, to speak to those sitting next to me on some useful subject. I always endeavour to pray for the whole neighbourhood, and I think that, in the course of time, I have, through God's mercy, seen some little benefit arise from the adoption of this plan. With regard to new comers into one's neighbourhood, I seek their acquaintance if I hear that they are persons who fear God, or if I am requested to do so by some friend, or, possibly, after meeting them at a friend's house. I should make a point of becoming acquainted with those in my own parish, unless there were circumstances of a character to prevent my wishing to introduce them to my family, when I should probably restrict my intercourse with them to that which my duty as a minister required.

CHAPTER XX.

1821, 1822.

THE 52ND AT DUBLIN.

The castle guard—The Montagus of the 71st and 52nd—Irritation of the King about a sentry—Amusing order handed down by the sentries on the bridge to the garden—Tracts and books for the men taken away by the captain of the guard—Some reason to hope they were made useful to him—Several anecdotes connected with that proceeding—Winterbottom and religious tracts at the bank guard; curious and important dialogue—Anecdote connected with Winterbottom's wound at Waterloo—Mention of his services in 52nd record—Peculiarities of religious people—Definition of a Methodist—A clergyman and his wife each considering the other to be free from sin—What a blessing that we have the first prayer of the liturgy—Expected Whiteboy attack on the barracks—On detachment at the Pigeon-house Fort—Boldness and discomfiture of rats—Detached to Wicklow—Rudiments of a savings' bank.

ONE of my strong recollections of Dublin is connected with what was called "the castle guard." It consisted of a captain, two subalterns, and one hundred men, with the King's colour, which was always attached to this guard, as the Lord Lieutenant was the King's representative. There was also a subaltern's guard of cavalry. It was my turn for this guard on one of the days of the King's stay at the castle. The officers of the guard then dined at the Board of Green Cloth, with three or four of the officers attached to the King's suite, and a very kind set of fellows I recollect they were. The 52nd were generally relieved at all the guards by the 71st Highland Light Infantry, which regiment had been in Adam's brigade with them at Waterloo. I never think of the castle guard at Dublin, without the most vivid recollection of that nice fellow, George Montagu, then an ensign in the 71st. I believe he more than once was the ensign of the guard when they were relieving us, and I think he was there on the occasion of our mounting guard over the King. In marching into the castle yard to take up their ground facing us, directly he caught my eye, he felt it impossible to avoid laughing. Whilst the sentries were being relieved, the King came down to his carriage, and was received by both the guards with presented arms and the dropping of the colours. I recollect his Majesty was very much annoyed and irritated in consequence of a sentry having been placed on the stairs, contrary, I think, to his orders. George Montagu, if he be still alive, will, I feel sure, kindly excuse this mention of him. His brother, John Montagu, was in the 52nd. He afterwards was Colonial Secretary at the Cape, and died there. He was a good and spirited officer, but did not remain long in the regiment. There are two anecdotes related of him in the 52nd record, which everyone who was with the 52nd in 1815 knows to be perfectly untrue; and how the talented editor could have admitted them, is only lamely accounted for by the explanation that they were pressed upon him by a person who professed to have a knowledge of the circumstances, but must have had a sadly confused recollection of them, and of the facts and circumstances connected with the regiment at the period referred to. George Montagu exchanged, after my days, as a captain into the 52nd, and, as I was assured lately by an old soldier, was greatly beloved by the men of the regiment, for his very great kindness towards them on all occasions. I was always interested in the Montagus, from my family having, from my childhood, been intimate with their uncle, Admiral Sir George Montagu, and all his family.

There was an amusing order handed on to each sentry stationed in turn on the bridge leading from the garden to the castle, which was always mentioned to me in the same words by the sentry at that particular spot, whenever, for months afterwards, as subaltern of the guard, I enquired what his orders were. It was in vain that I gave them the correct order again and again; the sentry on that spot always related it to me with the same mistake which I had, from the first, corrected. The dialogue was as follows:—*Officer:*—"What are your orders, my man?" *Sentry :*—" If anyone, not passing from the castle, wants to cross "this bridge, Sir, I am to stop him ; and there is a tame hare in "the garden, Sir: if it comes on to the bridge I am to *fire at it*, "and drive it back, Sir." There were two sentries in the garden, who had orders to fire at any persons attempting to get over the high garden walls.

When I went on guard, I made a practice of taking a large number of religious books and tracts of the "Religious Tract "Society" for the use of the men, and they were allowed to take them away with them when the guard was relieved. The commanding officer had before made the arrangement that any religious publications might be given to the men, which did not contain anything contrary to the doctrines of the Church of England. One day at the castle, soon after we had relieved the other guard, the captain of the 52nd guard, on passing the men's guard-room, saw the long table covered with little books and tracts, and calling the serjeant, enquired what they were and who had placed them there. On being told that my servant had done so, he sent for him, and asked by whose authority he had so acted; and on his telling him that his master had ordered him to do it, he had the tracts and books collected and brought to him, and then came and requested me not again to distribute tracts amongst the men of any guard which he commanded. I reminded him that I was acting in strict accordance with the permission of the commanding officer, and that he had no ground for complaint or interference. However, there the matter ended, and I heard nothing more of my tracts for some weeks. I then found out that they were still in existence, and in his possession, by hearing him, at some distance from me at mess, say, that he had fallen in with a turnpike-gate keeper, who was a greater swearer than any person he had ever met with, and that he had a great mind to give him one of Leeke's tracts. I often, in after days, wondered whether God, whose ways are not as our ways, had permitted him to display his natural dislike to, what he would term, these methodistical proceedings, in order by means of these very tracts, which he despised, and thought calculated to make soldiers unsoldierlike—in order by *them*, to lead him from darkness unto light, from sin to holiness, and from the power of Satan unto God. I never heard any more of the tracts; but as one of my chief objects in sending forth this publication is to give some account of God's mercies to myself, and of my poor attempts to lead others to receive His offered mercy in Christ, I may as well speak of the few things which give me a hope that this officer became, some years after, a very altered man. He was the person to whom I had lent my horse when I went into Germany, and who had been annoyed with Gawler for trying to lead the men to fear and serve God. We were on very good terms, notwithstanding my strange religious opinions, as he would consider them. On some particular day we were in the Phœnix Park, when I was sent as a subaltern to his company. In an advance in line, I perceived, from the rear, that the centre of the company was coming on a dirty place, about eight yards in diameter, into which several sewers emptied themselves, and called out to the men to "file round it," for they would have covered their white trowsers with black dirt up to their knees. Colonel C. Rowan, who saw some confusion in the company, but could not see what had occasioned it, came thundering down, exclaiming "What *is* No. 8 about?" I called out, from the rear, "*I* desired them to file round the obstacle, Sir." This barely satisfied him, for he was vexed at the apparent confusion, and the regiment was always very remarkable for the steadiness of its advance line. The officer commanding the company afterwards thanked me for taking upon myself the blame which was intended for it. After we got to Clonmel, in the autumn of 1822, one evening after mess I invited an officer, who had come in from an out-quarter for the night, to come to my room and get some tea, and I asked four or five others to join us. Amongst them was the officer who had taken my tracts at the castle guard. Just as we were about to begin tea, it occurred to me what an awkward business it would be to say grace before a set of fellows, who, perhaps, had never before heard of grace at tea. Although I felt the awkwardness of the thing, I felt that it was not right to omit it, and therefore merely said, "I always think it proper to " say grace before all my meals;" upon which they all gave their attention, and I repeated the grace which I had framed for

Y

myself, and which I have continued to use to this day:—" O Lord, "bless to us what we are about to partake of, and make us thank-"ful, for Christ's sake." They all behaved very well, and the purloiner of my tracts, by way of getting over the awkward feeling, said, "I must say, Leeke, you are a much better fellow than "I am." I had made an arrangement with the principal bookseller at Clonmel, to let me send to Dublin for a number of sound religious books, on any of which he was to have a good profit if they were sold, whilst I would take off his hands those which might remain unsold. One of the officers, G. H. Love, who had become very religiously disposed, and who knew of my books, told me some time afterwards, that one day when he was in the shop, the officer who had taken away my tracts came in, and told the bookseller that he wanted some book which would "enable him to understand the Bible," (I think that was his expression.) Love looked about, and found one of my books, called "Bickersteth's Scripture Help," which he recommended to him, and on his recommendation, he immediately purchased this very valuable book, after which Love brought from the shelf "Bicker-"steth on Prayer," another excellent book, and told him it was generally looked upon as a companion to the "Scripture Help." He bought this work also. I never, from that time, knew anything of his state of feeling with regard to religion, until very lately, when on mentioning some of the circumstances which I have just related to a pious lady who had had a large military acquaintance, being the widow of a field-officer in the artillery, I observed that she and her daughter exchanged looks which led me to ask, "Did you ever know Colonel ——?" She replied, "Yes, we knew him, and he gave my daughter that little Bible," pointing to a Bible on the table. She told me that they were one day calling on him, when they were stationed abroad, (he had been promoted into another regiment from the 52nd,) and on her daughter admiring the Bible he begged that she would accept it, saying, "I have a larger Bible which I use for my own "reading, but I have placed that smaller one on the table think-"ing, perhaps, that when some of the young officers are sitting "here waiting for me, they may take it up, and it, perhaps, may "do them good." All that they could tell me about his religious state beyond this was, that another colonel, who was a pious man, made use of these words to them respecting him:—" Yes, "——— is no doubt a good man." Colonel ——— has now been dead for many years. Whether the tracts so improperly taken, or the books which he purchased at Clonmell, had anything to do with this change or not, is of little consequence, but it is a great pleasure and mercy to be able to hope and think that he really did become a humble believer in the Lord Jesus Christ, for pardon and holiness, for comfort here and eternal life hereafter.

When any of us were on the bank guard, we usually had several of the officers of the regiment to call upon us. I think it consisted of a subaltern, and six-and-thirty men. I well recollect when I was one day on the bank guard, Winterbottom, who, after being adjutant of the 52nd from 1808 to 1821, had lately exchanged his position of senior or second lieutenant, I forget which, for that of paymaster, came into the officers' guard-room. In order to reach it, he had to pass up rather a long flight of steps fixed against the wall of the men's guard-room; over the rail of which he looked down upon it and saw some of my tracts and books lying about, and many of the men sitting and reading them. On reaching my guard-room, he threw himself into a chair in a state of some excitement, exclaiming, "Why, "Leeke, you are ruining the regiment." Now, Winterbottom and I were great allies. I had always regarded him as one of the best and most gallant soldiers that ever stept, and he had always treated me with very great kindness from the time of my joining the regiment as a mere boy. I recollect his telling me, some time after the return of the army of occupation from France, that, when on leave, he was one day telling his friends about the Battle of Waterloo, and that he made his mother cry, when he described the pitiable condition in which I appeared to be, on the morning of that day, and told her that I had just before left my mother, and how I had been lying out all night, and had been drenched with rain, &c., &c. This helps to show that he had no unkind feeling towards me, when he told me I was "ruining the "regiment," and I really felt very sorry for him at the moment. I could quite understand all that was passing in the mind of this fine, gallant soldier, for not so very long before, I should have had, under similar circumstances, the feeling that the reading the Bible, and tracts, and prayers, and *"psalm-singing,"* as the being religious was often termed, were calculated to interfere with, and even destroy, that gallant spirit and bearing, so conspicuous in the British soldier. The dialogue which took place between us, under these feelings and circumstances, was nearly word for word as follows:—

Winterbottom :—"Why, Leeke, you are ruining the regiment."

Leeke :—" You mean that the leading them to read these books "and to become religious, is likely to destroy their spirit as "soldiers."

Winterbottom :—" Yes, I do think so."

Leeke :—" Now, Winterbottom, just reflect for a moment. If " I should be the means of leading them to fear God, do you think " they would be less *orderly* than they are at present ? "

Winterbottom :—" No, of course they would not."

Leeke :—" If they should give up drunkenness, would that do "them any harm as soldiers ? "

Winterbottom :—" Of course not."

Leeke :—" Since *I* have begun to try and do what is pleasing "in the sight of God, do you think I am less attentive to my "duties as an officer than I used to be ? "

Winterbottom :—" No, if anything, I think you are more at-"tentive to them than you formerly were."

Leeke :—" If we should have any more campaigning, do "you think I should be less fearless in danger than I have "been ? "

Winterbottom :—" No."

Leeke :—" If our men are led to seek the pardon of their sins "through the atonement of their Saviour, and to become holy "through the teaching of His Spirit and His Word; and if, in " addition, they believed their sins were pardoned, and that they "should go to heaven when they died, do you think these feelings "would be calculated to make them more afraid of danger "and of death in battle, than they would have been without "them ? "

Winterbottom :—" No. I think they would not."

Leeke:—" Well you see, then, that my books and tracts, and
" any endeavours we may make to lead the men to fear God and
" walk in His ways, will not " ruin the regiment."

I was surprised and thankful to find, that this little quiet
talk appeared entirely to allay the perturbed feeling with which
Winterbottom entered the guard-room. During the time that we
remained in Dublin, he and our kind old Scotch quartermaster,
John Campbell, went with me very frequently on the Sunday to hear
those good men, Mr. Mathias and Mr. Nixon. Some of the other
officers went occasionally. Winterbottom and Campbell, although
so much my seniors, used to let me advise them and exhort them
on religious matters, as opportunity offered. One Sunday morning, when I was on duty as officer of the day, I was crossing the
barrack square with John Campbell, and whilst thinking of
something else, half whistled a tune in an under tone, when I
was very much amused by his taking the opportunity of good-humouredly paying me off for all my past exhortations to him, by
saying to me, in rather broad Scotch, " If ye were in my country,
" my lad, they would put ye in the stocks for whistling on Sunday."
Winterbottom, with all his gallant bearing, was a very bashful
man, and would sometimes blush, if anything drew attention
to him, up to the very roots of his hair. I recollect calling forth
one of his deepest blushes, by mentioning at the mess, some
years after it happened, the circumstance of my having, when as
a volunteer I went from Ostend to Lessines, fallen into conversation for a short time with one of the men, who, after speaking
of the daring conduct of Sir John Colborne in action, added "and
" Mr. Winterbottom is just like him, Sir."

With the names of Sir John Moore and Lord Seaton, that of
Winterbottom ought to be always remembered by his regiment
and country, as one of the most distinguished soldiers of his day.
As the 52nd record is likely only to be read by few persons, comparatively, I shall extract presently from it that portion which
mention's Winterbottom's services; but before I do so I will
transcribe the following, from a letter which I have lately received from an old New Brunswick friend, who is now one of the
highest judicial functionaries in that province:—" I heard the
" following anecdote from Mrs. Monius, the wife of Lieutenant-

"Colonel Monius,* of the 69th, when that regiment was here
"some years ago. She said that when Winterbottom was wounded
"in the head, (at Waterloo,) Monius bound up the wound with
"his own handkerchief. A considerable time after, when in
"England, Mrs. Monius was surprised by a visit from Winter-
"bottom, who announced his object by saying, that he called to
"return the *handkerchief* which Monius had so kindly lent him
"at Waterloo, at the same time presenting the lady with a very
"handsome *shawl*. Winterbottom married a Fredericton lady, a
"Miss Winslow, some of whose family reside at Woodstock, sixty
"miles above this, on the river St. John."

The following is an extract from the 52nd record:—

"On the 6th of November, 1838, the regiment disembarked
"at Barbadoes, and occupied the brick barracks, St. Anne's.

"About the middle of this month, the portion of the barracks
"allotted to the officers was visited by that fatal epidemic, the
"yellow fever, which continued its ravages for nearly six weeks,
"the sickness being confined alone to the officers' pavilion. Of
"fourteen officers present with the service companies, twelve
"were attacked, and three died, viz.—Paymaster John Winter-
"bottom, Lieutenant V. A. Surtees, and Ensign Edward Gough.
"The building was eventually condemned as unhealthy, and
"evacuated entirely, and no case of fever afterwards occurred.
"Paymaster John Winterbottom, who thus fell under the stroke
"of a pestilential disease, on the 26th of November in this year,
"was a veteran soldier, who had nobly borne his part in earning
"distinction for his regiment and for himself during nearly forty
"years of service.

"Born in the parish of Saddleworth, Yorkshire, in 1781,
"John Winterbottom was early obliged to help in the support of
"a very poor family, by cloth weaving. It was during a period
"of much distress among the operative weavers, that young
"Winterbottom enlisted into the 52nd, on the 17th of October, 1799.

"His first return to the home of his family was in 1814, dur-

* Eaton Monius was the youngest officer of the 52nd at Waterloo except myself. He was a good officer, and adjutant of the regiment for some time. He rose eventually to the rank of major-general, and obtained the colonelcy of the 8th regiment.

"ing the short peace which his exertions had helped to achieve,
and which put an end to the Peninsular War. On this occasion
"his fellow-parishioners presented to him, at a public dinner, a
"handsome gold snuff-box, together with expressions of their
"admiration of his worth and gallantry, such as drew from him
"a reply only in sentences broken by his feelings, under the ex-
"citement of an honour so gratifying. His ability as an execu-
"tive officer, his sterling integrity; high sense of honour, always
"coupled with that of his regiment, and readiness to oblige and
"instruct in their duty the younger officers, conveying instruction
"in a manner to encourage and inspire rather than to annoy or
"disgust, were so fully appreciated, that on his death one hundred
"and forty-three officers, most of whom had served with him,
"either in the same regiment or in the same brigade, subscribed
"to erect to his memory a handsome monumental tablet, which
"is now in his parish church at Saddleworth, and bears the fol-
"lowing inscription:—

"'John Winterbottom, Paymaster of the 52nd Light Infantry.
"Died at the Head-Quarters of the Regiment, in the Island of
"Barbadoes, on the 26th of November, 1838.

"Born at Saddleworth, 17th of November, 1781.

"Private Soldier, 52nd, 17th of October, 1799.

"Corporal, April, 1801.

"Serjeant, December, 1803.

"Serjeant-Major, 11th of June, 1805.

"Ensign and Adjutant, 24th of November, 1808.

"Lieutenant and Adjutant, 28th of February, 1810.

"Paymaster, 31st of May, 1821.'

"He served with distinction at the following battles and
"sieges:—

"As a Private at Ferrol; as Serjeant-Major at Copenhagen
"and Vimiero; as Adjutant at Corunna, the Coa, Busaco, Pombal,
"Redinha, Ciudad Rodrigo, Badajoz, Salamanca, San Munoz,
"Vittoria, the heights of Vera, Nivelles, the Nive, Orthes, Tarbes,
"Toulouse, and Waterloo, as well as in other actions of less note, in
"which the 52nd was engaged during the war; and he was never
"absent from his regiment except in consequence of wounds re-
"ceived at Redinha, Badajoz, and Waterloo."

There are, of course, many interesting events which I well remember, but which I could not for various reasons record in this work. I have endeavoured not to insert anything which would be calculated in any way to give pain or annoyance to any one. In my intercourse with my brother-officers and others, especially when speaking on religious subjects, I always endeavoured to avoid any peculiarity of look or expression which I knew, from my own feelings, was calculated to raise a prejudice against religious persons, in the minds of those who witnessed it. I mention it here, because I consider it to be of very great importance, that persons who are seriously disposed should be as natural as possible in their way of speaking and acting. I remember one of my brother-officers, when launching out rather vehemently against the ways of some religious men, whom he had met with, said, "I never knew one of them yet, except yourself, who had "not a ghastly smile on his countenance." I think it must have been at the same time and from the same person that I recollect the following somewhat clever reply. We were standing one day with two or three other men in the mess-room, when, in inveighing against some persons of whom he was speaking, he applied the term "Methodists" to them. By way of trying to stop him, I interposed the question, "What is a Methodist?" which he most quickly answered as follows:—"A Methodist! it means a "fellow who is always quoting St. Paul, as you and Gawler do."

I have always remembered the following circumstance, which occurred when I was making a call one morning at the house of a religious family. There happened to be several sets of callers, and, amongst others, was a very nice, intelligent young person, who lived about six or seven miles from Dublin. I had never met her before, and did not hear her name, nor have I ever seen or heard of her since. The conversation took a religious turn, and the unscriptural doctrine of perfection, held by the Wesleyan Methodists, was mentioned. This led the lady above-mentioned to observe, "Our clergyman and his wife both hold the doctrine "of perfection." I said, "Did any of you ever ask him if he "considered *himself* perfect?" "Yes," she replied, "and he says "of himself 'that he is a poor sinful man, leaving undone, every "'day, what he should do, and doing what he should not do.'"

When asked if he had ever met with a perfect person, he answers, "Yes, there is my wife, I consider her to be perfect in holiness." We enquired whether his wife considered herself perfect, and the lady said that she also spoke of herself in the same terms in which her husband described his feelings with regard to remaining sin, and sin being mixed up with all his best thoughts, words, and deeds. She added, that when the wife was asked if she had ever seen a person perfectly free from sin, she replied, "Yes, "there's my husband, I consider him to be perfectly free from "sin." I have often mentioned this anecdote since I heard it, and more especially for the benefit of married couples. Although it does not establish the doctrine of perfection, it shews that this clergyman and his wife must have led a most holy and happy life together. I daily think what a great mercy it is that, in the first prayer of the liturgy, we have the doctrine of remaining sin in all the children of God so clearly set forth, and that the most advanced Christians, as well as those who are just beginning to seek pardon and holiness, are therein invited, and taught daily, to humble themselves before God for the daily sins of their whole lives, from their very early years, down to the moment at which they are arrived.

An officer in barracks, and in such a place as Dublin, however much he may wish to acquire professional and other knowledge, meets with all kinds of hindrances in his attempts to improve himself. I managed, however, to do something in this way whilst I was there; and I recollect, with pleasure, the expressions of great approval with which a friend, much older than myself, greeted me when he called upon me at the Richmond barracks, on his return from Italy, and found my table covered with maps and books of reference, indications that, on that morning at least, I had not been idle.

The present Sir George Grey, our accomplished Home Secretary, was for a short time in Dublin, as the guest of Admiral Oliver; I had known him before, both at his father's and at our own house, but all I recollect of him in Dublin was that, on one occasion, I rode with him for some time in the Phœnix Park. He was my junior by a year or two.

One evening, in consequence of some information that an

attack was meditated, that night, on the Richmond barracks, by some thousands of Whiteboys, who, I suppose, thought to take us by surprise, suitable preparations were made for their reception; men were told off to occupy the officers' barracks, in case they should be wanted, and the sentries were doubled in some places, and their muskets loaded, and the troops were ready to turn out. These preparations could not have been made unless there had been some ground for expecting an attack; the night, however, passed over without anything happening.

In January, 1822, I went on detachment to the Pigeon-house, under the command of Captain Macpherson, of the 13th Regiment. He was a man of some reflexion, and we often spoke on religious subjects, and went to Mr. Mathias's church together. I trust our being together was profitable to both of us. A great portion of the Pigeon-house was built on piles, consequently, it literally swarmed with rats, with which gentlemen I had a very amusing encounter, which ended in their complete discomfiture. The barrack-rooms of the two infantry officers were on the ground floor, on either side of a passage, the six windows and door all facing the street, and the quay beyond it; the floor of my bedroom was, in more places than one, accessible to rats, and, I presume, to all the rats in the fort—no very pleasant idea! On the first night of our arrival, on going to bed, I put an extinguisher on a mould candle, which, together with the long candlestick, was about fourteen inches in height from the table on which it was placed. I was just dropping off to sleep, when I heard a noise which I supposed to proceed from mice or rats, and I frightened them away, and had just got to sleep again, when I was aroused by hearing my extinguisher fall to the ground; presently I heard it travelling along the floor on the opposite side of my room. Recollecting that my boots were close to the bed, I got hold of one of them, and immediately opened what I considered a somewhat effective fire on the enemy, at least, they retired very quickly, and in some confusion, but leaving no killed or wounded behind them. When, however, they considered the danger over, they renewed the attack, which I again repulsed by discharging the other boot at them. I heard scarcely anything more of my enemy during the night, but in the morning I found that not only the extinguisher had disappeared, but also the thick mould candle, on the top of which it had been fixed. I never saw it again, but if some antiquarian subaltern, stationed at the Pigeon-house, will take the trouble to search under the farthest end from the window of that room of the four which is nearest to Dublin, (supposing always those wretched rooms, and the still more wretched floor, to be yet in existence,) no doubt he will be amply rewarded for his trouble by finding, within a few feet of the middle of that end of the floor, a plated extinguisher, which, no doubt, the enemy left not far from their sally-port after they had cleared out from it the large amount of provision which they had captured at the same time. Their successful foraging expedition rather astonished me; for the sitting-room candlestick, in which the candle was firmly fixed, was at least seven inches high, and in getting the candle out they had not in the least disturbed it, nor had they left any small pieces of tallow near it, or along the floor. Here I must bring to a close the history of my first campaign against the rats, in which I must acknowledge that they came off victorious.

The second campaign I knew very well they would commence the very next night, and as I did not intend to be demolished by them, if I could help it, I reconnoitred the enemy's intrenchments, and looked about to see what means of defence or offence I could procure; I haplessly came across some brickbats on the outside of the building, and determined to make use of them, not with the view of firing away at the rats with them when they had gained access to my quarters, for I knew, in that case, I should get the worst of it, but for the purpose of hammering them into the holes, so as to prevent the possibility of the rats getting into the room at all. I retired to rest, as I thought, quite satisfied that I should not be intruded upon, as had been the case the night before; but I had only been in bed a few minutes, when there commenced a regular gnawing, by I know not what number of rats, at the edges of the flooring round the brickbats. Notwithstanding all I could do to frighten them away, this horrid noise continued till daylight came to my relief, so that I had almost a sleepless night; thus I got worsted in the second campaign.

The next day I ordered my servant to mix a quantity of mustard in a basin, and, by means of a long feather, I managed to saturate the wood around the brickbats with it, so that in no direction could the rats gnaw it without getting a good taste of the mustard. Soon after I had gone to bed, I heard, once or twice, a little gnawing for a few seconds, and then it ceased. This time I came off with flying colours, for I never saw or heard a rat after that night during the four or five weeks that I was quartered at the Pigeon-house. I wonder whether they forsook the place altogether! If they did, I might look upon myself as a second tutelar saint of Ireland.

One day, as I was sitting in my room with one of the artillery officers stationed at the fort, an officer passed the window, whom I at once recognised as Major Oliver. My friend, somewhat alarmed, said, "I think that's Major Oliver, I wonder what he is "doing here!" I answered, that he very probably was come to call upon me, as I was acquainted with him. He was anxious to get away before Major Oliver found out my quarter, which he was inquiring for, but said, as he was going, "I very much respect "Major Oliver, but I was one of the unfortunate men who signed "that paper."

I enjoyed very much the quiet and retirement of the Pigeon-house, for very quiet it was, except occasionally when the Irish were embarking for Liverpool. There were always a great many women and children amongst the passengers, and there were many friends who came to see them off. I had, consequently, many opportunities of conversing with the people, and of shewing them kindness in the way of relief, and of distributing useful religious books and tracts amongst them. Some of my happiest hours were spent there in reading and meditating on the Scriptures, and on "Young's Night Thoughts," and in prayer, as I walked on the extensive and beautifully paved sea-walls to the eastward of the fort.

I returned to the Richmond barracks about the 24th of February, 1822, and, towards the end of March, McNair's company was detached to Wicklow; Blois and I went with him. My kind friend Fitzgibbon came to see me there, and remained five or six days, and I went with him to the annual religious meetings at Dublin, where I met with Mr. Simeon, of Cambridge, and Dr. Marsh, of Colchester. In the neighbourhood of Wicklow we became acquainted with several nice families, and saw a great deal of the beautiful scenery of that county. At Wicklow I began to receive small sums of money from the men of the company to keep for them; this led to the formation of a regimental savings' bank a few months afterwards, and also, in 1824, to the first establishment of a savings' bank in the province of New Brunswick, in North America.

Being relieved by a company of the 86th, we returned from Wicklow to Dublin about the 6th of May, and I took up my quarters with the Gawlers, as there was no room for me in barracks. I remained with them for three weeks, when the regiment left Dublin for the south.

CHAPTER XXI.

1821, 1822.

DUBLIN. INTERESTING PARTICULARS RELATING TO THREE 52ND SOLDIERS.

Pat Kelly's proceedings in Spain and France—Remarkable visitation—Becomes a religious man—One of the guard of honour to the King—Selected as a trustworthy man—His suspicious death at the Pigeon-house—Dogherty—Houghton's remarkable case—Benefit arising from the distribution of the Scriptures—My visits to him in the hospital—He leaves the army—His letter to me—Enters Trinity College, Dublin—Becomes a devoted minister of the Church of England—His death.

AMONGST the religious men of the regiment there was one Pat Kelly, whose case was most remarkable and interesting; he had served in the Peninsula and at Waterloo, but was considered one of the most troublesome and disorderly soldiers we had. At one time, in the Peninsula, he got away from his regiment, and went and attached himself to the Spanish army, which was besieging the French in Saragossa, (this was usually called the second siege of Saragossa.) Here he astonished his friends the Spaniards by dancing on the parapets of one of the batteries, whilst the enemy "blazed away" at him, and by other feats of daring. After the siege was at an end he, with three or four other English soldiers, set off to join the English army. As they went through the country, they obtained supplies, for a short time, by giving out that they were the advanced guard of several hundred men who might be expected shortly to arrive, and for whom they ordered rations to be provided. This, of course, was not likely to last long, and they were arrested by the mayor of one of the towns, and sent up to the English army as deserters.

Kelly was to be tried for desertion, but, luckily for him, before he could be tried, a general action came on; he was a prisoner in the ranks, and, when an opportunity offered, he obtained permission to take the firelock and accoutrements of one of the men who had fallen: he behaved with considerable gallantry, and when the action was over he was forgiven. I recollect his being tried by a court-martial, and severely flogged, for breaking into a house at the time that we formed part of the army of occupation in France. I never knew anything more of him until some little time after I arrived in Dublin, when I heard the following remarkable story. Some months before, when he had been drinking, one of the serjeants did something which, if reported, was calculated to get him into trouble; Kelly was quite aware of this, and threatened that he would report him to one of the officers; the serjeant, knowing that he was quite capable of doing so, tried to pacify him, till Kelly ended by making use of the following imprecation, "He wished God might strike his tongue dumb in "his mouth, if he did not report him," though, as it afterwards turned out, he had, all the time, no intention of doing so. At night, when all the men in his room had retired to rest, and when he was sobered, he lay awake for some time, and he recollected the threat he had uttered, and the words he had used, and thought within himself, "suppose God *was* to strike me dumb?" He became alarmed, and tried to speak, when, to his great horror, he found that he was unable to utter a word. He made a moaning noise, which awoke his comrade in the same bed with him, and at last the whole room was aroused, and he was taken to the hospital, and the surgeon, Mr. Gibson, was sent for. On his arrival, he had some suspicion that Kelly, whom he knew to be a man of bad character, was only pretending that he was speechless; however, on examining his mouth, he found that his tongue was paralysed, and that the tip of it was turned down in a most extraordinary manner. He himself, and others who were present, were unable to turn their tongues at all in the same manner, and the most severe punishment which he could inflict, by applying caustic to the tongue, had no effect in producing any alteration in its state. They all looked upon it as having been inflicted by God upon the man on account of his sins. Some time after I heard this, I spoke to Gibson about it, and he, who was not a person at all likely to fall into any delusion in such a matter, gave me the details of what he had observed of the case, just as I have related them; he told me he could only look upon what had happened to Kelly as "a visitation from God."

Kelly remained in hospital, in a most wretched state of mind, for several days, feeling sure that God had sent him this affliction as a punishment for his wicked oath, and for all his numerous sins. At length it occurred to him that only He who had inflicted the punishment could restore him to the use of his speech, and he set himself to pray most earnestly that God would have pity on him, and take away this sore judgment from him. His own account was, that about a week after the awful stroke came upon him, whilst he was praying for relief, he found all at once, to his great delight, that he could speak again. He became quite an altered and religious man from that time.

From that time forth Kelly became an altered man in every respect; he had been a great drunkard, and so slovenly as a soldier, that he was continually getting into disgrace. It was some months after this change had occurred in him, that the King visited Dublin; and the change in his habits had then become so well known, that, on the occasion of a fête taking place in the Phœnix Park, Kelly was picked out as a clean, smart soldier, to be one of the guard of honour; and when, at the vice-regal lodge, the butler applied to the serjeant of the guard for a steady, sober man, to take charge of the ale which was provided for the numerous servants of the assembled company, he was selected as the most proper man for the purpose. When I first began to know him in his altered character, he was a very modest, unassuming man, apparently very anxious to do all that was right, and to lead his comrades to fear and honour God. I was told that, soon after the arrival of the regiment in Ireland, and some time after his change, he got a furlough, and went to see his friends in the north of Ireland. He was somewhat persecuted by them; and when he returned to the regiment, he mentioned to some of his friends, who took an interest in his religious state, that on one occasion, during his absence, he had been in liquor. It was considered by them that this sad fall back into the sin of drunkenness, when taken in connexion with his sorrow for it, and his confession of it, when it was not likely to be otherwise discovered, must not be considered as proving that a real change of heart had not taken place in him.

The last time I saw Kelly, he had come up to Dublin on leave, from the Pigeon-house fort; and, on that occasion, he requested me to give him a few useful and interesting books for the children of one of the artillery officers. This was, I think, about February, 1822. Either on that night, or on some subsequent night, poor Kelly lost his life as he was returning to the Pigeon-house. His wife had given him some considerable uneasiness with regard to another man, and, on the afternoon of his death, they had all been sitting in a public-house near, for the purpose of talking over their differences. It must be recollected that soldiers had scarcely any other place to which they could retire for such a purpose, so that his going there, on the occasion referred to, need not lead to the supposition that, by so doing, Kelly was giving way to temptation. His wife's account, the next day, was, that they all drank together, and that Kelly got regularly drunk, and, on their way to the Pigeon-house, became very much excited, and drew his bayonet, and rushed down from the causeway towards some stepping-stones over a channel on the sands, through which the tide flowed for some time before it overflowed the sands, and that they had lost sight of him. When questioned as to where he had got his money to get drunk with, she replied that it was with two shillings which it was known he had borrowed on that day. She went off to England about the second or third day after his death, declaring that she knew he was drowned, and that there was no use in her remaining in Ireland. On the night of Kelly's death, the other man returned to the Richmond barracks sober, just after the nine o'clock rollcall. There was a rather strange circumstance occurred, which I think it as well not to relate; at the time it attracted my attention, but it was not until afterwards that I connected it at all with his death. In about a month poor Kelly's body was found under the walls of the Pigeon-house fort, so eaten by fishes, that it was only known to be the body of a 52nd soldier by the number being on his breastplate and buttons. The two shillings, with which it was said he had got drunk, were found in his trowsers' pocket. It was not until after an inquest had been held, and a verdict returned, of "found drowned," or "accidental "death," that those, who knew something of the above circumstances, heard that the body had been found. It was then thought that, although there was some considerable grounds for suspecting that Kelly had come by his death unfairly, yet there was no proof of it.

Whilst the 52nd were at Dublin, the regiment was placed on a reduced establishment, and it was necessary to discharge several of the men. On this occasion I well remember a circumstance occurring, which I always looked upon as a rather remarkable answer to prayer. Amongst those selected to be discharged in Captain McNair's company was a man by the name of Dogherty, who had, I think, a wife and two children, and who was within two years of making up a service of fourteen years, so that the getting his discharge at that time was considered by him, and by many others, as a great hardship about to be inflicted on him; there were, however, some other reasons for selecting him which appeared to Colonel Charles Rowan to render it necessary, notwithstanding the hardship, that he should not be retained. We all felt very strongly about it, and we urged McNair to ask Colonel Rowan to let Dogherty remain; this he did, but Colonel Rowan said he could not, for several reasons, alter the arrangement. Afterwards Hall, the senior subaltern of the company, who felt great pity for the man, went to Rowan to see what he could do in the matter, but he met with the same answer. I think it was on the following day that I spoke to McNair again about it, and said, the poor fellow must not, after all, be allowed to go if it could in any way be avoided. He replied that both he and Hall had been to Rowan, who was not at all convinced by what they had said, that the man ought not to be discharged, but he added, "*you* can go, if you like, and see what you can do "with Rowan." I determined to do so, but first of all I committed the whole matter to God in prayer, and requested Him, if it was according to His will, that the commanding officer might see it in the same light in which we saw it. On going to him on the subject, I told him that I had ventured to come to him about this poor fellow Dogherty; that I knew McNair and Hall had spoken to him about his being discharged, and that I hardly felt it right, after what he had told them, to bother him any more on the subject, but that still I did not like to let the man be discharged without making one more effort in his favour. Colonel Rowan was not at all annoyed by my appeal to him, which one might almost have expected he would be, but was most kind about it, and, immediately that I had done speaking, said, " Leeke, "the man shall remain!" People who read this may be inclined to think that all this would happen very naturally, and that the commanding officer merely allowed himself to be persuaded by us to act in accordance with our wishes, but the more they become acquainted with the Scriptures, the more will they see that in *everything* we may make our requests known unto God, and that, in answer to our prayers, He often inclines the hearts of others to do what we desire, and, in various ways in His providence, brings about the most unlikely events and results.

A very interesting case of the great benefit arising from the practice of circulating the Scriptures amongst soldiers, occurred very shortly after my return to the 52nd at Dublin. It was the case of a man by the name of Houghton, who had been an attorney's clerk, and who had enlisted when the regiment was at Chester. In a little memoir of him, published several years afterwards, by the Rev. Roger Carus Wilson, this step is related as follows:—" At this period the 52nd Regiment of Light Infantry, "which had recently returned from France, was stationed at "Chester. The youthful wanderer heard of the laurels which "this regiment had won in the Peninsula campaigns, and at the "Battle of Waterloo. He viewed with inconsiderate delight "their smart appearance on parade. His imagination was at "once captivated with the honour, the enterprise, and—the idle- "ness of a military life; and, accordingly, without reflecting on "the pain he should thereby inflict on his family, he enlisted as "a private soldier."

When he had been upwards of two years in the 52nd, he began to be much troubled about his soul. The following passages from the memoir relate to this, and to some considerable benefit and comfort which, by God's mercy, he derived from some books lent or given to him by me:—

"During the month of September, and great part of October, "1821, he was laid up in the hospital, and he entertained but "faint hopes of recovery. But it pleased God to bless to "him, in a remarkable manner, this season of reflection, and to "make even a visitation so heavily afflictive the greatest benefit. "It proved the turning point of his life—the instrumental cause "of his passing 'from darkness to light, from the power of Satan "'unto God.' One day he was most unexpectedly induced to "read the Bible. He had asked for some book with which he "might beguile a restless hour, and when the Bible had been "given him, he had begged for some other book, adding, 'I can "'repeat all that:' but as no other was at hand, he was content "to pore over the sacred pages; and the study, thus casually "begun, soon became deeply interesting, affecting, and salutary "to his mind. He 'searched the Scriptures' at this time with "great earnestness, and in after life he frequently referred, with "grateful emotions, to the good which he now derived from them. "He was also much indebted to 'Doddridge's Rise and Progress "'of Religion in the Soul,' which an officer, who visited the "hospital, kindly placed in his hands. A spiritual appetite was "now created in him, through the divine mercy, and the proper "nutriment was thus providentially supplied. Gradually the "light of truth dawned upon his heart; the gospel of Jesus "Christ became the support of his soul, and the heavenly origin "of his new principles became apparent, in the holy and happy "tenor of his new life."

In his journal, under the date of October 20th, 1821, is the following entry, in which he refers to my books, and visits to the hospital, &c.:—" I have much, very much to be thankful for this "day; much to be sorry for in myself, much to be thankful for to "the Lord. In the morning I went to Mr. L——, for the purpose of purchasing, at his reduced prices, two copies of the 'Scripture 'Help,' which I most sincerely hope to render useful to my dear relations. Having expressed my desire, he, with the utmost kindness, presented me with the large edition of the "' Scripture Help,' and an abridgment of the 'Treatise on Prayer'

"*gratis*, pointed out to me the second chapter of St. Paul to the Gala-
"tians* as a standard of Christianity, and strongly recommended
"the diligent perusal of the whole epistle. If all gentlemen of
"fortune were like him, how essential would soon, by God's
"blessing, be the alteration in the manners of their dependants
"and inferiors.

"By God's blessing upon a severe fit of sickness, which he
"lately underwent, Mr. L—— is now an example of sobriety and
"seriousness, of piety and its fruits, to every officer in the regi-
"ment. He visits the hospital, supplies it with good books, and
"administers most excellent advice to every one whose sickness
"appears dangerous, and generally to all the patients. He
"supplies men in solitary confinement with sermons and religious
"tracts, in hopes of awakening them to a sense of their awful
"spiritual condition, and he freely distributes books to all who
"may be unable to purchase them at his reduced prices. What
"an example this to me! O that the Lord would be pleased to
"sanctify my illness with such a regeneration; that He would
"incline and enable me to employ my small means to such pur-
"poses, and bless them from my hands! Let me for a moment
"consider how good the Lord has shown Himself, and indulge the
"delightful hope of being able some time to make a complete
"dedication of my heart and soul to Him."

I could not very well omit to insert the above in such a work
as this, although I feel much humbled in doing so. It helps to
shew what some, at least, of the soldiers think of the poor, though
sincere and prayerful, efforts of their officers to lead them to fear
and honour God in seeking the salvation, and holiness, and comfort
of true religion. It will also, I trust, lead many, both officers
and civilians, who may read this work, to neglect no opportunity
which may offer itself, of striving to lead the careless, and ignorant, and wicked, to "seek the Lord while he may be found, &c.:"
Isaiah lv, 6, 7. God certainly does, in a most wonderful manner,
acknowledge and bless the poor, unworthy efforts which He puts
it into the hearts of His poor, sinful servants to make for His
honour, and for the good of people's souls. How much *unexpected*

---

* It must have been the latter part of that chapter, or possibly the third chapter.

encouragement also does He give to us to attend, at all times, with prayer for His blessing, to the commands contained in the first and sixth verses of the eleventh chapter of Ecclesiastes; and what a promise for our encouragement in this work He gives us in Isaiah lv, 10—13.

I did not know very much of Houghton, for almost immediately after he came out of hospital, towards the end of October, he procured his discharge; either his friends purchased it for him, or he was unfit for further service. I recollect he came to take leave of me, and to thank me for my kindness to him; and that I then gave him some religious books and tracts for distribution amongst his friends and neighbours. His subsequent history was very interesting. He had been well educated in his youth; and after some time he resumed his studies, and went through Trinity College, Dublin, and was eventually ordained a clergyman of the Church of England. He was a most efficient and devoted minister, but his health broke down, and he died full of faith, and peace, and joy, in the year 1830, at the age of twenty-eight.

I have lately found the following letter, which I received from Houghton about six weeks after he left the 52nd:—

"Preston, Lancashire, Dec. 7th, 1821.

"Sir,—Having received your kind permission to address you
" on my arrival at home, I can no longer neglect the performance
" of a duty which, I assure you, Sir, affords me the greatest plea-
" sure, of expressing my gratitude to you as the means, through
" Christ, of awakening me to a knowledge of Himself when I was
" dead in infidelity and sin. Your example convinced me that
" religion is not, as I had foolishly imagined, confined to the bigot
" and enthusiast, and founded upon weakness and ignorance;
" and I pray God that your light may continue to shine before
" men, for it is impossible to conceive the good effects which the
" Almighty may produce by it. For men who have not had the
" advantages of a liberal education, of whom the mass of society
" is composed, do conceive of it greater things than it really de-
" serves, and pay to persons endued with it a sort of involuntary
" respect and homage, by a close imitation of their manners, even
" when they are not conscious of doing so.

"As you had the goodness to express a desire to hear of my
"prospects, I beg to inform you that, with the advice of my
"friends, and my own decided inclination, I have re-commenced
"my classical studies, with the view of preparing myself for the
"church, and if it should please the Lord to admit such an
"unworthy member, I will spend my last breath in His service,
"and declare that it was good for me that I was afflicted. The
"tracts which you were so kind as to give me I hope to make
"useful, as I have obtained leave from the superintendent of the
"Sunday school to lend them to the boys. Our church is blessed
"with two pious gospel ministers, and we were near obtaining
"the Rev. Richard Marks, (now vicar of Great Missenden, Bucks.,)
"author of 'The Retrospect,' who offered himself to the curacy
"some years ago. You will, I hope, Sir, pardon my troubling
"you thus far, and believe me, with the sincerest prayers for
"your success in the Christian warfare,

"Your grateful, obedient servant,
"P. HOUGHTON."

CHAPTER XXII.

1822.

THE 52ND IN THE SOUTH OF IRELAND.

March from Dublin—Fair at Ballynahill—The county of Tipperary under the Insurrection Act—Detached to New Birmingham—The Rev. John Galway—Set up a school for the men—Two drunken men shot by sentry near Carrick—Refuse invitation to dine out on Sunday—Extracts from journal—The priest prohibits my tracts—Tracts given to beggars to sell—Benefit arising from this—Interesting details—Introduced to a very clever nailer—Comes to compare Roman Catholic catechism with Bible—Praying to angels—Hopeful state of several persons—Joined at night by a stranger on the road—The priest burns the tracts—Give Bibles and Douay Testaments—Instance lately discovered of good done by the tracts given to the soldiers—Relieved by Gawler—Clonmel, Ballynamult—Escort prisoners to Fermoy—On duty to Dublin—Return to New Birmingham for a short time—Account in after years of one of the New Birmingham converts—Converts become protestant Scripture readers—Establishment of a regimental savings' bank—Compliment to my efficiency—First epistle of St. Peter—Lord Seaton.

THE 52nd marched from Dublin, in two divisions, on the 27th and 28th of May, 1822, for the county of Tipperary. I was with that commanded by Colonel William Rowan,* which proceeded to Cashel. The head-quarter division was stationed at Clonmel. The night before we arrived at Cashel, we were at a place called Ballynahill; there was a fair there, and a regular row in the evening amongst some of the people, in which a man's stall was demolished, and he fired a shot at the mob, but did no mischief. I was witness to a curious dialogue on the occasion between Mr. Horne, a magistrate, and a very fine young man, who I suppose was a somewhat troublesome youth, but who on this occasion

* Now General Sir Wm. Rowan, K.C.B., Colonel of the 52nd; late Commander-in-Chief in Canada.

had taken the stall-owner's part, and had assisted in collecting and in taking care of his scattered wares. Mr. Horne was not aware of this, and spoke very sharply to him about his troublesome ways, and wished him to enlist. He said to him before us, "If these gentlemen will take you, and you will go with them, I "will give you a guinea out of my own pocket." The young fellow was very indignant about the proposal, and answered, "So "nothing will suit ye, Mr. Horan, but that I should 'list. No, no, "when I do go, I'll go daysent." The inhabitants of this part of Ireland struck me as being a very fine race of people; and this young man was one of the finest of them, so I had an eye to enlisting him, and on meeting him afterwards asked him if he was really wishing to enlist; he said yes, but that he did not like to go in that way. I told him to consider the matter, and that if he liked it I thought he could get into our regiment. He promised to come and see us off in the morning, and to come away with us provided another young man, who wished to enlist, would come also. He walked with me some distance the next morning, and said he would join us that night at Johnstown, or on the morrow at Cashel; we, however, saw no more of him.

The county of Tipperary was under the Insurrection Act, and we sent out numerous detachments under an officer to various posts, both from Cashel and Clonmel. My detachment proceeded to the village of New Birmingham, about three miles from Killenaule. The barracks for the officers and men were under the same roof, and were formed out of two large adjoining cottages. It was some time before we were supplied by the barrack-master with all the various articles required by a detachment. My principal window faced the bog of Allan, and on very wet days I sometimes took a sort of pleasure, in my loneliness, in seeing the showers chase each other without intermission across the bog; but the time, three months and a half, that I spent at New Birmingham, although I sometimes felt lonely, was a very profitable and interesting period of my life. I met with very great kindness from the Rev. John Galway, the curate of the parish, who resided in New Birmingham, though the church was four miles away. Two of the neighbouring gentry were also very kind. There was not much to do in the shape of military duty. The following extracts from a rough journal I then kept will give some idea of my manner of spending a portion of my time, and of my poor attempts to do some good to those around me, and will, perhaps, also shew that God did, in some good measure, deal with me according to that gracious promise contained in Proverbs xi, 25, "he that watereth shall be watered "also himself."

"June 9. Mr. Galway was kind enough to read prayers to the men. In the evening I read to them one of Burder's sermons on the knowledge of Christ. 10th. I dined early, and Mr. Galway and I took a long walk after dinner, and another after tea; during the last we had a very pleasing conversation on religious subjects. I do trust my stay here may be blessed to both of us; I humbly pray it may. May the Lord Almighty enable me to walk more and more closely with Him. I have indeed been greatly privileged for the last three or four days, my feelings having been very spiritual. Yesterday I had a very interesting conversation with a poor Roman Catholic farmer. I have promised to take him some books. 12th. Which I did to-day; he was very thankful for them; they were 'The King's Visit,' 'The 'Good Catholic,' and 'Short Prayers for every day in the week.' 13th. Established a school in the detachment; ten out of the twenty-one attended twice to-day; six of them read verse about in the Testament, I now and then explaining a little, and four others, two boys, and one of the women, were at their spelling and alphabet; the reading party looked out several of Chalmers's references.

"June 14th. My school goes on as well as I can wish. I trust that God's blessing is on it; if so, it will prosper; without His blessing it cannot. Besides reading twice a day with me, four of the men write in Serjeant Whamond's room. I had a visit from Sir John Tylden and Cosby on Wednesday. They tell me I have the best detachment of any. Love is at Feathard, Forbes at Mullinahone, Vivian at Scaw, near Carrick, and Campbell at New Inn. An unfortunate business happened the other night at Vivian's place. A man of his detachment was posted in front of the guard-room door with orders to let no one pass; two drunken fellows, returning from Carrick fair, would not pull up, though he repeatedly called to them; he fired, killed one and severely wounded the other. They were both on the same horse. The jury returned a verdict of 'Wilful murder,' and the man was committed to Kilkenny gaol. His trial will not come on till August. 15th. Received an invitation to dine with Mr. Langley to-morrow; refused on the ground of its being Sunday." He afterwards apologised for having invited me for that day. "23rd. Mr. Galway read prayers for us in the barrack-room, and gave us a faithful, but I cannot say a very awakening, sermon. In the evening we walked together, and I read 'Newton on the Pro- 'phecies.' How wonderfully are the prophecies concerning the Jews fulfilled. 'Oh the depths of the wisdom, &c:' Romans xi, 33. 24th. This day I have had great spiritual joy, and I am humbly thankful for it. What are the pleasures of the world, when compared with that joy which comes from above? That heart alone can feel it which looks on God as a reconciled father. May I from this day forth increase in the love and knowledge of that Saviour who died for me. May I love my God more and serve Him better every day. I humbly trust He will guide me with His Holy Spirit through life, and finally receive me to eternal happiness. This day has been a day of real happiness on earth. I have received great pleasure from an interesting conversation with Mr. Galway. I gave him about a hundred tracts to form a lending library for his Sunday school. A poor Roman Catholic, with whom I have had several interesting conversations, and to whom I have given some tracts, I hope much from. Watch and pray.

"June 26th. One of the men whom I confined for being drunk on parade, pretended to blow his brains out; he discharged his firelock with the top of the barrel close to his chin, and burnt himself very much, but as the ball was not in, did himself no further injury. Drank tea with Mr. Galway, and met Mrs. and the Misses Langley. Mr. Langley was out all night in search of Whiteboys. He took out Forbes's party, besides which several other parties were out. He succeeded in discovering a man supposed to be the original Captain Rock. He was admitted to bail for a minor offence, but it is probable he will be hanged yet for some of the crimes he has committed. A man, whom I saw, had given information to Mr. Langley, and in consequence of this the peasantry about Sliebneman became frightened, and gave up nearly two hundred stand of arms to different people.

"June 28th. Dined at Mr. Langley's at Coalbrook, three miles off. The whole family have some serious ideas; I promised to lend them 'The Retrospect' and 'Chalmers's Quarterly 'Papers.' Mr. Galway and I had a very pleasing conversation as we returned. I was mentioning that it sometimes occurred to me that I *might* be making myself too conspicuous as a strict man with regard to religion. 'Oh no,' he said, 'do not think so 'at all, but think of the good you may do in your situation. It 'must excite attention to these subjects when a young fellow, 'with a sword by his side, comes into a village, and, instead of 'lounging about and making a fool of himself, is observed to be 'anxious to encourage religion and morality among his men. 'You must observe that it has a beneficial influence even on the 'clergyman.' Frail and sinful as I am, perhaps I may be the *means*, if it be God's will, of stirring up a few of the people hereabouts to think more seriously of an eternal world.

"June 30th. Sunday. Mr. Galway gave us a very faithful sermon about praying for the Holy Spirit. In consequence of having been out all last night patroling, I felt heavy and sleepy in the middle of the day, and lay down for two or three hours. I feared much my Sabbath would pass away in an almost unprofitable manner. After dinner I read the first four chapters of St. John's Gospel with great pleasure, and I trust some benefit. I walked for about an hour: on my return I told my servant I would read a short sermon to him, and desired him to invite two or three of the men to come up, indeed as many as liked it. I went on my knees and prayed to God that He would put His Spirit into their hearts and incline many to come. How truly delightful it is to have one's prayers answered. I thought it probable that two or three might come, but all the men in the barracks and three women attended, about eighteen in all. My detachment consists of twenty-one men and six women; seven of them are Roman Catholics who did not come. I read Burder's second sermon, 'The broad and the narrow way.' May the Almighty Being, who graciously heard one part of my prayer, as graciously answer the other, that the Holy Spirit may be poured out on them, and that the sermon they have heard may be blest to them. May everyone of them be brought by that Holy Spirit into the narrow path that leads to eternal bliss. This evening, too, I have had sweet communion with my heavenly Father. I have also to-day received a pleasing letter from —— and ——; its style shews evidently that they are beginning to think seriously of eternal things. Oh! what cause have I for praise. 'O heavenly Father, may I from this day forth strive to live 'entirely to Thee, and may I seek Thy glory and the welfare of 'my poor fellow-creatures in all I do. Amen.' The more we seek our God in prayer the more blessed and happy we shall be.

"Sunday, July 7th. In the evening I talked to the men about a penny-a-week subscription to the Church Missionary Society, and told them that any who wished it might come to my morning and evening prayers." About ten men and women came the next morning.

"July 13th. Mr. Galway took the prayers for me, and read the thirteenth chapter of St. Luke; seven or eight of the men attended. Sunday, 14th. I have been trying to persuade the men to pray by themselves individually. May the Almighty pour His Holy Spirit on them and induce them to follow my advice. July 16th. I find the priest formally prohibited my little tracts last Sunday. Several have been brought back to me in consequence. It is quite pitiable to see how completely the priest has these poor fellows under his thumb, when one is convinced that he is leading them astray."

I see from my journal that I had at this time frequent interesting conversations with Roman Catholics, and that I circulated amongst them great numbers of tracts. One of my plans was to give several tracts to the beggars that they might sell them about the country; this practice was accompanied by prayer for God's blessing on them. One day, when I returned to my quarter my servant told me that a man had been wishing to see me very much, who had been there once before. In a day or two he called again, and told me that he had bought five tracts from a beggar woman to "whom I had given them to sell, and that he was much struck with them: he told me also he was sure he had been long astray. I was pointing out some passages to him in my Bible relating to the new birth, and his anxiety to turn to the references was quite delightful. I have promised to try and get him a Bible with references, and lent him 'Andrew 'Dunn,' 'Short Prayers for every day,' and another tract or two. I do hope and trust that this poor man will be brought to a knowledge of vital religion."

Some little time after I had had this first conversation with him I sent for him, that I might give him a Bible with references exactly like my own. He was delighted with it, and read and conversed with me for a long time on various points of religion. When he was going away he begged to be allowed to take my Bible with him, that he might copy out all the remarks which I had made in many parts of it. I permitted him to do this, and he returned my Bible in a few days. His name was Rawley, and he was a weaver.

About this time I became acquainted with one or two other interesting characters. As I was walking down the street of the village one day with Mr. Galway, he said, " If you will come with " me into this shop just below, I will shew you one of the most " clever fellows, for his station in life, that you ever met with." We accordingly entered the nailer's shop, and I was properly introduced to James Whelan. A nailer's shop in Ireland was a place in which several of the people assembled for the sake of a talk with each other. Not very long after I was first there, I turned into the shop one day for the purpose of trying to have some religious conversation with Whelan. There were four or five persons there. I forget now the exact turn which the conversation took, but I well recollect that he attempted to prove something which he advanced by the Roman Catholic catechism, when I observed that that was not in the Word of God. He replied that it was in their catechism, and that the catechism was taken from God's Word. I then addressed him very seriously and said, "You know enough of me to be aware that I " mean exactly what I say. Now, if you will come to my quarter " to-morrow, and bring your catechism with you, and can con- " vince me that what it contains is in accordance with the Word " of God, I promise you that I will become a Roman Catholic."

This was too tempting an offer for him to refuse it, besides which it was made in the presence of several of his neighbours, and it would have appeared very strange to them, if the man, to whom they had been accustomed to look up, had shewn himself afraid or unwilling to accept my challenge. He accordingly came to my quarter at the hour appointed, bringing his catechism with him. Rawley was also present by my invitation. I took down my Bible for the purpose of comparing the Roman Catholic catechism with it, when an unexpected difficulty arose. I told Whelan that I always made it my practice to pray for God's teaching and blessing whenever I read His Holy Word. He immediately objected, that he could not pray with a heretic. I told him that I could not examine God's Word without seeking His blessing on what I was about to do. There appeared to be some danger for a few seconds that our projected conference would come to nothing. It was in vain that Rawley said to him, "I assure you, "Jim, the gentleman's prayer is a very good one, and you will "like it." He could not pray with a heretic. At last I suggested that I and Rawley could offer up the prayer, and that he could join in it or not as he liked. To this he assented.

The prayer was a very simple one which I had composed for myself, and which I afterwards printed, that it might be placed in some copies of the Scriptures which I had procured for the people. I have one of the copies then printed lying before me. It was as follows:—

"Now that we are about to read Thy Word, Almighty God, "pour out Thy Holy Spirit into our hearts. Teach us the way "of salvation, and Thy will concerning our conduct in this life. "Grant this for our Saviour Christ's sake. Amen."

The very first point we turned to in his catechism was the doctrine of the worshipping of angels. We looked out the reference given in the catechism to prove this doctrine, which was the eighth verse of the last chapter of Revelation, and read it as follows:—" And I John saw these things, and heard them. And "when I had heard and seen, I fell down to worship before the "feet of the angel, which shewed me these things." And here ended the proof. Whelan immediately exclaimed, that the verse exactly agreed with what the catechism stated. I begged him to look at the next verse, and we read, "Then saith he unto me, "See thou do it not: for I am thy fellow-servant, and of thy "brethren the prophets, and of them which keep the sayings of "this book: worship God." On reading this the expression of his countenance changed most remarkably, and I felt convinced that I could read in it the very thoughts of his heart, which appeared to be, " Is it possible that my church, that which I have always "been taught to look upon as the true Church of God, is so "deceitful and so dishonest as to have recourse, in order to prove "a point, to such a remarkable suppression of the truth as this "which I have thus seen proved against her ?" I do not recollect anything more which passed between us on that occasion. A short time afterwards I gave to Whelan a Bible with references, similar to that which I had given to Rawley. I shall have to mention these two men again a few pages farther on.

I have always considered the following case as a rather remarkable one:—I had been employed all the forenoon, and during part of it had had a long and interesting conversation on religion with a Roman Catholic near our barracks; after which I went for a walk up the side of the mountain immediately behind the village; after a time, I observed a man some two hundred yards above me on the side of the mountain, but walking in the same direction. I was tired with the walk and long discussion which I had just had, and resolved to keep clear of this man, and to enjoy a quiet walk by myself; but the thought occurred to me that perhaps I should never again have an opportunity of speaking to this poor ignorant Roman Catholic, and I determined to alter my course so as to come across his path. I always tried to remember to ask for God's help and blessing on such occasions, and I probably did so then. I found him to be a quiet, intelligent man. His name was Noonan, and he lived in a village about two miles away on the other side of the mountain. After speaking to him for a short time, I gave him a few tracts, one of which I remember was "Andrew Dunn," which he afterwards told me had been eagerly read by a great many persons in his village. I shall have to speak again of him hereafter, but I may here say, that this meeting with him, and giving him the tracts, was the first step towards his throwing aside the errors and trammels of popery, and becoming an enlightened and pious Protestant.

The following is from my journal:—

"August 11th. About three weeks ago, twelve of my detachment, consisting of twenty-one, became subscribers of a penny a week to the Church Missionary Society: to-morrow we are to have a little missionary meeting. 12th. About fifteen of the men attended the missionary meeting. I tried to explain to them the object of the society, and read to them accounts of what had been done. I ended by praying for the extension of Christianity. The evening was very pleasing, and I trust profitable. September 5th. On the 2nd I received a fresh set of men. About eight of them have attended school very regularly as yet, and six or eight come up in the evening from eight to nine, when I read them a tract, and we read the Bible together and end with prayer. I do earnestly pray that the Almighty will pour out His Spirit on us, and bless what we are doing to the salvation of many of their souls. One young man, Ledgett, appears to be very serious; last night he arrived in the room just as I had finished reading a tract to the others, when, quite regardless of their being there, he knelt down in a corner of the room and prayed, I suppose for a blessing on what we were doing. I hope, from their not being surprised at it, that he is in the habit of kneeling down to say his prayers in the barrack-room. I have received great pleasure from knowing that the tracts, which I have given away here, have been the means of making four or five people very serious."

I think also that one family among the neighbouring gentry began to feel the importance of religion, much more than they had done before, in consequence of their intercourse with me, and through reading the books which I lent to them. On my return home from dining with them one night, as I was walking along a lonely part of the road, a man suddenly joined me, as if he had been waiting for me, and began to enter into conversation with me. I only recollect two things which he said, and my replies. He said he wondered I was not afraid to be on the road alone at that hour. I replied, at the same time touching my sword, "I have a trusty friend here in which I can place confi-

"dence." This was a soldier's speech, but I ought to have added, "God has promised to protect those who put their trust in Him," and I probably should have done so, had he not immediately said, "I wonder, Sir, you take so much trouble to distribute "such numbers of tracts amongst the people. You are not aware, "perhaps, that the priest regularly collects and burns them." To this I answered, "I don't care about his burning the tracts; he "does not get hold of them all, and I know you Irish people too "well to believe that the greater part of those which the priest "burns, are not read before they get into his hands." I never saw the priest, as he lived in a distant part of the parish, but after I had given the Bibles to Rawley and Whelan, he sent me a message to say that, if I would get him some Douay Testaments he would place them in the schools. I thought it better that they should have these Testaments than not have the Scriptures at all, although there were a few such translations as the following:—" Except ye do penance," instead of our authorized translation, " except ye repent." I therefore sent for two dozen of these Testaments, some few of which the priest had, and the rest were given to the people. After I had left New Birmingham, Gawler informed me that they would be glad of some more, but these I desired might be sold at sixpence each, as I thought the people would probably value them all the more if they paid for them. It will be seen, farther on, that this idea proved to be correct, under rather remarkable circumstances.

This appears to be the proper place in which to record the following, to me very interesting, account, as it is most probably connected with my distribution of tracts amongst the men of the regiment when it was stationed at Dublin :—A few months ago a man not living far from this parish, who knew I had been in the army but did not know in what regiment I had been, accosted me as I was walking home in the evening, and said he had long wished to consult me as to some money which he thought was due to him on account of his father, Samuel Baldwin, who belonged to the 52nd, and had died in 1826 in New Brunswick. In the course of conversation he told me the only thing he had which had belonged to his father was his military Testament. I sent him for this, as his house was not far off;

and I found the son's name written in it, and that he was born at Cashel, in 1822; but what interested me very much was to find an entry almost in the following words, taken from a tract which I well remember, and which I feel almost certain he must have received from me, either at Cashel or New Birmingham:—
" How do I know that the Bible is the Word of God? Bad men
" could not have written a book containing such holy precepts
" and commands. Good men would never have deceived man-
" kind by pretending that that was a revelation from God, which
" they knew had been fabricated by themselves." The tract was written by a clergyman named Marks, who had been a lieutenant in the navy. It is one of the Religious Tract Society's tracts, and is called "Conversation in a Boat between two Seamen." It contains some other short arguments proving the divine origin of the Bible; especially the fulfilment of the prophecies respecting the Jews, and of the prophecies and types which refer to Christ.

On the 25th of September I was relieved by Gawler in the command of the detachment at New Birmingham, and proceeded to Clonmel. I had much to be truly thankful for during my stay at New Birmingham. I was enabled not only to do something in the way of instructing our men and the Roman Catholics around me, but I had it in my power to befriend, to some extent, many of the poor of the village at a time of great destitution in that part of Ireland. My friend Gawler and Mrs. Gawler were also most kind to them, so that the priest from the altar told the people that they were bound to pray for Mr. Gawler and for Mr. Leeke.

Shortly after my arrival at Clonmel I went to Fermoy, in command of a large guard over a number of convicts, who were conveyed in carts. It was a most fatiguing march of twenty-four Irish miles, at the rate of not quite two miles an hour. Towards the middle of October, Kirwan Hill was taken ill at Ballynamult, and I volunteered to relieve him, and to remain in his place until the arrival of the other Hill from England. I remained there ten days and then returned to Clonmel. The Ballynamult barracks are capable of holding about 150 men, with a proportion of officers; they are situated in a very wild part of the county of

Waterford, near the Knockmeledown Mountains. There was not a gentleman's house within seven Irish miles; and it was a very solitary station, especially for the officer of the detachment, which, I think, consisted of forty men. I recollect many of them availed themselves of my permission to attend my daily Scripture reading and prayer.

At the end of November, 1822, I went to Dublin with a party of twenty-five invalids, and fell in with many of my old friends—Major Oliver, the Guinnesses, and Mr. and Mrs. Mathias; about three weeks or a month before, they had lost their eldest daughter, a truly religious young person, at the age of sixteen. Her mother, amongst other things which she mentioned as to the great comfort they had with regard to her state, told me that, a day or two before her death, she heard her say, when the room was quite quiet and she thought no one was in it, "O my precious, precious Saviour." I spent the Sunday with Mr. and Mrs. Mathias. I think it was the first time he had preached since his daughter's death. The following is from my journal:—"His sermon was very much calculated to touch the hearts of his congregation; he alluded in some degree to his recent loss, and said there were two sets of parents in the world, —those who were bringing up their children merely for this world, and those who were educating them for eternity. He said that death, when it made its appearance in a family, was an awful visitor, but those who feared God had consolations of the highest kind, which people of the world could not have. I felt much affected, for the last time I had been in that church, I had sat in that same pew with my poor young friend Annie."

I find the following entries in my journal:—"It was on the 4th and 5th of November that the row was about King William's statue. By order of the Lord-Lieutenant, the orangemen were prevented from dressing it for the first time. This gave rise to the disturbance at the theatre the other day, when the Lord-Lieutenant went there. Some one threw a quart bottle from the upper gallery, which, it was said, tore away some of the fringe from one of the cushions in his box. On the 23rd of December a party of us from Clonmel and Cashel went to Cahir, to dine with the 10th Hussars. I proceeded to New Birmingham on the 26th, to relieve Gawler, who went with his wife to England; he came back on the 9th, when I returned to Clonmel. At New Birmingham I found that two of the Roman Catholics to whom I had spoken and given tracts, Rawley and Noonan, had been regular attendants at Gawler's evening prayers for some time past, and had thereby 'entirely' offended the priest. I fancy they are both quite convinced that the Roman Catholic religion is full of error; they seem also to be anxiously searching the Scriptures. I had several arguments with Whelan, the nailer; a very clever man for his situation in life. I wanted him to read a little book of mine, and by my desire he took it to the priest and requested permission to read it. He was told by Father Meighan not to be too curious. A poor woman, who had once been at Gawler's family prayers, knelt two different Sundays at the chapel door, whilst the congregation were passing, by way of doing penance for that sin. The poor people at New Birmingham are still very wretched, although a great deal has been done for them. I gave Rawley £5 to purchase wool with. With this he is to keep thirteen women constantly employed in spinning. I supplied eight of them with wheels, and I hope this will be the means of adding a little to their support. I dined two or three times with John Galway, and he once with me. Our conversations on the subject of religion were very interesting, but I fear he does not yet see the necessity of endeavouring to do everything to the glory of God. I dined at Cashel on the 9th of January, 1823, and drank tea with Mr. and Mrs. Holmes. The next day I breakfasted with Cosby, at New Inn, and afterwards proceeded to Clonmel."

Here my journal for that period ends, and it was only very occasionally resumed in after times; but I must say a little more about my poor Roman Catholic friends, Rawley, Noonan, and Whelan, whom I never saw again, but whom I fully hope to meet at the right hand of our great Judge and Saviour, on that day when the trumpet shall sound, and those "who sleep in the "dust of the earth shall awake, some to everlasting life, and "some to shame and everlasting contempt."

After I left New Birmingham I sent the second two dozen of Douay Testaments, which were sold to the people. Gawler after some time offended the priest by a handbill, which he found it desirable to circulate in the village, and had the honour of being denounced from the altar. The priest ordered the people to return even the Douay Testaments, and singularly enough they brought to Gawler all those which I had given them, but refused to obey the priest's order with regard to those which they had purchased. Amongst those who brought back books, was Whelan the nailer, to whom I had given, as I have before mentioned, a Bible with references. When he brought it to my friend Gawler, he told him he had read from the beginning of the Bible to, I think, about the end of the second book of Kings. He added "I am a poor man, Sir, "but I do assure you I would rather give you ten pounds than "give you that book." "Why then do you not keep it?" replied Gawler. "Because my priest has ordered me not to do so," said Whelan. Gawler replied, "Your priest, who tells you not to "read God's Word, is only a man, whereas God Himself com- "mands you to search the Scriptures. Should you not obey God "rather than man?" Whelan, shrugging his shoulders in token of his feeling of helplessness, quietly said, "I must obey my priest, Sir." Some three or four years afterwards Rawley had an opportunity of sending a message to me, and a part of it was, I might depend upon it that Whelan was a Protestant at heart, though he was afraid to confess it openly.

Poor Rawley, the man who had bought my tracts from the beggar-woman, and to whom I had given a Bible, was a simple-minded, straightforward man. He suffered some considerable persecution from the Roman Catholics, and was waylaid one night and had his head injured by a blow with a spade. We sent him for a time to Kilkenny, commending him to the care of that excellent man, the Rev. Peter Roe, and afterwards I understood he became a scripture reader on Lord Mountcashel's estate. Some years after that, one of my sisters, who was married and living in the county of Kilkenny, mentioned in one of her letters that the clergyman of their parish, on accidentally hearing her maiden name, asked if she knew anything of a Mr. Leeke who had been quartered in the county of Tipperary several years before, and on learning that I was her brother, he told her that some little time before he had been sent for to visit a dying man, and that on arriving at the house he found about two hundred people assembled, and in a great state of excitement. They said the dying man was a Roman Catholic, and declared that he, Mr. Darby, should not see him, and threatened him if he attempted to go into the house. He said that they might do what they liked, but that he should certainly see the man. In the middle of the dispute, the priest arrived, and Mr. Darby and he arranged that they should both go into the dying man's room, and that whichever the man preferred should remain. He declared he was a Protestant, and wished the Protestant clergyman to remain with him. In the course of conversation, he several times mentioned the names of Mr. Gawler and Mr. Leeke, and how they had exerted themselves at New Birmingham, to lead the people to give up their sins and errors and to seek mercy through the atoning death of the Lord Jesus Christ. Mr. Darby said that he was not only a convert from popery, but a humble, penitent believer in the Saviour of sinners. I understood from my sister's letter that this was my poor friend Rawley. Some time after I received this letter I fell in with Mr. Darby, and he gave me the history of the case, as I have related it above, saying, however, that my sister had made one mistake, and that the man who died was not Rawley, but a convert of Rawley's.

Noonan was the man, from another village, whose path I crossed on the side of the mountain, and to whom I gave the tract called "Andrew Dunn." He attended Gawler's family prayers, and became a convert from popery, and a good man. He became a scripture reader on, I believe, Lord Cavan's estate, and was the means of doing much good there. It was reported of him, that he was held in all the greater estimation, "because he "made the people cry." He went in after years to Australia.

In November, 1822, I obtained leave from Major McNair, who was then in command of the regiment, to draw out rules for the establishment of a regimental savings' bank, and he requested me also to write the order on the subject for the orderly book, to be signed by him. I have my rough copy of the rules, but not of the order, now before me. The rules were duly lodged, according to the 57th of George III, c. 105, with the proper officer at Clonmel. I remember that the captains of the regiment were appointed trustees, and Winterbottom, who had become the paymaster, and I were the treasurers. On the first day on which money was paid in, upwards of four hundred pounds were received by us. I had heard of only one other savings' bank in the army at that time, and that was either in the 78th or 79th Highlanders. I was told, after my return from the military college, on our way to North America, that Sir John Tylden, some time after he came from leave and had assumed the command of the regiment, wrote to the Horse Guards, mentioning the establishment of a savings' bank in the regiment, and how acceptable it was to the men, and that he got a regular "rap "over the knuckles" for having ventured to take a step of such importance, without the permission of the Commander-in-Chief, (not that he had taken it,) and desiring him immediately to put a stop to the thing. When I rejoined the regiment from Sandhurst, and whilst I remained in it, I never heard anything more of a savings' bank.

I copy the following from the 52nd record:—"1843. Regi-"mental savings' banks had been established by Her Majesty's "gracious warrant of the 11th of October, and the 52nd "regimental savings' bank was begun by a regimental order, "dated 30th of November." It is very singular that in my rough draft of the "Rules for a 52nd Light Infantry Regimental Savings' Bank," it is stated to have been "established at Clonmel on the 30th of November, 1822," exactly, to a day, twenty-one years before the establishment of the other.

I am not sure that I ought to mention the following circumstance which took place at Clonmel. I will, however, write it down, and omit it in the publication of the work if on further consideration I think it desirable do so. I shall probably, however, retain it, for I feel it to be important to the cause of religion, as I have before stated, to shew that my religious views did not at all interfere with my efficiency as an officer. The circumstance was this:—One day the commanding officer ordered the company which I commanded to skirmish, and to conform to the movements of the battalion. He was so pleased with the manner in which I had handled the skirmishers, that when the men were dismissed, and most of the officers were standing around him in a group, he spoke of me as "the best light infantry officer in "the regiment." This was certainly an unusual thing for a commanding officer to do, but nevertheless the circumstance happened as I have related it. I fear the mention of it must be set down to the score of vanity, but that I cannot help. I suppose we are all vain at times; and I confess I was very proud of my regiment, and consequently very proud of being called "the best "light infantry officer" in the best light infantry regiment in the world, in "a regiment never surpassed in arms since arms were "first borne by men."* Of course I was aware that almost every officer in the regiment could handle a body of skirmishers as well as I could, and that most of them had much more experience than I had, still I have always remembered with gratification the above measure of praise dealt out to me on the parade-ground of the 52nd.

One other anecdote relating to my efficiency as an officer I am bound also, for the before-mentioned reason, not to omit; it occurred at nearly the same time as that mentioned in the last paragraph. The regiment was practising "street firing," both in advancing and retiring, and one of the older officers in command of a company made somewhat of a bungle of it, whilst I, with the company I commanded, executed the several movements with that precision and promptitude which they required. I was told that several of the officers, in talking the thing over afterwards, had expressed their wonder at the slowness, &c., of the older officer, and had particularly contrasted it with my smartness on the occasion. My readers will very naturally say of me, "His trumpeter has been long dead."

One of my pleasing recollections connected with Clonmel is the having learnt by heart the beautiful first epistle of St. Peter, during some of my quiet walks on the banks of the Suir. I think I have consequently always known more of that book than of any other portion of the Scriptures. I may here state also that

---

* If this work should ever fall into the hands of those who have served in the 43rd Light Infantry or in the old 95th Rifles, (now the Rifle Brigade,) those other fine and gallant regiments of the light division in Spain, they will kindly excuse this high-flown language, and set it down to that *esprit de corps*, which is so frequently imbibed by young officers, and which is often cherished by them to the latest day of their lives.

I do not recollect any commentary, or other religious book, that I ever read with greater pleasure and benefit than Archbishop Leighton's Commentary on this same first epistle of Peter. I should be thankful if I could induce my readers to study it, with much prayer to God that He would make it a blessing to them. Some years after the time I write of it was a favourite book with the great and good Lord Seaton.

CHAPTER XXIII.

1823.

SANDHURST.

Senior department at Sandhurst—Determined to work hard—Religious duties—Strict observance of the Lord's Day—Boerhave—Diggle's wound—Serjeant Houseley met him wounded at Waterloo—Diggle's anecdote about a toast in Sicily—My order to join 52nd, and to embark for America—Sir George Murray, the governor, opposes it, but without success—Asks me to dine with him on Sunday—Correspondence with the Horse Guards—Proceed to Cork—Find 52nd embarking.

IN May, 1822, whilst we were at Dublin, I applied to Colonel Charles Rowan, who commanded the 52nd as senior major, to get me leave to join the senior department of the military college at Sandhurst, that I might pursue my studies in fortification and military plan-drawing, which I had gained some knowledge of, before I entered the army, as one of the private pupils of Captain Malortie de Martemont, a French royalist, who was professor of fortification at the Woolwich Academy. Rowan told me he would readily do what I desired, but that I had much better make my application through Colborne, who was a friend of mine. This I did, and my name was forwarded by him to the Horse Guards, and it was notified to me, in a few weeks, that I should be admitted to study at the institution, taking my proper turn after those candidates whose names stood before mine, when a vacancy for me should occur.

I think I went to Sandhurst about the middle of February, 1823. Captain Lloyd of the 73rd Regiment and I, joined in hiring a small house exactly opposite to the large gates of the college, on the Bagshot road, and my servant, who had come with me from the regiment, and his wife, attended on us. Lloyd was a religiously-disposed man, and we got on most comfortably together. We had our family prayers, with great regularity, at seven in the morning, and at nine at night; and we took some considerable time also, every morning and evening, for prayer and meditation on God's Word in private. I believe that all this, and our strict observance of Sunday as a day on which we should not only abstain from secular pursuits and studies, but also endeavour to increase in the knowledge of God, and in holiness, brought down the blessing of God, in a remarkable manner, upon us, both as regarded our progress in religion, and in the military studies of the college, to which we determined to devote all our time and energies. At that time fifteen officers, from various regiments, were studying at the senior department. Lloyd and I worked hard each day, from eight o'clock in the morning till nine at night, scarcely taking any time for our dinner; and the progress we consequently made was remarked by the professors and others.

I rose at five each morning, and got to bed at eleven. This plan left a considerable portion of time each day for private prayer and reading of the Scripture, without at all interfering with our secular studies. I think I never, at any other time of my life, devoted so much of the morning and evening to religious duties, nor did I ever, at any other time, get through such an amount of hard work and study as I did during the few months that I remained at Sandhurst. I do not know that the following paragraphs, which I extract from "Buck's Anecdotes," were the means of my giving up so much time to religious duties, but the blessing which accrued from the practice recalls them to my mind:—

"The great Dr. Boerhave acknowledged that an hour spent "every morning in private prayer and meditation gave him spirit "and vigour for the business of the day, and kept his temper "active, patient, and calm.

"The famous Dr. Boerhave was once asked by a friend who "admired his patience under provocations, whether he knew what "*it* was to be angry, and by what means he had so entirely sup-

"pressed that impetuous and ungovernable passion? He "answered, with the utmost frankness and sincerity, that he "was naturally quick of resentment, but that he had, by daily "prayer and meditation, at length attained to this mastery over "himself."

Lloyd and I were very anxious to observe the Lord's Day in a proper manner, by "not doing our own ways, nor finding our "own pleasure, nor speaking our own words," the meaning of which command we understood to be, that we were not to be engaged in our usual occupations, nor were we to spend any part of the day in amusements, nor were we to engage unnecessarily in worldly conversation: Isaiah lviii, 13. We agreed to remind each other that we were deviating from our rule, if one or the other inadvertently introduced any worldly subject of conversation, being convinced that the day would be as much frittered away, as regarded any religious advantage to be derived from it, by such conversation, as it would be by engaging in our usual employments, or in travelling or amusements. I recollect, on one occasion, when walking in the wood behind our house, that we found we had, through inadvertence, been unnecessarily talking about worldly matters for a whole quarter of an hour. We always felt, and acted upon it, that works of necessity, mercy, and piety, not only might but ought to be done on that holy day.

A rather curious circumstance occurred at Sandhurst in connexion with my early rising. My servant, who went to bed an hour and a half earlier than I did, called me one morning, as I supposed, at the usual hour, five o'clock; I had gone to bed at eleven, and, as I always did, got up directly I was called. I happened, before I began to dress, to look at my watch, and found to my surprise that he had mistaken the hour, and had called me at twelve o'clock. I felt quite as much refreshed by my one hour's sound sleep, as I should have done had I slept for six hours. I was, however, not at all sorry to find that I might turn in again for five hours more.

It was a great pleasure to me to find Major and Mrs. Diggle at Sandhurst. He was a captain in the 52nd at Waterloo, and commanded No. 1, the right company of the regiment in that action, and was desperately wounded in the head in the charge on the French Imperial Guard. He recovered, but his wound was of such a nature, that he left the 52nd, and became captain of one of the companies of gentlemen cadets at Sandhurst. I was their guest for some time, till I had arranged about hiring the house which I occupied with Captain Lloyd of the 73rd.

Diggle of late years was a major-general, and silver-stick in waiting to the Queen. He was in the 52nd for several years, and saw some good service. He wore a silver plate, with black silk covering it, over his wound just above the left temple. I was perfectly astonished at the depth and width of the hole in his skull, when he took off the plate one day, at Sandhurst, to shew it to me. On that occasion I doubled up my forefinger, not a very small one, and laid it against the wound, and satisfied myself that if it could have been cut off at the knuckle joint, and placed on the skin over the brain at the bottom of the wound, I could have covered it over so as to let the plate fit down close over it, and lie evenly on the surrounding portion of the skull. He kept the musket-ball, and about a dozen or fourteen small portions of the skull in a box, the ball having been divided in two by the force of the blow. One of our old serjeants, (Houseley,) whom I shall speak of afterwards, told me a few weeks ago that at Waterloo, when he was returning from conveying Corporal Hood, whose heel was shot off, to the rear, which he was ordered to do on our 52nd squares retiring up the position from the neighbourhood of Hougomont, he met Captain Diggle, who had just been wounded, and, as he passed, heard him say to the men who were with him, "What will my poor wife do?"

Diggle was a very nice fellow, and was much liked by everybody in the regiment. I recollect that one day, at Sandhurst, he was observing that he often wondered how young officers got on in the army without getting into more scrapes than they did, and gave me the following account of a somewhat serious scrape in which he found himself soon after he first joined the 52nd in Sicily. There was a grand dinner given by the regiment to the general and several other persons, and after dinner many toasts were given, when Diggle, being somewhat excited, stood up and said, "Mr. President, will you allow *me* to propose a toast?" Everybody was silent; and the toast was proposed as follows:

"Mr. President, here is confusion to all commanding officers!" The whole of the party were horrified. He hardly knew how he got out of the scrape; he heard some of them say something about his being put in arrest, but the thing was passed over without any serious notice being taken of it.

The studies engaged in by the officers of the senior department at Sandhurst were especially suited to my taste. Professor Narien was an exceedingly pleasing man, and I think I had much more to do with him than with any of the other masters or professors. I believe there was one officer there, and only one, who pursued his work on the Sunday; it was said that he always did his fortification plans on that day. It particularly struck me that whilst Lloyd and I appeared to be especially prospered in our work, it was just the reverse with this officer. It perhaps may be thought that I say too much about myself, but Lloyd and I certainly were very generally known and spoken of, as setting an example in the way of diligence and progress, which was thought to be beneficial to that part of the Sandhurst establishment to which we were attached.

The military sketching was perhaps the most pleasing part of our work at Sandhurst. I well remember the very great pleasure I derived from finding, when I was just completing my first sketch, that, after having paced a round of several miles, and sketched the country bordering on my course, I found, on arriving at a particular point, that my pacing, &c., had been so correct, that it was impossible for it to have been more so.

One evening, I have some idea it was on a Sunday, the fine young plantations behind our house were maliciously set on fire; the fire had not made very great progress when we discovered it, and Lloyd and I, and my servant, with the help of another man, who came to the rescue, were enabled to beat it out before it had burnt more than half an acre of the wood. The proprietor sent his son the next morning to thank us for the service we had rendered him.

I knew scarcely any one in the neighbourhood of Sandhurst; but I once went to dine and sleep at General Orde's, who lived about four miles off. I had met him in town, in 1821, at Admiral Hawker's: he was a religious man, and a good officer. I remember his telling me the following circumstance, which helps to shew what a misunderstanding and fear there was at that time, at the Horse Guards, of men who were known to be strict in matters of religion. He told me that a little time before the Battle of Waterloo he had been offered the command of a brigade in our army in Flanders, to be composed of three of the finest regiments in the service, just returning from America—the 7th Fusiliers, the 29th Regiment, and the 43rd Light Infantry, a light division regiment—but he was required to promise something tantamount to his keeping his religious views to himself as far as his brigade was concerned. On these terms he felt that he could not accept the offer, and was constrained to refuse it, much to his mortification.

The officers of the senior department were not in any way mixed up with the cadets at Sandhurst. We now and then met some of them in their walks, and saw them in the college chapel on the Sunday; but I do not think I ever had an opportunity of speaking to any of them, except on one occasion, when I saw two or three serjeants of the establishment rather concealing themselves, and watching four or five of the cadets who were on what I knew to be the confines of their bounds. I then walked across the road, and called out to them over the hedge, "I think "you are not aware that some of your serjeants are watching you "at a very short distance from this." They immediately thanked me, and, jumping over a fence into their bounds, took the road to the college.

The officers of the senior department were not necessarily much thrown together, but I think we generally did our fortification plans in the same hall of study. I only recollect a few of them by name now, and perhaps they have since passed away; they were very nice, agreeable fellows, but I have only come across one of them since I left Sandhurst. One day, whilst we were at our drawing or fortification, two or three of them came to me and said they had observed that my way of going on was in some measure different from theirs, and they thought I was actuated by my views of religion; and they asked me to explain to them what those views were. I had never before had any opportunity of speaking to any of them, except Lloyd, on religious subjects, and was not sorry that the opportunity had now arrived for doing so. It is rather remarkable that, whilst I have a most accurate memory with regard to most things, I have not the least recollection of what I said to these men on that occasion, except that I acceded to their wish, and that they were very kind and civil about it. I think something must have occurred to prevent our continuing the conversation for more than two or three minutes.

In April, 1823, the 52nd received orders to hold themselves in readiness to proceed to North America early in June, and I received an order from the commanding officer, Sir John Tylden, through the adjutant, to join the regiment, and accompany them to America, and stating, that if I wished to remain at Sandhurst, I could do so only by going on half-pay, and that he should apply to the Horse Guards for a half-pay lieutenancy for me. This letter I took at once to General Sir George Murray, who was governor of Sandhurst. He was very kind, and told me that commanding officers would be commanding officers, but that the commanding officer of the 52nd had nothing to do with ordering me to leave Sandhurst, and join my regiment. He desired me to write as civil a letter as I could in reply to the adjutant's communication, and that he would write to the Horse Guards on the subject.

Sir George Murray occasionally invited an officer or two of the senior department to dine with him, and the day he usually fixed on was Sunday. I had not yet received an invitation, but when I had finished the above-mentioned conversation with him, and was coming away, he said, "Mr. Leeke, you will dine with "me on Sunday?" This came very unexpectedly upon me, but I immediately thanked him, and said that I made it a rule never to dine out on Sundays. He was evidently somewhat "taken aback," as we say, by my reply, and merely said, "Oh! "it's of no consequence." This made no difference in his kindness to me during the few weeks that I remained at Sandhurst after this, though he did not again ask me to dine with him. My kind and good friend Admiral Hawker had been flag captain to William IV, when, as Lord High Admiral, he hoisted his flag for a time in the Britannia, at Plymouth. After he came to the throne, Admiral Hawker was invited, or commanded, on one occasion, to dine with the King on a Sunday. He stated that he had conscientious scruples to doing this on the Lord's Day, and the King took it very good-naturedly, and begged him to dine with him on the following Thursday instead, which he did.

Sir George Murray wrote at once to the Horse Guards, and by return of post received the following reply:—

"Horse Guards, 26th April, 1823.

"MY DEAR GENERAL,

" By the Commander-in-Chief's desire, I have the honour to
" enclose, (in reference to your letter of yesterday,) for your inform-
"ation and guidance, the copy of an official communication which
" is to be made this day by me to the officer commanding the
" 52nd regiment, notifying that Ensign Leeke is to remain at the
" college to complete his studies.

"JOHN MACDONALD, D.A.G."

I naturally thought that this settled the matter, but two or three weeks afterwards it occurred to me that, as a half-pay lieutenancy had been applied for, I had better see Sir Herbert Taylor, the Commander-in-Chief's military secretary, and tell him I did not wish for such promotion. I accordingly went to town, and attended his levée. After remaining there about an hour amongst a large number of officers, one of the attendants came to say that Sir Herbert Taylor would be obliged if I and two other officers, whose names were called out, would go and see Major Maling, the assistant-secretary. On entering his office, he put the following letter into my hand, saying, "There, Sir, " is a letter which, I think, will set your mind at rest:—"

"Horse Guards, 17th May, 1823.

" SIR,—I am directed by the Commander-in-Chief to acquaint
"you that, upon your lodging the sum of £250 in the hands of
" Messrs. Greenwood, Cox, and Co., His Royal Highness will
"submit your name to His Majesty for the purchase of a half-pay
"lieutenancy in the 49th Regiment.

"I have the honour to be, &c.,
"Ensign Leeke, 52nd Regiment.   H. TAYLOR."

I told Major Maling that I had come for the very purpose of

declining the purchase of a half-pay lieutenancy. He brought me Tylden's original letter, with one corner of it turned down, on which the Duke of York had written to the following effect; I am not sure of the exact words :—" This officer to have the pro-
" motion requested for him, or to join his regiment.—FREDERICK."

On my asking if I could have some little time to consult Sir John Colborne on the subject, he said he thought I might take about a week, the time I mentioned, for that purpose, and opening a door into another office, he called out, "Ensign Leeke's promo-
"tion is not to appear in the Gazette to-night."

In about a week I received the following letter from Sir John Colborne :—

"Guernsey, May 23rd, 1823.

"MY DEAR LEEKE,

"I have this moment received your letter, and scarcely know
"what advice to give, so much depends on whether you really
"are not a little disgusted or tired with your profession. I should
"rather be inclined, were the case my own, to join the regiment,
"and proceed to America. You must get a lieutenancy soon in
"the 52nd. The purchasing in another regiment would be
"throwing away money, with a chance of being sent to a colony
"more disagreeable than Nova Scotia. To retire to half-pay
"would be a very unsatisfactory measure, unless you make up
"your mind to bid adieu to a profession to which you owe nothing,
"and in which you have spent many years, without having gained
"any advantage, and without a prospect of obtaining that rank or
"remuneration which might induce you to sacrifice the best part
"of your life. However, in our very precarious profession, we
"are placed frequently in a situation from which it would be
"absurd to escape, unpromising as the prospect may appear. I
"am almost tempted to say, keep your money, and go to America ;
"you can always purchase half-pay, and you may not dislike
"Halifax for some years. Of all this you are the best judge ;
"but either remain in the 52nd, or accept the half-pay lieutenancy
"with the view of quitting the army. I believe Campbell has
"arranged an exchange.

"Very sincerely yours,
"J. COLBORNE."

On the receipt of this letter from Sir John Colborne, (afterwards Lord Seaton,) I wrote as follows to Sir Herbert Taylor:—

"R. M. College, Sandhurst, May 27th, 1823.

"SIR,—In answer to your letter of the 17th, relating to the "purchase of a half-pay lieutenancy in the 49th Regiment, I "have the honour to inform you that this promotion is not at all "what I wish, and that the application for it was made entirely "without my desiring it. Understanding from the adjutant of "the 52nd that such an application had been made by the com-"manding officer, I went to the Horse Guards on the 19th instant, "with the intention of informing you that I should rather remain "in my present regiment, when your letter was put into my hand "by Major Maling. I should have answered it immediately, had "I not wished to consult Sir John Colborne previously to doing "so. I have now been eight years in the 52nd, and am much "attached to it, and should prefer remaining till a lieutenancy "becomes vacant in it, to the purchasing even a *full-pay lieu-* "*tenancy* in another regiment, except with the prospect of further "promotion, or immediate restoration to my old corps. I am "aware that Sir John Tylden, in applying that I should either "join my regiment, or be permitted to purchase half-pay promo-"tion, mentioned the long period during which I was absent from "my regimental duties some time ago. I think it right to state "to you, for the information of His Royal Highness the Com-"mander-in-Chief, that with the exception of three months' leave, "which I had in 1816, I have not been absent from my regiment, "except in consequence of a severe illness, and in order to acquire "a knowledge of French and German.

"I much wish to remain at this college, and I trust I shall be "allowed to do so; at the same time, if it be necessary, I shall "cheerfully return to my regimental duties.

"I have the honour to be, &c.,
"WM. LEEKE, Ensign, 52nd Light Infantry."

To this letter I received the following reply from Sir Herbert Taylor:—

"Horse Guards, May 29th, 1823.

"SIR,—I am directed to acquaint you, in reply to your letter "*of* the 27th instant, that the Commander-in-Chief has no ob-

"jection to cancel your promotion, the candidates for which are
"very numerous, but His Royal Highness cannot, under the
"representation made by your commanding officer, allow you to
"be any longer absent from your regimental duty. If, therefore,
"you choose to continue as an ensign in the 52nd Foot, you must
"join immediately, and proceed with them to Nova Scotia. An
"early answer is requested.

"I have the honour to be, &c.,
"HERBERT TAYLOR."

Sir George Murray felt very strongly, I have reason to think, on the subject of my having the somewhat cruel alternative set before me, of giving up the 52nd, or relinquishing my studies at Sandhurst. He, as the Duke of Wellington's quartermaster-general in Spain, knew the 52nd far better than the Duke of York or Sir Herbert Taylor could know them; and he knew something of my conduct and progress at Sandhurst, and was anxious that I should be differently treated. He consequently wrote strongly to the Horse Guards, urging that I should be permitted to remain at Sandhurst, and enclosing the correspondence which had taken place between the adjutant and myself. To this communication he received the following reply:—

"Horse Guards, 3rd June, 1823.

"MY DEAR GENERAL,
"I have submitted your letter of the 31st ultimo, and its en-
"closures, herein returned, to the Commander-in-Chief, who orders
"me to say, that if the opportunity of recommending Ensign
"Leeke for the purchase of promotion had not offered, His Royal
"Highness would not have required him to join his corps, or to
"retire on half-pay as ensign. As it is, an alternative has been
"offered to him, of which there is scarcely an officer in the service
"who would not avail himself, and His Royal Highness, adverting
"to the manner in which he has endeavoured to consult that
"officer's wish to remain at the college, without losing sight of
"what is due to the efficiency of regiments, to which he attaches
"also great importance, cannot but consider this holding out
"against such arrangement most unreasonable, and must therefore
"abide by what has been communicated in my letter of the 29th
"ultimo to Ensign Leeke.

"His Royal Highness directs me further to observe that En-
"sign Leeke's application in May, 1822, for admission to the
"college, should have been made through the officer then com-
"manding the 52nd Regiment, and not through Sir John Colborne,
"who, being on the staff at Guernsey, could have no concern with
"it, and His Royal Highnesss is not surprised at Sir J. Tylden's
"noticing with displeasure the style of Ensign Leeke's letter of
"the 25th of April.

"I remain, my dear general, sincerely yours,
"HT. TAYLOR.
"M. General Sir George Murray, G.C.B."

The Duke of York, in coming to this conclusion, must, I think, have lost sight of the fact that I was the senior ensign of my regiment, and that, although I had always been for purchase, I had been upwards of eight years an ensign.

I was sketching at some little distance from the college, when Sir George Murray sent me the above letter, in the middle of the day, on the 5th of June, that I might act upon it. I immediately packed up my things and took leave of my friends, and started by the night mail for Bristol; for I was afraid the 52nd would start from Cork before I should reach them. Poor Mr. Narrien, the principal professor at Sandhurst, when he took leave of me, with tears in his eyes said, "we are losing our best hand."*

---

* Mr. Narrien was at Sandhurst for forty years as astronomer and professor. After his death his bust was placed, I believe, in one of the halls of study, as a memento of one who was very much respected and beloved by all who knew him. I received the following letter from him many years after I left Sandhurst, in reply to a letter of introduction to him which I had given to my friend the late Sir Andrew Agnew, when his son was thinking of becoming a student at the senior department of the military college:—

"Royal Military College, October 9th, 1841.
"MY DEAR SIR,—It gave me great pleasure to receive from you the kind letter "which Sir Andrew Agnew did me the favour to deliver, and though eighteen "years have elapsed since I remembered you among my pupils, I have not for-"gotten the regret which I felt at your departure, and the expression—'you feared "'that we should meet no more in this world.' This anticipation may indeed "be verified, inasmuch as I am confined to this spot, and you may not have any "occasion to revisit the dark heaths and fir groves of Bagshot. Yet I know that "you feel, and I may be allowed to say that I also feel, that we are and were, "even when separated by the Atlantic, under the protection of the same good "Providence, like children under one father. Therefore to us a separation by a

Thus ended my studies at the senior department of the military college, after a short stay there of rather less than four months. How wonderfully does God, in His providential dealings with us, make the most trifling circumstances subservient to affecting the whole course of our future lives. The day after I left Sandhurst, I addressed the following letter to Sir Herbert Taylor:—

"Bristol, June 6th, 1823.

"Sir,—I have the honour to inform you that, in consequence
" of your communication of the 4th ultimo to Sir George Murray,
" I thought it my duty to endeavour to join my regiment as soon
" as possible; I am thus far on my road, and hope to join on the
" 8th or 9th. I am very sorry that His Royal Highness the Com-
" mander-in-Chief deems my conduct in this affair unreasonable.
" I had not the most distant idea that, in acting as I did, I was
" holding out against any arrangement made by His Royal High-
" ness. Had I been aware that His Royal Highness thought it
" expedient that I should purchase the half-pay lieutenancy, I
" should not have declined it. I really thought the offer of this
" step was made to me under the supposition that I had applied
" for it. I imagined I was doing what was right, and most con-
" sulting my interest, in desiring to remain in the 52nd. I hope
" this explanation will prevent me from suffering in the opinion
" of the Commander-in-Chief. I have only to add that I am
" ready at all times to be disposed of in any manner which His

" little land or water is of small moment, seeing that we hope for the advent of
" that day when all men shall be united in one family. Here is our consolation.
" But it is impertinent in me to dwell on this subject. I hope to have the gratifi-
" cation of seeing Captain Agnew in our hall of study next January; and I have
" no doubt that I shall be able to inspire him with a taste for science, at least I
" will do my best to produce that effect, which will, I am confident, open for him
" a source of pleasure, both in the enjoyment which the world attaches to the
" possession of knowledge, and in the consciousness of having fulfilled one end of
" our being, which is, that we cultivate the faculties given us by our Creator.
" A thousand thanks for your very flattering invitation, and I wish I could
" say that I thought it would be in my power to accept what would afford me the
" highest pleasure. This impossibility does not, however, diminish the grateful
" sense I entertain of your kindness, and wishing that you may long enjoy every
" earthly blessing,

"I remain, my dear Sir, ever faithfully yours,
"John Narrien."

"Royal Highness may deem beneficial to me, or conducive to the "good of the service.

"I have the honour to remain, &c.,
"WM. LEEKE, Ensign, 52nd Light Infantry."

Before I sailed from the Cove of Cork, I received the following reply to the foregoing letter :—

"Horse Guards, 9th June, 1823.

"SIR,—I have submitted your letter of the 6th instant to the "Commander-in-Chief, who orders me to say that he is perfectly "satisfied with your statement. His Royal Highness had sanc-"tioned your purchasing a half-pay lieutenancy in order to meet "your wishes to remain at the college, and had you availed your-"self of it, you would, at the expiration of your stay there, have "been brought up on full-pay. The arrangement would there-"fore have forwarded your general interests, without interrupting "your studies, and without affecting the efficiency of your corps.
"I am, &c.,
"Ensign Leeke, 52nd Regiment.   HT. TAYLOR."

Thus ended for a time my correspondence with the Horse Guards.

Immediately after this, Ensign Hill of the 52nd, nephew of Lieutenant-General Lord Hill, afterwards Commander-in-Chief, who was four years my junior in the regiment without including the two years given by His Majesty for Waterloo, was allowed to purchase the half-pay lieutenancy in the 49th, and to exchange back into the 52nd, so that when I got my lieutenancy by purchase in the 52nd in the following November I had, as my immediate senior in the list of lieutenants, a man who had served only four years, whilst I had served eight years as ensign in the regiment. Hill was a very good fellow, and then and afterwards was a good officer; and there was nothing wrong in their letting him purchase the lieutenancy in the 49th, but to allow him to do so with the understanding that he should exchange back again immediately into the 52nd, a boon which they had refused to me, although I had stated that I should be glad to accept it, this, and the placing him above one so much his senior, and refusing afterwards to rectify it by placing me above him in the list of lieutenants of the regiment, on my obtaining my lieutenancy a few months afterwards, I must always regard as a most cruel, unjust, and tyrannical proceeding as ever they were guilty of at the Horse Guards; a proceeding quite sufficient to disgust any-one with the service. It will be seen afterwards, that soon after we were settled in New Brunswick, when I became aware of all that had been done in this matter, I memorialized the Duke of York on the subject.

CHAPTER XXIV.

1823.

THE 52ND GO TO NEWFOUNDLAND AND NEW BRUNSWICK.

Explanation with Sir John Tylden—Proceed with three companies to Newfoundland—Off Kinsale and Castle Townsend—Sea sickness—Calm—Visit timber vessel—Sudden squall—Shark—A bonnet overboard—Cards—Bible—Banks of Newfoundland—Fogs—Vessels—74th at St. John's—Found an order to proceed to New Brunswick—Naval officer—Rencontre—Frigate—Go on board—Leave Newfoundland—Bay of Fundy—St. John's—Annapolis—Proceed with one company to St. Andrew's—Barracks—Expel vermin—Level a road—Prayer for the people—Snow-shoes—Frost-bites—Kindness of the people—Many joined us in meeting to read the Scriptures—Party kept up for many years.

ON landing at the Cove of Cork from the Bristol packet, I found that the first detachment of the 52nd had embarked, and that Sir John Tylden was just going off to visit the transport; so, as I knew nothing about my exact destination, I went off with him that he might enlighten me on the subject. In the first place he told me that they were not at all expecting me from Sandhurst, and that the last they had heard of me was that I was to remain there. In the course of conversation, something I said led him to ask me, "Did you not then go to Sandhurst through "Colborne's interest contrary to Rowan's wish, who was the commanding officer when your application was made?" On my telling him that I had applied first of all to Rowan, who told me I had much better get Colborne to make the application for me, Tylden said he had been altogether under a misapprehension about it, and appeared to be sorry that his application had interfered with my plans. I have an idea that his mistake arose from this, that McNair, the second major, who was the commanding officer when I might expect on any day to receive my summons to go to Sandhurst, tried hard to persuade me to give up the going there altogether; but this, of course, I could not do. I was on detachment at Ballynamult in the Knockmeledown mountains, when the order arrived, and I received a letter from the adjutant commencing, "Your order to go to Sandhurst has "arrived. We are all in confusion, McNair is furious." I believe at that moment there was something calculated to make a commanding officer very angry, for so many were the detachments, and consequently so few were the officers at head quarters, that it was very difficult to spare a subaltern from the regiment, with anything in the shape of undisturbed feelings.

I found that six companies of the 52nd were going to New Brunswick, three to Newfoundland, and one to Annapolis in Nova Scotia. McNair commanded the Newfoundland party, and Kirwan Hill, myself, W. Forbes, and Assistant-Surgeon Macartney were the officers. Gawler was to join us afterwards. I think we were the last portion of the regiment to sail. I recollect feeling very melancholy just as we were casting off from the quay to drop down to the mouth of the harbour; but when I looked at the men, and thought of their feelings at the prospect of being away from their country for several years, whilst I might probably return at a less distant period, it helped to cheer me up.

As we ran along the southern coast of Ireland, some fishermen came on board to sell us some fish. When I found they came from Kinsale I asked them if they knew Mr. Townsend of Castle Townsend; and on their saying that they did, I hastily wrote their names and the date, and a line or two in the cover of a small book, whilst the fishermen held on to the transport, and committed it to their care. I heard, upwards of thirty years afterwards, that it safely reached Mr. and Mrs. Townsend. They were kind and valued friends whom I had known at Nice, in the winter of 1820.

Our voyage to Newfoundland in the sailing transport, Loyal Briton, appeared very tedious, and I do not recollect very many incidents connected with it. One of our officers suffered for a long time from sea-sickness; and I believe we all felt so queer in a gale of wind which we had, that we did not eat much for a day or two. Our friend who had been so very sea-sick for a week or ten days, suddenly became quite free from it one morning, and we often accused him afterwards of having devoured two cold ducks at his breakfast on that day.

McNair had a small enclosed sleeping-place, which was dignified by the appellation of "a state room;" the other four officers occupied open berths on each side of the cabin. I think we were more than four weeks in reaching Newfoundland. We were becalmed once or twice. On one of these occasions four of us started in the ship's boat to cut off a timber vessel, on her way to England, that we might put letters on board her. She was six miles away when we started, and there was just enough wind to make the sails flap, and to enable both ships to keep their heads in the direction of the country each was bound to. There was something grand and interesting to us landsmen in pulling in a little boat over the long smooth swell of the Atlantic. When down in the trough of the swell, both ships were hidden from us. The kind old captain of the timber vessel was very glad to see us, and gave us some gin and water to drink, the most detestable beverage I ever tasted. We ought to have thought of taking him some little present. When we had spent half an hour with him, the ships had neared each other so much, that it was time for us to take leave of him and return to our transport.

One night when we had been becalmed during the day, we were aroused by a tremendous row and confusion on deck. By the time I had slipped some things on and had run up, I found the ship was going before the wind with all sails set, through a smooth sea, at a most tremendous rate; I should say at the rate of upwards of twenty miles an hour. She had been caught in a sudden and heavy squall, accompanied by thunder and lightning. They said we had had a very narrow escape of being dismasted.

We were ten days or a fortnight at sea before we saw a shark; a hook and line were soon put over the stern for it, and in a few seconds it was caught, but before it could be hauled out of the water, it bit through the cord above the hook and escaped.

In a few minutes another hook was lowered, with a couple of yards of chain between it and the rope, and in less than half a minute the same shark was taken and brought on board, with the first hook sticking in his jaws. It was a very young one.

We were told afterwards that some of the men and officers in one of the other transports bound for Halifax, were bathing one day, and that, a slight breeze springing up, they all got on board as quickly as possible, one of the officers being the last and the ship making some way through the water. He had scarcely got on deck when a friendly shark made its appearance. It has occurred to me, as I write this, that had he, poor fellow, been caught by the shark, I should probably be now in the army; whereas I have been out of it forty years. I am very glad that he escaped and is still alive. But what a difference does a trifle of time, or any other trifle, continually make in the whole future course of a man's life. Surely the Scriptures and our own experience teach us that God over-rules and directs every little circumstance, as well as every more important circumstance, of our lives. If God only directed the great events of our lives, He would have very little to do with the life of each person; for what we consider great events occur very seldom; whereas our lives are chiefly made up of all the various little occurrences which follow each other every minute and every second. And does not God shew us that He directs and over-rules every event of a man's life, when He tells us that, "one sparrow shall not "fall to the ground without our heavenly Father," and "the "very hairs of your head are all numbered?" Matthew x, 29, 30.

I remember on one occasion, when we were going about six knots an hour, a serjeant's wife had the misfortune to lose a very nice bonnet overboard; and, as it drifted away in the wake of the ship, we some of us proposed that the boat should be lowered to pick it up, but McNair, very properly perhaps, would not permit it; thinking that we had no right to run the slightest risk of delay or accident for a woman's bonnet. I won't say it was heart-rending to see it for a good quarter of an hour still floating in our wake till we lost sight of it; but the loss of her best bonnet, which it appeared to be, was no doubt considered a very serious one by the poor woman.

On the banks of Newfoundland we met with the usual fogs, which made a part of our voyage anything but agreeable. The rigging, as it cuts the fog, brings down the moisture in the shape of a continued drizzling rain; added to this, the fog is so thick that a vessel sailing at the rate of eight or nine knots an hour, is in constant danger of running into some of the vessels at anchor for the purpose of fishing. We kept a bugler at work, sounding a few notes at short intervals; sometimes the ship's bell was sounded. In return we occasionally heard the sound of a drum or bell. And these sounds were always sufficiently distinct to enable us to judge how far the vessels at anchor were clear of the direction in which we were sailing. We only saw two or three of them; they were chiefly French.

The first time we cast the lead on the banks, it was accompanied by several well-baited hooks, and we brought up three very fine fish.

I think it was when we were about half way between Ireland and Newfoundland, that I one day saw what no other person on board saw, and what, after making several enquiries, I found none of those I spoke to had ever seen:—I saw, at a distance of two or three miles from the ship, when there was half a gale of wind, and the sea was rough, a large whale jump clean out of the water, so that I could clearly see the horizon under it. Perhaps this sort of thing may often have been seen at the whale fisheries.

We only saw one iceberg on our voyage to Newfoundland; the morning was very cold, although it was the middle of summer, and the coldness of the atmosphere was accounted for when the iceberg hove in sight. We passed it at the distance of half a mile; the sun was shining on it, and it appeared very magnificent and beautiful as we observed it from our cabin windows whilst we were dressing.

The having five officers constantly occupying the small cabin of a transport, about twelve feet square, renders it very desirable that all should be good-tempered fellows; and I think we were very fortunate in that respect. The having but one small table to write at or to read by, created a difficulty which will be readily understood by my readers. When it became dark, or in wet weather, we were generally all together below. For a long time at first one of the five suffered so much from sea-sickness, that he could not join the others at the table. All the remainder of the party except myself wished to amuse themselves almost every night, except Sunday, by playing at cards. This I could not join them in, for reasons which I think I have before given, and it was rather a curious sight to see my three friends occupying three sides of the table, and playing at whist with the cards of the dummy spread out on the fourth side, a portion of which I also occupied, that I might have the use of one of the candles to read by. As they often played at cards for several hours, I usually had to spend a portion of that time in my evening reading of the Scriptures. It was not looked upon by the others as a parading of my religion, but rather, if I must read the Bible, as a case of necessity. Our occupations were in singular contrast, but we got on very well together; and I think the time thus spent was not without its blessing and benefit to me. Two or three times at first one or another would grumble out, that it was very ill-natured of me not to help them in their difficulty. And then in return I would ask them, how they could so regularly waste their time, and how they could expect a blessing from God, if they so entirely neglected His holy Word and the care of their souls. Then again they would tell me that I had no right to interfere with them and their religion, and I replied that neither had they any right to interfere with my religion and my reading of the Scriptures. All this was said without any acrimony or unkindness; but just in the off-hand way in which we had always been in the habit of talking to each other. I am sorry to say that divine service was not performed on the Sunday, during the whole time we were in the Loyal Briton, although I requested it, and the weather generally was favourable for it. Three or four years before I should have been equally careless about it.

There was a thick fog as we were nearing the harbour of St. John's, Newfoundland, and the captain of the transport determined to lie to when, according to his reckoning, we were within six miles of it. Strange to say, he never thought of sending a man aloft, until we begged him to do so. They told us afterwards that the look-out men on shore had seen our top-masts above the fog all the morning. It seems strange again that no arrangement existed for giving warning to a ship thus situated that land and breakers were near. We got the master also to get up a small cannon from the hold; and immediately after it was fired, the fog broke and dispersed, and we found ourselves just in the position which the captain had reckoned on.

We soon entered the capacious harbour of St. John's, and found there an English frigate, the Egeria, and three companies of the 74th Regiment, under the command of Major Mein, brother of Mein of the 52nd. We were very much pleased to find that an order had arrived before us from Halifax, that we were to proceed to St. John's, New Brunswick, whither the rest of the regiment had been sent from Halifax. The companies of the 74th were to remain at Newfoundland until they should be relieved by three companies to be immediately raised, and to be called the Royal Newfoundland Veteran Companies. We remained at St. John's about three clear days, as some old stores were to be sent to England in our transport. The harbour was tolerably redolent of the smell of decayed fish, which we were able to bear very manfully, knowing how soon we should escape from it. I recollect we were disappointed not to meet with a single specimen of a handsome dog. The more we saw of St. John's the more pleased we were at the idea of escaping from it. I only recollect landing once, and the leaving a large parcel of tracts and books with a person who promised to see that they were distributed.

I think it was on the second day that a party of sailors, under the command of an officer of the Egeria, were employed in transferring old stores from a lighter to the hold of the transport. After the duty was over, the officer joined our dinner party. He had known a near relative of one of our officers, and this led to their sitting and talking hour after hour to a very late hour of the night, and it became exceedingly tiresome to the rest of our party, who were forced to be almost entirely on deck. In vain did we send a message from time to time to say that the Egeria's boat was alongside; the reply always was, "Tell them to wait." And our friends did not take the hint, when a cock was selected from our poultry and let down through the skylight, to indicate to them that the morning was approaching. They had both taken too much wine, a thing the 52nd officer was never known to do at any other time.

Having had plenty of time for my prayers, &c., on deck, I determined at last that I would go to bed, and, expecting, from something which had already been said on the subject, that they would manifest some opposition to my doing so, I prepared myself for it, so that I could, in a few seconds, divest myself of the remainder of my things, and get into bed, before they were well aware of what I was doing. When they found that I was in bed they were very much affronted, said that it was a regular insult, and that they would pull me out again. My berth was the upper berth on the starboard side of the cabin, and the nearest one to the stern windows: no one occupied the lower berth of the two. I thought these two fellows would have some difficulty in pulling me out of the berth, and lay on my back, with the corner of a pillow twisted round my fingers, so that I could use it with some considerable force. The sailor led the attack, and came on in the direction of the middle of the berth, which enabled me, by raising myself a little on my left arm, to deal him a blow with the pillow on his neck which sent him reeling away. They then, very considerately for themselves, gave up the attack, saying I was a very good fellow, and that they would let me alone. The lieutenant of the Egeria soon after took his departure.

I think it was the day after the above occurrence, and the afternoon or evening before we left St. John's, Newfoundland, that, as four of us were pulling in the ship's boat up the harbour, they hailed us from the Egeria and begged us to come on board. This we did in our shirt sleeves, for we had left our coats in the transport. The officers invited us to go below and take a glass of wine, which we consented to do; but we were not expecting to find a somewhat large party assembled. After some little time some of them proposed that, as we were without our coats, they should doff theirs also, out of respect to us. This the first lieutenant resisted at first, as it was contrary to the etiquette of the service that they should do so at their mess table, but at last he consented, and was the first to throw off his own coat.

They gave several toasts, and the noise which was made must have been heard over the whole harbour and town. When we went on deck, the seamen sang several songs for our amusement.

Owing to contrary winds and calms, our voyage from Newfoundland to St. John's, New Brunswick, was nearly as long, in point of time, as that from England to Newfoundland. We passed within seven miles of Halifax, but did not see it or any part of Nova Scotia, owing to the continued fogs. The currents are very strong in the neighbourhood of Cape Sable, the southern point of Nova Scotia, and also in the Bay of Fundy. When we supposed ourselves to be six miles to the northward of Cape Sable, we suddenly came across a ship in the fog, and they had just time, before we lost sight of them, to chalk on a board for our information, "Cape Sable north and by west, seven miles." We soon stood up the Bay of Fundy and the fog cleared away, giving us a pleasing view of the coast of the state of Maine, and of the Island of Grand Manan.

We reached St. John's, New Brunswick, about the 20th of August, 1823. All the regiment had now assembled in New Brunswick, and had there been only the 52nd in the province, Sir John Tylden, who commanded the regiment, would have been the Commander-in-Chief and acting governor of New Brunswick, but there happened to be a few artillerymen in the province, and thus Brevet-Lieutenant-Colonel William Rowan, who was a captain in the regiment, but a senior lieutenant-colonel in the army to Tylden, took the command of all the troops in New Brunswick, and proceeded also to Fredericton, the capital, as acting governor, ordering Tylden to remain at St. John's with three companies. This is one instance of the awkwardness of the system of allowing brevet rank to exist in the army.

I was ordered to St. Andrew's, with the company I was commanding, and we embarked for that purpose in one of the other transports, the Vibilia; but first of all we went over to Annapolis, in Nova Scotia, with Major Love's company,* which was to be

---

* On the very day on which this was written, the following notice appeared in the obituary of the "Times:"—On the 13th instant, (January, 1866,) at 17, Ovington Square, General Sir James Frederick Love, G.C.B., K.H., Colonel 43rd Light Infantry.

stationed there. Sunday was the day on which we sailed, or the day before, and finding myself the commanding officer on board, I had a church parade, and read part of the service and one of Burder's village sermons to the men. As we entered the Bay of Passamaquoddy, (an Indian name,) from the Bay of Fundy, we found the strongest tide running out which I have ever seen; we could scarcely make head against it with the help of a strong breeze.

St. Andrew's is a small town on the northern coast of Passamaquoddy Bay, which separates it from the State of Maine, the most northern state of the United States. Opposite to St. Andrew's, the bay is about three miles across. Many of the principal inhabitants were the descendants of the royalists, who had retired there at the close of the War of Independence, as the Americans call it, in 1782. It contained, when we were there, between two and three thousand inhabitants, and appeared to be a thriving and increasing town, carrying on a good trade by means of timber vessels and other smaller craft.

On disembarking from the transport, I found a company of the 74th, under the command of Captain Jones. He had been there some time, and had married a lady from the neighbourhood of St. Andrew's. The 74th made our men as comfortable as they could in the barracks for a couple of days, and then left us in possession and embarked in the vessel in which we had arrived. One thing which struck me, during the first few days of my being at St. Andrew's, as very singular, was the habit in many of the houses of leaving the outer doors unfastened at night. It spoke well for the honesty and quiet behaviour of the inhabitants. There being no rooms for officers in the barracks, I went into lodgings, but I think I very soon, in the expectation that Gawler and his wife, on their arrival, would like to join me in occupying the same abode, engaged a furnished house in one of the main streets of the place, in which they continued to reside long after I left St. Andrew's. They had been detained a long time at Liverpool, and did not arrive in New Brunswick until I had been there several weeks.

I think I have mentioned before, that my plan with regard to this work is to write down almost all the events I can recollect, which happened forty and fifty years ago, and which I can properly mention without occasioning annoyance to myself or others; and then, before I publish it, to cross out freely whatever, from any cause, I may feel had better be omitted.

My first trouble at St Andrew's was that the barracks were reported to be full of bugs. The men could not sleep even on the floors of the rooms without insulating their beds, by drawing around each a *cordon*, if I may use the expression, of water. When the floor got at all dry, the animals could pass over and attack their prey. It was so bad, and appeared to be so incurable, that I at once reported it to Sir John Tylden, who was at St. John's, seventy or eighty miles to the northward of St. Andrew's. He replied that he shortly intended to visit all the stations of the regiment, accompanied by an engineer officer, and that if our barracks were found to be as bad as I represented them to be, they should be condemned.

I then set myself to work to devise some plan by which we might possibly get rid of the bugs without putting the country to the expense of erecting new barracks. I thought it possible that they were not to any extent in the wood-work of the building, but had chiefly located themselves in the bedsteads. I therefore determined to commence by having every joist of every bedstead taken to pieces, and to superintend the operations myself. I had a bucket filled with a strong solution of vitriol, so that when the different parts of the bedsteads were separated, the ends might be well saturated with it. Every bedstead was brought out and taken to pieces on the green in front of the barracks, and everybody was perfectly astonished at the immense quantities of bugs which we discovered. Even within those joists, into which it would be hardly possible to insert the fine point of a knife, large clusters of them were found; some of the clusters were as large as a good-sized walnut. They were well dosed with the solution of vitriol, and, I believe, all were destroyed. Some of the larger bugs which fell on the grass attempted to walk off, but a drop of the solution, applied by means of a pointed stick, in almost every case made them instantly turn on their backs and die. Two or three sturdy fellows, I observed, had to be touched two or three times before they were settled. This account may possibly be useful to some persons, whose furniture may be infested by these annoying insects. But the upshot of the experiment was that no bug was seen again in the barracks until about nine months after, and that was on the very day before that on which I left St. Andrew's altogether.

The mention of the first bug having been seen in the barracks the day before I left St. Andrew's, reminds me that I learnt afterwards that the first desertion took place the day after I left that place. Desertions have always been common from the regiments stationed near the frontier of the United States, many of them arising from the fact that some of the men have had relations living in the Northern States. I forget if the desertion I have just mentioned was that of a man who was very cleverly recaptured by Gawler at Eastport. He heard that the man was there, and that he was fraternizing with some of the United States soldiers. He went to Eastport by the packet in the morning, and laid his plans so well that, just before it sailed for St. Andrew's in the evening, the man was allured on board by one or two persons to see the vessel, not knowing that it was the St. Andrew's packet. When he had got on deck, they quietly pushed off and left him. There was scarcely anybody on board besides Gawler, who was in the cabin below; the deserter went down into the cabin, and on seeing Gawler, who had taken up a candle from the table, rushed at him, and knocked the candle out of his hand. A young New-Brunswicker, a passenger, immediately jumped down, grappled with, and secured the man, who was brought back a prisoner to St. Andrew's.

The barracks were, I should suppose, a quarter or a third of a mile from that part of the town in which the Gawlers and I resided. Before they came, as there was only one road to the town, and that not a very good one, I employed the men at times in levelling another piece of ground which had been fenced off for a road, but had never been made. It afforded a much nearer communication with one part of the town than the other road did. I was informed that for some years it was called Mr. Leeke's road, but I suppose it has long since had some other more convenient appellation.

The barracks were on the top of a not very steep hill, along the base of which, and between it and the sea, ran the town. Of course I visited the barracks very regularly, and the men were paraded by Gawler or myself each day. Before he arrived I remember two things which rather amused me. In drilling the company one morning, I sent them in skirmishing order along the top of the hill, to the westward of the barracks, into a wood. I was, perhaps, 150 or 200 yards from them, and was surprised to see them, directly they got into the wood, striking in different directions, at something or other, with the butt ends of their muskets; but what it was I could not imagine, for the whole company was at work, and could not have displayed greater energy if they had found a company of their old antagonists, the Imperial Guard, lying in ambush for them just within the boundary of the wood. On my bugler sounding the retreat, I think they were not at all disinclined to retire. I was informed afterwards that their invasion of the wood had disturbed quite an army of large snakes, which started off in all directions before them.

There were a large number of what we called snow-shoes in the barrack store, almost a sufficient number to furnish the whole company with a pair. The snow-shoe is very much like a racket bat, but larger; the foot is placed on the catgut in the centre, and then the shoe is strapped tightly on. It is very difficult, till people are accustomed to it, to walk on snow-shoes without their striking against each other, or in the snow; in walking they must be kept clear of each other, and be placed flat on the top of the snow. I think they were nearly a foot and a half in length, and rather more than a foot in width: any carelessness in walking insures a regular fall into the snow.

One morning, soon after there had been a heavy fall of snow, so that the ground was well covered, the company paraded in fatigue dress, without arms, and a pair of snow-shoes were served out to each man. When the men were drawn up in a single rank facing to the eastward, along the top of the hill, and it was ascertained that all the shoes were properly tied on, I told them we would see which of us could first reach the third fence from us. The fences were of posts and rails, and I think the third fence may have been 200 yards away. All started in great glee, and before we reached the first fence, I think fully two-thirds of our fine fellows were with their faces in the snow, the usual way of bringing up, or on their beam ends. Only three of us reached the second fence. When we had cleared it, and were fairly off for the goal, I began to think it would be a great feather in my cap if, on this our first trial of walking on snow-shoes, I should beat the whole of the company. The thought had no sooner crossed my mind, than immediately the old adage, " pride shall " have a fall," was fulfilled in my case, by my going head foremost into the snow. Several weeks afterwards the same thing happened to Gawler. I had been giving him an account of the above race in snow-shoes, and he wished to try them, and we started together to walk in them from the barracks to our house. The road was rather uneven, notwithstanding the snow, and sloped down to the town. We got about half way along it very nicely, when Gawler said, "I think I am getting on pretty well," and the next moment pitched over with his face in the snow, the fall being all the heavier by reason of its being forward on the slope.

The sleighing was a very pleasant mode of travelling, and the complete upset and emptying of the sleigh of all its contents, men, women, and children, cloaks, &c., was often very amusing, and seldom attended with danger. By far the most interesting sleighing to me was that on the river, where we could get along as fast as the horses could lay legs to the ice, the shoes being turned up so that they had secure footing on the ice. We found that our feet were kept perfectly warm in the sleighs, and on parade, when we wore the common Wellington boots, rather thin than thick, with warm cloth boots over them, and when we had started with warm feet. This was the case when the thermometer was at ten below zero. We wore boots of light coloured thick cloth, fastened with three or four silver regimental buttons. When sitting in the house, or walking, I could keep myself perfectly warm with a flannel shirt next the skin, then a calico shirt, and over that another good flannel shirt, and then the surtout coat and waistcoat which people usually wear in England.

In walking in the woods, which I occasionally did, and in which I never found the undrifted snow more than knee-deep, I think I did not wear cloth boots over the others; but when I came to take them off afterwards, I almost always found that the effort (they being wet, and difficult to get off) produced severe cramp in the calf of the leg. We wore fur over our ears. I never, during the whole winter, got frost-bitten, nor do I recollect more than one man belonging to our St. Andrew's party who complained of it, and he got the fingers of his right hand frost-bitten from trailing his musket too long, but they were soon set to rights. I once met a man in whose cheek I saw the evident mark of a frost-bite, a round, whitish spot, and rather astonished him by saying, directly I came up to him, "You are a stranger "in America, I think, and you are not aware that your face is "frost-bitten?" I then gave him directions how to proceed—on no account to go near a fire, but to get the part well rubbed with snow till the frost-bite should disappear. I think there was a house at hand, and that it was not necessary that I should commence operations on his face myself. He was very much obliged to me for my kindness.

The cold was very severe at times during the winter of 1823, although it was spoken of as a milder winter than usual. Our house, as most of the houses were, was built of wood, and certainly the cold found its way into it. I well remember, one morning, sitting at breakfast with my chair close to a good fire, and that my cup, which was full of tea, was frozen to the saucer on the table within a yard of the fire.

I read a good deal whilst I was at St. Andrew's, and generally rose at five in the morning. As I had my bed-room fire laid over night so that it would burn up and become a good fire immediately on my lighting it, I was enabled to pursue this plan of early rising notwithstanding that the cold was so intense that the top of the sheet was stiffened by the breath from my mouth being frozen on it. We had no coal at St. Andrew's, but a very plentiful supply of fire-wood.

The principal families of the town were remarkably kind and attentive to us. Before the arrival of the Gawlers I received several invitations. It seemed rather curious, considering my rank, that some of the notes addressed to me, were addressed to "The Commandant of St. Andrew's." I forget on what occasion it was, but I recollect being invited, as commandant, to a large public dinner, and being treated with some considerable respect there. Captains were rather plentiful at St. Andrew's, for every master of the dozens of vessels at anchor in the port was a "captain," but an ensign was a "rara avis in terrâ," (I cannot add "nigroque simillima cygno,") and therefore he was made much of. One of the first notes I received was from the race committee, requesting me to allow the only bugler we had (the others were all at head quarters) to attend the races for the purpose of starting the horses. This I could not permit, for several reasons, and I was glad to find that the bugler himself had a very great dislike to be so employed.

We found religion to be at a very low ebb in St. Andrew's; the only clergyman there was a good-natured man, but he had some very confused ideas about religion. There was a respect for it amongst the persons we were acquainted with, and amongst the people generally, but there was scarcely any correct idea of the way of salvation through Christ, and of the change of heart, that true repentance, which always accompanies it; nor did they understand that the Word of God was to be read and meditated on each day with prayer, that, by the teaching of the Holy Spirit, it might be for the continual nourishment and growth of the soul in faith, and holiness, and comfort: 1 Peter ii, 2. Though it may appear to many of the readers of this book to have been a great piece of presumption on our part, yet we did really desire to consider ourselves as a sort of missionaries sent, in the providence of God, to the kind people of this place; and I have no doubt that God did, in His great mercy, in answer to our prayers, greatly bless our poor and feeble efforts for their religious benefit.

In relating God's goodness in this matter, I perhaps hardly need disclaim any desire to make myself of any importance with regard to it. If I know myself at all, my chief desire is that the relation of what follows may be the means of doing good to others, and especially that it may, with God's blessing, lead the officers and others of our army and navy, who go forth to the various portions of our extended empire, to consider their responsibilities with regard to the people they may come in contact with; that they should endeavour to set them a holy, and not a vicious, example, and to help forward the cause of God, and not of Satan, amongst them. I trust, also, it may prove to be some encouragement to those who desire to do good to the souls of their fellow-creatures, to endeavour to do so in season, and even out of season, looking up to God to bless every effort they make. I feel very confident that no effort thus made shall be altogether useless. I have many times seen that promise fulfilled, which we find in Ecclesiastes xi, 1 : "Cast thy bread upon the waters, and thou "shalt find it after many days :" see also Ecclesiastes xi, 6. At all events, our prayers and endeavours will bring a blessing on our own souls. It, perhaps, would not be good for us to hear much of benefit accruing to the souls of others through our efforts, but our heavenly Father does not altogether withhold this sort of encouragement from us, but gives it in the measure which He sees to be best for us. I think the effect of hearing of God having sent any spiritual benefit to anyone, through me, has been great pleasure and thankfulness, accompanied by a deep feeling of humility, that He should have conferred such honour on such a poor, unworthy sinner as I am.

I think the fact, that both the officers who were stationed at St. Andrew's were religiously-disposed men, not only attracted the attention of the people, but also made a great impression upon them. It was generally necessary that I should spend an hour or more at the barracks on the Sunday mornings before we marched to church, and I well remember that I made it my practice, as I walked up and down on the top of the hill, and looked on the town below, to pray for the people in the words of Isaiah xxxv, 1, that God would be pleased to make that "wilder-"ness and solitary place to be glad," and that " desert to rejoice, " and to blossom as the rose."

It will be necessary for me here to mention that we received invitations from all the gentry of the town to dine or drink tea with them, and that we accepted them all. On one or two occasions cards were introduced, and we were solicited to play ; but this, with our opinion of the evil frequently resulting from card-playing, we of course could not do. At one of the parties I was invited to mention what my objection to playing at cards arose from, which I then freely did. Soon after we had visited most of the families, it occurred to me that it would be a very desirable and useful thing if we could get them to meet us for the purpose of reading the Scriptures together. The Gawlers and I talked the matter over, and the result was, that I undertook to go to each family and mention our wish to them. I told them I was come to make a proposal to them; that they and the other families had been exceedingly kind to us in asking us to come and see them; that they would have observed that we had freely availed ourselves of their invitations, although at some of the houses we had excused ourselves from joining in some of the things which were going forward; and that, by way of making some return for their kindness, we had to propose to them that they should do us the favour of drinking tea with us on the following Wednesday evening, and that after tea we should read the Word of God together; and further, that we should afterwards meet at each other's houses for the same purpose on the Wednesday in each week. To our great surprise and pleasure the invitation was everywhere received with all due respect and civility, and about half the families accepted it. We had reason to believe that it was of much real benefit to many, if not to all, who attended it. I think it was in the autumn of 1824 that the Bishop of Nova Scotia held a confirmation at St. Andrew's, and then, especially, I understood that the meeting was evidently a great help and comfort to many who were about to be confirmed. There had not been a confirmation there for more than thirty years, and, on the occasion just referred to, numbers of all ages were confirmed. Some six or seven years ago one of the party, a truly religious lady, in writing to Mrs. Gawler, said, "You will be pleased to "hear that the Wednesday evening meeting for reading the Scrip- "tures is still kept up." It was, of course, a great pleasure to us to hear this, after the lapse of five-and-thirty years from its commencement. One of the gentlemen I spoke to, who excused himself from joining the party, told me a few years afterwards, in England, that he felt very angry when I made the proposal to him, and thought we were taking a very great liberty by thus interfering with him and his religion, although he did not venture to express that to me. He added that, some time afterwards, when he came to reflect on all that the Gawlers and I had been doing in the place, it was the means of leading him to very serious thought and consideration about his own religious state, and that it ended in his becoming a very altered man: he is now one of the principal persons in the colony of New Brunswick. I must not exactly give the names of those in whose religious state we were very much interested; it might not be agreeable to them. The Gawlers, in writing to me during the two years that they remained at St. Andrew's after I left it, described what they conceived to be their progress by a number of lines, varying from one to six, drawn under each name.

After I left St. Andrew's, Captain and Mrs. Gawler established a very flourishing Sunday school there, there having been none before, which met with the approval and support of the governor, Sir Howard Douglas. The only public establishment which I think I was the principal author and promoter of, was a savings' bank for Charlotte county, which was the county in which St. Andrew's stood. This led to the establishment of savings' banks throughout the colony.

CHAPTER XXV.

1823, 1824.

ST. ANDREW'S, NEW BRUNSWICK.

Benefit of religious tracts—One lent in twenty-two houses—Man with cart—Tract given to one man, the means of the conversion of another—Sermons—Mr. Simeon—Description of a good minister—H.M.S. Sparrowhawk—Smuggled provisions—Smuggled fowl for dinner—Meat preserved by becoming frozen—Expedition into the uncleared woods—American General—Charlotte county militia—Voyage to St. John's—Find half the town on fire—Of some use in stopping the conflagration—Armine Mountain.

MY first attempt to do any good to the people by means of giving them tracts was as follows:—I set off one morning on the St. John's road and leaving it at a certain point I followed a road inclining to the left. On coming to two or three small farm houses, I went into one of them, offering up the prayer which our Saviour desired His disciples to use when He sent them forth among the people, " Peace be to this house." I found a woman sweeping the floor, who told me she was housekeeper to the owner of the house, who was then away. After trying to give her some good advice, I left with her three small tracts, one of which was entitled " Con-"versation in a Boat between two Seamen," one of the Religious Tract Society's works. The man afterwards tried to find me at home, at St. Andrew's, several times before he succeeded. He informed me that he had been brought up religiously in Scotland, when he was young; but that the kind of life he lived as a hawker, since his arrival in New Brunswick, had led to his becoming utterly careless about religion. And that this tract had been the means, by God's blessing, of arousing him to a consideration of his danger, and to a determination to try and lead a holy life for the time to come. He had lent the little tract, above mentioned, in a hamlet beyond him, and it had such an effect upon the inmates of the twenty-two cottages, of which it consisted, that he came to request me to purchase for them twenty-two Bibles and Testaments, that each house might be supplied with a copy of the Bible or Testament. He continued to go on very satisfactorily afterwards.

I forget whether it was on my return from this man's house, or on another occasion, that I met on the road a man driving a cart and two horses. Thinking I might never have an opportunity of seeing him or speaking to him again, and that my accosting him would be taken kindly by him, I stopped him for two or three minutes, and spoke to him, as seriously as I could, about the state of his soul, and about his God and Saviour, and about eternity. I never saw him again; but some few weeks afterwards I recollect a very tall man called upon me, who told me that he lived up in the woods about nine miles off, and that he had been anxious to come and find me out, as the man whom I had met with the cart had told him what I had said to him, and that it had made him wish to speak to me about his own religious state. He said the man whom I had met also told him that directly I was out of sight he stopped his cart and horses again, and went into the wood at the side of the road, and fell on his knees and prayed earnestly to God to save his soul.

I never saw either of them afterwards, but it may not be without its use that I should mention that the man who came down from the woods spoke in what we should call a regular canting tone, and also through his nose, so that his way of speaking was most disagreeable. I was then struck with the great importance of making great allowance for any peculiarity of manner which might discover itself in persons, especially when they might be speaking on religious subjects. We ourselves should of course avoid, as much as possible, any peculiarity of manner, or of speaking, which is calculated to annoy other people; but the consideration, that really good people do often fall into these peculiarities, should lead us to bear with them, however trying and annoying they may be to us. This man had all the appearance of being sincere. Perhaps that which is spoken of the Saviour in Isaiah xi, 2, 3, may be intended to teach us the above lesson, as well as that of always endeavouring to put the best construction on every person's conduct, however much appearances may be against him.

On the same road another interesting circumstance occurred. One Sunday afternoon Gawler and I were taking a quiet walk, when not far from the town we observed a man on crutches, who had come through the belt of wood from his house and clearing within it, and was standing on the road. I accosted the man whilst Gawler walked quietly on; I spoke to him on religious subjects, and then gave him a hand-bill, about the size of a pound note, on which was printed a short but very striking address on eternity, issued by the Religious Tract Society. After saying a few words to him and promising to call upon him, I proceeded to overtake Gawler. I very well remember that as I walked up the hill, before I overtook him, I prayed that the reading the tract and what had been said to the man might be blessed to his eternal welfare. On turning round after we had reached the top of the rising ground, we saw that two men were reading the tract together, another man having joined him from the house or wood. I saw the man, who had broken his leg three or four times; at first he appeared to be seriously impressed, but as he got better this seemed to pass off. Some time after I had returned to England, in one of Gawler's letters was the following sentence: "John ———, to whom you were made effectually useful by giving "a tract to another man one Sunday afternoon, when you were "walking with me on the St. John's road, desires to be kindly "remembered to you." Thus in God's providence, this little messenger, containing divine truth, came into this man's hands, when it was not at all intended for him. I heard about him several times from the Gawlers; they had no doubt about his being a truly good and religious man; and he always attributed his great change to this tract having fallen into his hands. I do not distinctly recollect any other cases in which the circulating of books and tracts at St. Andrew's was productive of benefit. We set up a lending library there, principally consisting of useful and simple religious books, and when I left St. Andrew's, our friends there intrusted to me a very sufficient sum which I was to lay out in purchasing books for the purpose of increasing the library. Our friends were very kind to us and very grateful for our poor attempts to do them good, and to sow that seed amongst them which a gracious God, by His Almighty power, has made effectual, as we believe, to the salvation of many souls. I know not why I should not state it, though I hesitate to do so, that one of these friends, writing about a year and a half ago to Mrs. Gawler, expresses herself thus:—"The people seem to be "awakening; there are some really praying souls amongst us; I "think it is in answer to the prayers of your dear husband and "Mr. Leeke, and other Christian friends, that mercies are vouch- "safed to St. Andrew's. There is certainly more spiritual life "among us. Continue your prayers for us, dear friends. God "blessed your coming amongst us at first. How affectionately "you are still remembered by many in this place."

More recently, the following passages occurred in other letters: "The names of Colonel and Mrs. Gawler and Mr. Leeke are "household words with us." "The photographs Mr. Leeke sent "of his house and family are very much admired. It is a great "pleasure to shew them to our friends. The house covered with "ivy and the family in front of it is a beautiful picture."

I had not been long at St. Andrew's when one morning the clergyman called upon me, and let out that he was intending to preach a sermon, on the following Sunday, on the subject of the Good Centurion, and that he should introduce something about me in it. I of course laughed at the idea, and told him that it would be most improper. It was with great reluctance, however, that he gave up his project. His views were not at all clear upon the doctrines of salvation by faith only, and of holy works as the fruits of faith, and we had frequent discussions about his sermons, which, although he must have been many years my senior, he very kindly engaged in with me. He sometimes preached some very excellent sermons. One Sunday morning he preached one of these, and that very evening we read the same sermon, in the work of an old author, at our family prayers. This sermon was very clear upon the above-mentioned points; and in our subsequent discussions I always referred to what he had stated in that sermon; and when he felt himself pressed, he said that was an old sermon which had been written several years ago. He used to give me his sermons to read, and that I might mark the passages which I thought erroneous, so that we might go over them together afterwards.

I suppose that all ministers do occasionally, and perhaps some frequently, preach sermons which they have not composed themselves; all must be indebted for almost all the *ideas* they have to those who have gone before them. There is an old saying too, that it is better for a man to preach a good sermon of another man's than a bad one of his own. An experienced man, when I first took orders and had to prepare two sermons for each Sunday, besides several lectures for evenings in the week, strongly advised me only to compose one of the sermons, and to take the most suitable sermon for my people which I could find amongst the published sermons of others. One friend recommended Simeon's sermons as a study and pattern; and certainly his twenty-one volumes, comprising upwards of 2500 sermons on texts taken, I believe, from every book of the Old and New Testaments, contain a body of sound divinity for which the church at large, and all ministers of the gospel, will have reason to be thankful to Almighty God to the end of time and to all eternity. One special beauty and excellence, and I may almost say peculiarity, in Mr. Simeon's sermons is, that he keeps close to his text in each sermon, and follows out the meaning of each portion so as to produce that singular, beautiful, and pleasing variety for which his sermons are so remarkable. The Rev. Charles Simeon was for several years the Senior Fellow of King's College, Cambridge, and many of his sermons were preached before the university.

There are several dangers, if they may be so called, in preaching the sermons of other ministers. The chief danger is that a man may grow idle, and not give that time and attention to the composition of sermons which is so calculated to increase his own knowledge of the word of God, and to bring blessings to his own soul, and also to make him a blessing to others. Another danger is, that if his hearers discover that he occasionally borrows another person's sermon, they will be apt to think all his sermons are borrowed, and not to give him credit for those sound and useful sermons which may have been composed with much labour and prayer. Everybody has heard of some curious troubles that ministers have got into, when they have ventured to preach the published sermons of others. Besides the instance mentioned above, I only personally know of one other, much more awkward, circumstance of the kind :—A very clever, and very hardworking and over-worked professor, when the select preacher for the time, preached a most clever and useful sermon in the university pulpit at Cambridge, on two well-known passages which, apparently, contradicted each other. The vice-chancellor was so well pleased with the sermon, and thought it so calculated to do good to the members of the university, that he requested the professor to preach it over again on the following Sunday. This request he could scarcely help complying with, and the sermon was preached for the second time; but the next morning it was buzzed about that it was one of Romaine's sermons. It was rather a hazardous thing for a man to venture upon before such a congregation, but I do not know that he suffered for his temerity, for I had some reason to think it possible that he never found out that his "pious fraud" (I think we may so call it) had been discovered.

It has always appeared to me that ministers should get out of the habit of using written sermons as soon as possible. Let them study the Word of God with prayer, and become well acquainted with the passage they are intending to preach upon, and they will, after a little time, find that there is not so much difficulty in what is called extempore preaching, as they had anticipated. With regard to eloquence, I think they should give themselves little trouble and less concern. Let them, in dependence upon the help and strength of the Holy Spirit, and seeking to have their hearts filled with love to God and to the souls of men, endeavour humbly to unfold the truths of God's Word to their people, and they shall not be without a blessing on their work. We should not too much undervalue eloquence; but I think directly either the congregation or the minister himself begins in any degree to trust to his eloquence, or to any other gift he may possess, there is the greatest danger that it may interfere with and prevent that blessing on the word preached, which ministers and people should invariably pray for and expect. I have always been much pleased with the description given of a good minister in the Pilgrim's Progress, " Christian saw the picture of "a very grave person hang up against the wall, [in the Interpreter's "house,] and this was the fashion of it:—It had eyes lifted up to "heaven, the best of books in its hand, the law of truth was "written upon its lips, the world was behind its back; it stood as "if it pleaded with men, and a crown of gold did hang over its "head." Let us pray that all bishops, priests, and deacons, and all ministers of the gospel, may be of the character and spirit thus so beautifully delineated. With regard to eloquence, if ministers have it not, let them not be thereby cast down. St. Paul was not an eloquent man, but who was more useful or more honoured of God? He says of himself, in 1st Corinthians, ii, 3, " I was with "you in weakness, in fear, and in much trembling; and my "speech and my preaching was not with enticing words of man's "wisdom, but in demonstration of the Spirit and of power; that "your faith should not stand in the wisdom of men, but in the "power of God." St. Paul also says of himself and other ministers, in 2 Corinthians iv, 7, "We have this treasure in earthen "vessels, that the excellency of the power may be of God, and "not of us."

I fear I have greatly wandered from my recollections of St. Andrew's, but I have felt constrained to follow out these other subjects to a certain extent; and what I have written must remain where it is, for I have not the time which will enable me to arrange what I write in what might appear to be more correct order.

One Sunday morning we were rather surprised by seeing several naval officers at church, for we were not aware that the Sparrowhawk, Captain Dundas, had looked in upon us, and was in St. Andrew's harbour. The little child of the Gawlers was just dead, so that the calling upon the commander devolved on me. He was very kind, and gave me some luncheon; but as they sailed in a day or two, we saw nothing more of them.

There were several articles of consumption which might have been passed from the United States into the province of New Brunswick, and *vice versâ*, to the benefit of both countries, but they were, as appeared to us very foolishly, prohibited. Amongst these were meat and dead poultry. In North America, in the winter, these things are frozen for the purpose of keeping them, and they may in this way be kept for weeks and months. They are unfrozen by being placed for a sufficient time in *cold* water, and then they are as good and as fit for use as they would have been if they had only been killed a few days.

Rather a singular circumstance occurred to me in connexion with this prohibition to the entrance of dead poultry by the New Brunswick custom-regulations. I was invited to take a family dinner with some of our kind friends, the family consisting only of the gentleman and his wife. Just before we sat down to dinner, a very fine roast capon made its appearance, and very tempting it looked to hungry people. I was just anticipating a very pleasant attack upon it, when the master of the house innocently observed, " We are indebted to our neighbours on the " other side of the bay for this fine capon," which meant that it had been smuggled. Had nothing been said about it, I should, of course, have partaken of it. As it may be supposed, I was very sorry for the disappointment of my host and hostess when they found I did not think it right to eat of the principal article of food which they had provided for my entertainment. But there was no help for it, as I did not think it right to partake of that which I knew to be smuggled. I think, as the party consisted of only three persons, it is possible there was not any other sort of meat at the table, which would make it all the more annoying to my friends.

Gawler and I determined one morning to make an exploring expedition into the woods, and after going along the St. John's road for some distance, we took a track to the left, and followed it for some considerable distance, when, turning to the left again, we soon found ourselves, to our heart's content, in the midst of a wild, uncleared American forest. Trees of every size had fallen over each other in all kinds of directions. I think the part we got into was called, "The Cedar Swamp." There was not so much difficulty in getting on when we were careless about the direction we went in, but when we decided on returning home, and arranged to separate and to make our several ways as well as we could to a certain point which we were acquainted with, at which two roads met, it was necessary that we should proceed in a particular direction, and then began the difficulty of making progress. The tacking of a ship, with the wind right ahead, was nothing to it. We had only the sun, seen through the tops of the trees, to guide us, but that was quite sufficient. Whilst we kept the direction which formed an angle with the direction the sun was in, to our right and rear of about 135 degrees, we knew that we were not far wrong. Trees that had been lying there for scores of years, in all imaginable stages of decay, and lying over and under each other in all directions, seemed to oppose almost insurmountable difficulties to our progress. But although it was a tedious business, there was no real difficulty in making our way. We could advance, perhaps, ten or fifteen feet along a fallen tree, six feet from the ground, in the right direction, and then find our way barred by the trunk and branches of another tree lying at right angles with it, and five or six feet above it; then, after climbing on to it and choosing whether we would go to its root or top, we had to make our way along its trunk, twenty or thirty, or more feet, till we could descend to some other tree that promised either itself to give us a better advance in the right direction, or to conduct us to one that would. I know not whether this will give my readers anything like an idea of what a walk in an uncleared American forest is, but I have done my best to describe it. Another peculiarity met with in these forests, sometimes at every few yards, is the vast number of high dead trees which are standing, and which a slight push will send to the ground. The first I met with was on a rather steep descent in the wood; it might be ten inches in diameter and forty feet high. I was very much astonished to find, on putting my hand against it to stop myself, that the whole trunk went right away before me to the ground. I pushed numbers of them down, but there was this danger attending the doing so, which, however, could be easily avoided, that, when the tree was pushed to the ground, in most cases, a portion of the top came off, and came straight down, and was generally of sufficient size and weight to seriously injure the person underneath, if it happened to fall on his head. We were, I think, nearly a mile from the point we arranged to make for when we separated, and we thought ourselves rather clever, when, without having seen each other, we found we had struck the two roads, one of us the one road and the other the other, both within eighty yards of their point of junction.

They told us that bears seldom visited that part of New Brunswick; but the foot-marks of two bears were discovered that winter on the sand or snow, in a creek about two miles to the northward of the town. I sometimes used to think they would be "ugly customers" to meet with, unarmed as we always were. However, I never heard of anyone who had seen them.

I used to read to those of our soldiers who liked to attend, on the Sunday evening, and also on some evening in the week. At one time I read "Robinson's Scripture Characters" to them. We always had a prayer also, but whether I used some of the church prayers or not I do not recollect. I knew of one man only who thought he was first led to think seriously about the salvation of his soul, by attending those reading parties.

We had very little intercourse with the state of Maine, on the other side of the bay of Passamaquoddy. There was a communication between Eastport, a small town about ten miles from St. Andrew's, by means of a small decked vessel; I am not sure that it went there every day. There was also a large village called Robinstown, on the opposite side of the bay, through which we got our letters from England. I once went over there with Gawler, and we were somewhat amused to find, that the landlord of the small inn, or large public-house, there, had been a general officer in the United States service, and had commanded all that district for two hundred miles back as far as the river Penobscot, and had also ceded it to the English general Sir John Sherbrooke, in the late war ending in 1815. He was a very pleasant and quiet person, and ordered a separate dinner for us and himself and another person, which was intended as a mark of attention to us. Whilst we were standing and talking to him, a man came up and said to him, "General, I shall be "glad if you will order my horse a feed of corn," which sounded rather oddly in the ears of English officers.

Whilst I was at St. Andrew's, the Charlotte County Militia assembled there for their annual training, and we looked forward to it with some degree of interest. Several of the officers resided at St. Andrew's. Some of them requested us not to come and see them when they were assembled on parade, but we told them it was too grand an affair for us to miss. They had, I think, a grenadier and also a rifle company, and were a fine body of men, but, as might be expected from the short time they were assembled, and from the want of proper drilling, they knew scarcely anything about marching, or the use of their firelocks. One day when Gawler and I and several of our men were looking on, they accepted our offer to shew the rifle company, I think it was, how to move a little in skirmishing order, and we made our men fall in and be intermingled with them. The little drill they got in this way they appeared to be much pleased with. But on our inviting them to assemble frequently and place themselves under our instruction, with the promise that if they did so, we would make them one of the best light infantry companies in the world, (which we could have done in the course of time,) they found there were difficulties in the way of their assembling which precluded them from accepting the invitation. I suppose most of the rifle company belonged to St. Andrew's, for otherwise our proposal would have been useless. I was quite grieved to see the state in which our militia were left, until I went into the United States some time afterwards, and found that their militia were, if possible, in a still more inefficient state. I suppose in these days all these matters are properly attended to. During the war I understood that the inhabitants, on each side of the border, did not at all interfere with each other; and higher up the bay, and on the river above it towards St. Stephen's, they were in much closer proximity than in the immediate neighbourhood of St. Andrew's. This, perhaps, would account in some measure for the carelessness which was manifested when I was there, relative to the training of the militia.

St. Stephen's was a settlement up the river at some distance, perhaps fifteen miles, from St. Andrew's. Dr. Thompson was a good and pains-taking clergyman there; his younger brother was the good clergyman of Machidavie, (I forget how it is spelt,) a settlement in another direction, north-east, I think, of St. Andrew's. Dr. Thompson made, what I considered at the time, a very singular request of me, when I was about to leave New Brunswick; it was, that I would try and get a large tract, a thousand acres, of the government reserved land for him; he considered he had a claim upon government in consequence of services which he had rendered when residing in the north of Ireland. I thought he might almost as well have asked me to get him a peerage; however, I received his papers containing the particulars of the services rendered to the government, and had not been long in England, when, on mentioning the subject to a near relative, he offered to give me a letter to one of the chief men in the Colonial Office, who was an intimate friend of his. Armed with this important missive, I went to the Colonial Office, and saw the under-secretary, or chief clerk, I forget which. He promised to look into the papers, and let me hear from him in a few days. The finale was, that my friend obtained the grant of the thousand acres, which were all the more valuable to him, as they were close to his own house and to a good road, which latter advantage greatly enhances the value of grants of land in the colonies.

I had occasion, before I returned to England, to go up to St. John's for a few days. It was about seventy miles off, and I went in the packet up the bay of Fundy. I recollect a curious story which the captain or some other person on board the packet told us. He knew the case of a small vessel, in consequence of the wind being dead against them, having put into a small inlet, which we were then passing, in which it anchored for the night; and that, in the middle of the night, the crew all at once found the vessel dashing out of the inlet, and going to sea at the rate, I think he said, of a hundred miles an hour. It was supposed that a whale had got entangled in the cable, and had started off with the vessel. It sounds like what is usually called an "American story;" at all events, according to an old 52nd saying, "It's very like a whale."

We neared Partridge Island and the harbour of St. John's in the middle of the night, and, from some considerable distance, saw that there was a large fire, which we could not account for, either in or near St. John's. As we stood up the harbour, with a good breeze from the southward, we soon perceived that nearly half the town was on fire. We stood on past the town, and landed beyond the fire. I immediately jumped on shore, and running up to the fire, found that several of the lower streets towards the harbour had been burnt for a very considerable distance. Tylden, I recollect, expressed his astonishment, in no very measured terms, at seeing me make my appearance in the midst of this terrible fire. I think I did some considerable service there, for perceiving that the fire was increasing, and that nothing effectual was done to stop it, and that it spread from street to street by means of the dry palings which separated the gardens between the streets, along which palings it was rapidly carried up the hill by the southerly wind, I collected some twenty of the soldiers, and extending them a few paces from each other, we advanced in line against the palings, kicking one after another of these slight fences flat down, and thus prevented the wind from taking the fire along them, as it had done along the other fences. I believe this had very much to do with stopping the fire: indeed, but for this proceeding, the houses in the street above (the houses were chiefly of wood) would certainly have been burnt, for in several places the fire was already beginning to rush along the partitions when we came to them. I fear my services on the occasion were not known, and that it is now too late for me to expect that the inhabitants of St. John's shall acknowledge them by giving me a vote of thanks, or reward them by getting the government to give me a grant of some thousands of acres of their best reserved land.

Some new officers had joined the 52nd since their arrival in New Brunswick, and I particularly recollect meeting Mountain there, and being very much pleased with him during the few days I remained at St. John's. I remember that each day at mess he made a point of asking me to take some wine with him, and I have thought that perhaps it was for the purpose of shewing that he valued that character which I had as a religious man, and which others might possibly have spoken of in terms of ridicule. Many years afterwards I met with him, when he had himself come out openly as a man who feared God. His father and brother were bishops of Quebec. I copy the following about Armine Mountain from the 52nd record :—

"Amongst the regimental changes this year (1825) was that "of Lieut. A. H. S. Mountain, from the 52nd, to be captain un- "attached, on the 26th of May. This officer afterwards rose to " to be colonel and adjutant-general of H. M. forces in India, and "his biographer thus writes :—

"'The regret of the 52nd at losing young Mountain was ex- "'treme, and exertions were made by the officers to arrange some "'means by which he could procure a company in their corps, but "'it could not be accomplished, and he never rejoined that regi- "'ment. He always, however, looked upon the time spent with "'the 52nd as the foundation of his military experience, and when, "'in the course of service, he obtained the command of a regiment, "'his aim ever was to introduce the high feeling of honour, the "'*esprit de corps*, and gentlemanlike conduct, which had been fos- "'tered in that distinguished regiment.'"

It is a well-known fact that whenever regiments proceed to any of the colonies where rum is cheap, some of the men will drink of it till they bring themselves very rapidly to the grave. The new rum which they purchase, and often that which is supplied by the contractors, is particularly injurious; some three or four of our men lost their lives from drinking the new rum, soon after our arrival in New Brunswick. Either on this occasion, or when I first came to St. John's, I recollect seeing a crowd of persons in the street, and a few soldiers amongst them. On my coming up to them, I found a man, half mad with drink, standing with his bayonet drawn, and setting at defiance a corporal and a file of men, who had been sent to take him to the guard-room. This is always a most painful and awkward position for a non-commissioned officer to be placed in; I once knew a similar case which ended in the death of the man in custody. On my coming to the crowd, I went up to the man, and merely said "Hollo! what is all this about?" and he immediately returned his bayonet to the scabbard, saying, "Now there is an officer, I "will give in," and went off quietly with the men of the guard.

Trying circumstances, connected with my promotion and the half-pay lieutenancy I had refused, which I will explain in a subsequent chapter, rendered it desirable that I should proceed *to England*; and this step, which had been long determined on, in the event of my receiving an unfavourable reply to a memorial I had forwarded to the Duke of York, was taken immediately after my return from St. John's. I was very sorry to leave all my kind friends at St. Andrew's, especially the Gawlers, but I had great reason to be most thankful for all the mercy and goodness which God had been pleased to manifest to me during my residence at that place, both as regarded my own religious state, and the work which He had enabled me to participate in with my dear friends the Gawlers, with a view to the religious benefit of others.

It was a very considerable trial to me to leave Sandhurst; but I have been enabled to see clearly that the great Disposer and Over-ruler of all events did, in His wisdom and loving-kindness, send me to America; and in many a mortification, and in much more severe trials which have occurred to me since then, I have constantly seen the same loving-kindness and wisdom in all His dispensations towards me. "It is not in man that walketh "to direct his steps."

END OF THE FIRST VOLUME.

Printed in the United States
85502LV00003B/53/A